THE INSIDERS'® GUIDE TO

Golf in the Carolinas

COVERING COURSES IN NORTH AND SOUTH CAROLINA

THE
INSIDERS'® → GUIDE ←
TO
Golf in the
Carolinas

COVERING COURSES IN NORTH AND SOUTH CAROLINA

by
Mitch Willard
&
Scott Martin

The Insiders' Guides® Inc.

Co-published and marketed by:
Knight Publishing Company, Inc.
P.O. Box 31288
600 South Tryon Street
Charlotte, NC 28232
(704) 358-5922

Co-published and distributed by:
The Insiders' Guides Inc.
The Waterfront • Suites 12 &13
P.O. 2057
Manteo, NC 27954
(919) 473-6100

•

FIRST EDITION
1st printing

•

Copyright ©1995
by Knight Publishing Company, Inc.

•

Printed in the United States
of America

•

ISBN 0-912367-87-3

Knight Publishing Company, Inc.
Subsidiary Publications Division

Director, Subsidiary Publications
Stewart Spencer

Manager
Linda Sluder

Advertising support from
the following companies:
**The Insiders' Guides Inc.
By the Sea Publications
Great Direct Concepts
The Myrtle Beach Sun News**

The Insiders' Guides® Inc.

Publisher/Managing Editor
Beth P. Storie

President/General Manager
Michael McOwen

Vice President/Advertising
Murray Kasmenn

Partnership Services Director
Giles Bissonnette

Creative Services Director
Mike Lay

Sales and Marketing Director
Julie Ross

On-line Services Director
David Haynes

Managing Editor
Theresa Chavez

Project Editor
Dan DeGregory

Project Artist
Mike Lay

Fulfillment Director
Gina Twiford

Controller
Claudette Forney

Foreward

By Davis Love III

I've played golf all over the United States and all over the world but I can't think of two states where there's a better concentration of courses than in North and South Carolina. *The Insiders' Guide® to Golf in the Carolinas* provides an introduction to the many fine courses available to a very fortunate public.

With such a great climate and with so many excellent courses at their disposal, people in the Carolinas take their golf seriously while still having a lot of fun. The result is a wealth of outstanding places to play coupled with a commitment to good maintenance. I'm sure it comes as no surprise to anyone that more and more golfers from across the country and around the world are discovering that the Carolinas are great places for a golf vacation anytime of the year.

Credit: PGA Tour

Davis Love III

Perhaps what makes golf in the Carolinas so special is the variety of terrain. You could play a round at a beach course in the Lowcountry of South Carolina then catch a plane to Asheville and play your afternoon game on a magnificent mountain course. The next day, you could play amid the ancient hardwoods of the Piedmont then round out your excursion in the Sandhills where you'll find Pinehurst, the golf capital of the world.

Then there's the tradition. The great Donald Ross lived and worked in North Carolina. In a number of towns and cities you'll find clubs and courses where golf dates back to before the turn of the century. The world's famous golf course architects have built some of their best courses in the Carolinas. Prominent professionals and amateurs from around the world have been coming to the Carolinas for nearly a hundred years to compete in tournaments and championships. Every great golfer has played and competed here at one stage in his or her career.

Each year brings new courses and new resorts to the Carolinas. Each year brings new champions. And each year you'll find old courses gaining new leases on life with loving redesigns.

The Insiders' Guide® to Golf in the Carolinas provides an introduction to what makes golf so wonderful in North and South Carolina. Now it's up to you to use it, enjoy it and discover for yourself the infinite variety and magnificence of golf in the Carolinas.

Hit it well!

Ed. note: *Davis Love III* is currently one of the top golfers on the PGA Tour. He picked up his first club while his father was the head professional at Charlotte Country Club. Davis attended the University of North Carolina on a golf scholarship and won an ACC Championship. He also won the North and South Amateur Championship at Pinehurst #2 and was a member of the Walker Cup team in 1985. He passed through qualifying school on his first attempt and turned professional that same year. Since then, Davis has won numerous tournaments, including the MCI Heritage Classic in South Carolina, The International, The Kmart Greater Greensboro Open, the Players Championship and the Las Vegas Invitational, and has accumulated close to $5 million in tournament earnings. Davis has led the PGA Tour in driving average twice and in 1993 was a member of the victorious U.S. Ryder Cup team. He currently lives in Sea Island, Georgia.

Preface

Welcome to the Carolinas!

Golf is played with a passion here, and we invite you to sample the Southern hospitality on and off the courses.

In North and South Carolina you have the best choices of golf courses in the world. We have studied and played them to provide this guide for choosing your own courses and for planning your golf vacation. The courses within each chapter are listed in alphabetical order for quick and easy reference. The chapters are organized to take you geographically from one end of each state to the other. (Note that the North Carolina Mountains and South Carolina Midlands chapters are within themselves divided geographically since each covers such an expansive area.) We recommend enough variety of courses to suit every interest, whether you are a scratch golfer looking for the toughest challenges or a true beginner ready to learn. Even if you don't want to play, we recommend some tournaments that you can enjoy watching.

We wanted this guide to go beyond just providing great golfing information. We know that not *everyone* is a golf nut, so in each chapter we've given you details about other fun things to do. Plus, we've provided details about recommended accommodations and restaurants in each area to make planning your golfing getaway easier or to assure that you take fuller advantage of what each area has to offer.

Many of the accommodations we recommend at the end of each chapter will include golf in a package for you. Others may be more suitable for your non-golfing family or traveling companions with other interests (but don't worry — we've kept the recommended accommodations close to your courses for quick access).

We suggest restaurants suitable for any of the golfers we know, and we offer a medley of family activities in every location. Golf can be combined easily with other interests, and much is available to every visitor to the Carolinas.

The Insiders' Guide® to Golf in the Carolinas is intended to tempt you with enough basic information to help you understand our states' golfing mentality and add to your golfing pleasure. Please keep in mind that the greens fees for golf vary with the seasons, especially throughout much of the coastal area, with the more expensive golf being found during spring and fall. Also, rates typically increase a few dollars each year. We encourage you to call in advance for tee times and inquire about the cost as well as any special rates that may be available.

Although walk-ons are accepted at many Carolina courses, it's important to book tee times in advance if golf is the main purpose of your trip, especially if the choice of course or time of day is important to you.

Accommodations should be booked in advance to ensure availability, and be sure to inquire about golf packages, senior citizen discounts or other specials based on your length of stay. When calling for reservations, be sure to clarify the lodging's policy regarding cancellations. Unless otherwise noted, all accommodations accept most major credit cards.

The following price code key gives a general idea of the accommodation rates for the lowest charge for one room for two people for the places we note in each chapter.

ACCOMMODATIONS RATING KEY
$50 to $75	$
$76 to $101	$$
$102 to $127	$$$
$128 to $153	$$$$
$154 and more	$$$$$

The following key explains the price range for an average meal for two at our recommended restaurants. As with accommodations, all restaurants accept at least MasterCard and Visa unless otherwise noted.

RESTAURANTS RATING KEY
Less than $20	$
$21 to $35	$$
$36 to $50	$$$
$51 and more	$$$$

We wish you par or better on your golfing excursions. And we hope all your non-golfing companions have (almost) as much fun as you golfers do. Let us know about your Insider experiences from following our recommendations in this guide so we can provide the best information possible in our annual updates.

How This Book Was Written

The authors of *The Insiders' Guide® to Golf in the Carolinas* visited each of the courses written about in this book. Inspections and reviews took place from May to October 1995. Scott Martin covered courses in North and South Carolina west of Interstate 95, and Mitch Willard covered courses to the east.

Courses were assessed either by playing a round or by riding a cart and surveying the layout. The positive aspects of the course were stressed in the belief that there's something commendable about every golf course, no matter how it may appear upon first inspection. It was physically impossible to review every public-access golf course in North and South Carolina (there are close to 600!). But we hope that this book provides an excellent selection. We certainly tried! In slightly more than four months, Scott Martin alone played or saw more than 730 miles of golf courses! And Mitch Willard played or saw more than 2,950 holes! (Whew.)

As always, we welcome your comments and suggestions and encourage you to drop us a line:

Insiders' Guides Inc.
P.O. Box 2057
Manteo, North Carolina 27954

Happy golfing!

About the Authors

Mitch Willard is a freelance writer in North Myrtle Beach, South Carolina. He plays golf every possible moment throughout the Carolinas, Virginia, Tennessee, California, Scotland or wherever an assignment or a whim may take him. Although steadily improving his game, he can sometimes write about it better than play it, and he always has excelled at watching or reading about it.

Mitch spent his first 40 years based in Lynchburg, Virginia, where he earned a master's degree in education and taught elementary school, then college, for more than 13 years. During that time he also learned to play golf and wrote numerous sports-related features for a variety of publications. The sports writing interest was born in high school when he was sports editor and photographer for the *High Times* newspaper.

A dedicated runner and fitness buff, Mitch enjoyed road racing for 17 years, then finally recognized that his aching feet would improve on the golf course but not on the road. When he moved to North Myrtle Beach more than three years ago, his love of golf intensified. Too many courses are readily available and affordable to deny the passion. He travels frequently for golf experiences and other business. Whenever an opportunity arises, a golf course always beckons. When not golfing or writing about it, he actually enjoys his real job as a Realtor, and he will talk to anybody about buying and selling property in any state.

His wife is a beginning golfer who is enthusiastic about his golfing and his writing interests. They have fun traveling together and discovering new material for travel or sports writing. Their trip to St. Andrews, the home of golf in Scotland, during the research for this book, provided additional inspiration if not reverence for the game. Walking the links, seeing the home of the Royal and Ancient Golf Club and learning exactly how and where the phenomenon all began in 1400 CE brought an almost-religious experience into his life.

Mitch returned to his familiar courses in the Carolinas and to writing this book with renewed fervor and a true sense of belonging to the universal experience called golf.

Scott Martin was born in Cincinnati, Ohio, and raised in Montreal, Canada, and London, England. In 1984, he was awarded a Morehead Scholarship to the University of North Carolina at Chapel Hill where he took creative writing classes with Bland Simpson and Max Steele. He graduated from UNC with a BA in comparative literature. Following graduation, Scott spent almost a year in Denver, Colorado, where he coached high school soccer, took his first writing job and learned how to ski moguls.

From Colorado, Scott moved to Charlotte, North Carolina, where he worked as a copywriter and typesetter. He then set out on his own as a freelance writer, specializing in preparing manuals for financial institutions such as Barclays American Mortgage and NationsBank. He also wrote articles for a number of local publications such as *Break* magazine and the *Charlotte Observer*. In 1992, he became editor of *SouthPark Update* magazine. And in 1995 he joined Knight Publishing's Subsidiary Publications department.

Scott took up golf seriously in 1992 and is a self-confessed addict. In little more than three years, he has lowered his handicap from 28 to 13 and hopes to bring it down even further following his numerous travels and playing time as a golf writer for *The Insiders' Guides® to Golf in the Carolinas*. During the research for this book, Scott played golf at public and private courses throughout North and South Carolina and logged time on more than 730 miles of fairways and greens.

Outside work and golf, Scott is a member of the Charlotte Cricket Club and twice has completed the Charlotte Observer Marathon in less than four hours.

Acknowledgments

Writing *The Insiders' Guide® to Golf in the Carolinas* was a labor of love and a wonderful experience. What golfer would not want the opportunity to talk about and play some of the finest and best-known courses in the world?

First of all, I must thank my lovely wife, Liz, who constantly gave me encouragement and wonderful ideas that always seemed to come at just the right time — when they were needed the most. Without her, this book could not have been written so easily.

The staff and editors of Insiders' Guides Inc. also need a special nod of thanks for all of their help. The atmosphere in their offices in Manteo, North Carolina, exudes information and ideas. Beth and Dan and the whole staff are ultimate professionals. Their help was tremendous. Along those same lines, let me also thank Linda and Stewart at the *Charlotte Observer*. After our first meeting, while aware of the hard work ahead, I was also aware of the constant support that all of them would and did give me.

This book could not have been written, of course, without the time and kindness of the club professionals at the golf courses. Some of the staff and workers at a few of the courses were curt and did not always have time to talk to someone who wanted to know the nuances and intricacies of their course. But others, and I should say most of the people with whom I talked, were as nice and helpful as they could possibly be.

Some really stand out: David Donovan at the Pointe, Bryan Sullivan at Sea Scape, Danny Agapion at Nags Head Golf Links, Steve Jernigan at Goose Creek, Sam Timms at Baytree, Dick Hester at Azalea Sands, everyone at Pine Lakes in Myrtle Beach, The Links Group, and all the folks at Myrtlewood made the task of information-gathering a joy.

Suffice it to say, everyone from the club professionals to the staff at the clubs and the rangers is very proud of their courses, and rightfully so. Most are glad to tell you about the course, and it gives them the perfect opportunity to do a little bragging about their home turf. After all, the Carolinas offer some of the best golfing opportunities in the world.

I would like to also thank my personal friends — Fred Hickey, Rocky Burton, Jim Wilkes and Bob Carson — who gave me their constant encouragement and shared with me their knowledge and their time to talk and play golf. I am very lucky to have such supportive friends. Also Sam Patrick, a native of Scotland, was the perfect partner at St. Andrews.   — Mitch

Many, many, people throughout the Carolinas provided assistance with this book. I would particularly like to thank Holly Spofford Bell at Pine Needles, Luellen Cobb at Mid Pines, David Rucker at Myers Park Country Club, Peter Rucker at Hound Ears, Bill Hensley, Todd Smith at Charlotte Golf Links and The Divide,

Beth Storie and Dan DeGregory at Insiders' Guides Inc., Stewart Spencer and Linda Sluder at the Charlotte Observer, Tom Kirk-Conrad at Foxfire Resort, Dave Tomsky and Dal Raiford at The Grove Park Inn, Ron Whitten at *Golf Digest*, Karen Miller, Melanie McGavran, Dennis Farley at The Squire's Pub in Southern Pines, David Craig, Chuck Cordell, Larry Williams (Bam!), Melody Dossenbach at Pinehurst Resort and Country Club, Irwin Smallwood, Dr. and Mrs. Walter Morris, Sylvain Blouin, Malcolm and Lauren Campbell, Chuck Lotz, Michael Pfaff, Alan Knott, Jay Allred, Ron Green Jr., Dave Reece at Stoney Creek, Tom Jackson, Russell Breeden, H. C. Bissell, Ned Curran, James Fawcett, Americus "Max" Lamberti at Pinehurst #2, Petey Miller, and Mr. and Mrs. Hector Ingram of Wilmington, North Carolina. And a special thanks to James J. Bissell for my back-cover photo.

I would also like to thank the numerous hard-working and amenable club professionals who graciously allowed me, often at a moment's notice, to play and review their golf courses. If there is a profession whose members are friendlier and more approachable, please let me know.

Throughout this book, you will find references to *Architects of Golf* (HarperCollins; 1981, 1993), researched and authored by Ron Whitten and Geoffrey Cornish. This 648-page volume is a must for any golfer interested in golf course architecture and design. It includes a history of golf course architecture, profiles of notable golf course architects from around the world and a list of their courses plus a comprehensive list of golf courses and their designers. It's a wonderful book that lovingly details the artists who create (and have created) the golf courses so many golfers enjoy every day.

Finally, I would like to dedicate this book to Thomas Martin as well as to the greenskeepers, golf course architects, entrepreneurs, pros, volunteers, rangers, manufacturers and others who work so hard and successfully to make excellent golf available to so many in North and South Carolina. Thank you all!   — Scott

Table of Contents

Directory of Maps

*More than 90,000 people attended the SENIOR TOUR Championship,
played for the first time in Myrtle Beach in November of 1994.*

Inside
Tournaments in the Carolinas

Tournaments come in every variety and take place at almost every course. You can probably play in some kind of tournament in the Carolinas any weekend you choose if you check around in advance. For instance, read about the International Summer Family Fun Tournaments, played all summer in Myrtle Beach, South Carolina, in our Family Golf Trips chapter.

If actually competing is more participation than you desire, join the galleries for some of the finest tournaments on spectacular scenic courses. Following are a few picks that we highly recommend.

SENIOR TOUR Championship

The Energizer SENIOR TOUR Championship will be played in Myrtle Beach every November for an indefinite number of years. It's the year-end tournament for the cream of the crop of golfers and an absolute grand finale for spectators who throng to the Grand Strand during the second week of the month.

The Energizer SENIOR TOUR Championship is a 72-hole tournament that features the top 31 money leaders on the PGA SENIOR TOUR. In 1995, the top 16 Super Senior players (60 years of age and older) were featured in a simultaneous, but separate, championship tournament. The largest purse of any PGA senior event and the largest combined purse of the super senior and senior tournaments were up for grabs.

It's played at the famed Dunes Golf & Beach Club where the 9th and the 18th holes (and almost all of the bars) overlook the ocean.

Anyone who loves to watch premium golf will go nuts over this tournament. Set against a sunny backdrop of warm and glorious fall days on one of the world's best and prettiest golf courses, spectators can watch the year's accumulation of champions vie for the top spot. Despite the tournament pressure and the tough course, players take time out for autographs and conversation and relax by the Atlantic while the world's television cameras tell their stories. If you're lucky, you can watch the tournament then shuttle back to your home or hotel and watch it again on ESPN. Is that too much, or what! If you're really smart, you'll plan at least part of your vacation for early November. You can even play 18 holes a day (except at the Dunes Club, of course), then watch the seniors and super seniors finish their rounds.

We must admit that most of our favorite players are currently on the PGA SENIOR TOUR (does that mean *we're* getting older?!). It features the all-time greats — some who get better with age and many who have developed the personalities that attract loyal followers.

Ticket information is available from the PGA by calling (803) 444-4STC.

Accommodations offering ticket packages are listed in Myrtle Beach Golf Holiday's *Vacation Planner*. To obtain a free copy, call (800) 845-GOLF. Myrtle Beach Golf Holiday is the host organization for the tournament.

Heritage Classic

The Heritage Classic has been played annually in April at Harbour Town Golf Links at Sea Pines Resort on Hilton Head, South Carolina, since 1969. The plaid winner's jacket has been donned by some of golf's true greats. The pros choose to play here because of the island's charm as well as the course's challenge, and the venue is the spectator's choice for the tradition and distinction that accompany this tournament.

The course, designed by Pete Dye and Jack Nicklaus in 1969, is continually listed in any ranking of top layouts. The greens are small and well-protected. The 18th hole is one of the country's most recognized, and the wind from the sound usually becomes a factor.

Call Sea Pines Resort at (800) 925-4653 for information.

DuPont World Amateur Handicap Championship

Anyone with an established handicap, no matter what it is, can play in this tournament. And anyone can win it!

The DuPont World Amateur Handicap Championship, the world's largest amateur golf tournament, is played the last week in August every year. It will be played for its 13th year in Myrtle Beach, South Carolina, in 1996, on more than 50 courses. It's a four-day, 72-hole flighted tournament open to any amateur with a verified USGA handicap (or foreign equivalent).

The DuPont Company of Wilmington, Delaware, is the title sponsor of the tournament, which is owned by Myrtle Beach Golf Holiday and managed by Golf Digest Sports Marketing.

All types of golfers from all locations compete in the World Am. It began with 680 golfers and grew to more than 4,000 in 1995. Scores of participants return year after year to renew golfing friendships and to play in a fun tournament. What a spectacle it is when they all bring their guests and gather in the convention center each evening to view scores and swap stories. Just the socialization itself, lubricated by lots of free-flowing drink, is enough to bring most folks back annually.

Players fly and drive to Myrtle Beach from every state and 20 or more foreign countries. The greatest number of golfers, of course, play in the men's division,

Any Golfer's Home Course

The Royal and Ancient Golf Club of St. Andrews has hosted many Open Championships.

If you are reading this book you are undoubtedly a golfer — or planning to become one. If you are either, you owe it to yourself to visit the mecca of golf someday, where the game was first played, St. Andrews' Old Course. With today's airfares, the trip might cost less than you think if you plan ahead and check for special deals, and the adventures you have will be unforgettable. You will probably want to fly into Glasgow, Scotland, and hire a car for an easy drive to St. Andrews.

At St. Andrews you will almost certainly feel that you are at your *home* course. Playing golf here is an unbelievable experience. Just walking the Old Course is an incredible rush. To walk the course — or step down into one of the bunkers — that has played host to some of the most famous shots in golfing history is a fabulous feeling. Only by doing this can you truly appreciate the shot-making ability of Hogan, Nicklaus, Palmer or Watson.

According to John Philp, a professional with the Links Group at St. Andrews, "... no professional would say that the Old Course is the best links in the world. But it's the atmosphere that makes it."

You have easy access to the Old Course. It is on public land, and you can take a walk on it any day after all play has finished. When you are walking on the fairways and greens of St. Andrews, you will absolutely be in awe of your surroundings.

Getting a tee time at the Old Course is a hassle to those of us who are accustomed to calling the course a day or two in advance of wanting to play. A strict procedure must be followed. You may write to the Links Management Committee, St. Andrews, Scotland KY16 9JA and request a tee time. Or, if you don't have any luck getting a tee time this way, you may want to show up at the course and put your name in the hat for any tee times open for that day. For assistance in booking your golf or accommodations in the United Kingdom or neighboring countries, you will find all the help you need with Graeme Pook at Executive Golf & Leisure at 16 Melville Terrace, Stirling, Scotland FK8 2NE, telephone (44) 1786-451464.

Don't leave home without plenty of money. Golf at the Old Course costs about $120, but this does include a caddie, who is a major part of your game. Also, in order to play the Old Course, you must have a USGA handicap card. Ask your local pro about this.

If you don't succeed in getting your tee time at the Old Course, don't despair because you can play the adjacent New Course without too much trouble. If you play there and your golfing appetite is still not fulfilled, you have a number of other choices, one of which should go to the top of your list. Take a 30-minute drive to Angus. There, you have what Walter Woods, custodian of the Old Course for the last 21 years, calls "the number one course in the world" — Carnoustie Championship Course. Plus when you watch the British Open on television in 1999, you can tell all your friends you played there way back when. Getting a tee time in Carnoustie is not as difficult as getting on in St. Andrews.

A short drive down the coast is the Kirkcaldy District, with 11 courses in a 12-mile radius. Also nearby are Leven Links, Ladybank Golf Club, Lundin Golf Club and Scotscraig Golf Club. All of these are great courses and are used many times during qualifying rounds for the British Open.

A final word to the wise: Don't go to Scotland thinking you may get a great deal on golf equipment. A set of name-brand golf clubs sells for about $1,400. For a sleeve of golf balls, you will pay about what Americans expect to pay for a box of 12 or 15 balls. But, be aware that you don't have to put up with the hassle of lugging your own clubs across the Atlantic; almost all the courses and the golf shops rent them.

So if your appetite has been whetted, don't hesitate. Make your reservations now for your golf excursion. Or better yet, plan on going to a future British Open. In 1996 it will be held at Royal Lytham & St. Annes; in 1997 at Royal Troon; in 1998 at Royal Birkdale; and in 1999 at Carnoustie.

although senior men and super seniors are loyal to the tournament, and the numbers of women increase every year, partially due to more recognition from increased marketing efforts.

Participants have been as old as 86 and as young as 16.

The grand prize is often something super-snazzy, such as a Lincoln luxury automobile. All entrants are eligible for this grand prize as well as thousands of dollars worth of drawing prizes.

For entry information, call (800) 833-8798. In Connecticut or outside the United States, call (203) 373-7162.

PING Myrtle Beach Junior Classic

The PING Myrtle Beach Junior Classic will be played for the eighth year in June 1996. It's one of 34 tournaments nationwide conducted by the American Junior

Golf Association (AJGA) and is one of the most popular stops on the tour.

Nearly 500 golfers between the ages of 13 and 18 apply annually, and 106 are selected by the AJGA. Another 14 are selected during the first-day qualifying round. Participants typically represent at least 17 states.

Myrtlewood Golf Club is host for the 54-hole tournament.

For information on the tournament, promoted by Myrtle Beach Golf Holiday, contact tournament chairman George Hilliard at (800) 845-GOLF.

Paine Webber Invitational Seniors Tournament

The PGA SENIOR TOUR makes one of its more lucrative stops in Charlotte at the TPC at Piper Glen. Arnold Palmer designed the course (with Ed Seay) and serves as tournament host. He personally invites some of the bigger names on the tour. Past competitors include Chi Chi Rodriguez, Gary Player, Ray Floyd, Lee Trevino, Jim Dent, Bob Charles and Bob Murphy. The tournament is typically held in the first few weeks of summer — before it gets too hot.

The Paine Webber Invitational has been quite a popular event with Charlotte golf fans — and with good reason. It's a chance to see some players who, in their prime, were among the finest in the world. The course at Piper Glen is something to behold, as are the houses that surround the track. Most spectators watch the back nine, where you'll find some of the more diffi-

cult holes on the course. A great place to stake out a spot is the green on the par 5 16th, as most of the pros can reach the green complex in two shots. Then the short game clinic take place. Most players get up and down (somehow) for birdie, proving why they are professionals — and reminding many of us spectators why we are amateurs.

Another fun place to watch is the par 3 17th. It's a short iron shot downhill to a multilevel green backed by water. The comment you'll hear the most from the gallery is, "Look how easily they swing — I'm going to swing less hard from now on!" Right. It's also reassuring to see the pros goof . . . you quickly realize that even those who play golf for a living are human.

As some of the bigger names on the regular tour are now playing the senior tour, this tournament is bound to grow in popularity. Most of the players seem to enjoy TPC at Piper Glen, Arnold Palmer is a big magnet, the money and extracurriculars here are good and the galleries are well-behaved, jovial and knowledgeable.

For more information, call (704) 543-9677.

Fieldcrest Cannon LPGA Classic

The Fieldcrest Cannon Classic is a new stop on the LPGA Tour. If all goes well, tournament organizers and sponsors hope it will become an annual event.

How to Get Here

Travel to the Carolinas is delightful by car from anywhere because the road system is well-maintained and so much of nature is displayed for your enjoyment from the roadways in these two states.

Interstate 95 traverses both states from north to south. Also going north and south is Interstate 85, which passes through Greensboro and Charlotte in North Carolina and through Greenville in South Carolina. Interstate 40 bisects North Carolina, giving you an opportunity to see Asheville in the western part of the state, historic Winston-Salem and Old Salem in the Piedmont, the well-known Triangle area that includes Raleigh, Durham and Chapel Hill and Wilmington where the interstate ends in the east. Interstate 77 goes through western North Carolina, crosses I-40 and stops in Columbia, South Carolina. Interstate 20 crosses the South Carolina border at Augusta, Georgia, goes through Columbia and stops in Florence, South Carolina. Interstate 26 runs diagonally across South Carolina from Greenville in the Piedmont to the Lowcountry and Charleston.

Raleigh-Durham, Wilmington, Charlotte and Charleston boast international airports. Asheville and Greensboro in North Carolina and Columbia, Myrtle Beach, Florence and Greenville/Spartanburg in South Carolina all have domestic airports offering various jet and connector flights daily. If you choose to travel by air, you will probably first arrive in Charlotte — a major hub. This is convenient, as Charlotte is on the border of the two states, and you can rent a car, enjoy the scenery and be almost anywhere in either state within 4½ hours.

No matter what mode of transportation you choose, the Carolinas offer you an opportunity to view all aspects of Mother Nature, from the Great Smoky Mountains of North Carolina to the Lowcountry and beaches of South Carolina. And the states' efficient interstate system will make it possible for you to get to your chosen golf courses as fast as possible.

The inaugural 1995 tournament — the first LPGA event in Charlotte — was staged in the fall at The Peninsula Club on Lake Norman. Rees Jones designed this challenging private course.

Some of the stars of the LPGA Tour at this event: Nancy Lopez, Betsy King, Dottie Mochrie, Beth Daniel, Pat Bradley and Patti Sheehan. Quite a field.

For more information, call (704) 378-4410.

Insiders' Tips

Don't substitute lessons for practice. Lessons should guide your practice.

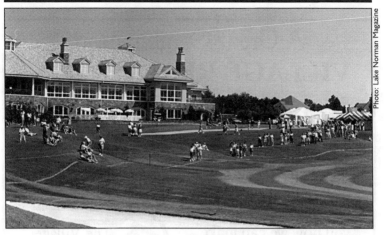

Spectators were numerous at the Fieldcrest Cannon LPGA Classic, played in September at The Peninsula Club.

Kmart Greater Greensboro Open

Two weeks after The Masters, the professionals on what Insiders call the "Big Boys Tour" come to Greensboro for the Kmart Greater Greensboro Open. It's not a major, nor is it one of the biggest events on tour. Nonetheless, it's a popular tournament that attracts an excellent field. Past winners of the tournament include Sandy Lyle and Davis Love III.

The tournament is played at Forest Oaks Country Club near Greensboro. The course was designed by Ellis Maples and is set up to make it as difficult as possible for the pros. You'll find the tees all the way back at the tips of the tee boxes. The rough is deep, and the greens are extremely fast. Despite these hurdles, the pros still manage to fire under par just about all day. If you've never attended a PGA tournament — and seen just how far the big boys hit the ball and how well they putt — then you should check out the GGO in person.

For tickets and information, call (910) 379-1570.

Vantage Championship

On the last weekend of September each year, the top 78 money winners on the PGA SENIOR TOUR gather at the Championship Course at Tanglewood to play in one of the richest and most popular events on that tour: the Vantage Championship. You'll see Trevino, Floyd, Irwin, Dent, Charles and the other successful pros who are older than 50 and still able to play some serious golf.

It's worth attending this tournament to see the Seniors play on the difficult yet picturesque Championship Course at Tanglewood. It's a public course (see our Triad chapter), so you might want to play it a couple of weeks before the tournament then see how the pros approach the same hole on which you scored double bogey.

For ticket and other information, call (910) 766-2400.

Inside
The Outer Banks
of North Carolina

The Outer Banks of North Carolina make us think of sand dunes, fishing communities, hammocks, hang gliding, wind surfing and glorious, relaxing family vacations. It's also the newest and best-kept secret of the golfing world. Popular and upscale as well as mid-range, the courses offer excellent golfing experiences, and the surrounding beach communities offer everything else for a complete vacation.

The Outer Banks north of Oregon Inlet include Corolla, Duck, Southern Shores, Kitty Hawk, Kill Devil Hills and Nags Head; Roanoke Island to the west includes Manteo and Wanchese; and to the south are Hatteras and Ocracoke islands. All of the golf courses are more accessible from Manteo, Duck, Southern Shores, Kill Devil Hills, Kitty Hawk or Nags Head. Then go south to Hatteras or Ocracoke for some easy days of pure relaxation, maybe with a fishing pole or just a good book.

Note that the area code for all golf courses and businesses listed in this chapter is 919.

Also note that the MP found in many addresses in this chapter stands for mile post, a common location designator on the Outer Banks. Mile Post 1 starts in Kitty Hawk, on the northern end of the Banks. The mile post markers end in South Nags Head, at MP 21.

Outer Banks Golf

CURRITUCK CLUB

N.C. Hwy. 12   261-5261
Corolla   (800) 465-3972

This is the new talk of the town. Carolinas Golf Group is building the Currituck Club on a 600-acre development that will be Corolla's only golf-resort community. It promises the upscale ambiance appropriate for the Outer Banks gentry and like visitors. The land has been used by a historic shooting club since the mid-1800s, and that will be preserved on one end of the development. The dense vegetation along the sand and several spectacular dunes provide an opportunity for a true links-style layout. It's the last piece of land of its kind along the Outer Banks.

The 18-hole Rees Jones course is scheduled to open in July 1996. It will offer a limited number of memberships beginning with property owners. Public-fee play will be welcomed daily. We would recommend playing it right away, as this course is sure to be busy and popular once the word gets out. The community will include a clubhouse, 5 miles of bike trails and private beach access. Course yardage and fees were not available when we went to press.

GOLF COURSES ON THE OUTER BANKS OF NORTH CAROLINA

Course	Type	# Holes	Par	Slope	Yards	Walking	Booking	Cost w/ Cart
Currituck Club	semiprivate	18	n/a	n/a	n/a	n/a	n/a	n/a
Duck Woods Country Club	semiprivate	18	72	129	6161	yes	2 days	$52
Goose Creek Golf & Country Club	semiprivate	18	72	109	5943	no	2 days	$28-$38
Nags Head Golf Links	semiprivate	18	71	126	5717	no	365 days	$75
The Pointe Golf Club	semiprivate	18	71	109	5426	yes	call	$37-$52
Sea Scape Golf Resort	semiprivate	18	72	123	6052	no	90 days	$40-60

The Outer Banks

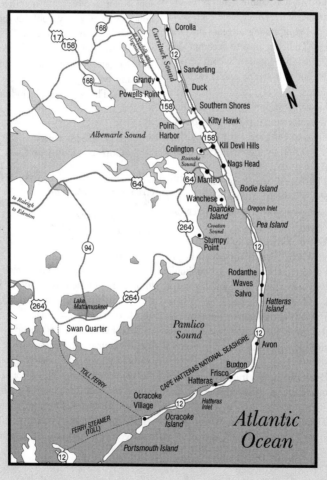

DUCK WOODS COUNTRY CLUB

50 Dogwood Tr.
Kitty Hawk   261-2609
Championship Yardage: 6578
Slope: 132   Par: 72
Men's Yardage: 6161
Slope: 129   Par: 72
Ladies' Yardage: 5407
Slope: 127   Par: 73

This 18-hole country club is the oldest course on the Outer Banks; it boasts a pristine setting among tall pines and other foliage. The club aims to accommodate its 900 members, many of whom are non-locals, but will accept public play year round.

Housing surrounds parts of the course but does not inhibit play. You shouldn't be afraid to cut loose with a long shot; you won't find a window close enough to break.

The course was designed by Ellis Maples. Fairways are narrow, and water comes into play on 14 holes. Greens are bentgrass.

You should warm up before playing Duck Woods because the course begins with a bang: a 481-yard par 5. You should stay warm for the entire round because it ends with a 506-yard par 5. Shot placement is key on this course. For example, on the par 5 14th, where water dissects the fairway, you must lay up in front of the water.

Duck Woods is a friendly but unforgiving course; every shot must be placed carefully.

The driving range and putting green are open to the public the day of play only. Target greens and a practice bunker are new.

Club rentals are available. The pro shop is not always well-stocked with golfing gear or apparel other than balls and tees. A clubhouse, locker rooms for men and women, a bar and restaurant are available to members. Beer and wine are sold to nonmembers, but no other alcoholic beverages are available, as the club does not hold a liquor license.

Walking is not allowed. Booking is accepted one week in advance for members and two days in advance for nonmembers. The greens fee, including cart, is $52 year round.

GOOSE CREEK
GOLF AND COUNTRY CLUB

U.S. Hwy. 158   453-4008
Grandy   (800) 443-4008
Championship Yardage: 6191
Slope: 114   Par: 72
Men's Yardage: 5943
Slope: 109   Par: 72
Ladies' Yardage: 5558
Slope: 116   Par: 72

On the score card, Goose Creek's philosophy is summed up: "Golf is a fun, relaxing, competitive sport. Enjoy Goose Creek to its fullest potential."

Goose Creek is one of the most player-friendly courses we have seen. The main objective is for golfers to have a good time and come back again. This is not a course where you will lose countless balls and go home frustrated. This course is for the whole family. Family golf outings are encouraged, and children are welcome dur-

ing a recommended time frame conducive to young golfers who are learning the game.

The clubhouse is a former hunting lodge. The owners have converted the small bedrooms into private locker rooms for players. The homey atmosphere is derived from the owners' receptive attitudes as well as from the ambiance of the pine-paneled lounge and snack bar — retaining the feel of the lodge living room and kitchen.

Steve and Bill Jernigan built the course three years ago with a Jerry Turner and Associates design, and the brothers have enjoyed it so much they have committed to another 18-hole course adjoining this layout. Barnett's Creek promises to be the first golf course community on the Currituck mainland. Plans are under

way for the 1997 opening. The Jernigans believe in their golfing concepts and are interested in the development of packages to bring more golfers to the Outer Banks for the fun aspects of the game in a comfortable Southern-style atmosphere.

Bermudagrass greens and fairways grace the flat Goose Creek course, which is not a typical beach layout. The tree-lined fairways are tighter on the front nine and more undulating and open on the back. Greens are relatively small.

No. 13 is considered the signature. During the fall and winter the wind in your face presents the difficulty; during summer the wind is at your back, thus the hole plays differently. A few water hazards exist and could come into play on five holes.

After playing Goose Creek, you

should feel confident and upbeat about your game. It's a course for high handicappers as well as for seasoned golfers.

A driving range and practice green are available.

Walking is allowed for members only. Greens fees range from $28 during late afternoons to $38 for prime morning tee times. A three-day golf pass is offered for $99.

NAGS HEAD GOLF LINKS

Village at Nags Head
5615 S. Seachase Dr.

Off U.S. Hwy. 158, MP 15	441-8073
Nags Head	(800) 851-9404
Championship Yardage: 6126	
Slope: 130	Par: 71
Men's Yardage: 5717	
Slope: 126	Par: 71
Other Yardage: 5354	
Slope: 123	Par: 71
Ladies' Yardage: 4415	
Slope: 117	Par: 71

This course offers enticing beauty along the Roanoke Sound. Views of the water are spectacular on almost every hole. Architect Bob Moore used the old adage "Don't mess with Mother Nature" when he designed this course, and he left intact almost all of the natural setting.

With the wind whipping around the course, its proximity to the ocean and its design, this course could easily be mistaken for true Scottish links. If your ball travels out of the fairway, plan to spend time searching the dense undergrowth. The distance is fully realized because of the strength and influence of the constant winds. This is especially true on the 583-yard par 5 18th. It runs dangerously close to the Roanoke Sound and, therefore, truly tests your skills as a golfer. This course is difficult, and a less experienced golfer may want to play from the Other tees. You also may want to leave your

woods in the bag and play only with irons because, many times, your drive will get caught in the wind and blown off-line.

In addition to the wind, water and wetlands present challenges, coming into play on all but four holes. Nags Head Golf Links requires both muscle and mind. Houses on the course may present a fear of breaking glass if you don't have control of your tee shots. After hitting each tee shot, you might need to look to the sky and say a quick prayer that your shot lands somewhere near where you'd aimed.

Of the five par 3s, none is a "gimme." The cruelest par 3 is on the 221-yard 15th. With one quick gust of wind, your ball could either be in sand on the right or in the pond in front of the green. This course changes almost minute by minute. You can be standing on the tee box with wind hitting you in your face, take a quick glance at the flag and notice the wind blowing the exact opposite direction on the green.

Nags Head Golf Links has a pro shop, bar, restaurant, driving range, putting green and rental clubs. The Links Grill overlooks the 9th green and Roanoke Sound.

Walking is not allowed. Greens fees average $75. A nine-hole shoot-out is played every Sunday afternoon from May through September. Kids play free. And tee times may be booked up to 12 months in advance.

This is a golfing experience that every golfer should appreciate regardless of ability. A round here will make your visit to the Outer Banks unforgettable. It's the place to remember: Golf is just a game. But golf on this beautiful course, regardless of your score, is a game worth playing.

Danny Agapion is a super profes-

Photo: Village at Nags Head

Wind off the water presents an interesting challenge to Outer Banks golfers.

sional, and you will be welcome at Nags Head Golf Links.

POINTE GOLF CLUB

U.S. Hwy. 158 E.
Powells Point   491-8388
Championship Yardage: 6320
Slope: 120   Par: 71
Men's Yardage: 5911
Slope: 113   Par: 71
Other Yardage: 5428
Slope: 108   Par: 71
Ladies' Yardage: 4862
Slope: 110   Par: 71

Pointe Golf Club just opened on July 1, 1995, and according to David A. Donovan III, the resident pro, it is expected to be as nice as any course in the country by next year. Donovan brings just the professionalism and personality the course deserves.

A Russell Breeden design, it's the first course in the country to have the A1 bentgrass. This new disease-resistant, dense grass has been researched extensively at Penn State University, and Keith Hall, Pointe owner and president of United Turf, is a perfectionist when it comes to lush grass. The site of the course formerly was a turf farm, thus a special bit of attention was given these perfect greens. Hall and his staff are devoted to providing the finest course conditions, including the concrete cart paths.

No development surrounds this course as our book goes to press, although a few scattered farmhouses add to the character of this rural Carolina-mainland community.

The course is a traditional design, built for speed of play. Water hazards could come into play laterally on 15 holes.

The signature hole is No. 6, a 457-yard par 4 with a carry over wetlands, a blind shot to the fairway, water, bunkers and slopes to the right.

The 18th hole plays an exciting 619 yards from the back tees. Your drive has to hit the fairway. Three perfect shots will make your birdie for the day.

A driving range, practice bunker, full-size putting green, clubhouse, pro shop and restaurant are available. The newness of the facilities is quite classy, and you will certainly appreciate the course's beauty.

Walking is allowed after noon for greens fee pass-holders from October 1 until May

Alternative Routes to the Outer Banks

As golf courses of the Outer Banks become a dominant attraction, the need for several access routes is apparent. Let's face it, most of us want to know, "How long does it take to get there?" Well, improvements are on the way. The Wright Memorial Bridge, the main access to the Outer Banks from points north, is being expanded from two to four lanes. Four lanes were open on a limited basis during the summer of 1995, which was a vast improvement, especially during busy weekends. Following off-season improvements to the original two-lane span — the new two-lane span will remain open, of course — four lanes should be completely ready by the spring of 1996.

The Monitor-Merrimac Memorial Bridge-Tunnel in Hampton Roads is a recent timesaving improvement. If you are coming from the Washington, D.C., area, take I-95 S. to I-295 north of Richmond, and follow signs to I-64 E. toward Norfolk and Virginia Beach. Follow I-64 E. until you get to Hampton. Then go south on I-664 toward Newport News and through the tunnel; then take I-64 toward Norfolk/Virginia Beach; go south on U.S. Highway 17 at Deep Creek, Virginia, to South Mills, North Carolina. Pick up N.C. Highway 343 S. to U.S. 158 E., which will take you directly to the Outer Banks.

An alternative from Hampton is to follow I-64 E. to Exit 290B (Battlefield Boulevard S.). Proceed past Chesapeake General Hospital (on the right) and exit right onto Va. Highway 168 S. Remain on Va. 168 into North Carolina; it eventually merges with U.S. 158 E. at Barco. Then follow U.S. 158 E. to the Outer Banks.

From points west and south, take I-95 to Rocky Mount, North Carolina, and pick up U.S. Highway 64 E. This route will take you to Manns Harbor, across the William B. Umstead Bridge to the north end of Roanoke Island and into Manteo. Follow U.S. 64 E. through Manteo and across the Manteo-Nags Head Causeway to access the beaches. At Whalebone Junction take N.C. 12 south to reach Oregon Inlet and Hatteras Island or U.S. 158 to Nags Head, Kill Devil Hills, Kitty Hawk, Southern Shores, Duck or Corolla.

While there are currently just three vehicle access points to the Outer Banks — the Wright Memorial and William B. Umstead bridges and the ferry to Ocracoke — there are certainly alternate routes on the mainland, some of which may help you discover new and wonderful things. Who knows . . . you might find a way to take a couple of minutes off the trip back home.

24. Call to inquire about the various packages for purchasing couples, junior or individual passes. Greens fees are $52 in peak season and $37 after October. Packages are available through area rental companies.

SEA SCAPE GOLF CLUB
300 Eckner St.
Off U.S. Hwy. 158 E., MP 2½
Kitty Hawk   261-2158
Championship Yardage: 6408
Slope: 127   Par: 72
Men's Yardage: 6052

Slope: 123   *Par: 72*
Ladies' Yardage: 5536
Slope: 114   *Par: 73*

The Scottish links-style course is cut into the maritime forests of Kitty Hawk and the signature dunes of the Outer Banks. It was designed by Art Wall, with bermudagrass greens and fairways. The fairways are somewhat wide.

Sea Scape is the second-oldest course on the Outer Banks, and it has aged beautifully since 1965. At Sea Scape, as at virtually all seaside courses, but particularly those on the Outer Banks, you not only play the course but the wind as well. The course derives its character from the natural surroundings, with water views from almost every hole. If the wind is unforgiving and your shot lands in the rough, you will be looking for it in sand and sea oats as well as scrub.

The most challenging hole is No. 11. It's long and always plays against the prevailing wind. The par 3 141-yard 9th is aesthetically appealing from its elevated tee. Club selection is imperative here depending on the direction of the wind. Your shot could easily bounce off the road if you have a good tail wind. With its five par 3s and five par 5s, Sea Scape is a true test of your golfing ability as well as your patience. Housing along Sea Scape is sometimes close and surrounded by woods.

This course will present some differences in 1996 due to bulkheading and other structural changes on several holes. Sea Scape has a teaching center, club fitting, rental clubs, a driving range, bar, restaurant and a fully stocked pro shop. Bryan Sullivan has been the professional for many years, and he has loads of knowledge about the course and always takes the time to discuss its intricacies.

Walking is not allowed. Greens fees range from $40 to $60, including cart. Advance tee times are available whenever you call, which means to call well in advance of your arrival if you plan to be here during the busy summer season.

Around the Outer Banks...

Tourism is king on these once barren, now booming barrier islands. As a result, the type, price range and selection of accommodations, restaurants and activities span the gamut. Regardless of your personal preferences and tastes, there's something here to satisfy you and yours.

Explore the options, especially in the off-season, when locals' spirits rise, and temperatures and lodging rates fall into a comfortable range. We suggest you pick up a copy of *The Insiders' Guide® to North Carolina's Outer Banks* to help in your search for a wonderful stay. These books are available in bookstores nationwide or through direct order — use the handy order form at the back of this book. Or, check out the Insiders' Guide Homepage on the Internet at www.insiders.com/outerbanks. And if you find yourself on Roanoke Island, stop by Insiders' Guides Inc. headquarters on the Manteo Waterfront, meet the folks who help bring you

Count your clubs before beginning play and be sure to take the same number home with you.

these invaluable guidebooks, and let them know how they're doing — they'll welcome your feedback.

Fun Things To Do

On the Outer Banks, you're sure to enjoy the beaches and the sand dunes, unlike those anywhere else in the world. You should do some fishing, even on a golf trip, because that's the greatest lure for most vacationers here, so there must be something to it, right? In fact, these barrier islands are renowned for offering some of the best fishing opportunities in the world. Call **Oregon Inlet Fishing Center** at 441-6301 or **Pirate's Cove Marina** at 473-3906 to get out on the water. Or stop by one of the many fishing shops to get the gear you'll need for shore or pier fishing.

If angling isn't your activity, enjoy any one of the many quaint villages, where biking or strolling are better than driving. Appreciate the native arts and crafts in the numerous art galleries, shops and boutiques prevalent all along the Outer Banks. You will find some enticing buys to remind you of your vacation here.

The **Wright Brothers Memorial** in Kill Devil Hills will teach you all about our first flight in a heavier-than-air plane. Plan on spending several hours at this educational and interesting site. National Park Service interpreters lead you through the historic events that started humankind's love affair with air travel, and the monument near the location of those first flights

in a worthwhile stop. A small entrance fee is charged.

Dowdy's Amusement Park in Nags Head is open during the summer, with a Ferris wheel and rides for the kid in all of us.

Hang gliding and windsurfing are important sports on the Outer Banks, for good reason: The wind here is as consistently good as anywhere on earth for related recreational activities. Surfers also find consistent seasonal breaks at a number of spots, especially on Hatteras Island. Shops to get you catching the big one, be it wave or wind, are all over the place.

The Lost Colony historical drama tells the story of the first attempt at English settlement in the New World. Summer nights are enchanting when you enter the outdoor amphitheater and immerse yourself in the mystery. Call (800) 488-5012 or 473-3414 for information about tickets for scheduled performances from mid-June through late August, nightly except Sundays. The Waterside Theatre is located on the north end of historic Roanoke Island.

The **North Carolina Aquarium** on Roanoke Island is open daily. Become acquainted with crabs, sharks, Loggerhead turtles and other marine creatures from the nearby Atlantic. Call 473-3494 for information about hours and admission.

The *Elizabeth II* is a representative 16th-century sailing ship, commemorating Sir Walter Raleigh's Roanoke Voyages. The **Elizabeth II State Historic Site**

Insiders' Tips

Always mark your ball before lifting it.

Ferry Thee Well

Photo: Phil Ruckle

Travelers on the ferry between Hatteras and Ocracoke experience close encounters of the feathery kind.

Standing on any tee box at almost any golf course along the Outer Banks, you can look around to see some of the most fantastic scenery in the world. The intrinsic beauty of the ocean is awe inspiring.

Another way to capture the flavor of the area is to take a drive from the northern banks south along N.C. Highway 12 through Pea Island National Wildlife Refuge to Hatteras Village at the southernmost tip of Hatteras Island. Then take advantage of the North Carolina ferry system, which will shuttle you to Ocracoke Island. Of course, ferries also run between Ocracoke Village and points on the North Carolina mainland, so visitors accessing the Outer banks from points south can also enjoy this service. It is truly a wonderful experience, and we think it will be one of the small but meaningful pleasures of your trip.

The North Carolina Department of Transportation Ferry Division operates seven routes within their system. It is not only a great excursion but a valuable service to citizens and visitors of the Outer Banks. The ferry service runs its fleet of more that 20 vessels year round. Some trips take as little as 45 minutes. Others last as long as 2½ hours. Don't feel like you have to take these rides only in the daylight hours. We took the ferry ride from Cedar Island to Ocracoke on the last ferry of the day — 8:30 PM. Granted, it was a clear night, but the sky put on a great display of lights that can only be appreciated at sea.

The ferry system in North Carolina began on the Outer Banks in the 1920s and was run by a private enterprise. The first ferries took passengers across Oregon Inlet. After 13 years of subsidizing the privately owned ferry system, the state took over the service in 1947.

Call (800) BY FERRY for information about reservations, varying costs and schedules. The trip from Cedar Island to Ocracoke Island costs $10 per car, and the ferry from Ocracoke to Hatteras Island is free.

is a museum about life in the 16th century. It's easy to find on Ice Plant Island, across from Insiders' Guides Inc. headquarters on the Waterfront in Manteo; it's worth a visit. Call 473-1144 for information on admission and changing hours.

The **Elizabethan Gardens** were initiated in 1951 by the state garden club as a memorial to the people of Sir Walter Raleigh's lost colony. Herbs, wild and native flowers and statuary combine with the history and mystery for a fantastic and beautiful adventure. Call 473-3234 for information on admission and hours. And, if you go, bring a camera.

Are you a shopping fool? Then check out **Soundings Factory Stores** on U.S. 158 in Nags Head, where you'll find discount prices everyday on name brands like Bass, Bugle Boy, Van Heusen, Corning, Pfaltzgraf and more. Browse through several collections of boutiques on the northern beaches from Corolla to Duck: **Scarborough Faire**, **Wee Winks Square**, **Osprey Landing**, the **Waterfront Shops**, **TimBuck II** and **Corolla Light Village**, to name just a handful.

The **Cape Hatteras Lighthouse** in Cape Point is probably the most recognizable symbol of the Outer Banks. Explore the visitors center with its interesting exhibits and gifts or climb the 268 steps to the top of this 180-foot, black and white spiral-striped structure. The light still flashes its warning to mariners, and a visit here will fascinate young and old.

Where To Eat

BLUE POINT BAR & GRILL
The Waterfront Shops
Duck   261-8090
$$$

This is one of the locals' favorite places for imaginative, expertly prepared food, served in an atmosphere that doesn't take itself too seriously. The menu centers on what's fresh, not just a set selection. Be prepared to try tuna is a way that you never would have thought up yourself but after eating wish you could duplicate. Enjoy a steak and potato dinner that's anything but usual. And, if you usually don't have dessert, make an exception here. Reservations are a must, as is a visit to this fine establishment.

ELIZABETH'S CAFE & WINERY
At Scarborough Faire
Off N.C. Hwy. 12
Duck   261-6145
$$-$$$

As the name implies, wine is a primary focus here. If you like wine and want to learn a few things, you'll appreciate the choices at this warm and casual establishment, recognized three times this decade by *The Wine Spectator* magazine. The changing menu offers eclectic French and California dishes. Fresh seafood is prepared with fresh ingredients in creative and varied ways, and all desserts are homemade and delicious.

Lunch and dinner are served. Call for information about hours, which change seasonally, and ask about wine tastings or specials during the summer. Elizabeth's has a strict no-smoking policy.

FISHBONES RAW BAR & RESTAURANT
Scarborough Ln.
Duck   261-6991
$-$$$

Fishbones is located in the Scarborough Lane Shoppes next to Scarborough Faire. It opened in the summer of 1995. This restaurant has one of the best raw bars we experienced in the area. The oysters are reasonably priced and icy cold. Some raw bars serve oysters plucked from a can and placed on a shell

— not at Fishbones. You can sit at the bar and watch the bartender shuck them on the spot. You might want to initially ask for extra cocktail sauce, because it's *that* good, as are the Bloody Mary's — hot and spicy. The raw bar is open all day.

Fishbones also serves the usual burgers and chicken entrees for lunch. However, for an alternative, you might give the veggie burger a try. It will make your mother happy . . . you'll have had your vegetables.

If you can't get there for lunch or the raw bar, go to Fishbones for dinner. The tuna steak is fresh everyday, and it's great — we think Fishbones soon will be known for this seafood treat. Evenings during the season, live music adds to the already nice atmosphere.

Before you leave, check out the array of T-shirts. You'll want one to remind you of your wonderful time here.

AWFUL ARTHUR'S

Beach Rd. (N.C. Hwy. 12), MP 6
Kill Devil Hills 441-5955
$$

Awful Arthur's is popular for steamed seafood and beer . . . lots of each. Locals keep it busy, but all those folks crowded around the bar can't *all* be locals! It's a casual, very typical beach place.

GOOMBAY'S GRILLE AND RAW BAR

Beach Rd., MP 7½
Kill Devil Hills 441-6001
$ $

Come to this fun spot if you're looking for a great time to go with your great food. It's noisy at times, but it's the sound of people having fun, so just join in. The food is built around a Caribbean theme (as is the colorful decor) and centers on fresh seafood and pastas. Our absolute favorite chicken wing appetizers are found here. There's a full line of beer, wine and spirits to wash it all down. For

the price, quality of food and fun atmosphere, this place is hard to beat.

THE DUNES

U.S. Hwy. 158, MP 16½
Nags Head 441-1600
$

Delicious seafood is served with a salad bar, and everyone can find something good for dinner. Breakfast and lunch are popular here too. Keep an eye out for the all-you-can-eat specials (we'd never miss the soft-shell crab nights). The Dunes is also known for its friendly service.

KELLY'S OUTER BANKS RESTAURANT & TAVERN

U.S. 158, MP 10½
Nags Head 441-4116
$$$

There are those people who feel their Outer Banks experience isn't complete without a visit to Kelly's. What keeps them coming to this place in droves? Well, it could be the great seafood or the extra-fun atmosphere or the bar where you can dance the night away to live bands. Maybe it's that you see all your friends here. Go see for yourself. And tell Collis, the big guy who watches over the front door, that the Insiders sent you.

OWENS RESTAURANT

Beach Rd., MP 16½
Nags Head 441-7309
$$-$$$

This restaurant is a tradition on the Outer Banks for fine dining and attentive service. The seafood reigns supreme here, and it is prepared to perfection. Try the crab cakes — they melt in your mouth. And the beef is top on the list if seafood isn't what you're in the mood for. The wine list is substantial, or you can enjoy a drink from the upstairs piano bar. One visit to Owens and we bet it will become a dining tradition for you too.

1587

At the Tranquil House Inn
Queen Elizabeth St.
Manteo   473-1587
$$$$

Named after the year the English colonists attempted to permanently settle Roanoke Island, 1587 is one of the finest restaurants on the Outer Banks. The presentation is superb and meets the chefs' goals of standing apart from the mainstream. In fact, this is truly one of the best dining experiences we've had anywhere.

Savor some of the best-prepared delicacies at 1587, creations of culinary artists Jason Melton and Erik Speer. We enjoyed two specials: grilled duck steak with wild rice-cranberry griddle cake and sour cherry-pecan marsala sauce; and pan roasted leg of lamb in herb crust with charred late summer vegetables and sweet potato napolean with zinfandel cracked-peppercorn jus. Don't be in a rush. This is an experience, not just a meal.

CLARA'S SEAFOOD GRILL AND STEAM BAR

At the Waterfront
Manteo   473-1727
$-$$$

Views across Shallowbag Bay are a treat during lunch or dinner. Sunday brunch is a good time to come here for a made-to-order omelette; or come late night for local gatherings. Chowders and soups, especially the she-crab, are good any time of day. And the steam bar puts out some mighty fine oysters, clams and shrimp (or steamed veggies if you're watching your fat intake). Black beans and rice are almost as popular here as in Charleston, South Carolina, or New Orleans, Louisiana. Of course, this dish begs for an accompaniment: blackened fish of the day. Yum!

WEEPING RADISH BREWERY & BAVARIAN RESTAURANT

U.S. Hwy. 64
Manteo   473-1157
$$

The most important thing here is the beer — varieties and flavors you'd never dream of. Enjoy some samples with a hearty Bavarian meal, or go during the afternoon for brewery tours.

THE FROGGY DOG RESTAURANT

N.C. Hwy. 12
Avon   995-4106
$-$$

Go for breakfast, lunch or dinner at The Froggy Dog. Check out entertainment nightly at its Lilly Pad Lounge. And drop in daily for the happy-hour steamed shrimp. It's open every day year round, which is important on Hatteras Island: Not many establishments here stay open all year. The steaks and chicken are good if you ever tire of seafood.

THE PILOT HOUSE

N.C. Hwy. 12
Buxton   995-5664
$$$

This restaurant provides a lovely view of the sound, and the seafood is fresh and well-prepared. Seafood bisque is a specialty. The restaurant is open for dinner only during the summer.

HOWARD'S PUB AND RAW BAR

N.C. Hwy. 12
Ocracoke   928-4441
$

Probably the only place on Ocracoke Island open for a late-night visit in the off-season, everyone congregates here; it's a good destination for casual fun, occasional live music and dancing. The raw bar is popular (for good reason), and simple, tasty burgers and sandwiches are served day and night. Beer and wine also are served.

THE PELICAN RESTAURANT
N.C. Hwy. 12
Ocracoke Village   928-7431
$$

Breakfast, lunch and dinner are served in this neat old cottage near the center of Ocracoke. It's a casual and pleasant place, and folks often enjoy a beer or glass of wine while waiting for a table. Seafood specials are a good bet for dinner; sandwiches, soups and salads for lunch; or try the crab cake Benedict, a real breakfast treat. It's only open during the summer season, so call before making plans.

An Outer Banks resident enjoys a round of golf at Sea Scape.

Where To Stay

ADVICE 5¢
111 Scarborough Ln.
Duck   255-1050
$$$$

This charming bed and breakfast opened in 1995 and offers four guest rooms and one suite, all with private baths, rocking chairs and decks. The suite includes color cable TV, stereo and a Jacuzzi. The atmosphere is warm and inviting, as is the hospitality you'll receive from the owners, Nancy Caviness and Donna Black. Quiet-time activities, such as games, puzzles and books, are at hand. And you're allowed to use locking storage for your gear — golf clubs, surf boards or fishing poles. A continental breakfast is served in the morning, and an afternoon tea tempts guests with homemade goodies and hot and cold drinks.

3 SEASONS GUEST HOUSE
U.S. Hwy. 158, MP 2   261-4791
Kitty Hawk   (800) 847-3373
$$$

This is the perfect bed and breakfast inn if you want to play Seascape Golf Course every day. The house overlooks the 9th green and is across the street from the clubhouse and pro shop. The ocean is just a few blocks away too. Bicycles, a common area, a Jacuzzi, complimentary cocktails and full breakfast add just about anything you could want for a great golf vacation. Other courses are only a few minutes away.

CHEROKEE INN BED AND BREAKFAST
Beach Rd. (N.C. Hwy. 12), MP 8   441-6127
Kill Devil Hills   (800) 554-2764
$$-$$$

This former hunting and fishing lodge across the road from the beach offers six rooms with private baths, televisions and comfortable furnishings. The atmosphere is homey, and guests may borrow bikes or gather on the porch for conversation.

SURF SIDE MOTEL

Beach Rd., MP 16
Nags Head   441-2105, (800) 552-7873
$$-$$$$

The friendly folks at this oceanfront hotel will go out of their way to make your Outer Banks experience a good one. The rooms in the five-story structure all have ocean views, and some even have sound views. Standard in all rooms are refrigerators, color cable TV and phones, and all rooms have private balconies. Why not book the honeymoon suite (you can make this visit a second honeymoon!), which offers a king-size bed and private Jacuzzi? Complimentary coffee and sweets are provided for early morning convenience, and an afternoon wine and cheese get-together is the perfect way to end a great day on the golf course. Indoor and outdoor pools and strolls on the beach are other convenient recreations.

THE NAGS HEAD INN

Beach Rd. (N.C. Hwy. 12), MP 14 441-0454
Nags Head   (800) 327-8881
$$$$

This crisp, white oceanfront hotel is near the golf courses and the Oregon Inlet Fishing Center as well as Nags Head, Kill Devil Hills and Roanoke Island attractions. Amenities include an indoor/outdoor pool and refrigerators in every room plus a wide, inviting beach expanse.

SCARBOROUGH INN

U.S. Hwy. 64
Manteo   473-3979
$-$$

This is one of our favorite places if traveling without very young children or large groups of golfers. Furnished with authentic antiques, it's a charming and friendly atmosphere, carefully created and preserved by the family. Sally and Phil Scarborough recently turned the daily operation over to their son, Fields, and his wife, Rebecca. Although on the main street of the delightful village, the inn is tucked away and private, more so than at larger hotels on the beaches. Breakfast is continental. Borrow a bicycle and explore historic Roanoke Island, or just walk across the street for some food or drink. They also just opened the Scarborough House, in a lovely area of town, if the inn is full.

WHITE DOE INN

Sir Walter Raleigh St.
Manteo   473-9851, (800) 473-6091
$$$$

When you're looking for luxurious accommodations with the personal attention that comes from a bed and breakfast, look no further than the White Doe Inn. The owners of this Queen Anne-style house lovingly restored the property and added modern conveniences and niceties such as fireplaces (in every room), antique furniture, tile bathrooms (one with a Jacuzzi), stained-glass windows, lovely linens and finishing touches like Godiva chocolates on your pillow.

The inn is in a quiet neighborhood in Manteo — a perfect starting point for exploring all that Roanoke Island has to offer (see our "Fun Things To Do" section).

A full breakfast is served each morning, and afternoon tea and coffee with sweets are offered in the afternoon. Guests may take the inn's bicycles out for a spin on the 6-mile Manteo Bike Path or just sit in the front porch swing and watch the goings-on of this charming little town.

LIGHTHOUSE VIEW MOTEL

N.C. Hwy. 12
Buxton   995-5680
$$-$$$

Oceanfront or oceanside units include your choice of efficiencies, duplexes, motel-style rooms, villas or cottages.

Windsurfers, surfers and fishing vacationers all enjoy this motel, which is in close proximity to the landmark Cape Hatteras Lighthouse, to the renowned windsurfing mecca, Canadian Hole, and to a myriad of restaurants and shops.

CAPE HATTERAS MOTEL
N.C. Hwy. 12
Buxton   995-5611
$$$-$$$$

Owners Carol and Dave Dawson offer basic rooms as well as efficiencies that sleep six. Nearby Canadian Hole is a notable venue for windsurfers. The motel is also popular among anglers, beachcombers and surfers. Guests enjoy an outdoor swimming pool and spa.

BERKELEY CENTER
N.C. Hwy. 12
Ocracoke Village   928-5911
$$-$$$ *No credit cards*

This is a nine-room bed and breakfast inn, outstanding for its hand-carved paneling of redwood, pine, cypress and cedar. This inn is tucked away from everything, and rooms are quietly furnished without telephones or televisions for the times you really want to escape. The living and dining rooms, with their country estate-type atmospheres, are gathering spots for content guests.

OUTER BANKS GOLF GETAWAYS
U.S. Hwy. 158, MP 2   255-1074
Kitty Hawk   (800) 916-OBGG
$$-$$$$

This real estate company packages golf at four Outer Banks courses and offers private homes and condominiums from simple oceanside retreats to spacious homes for large groups. Tee times are confirmed in advance for you, and private or group lessons or club rentals can be scheduled. All packages include accommodations, breakfast allocation, one round of golf per day, linens, towels and departure cleaning. Non-golfer rates also are available.

We recommend Outer Banks Golf Getaways if you travel with a group of golfers or possibly a large family. The ease of booking your golf and accommodations with one phone call is appealing for simple vacation planning.

Golf Equipment

Teed Off in Kitty Hawk is one of the few places to buy golf equipment or apparel except for the fine pro shops. Otherwise you'll find everything you need at the pro shops, especially those at **Nags Head Golf Links** and **Sea Scape**.

Photo: Mitch Willard

The clubhouse at The Sound.

Inside
New Bern, Edenton and Eastern North Carolina

Much of Eastern North Carolina is rural, and the scattered towns all have their own character that derives from their industries of agriculture, fishing, clothing manufacturing, boat building, cabinet making and, in the case of Jacksonville, the military base Camp Lejeune. The area is not one you would primarily choose for a golf vacation, but you will find quality courses that are well worth your time. The locale is quiet, and most courses are just enough off the beaten path to be truly appreciated.

Bath is North Carolina's first town, founded in 1705, and the notorious pirate Blackbeard was reported to have been one of the early residents here. Today you can enjoy the historic district with the state's oldest church and three restored historic house museums from the 18th and 19th centuries.

The river town of New Bern is the second-oldest city in North Carolina, named by its Swiss settlers in 1710 after the Swiss capital of Bern. The black bear emblem roaming through the town also came from Bern. The city sits at the confluence of the Neuse and Trent rivers, both of which influence most of the area's recreational pursuits. New Bern's downtown has been carefully restored to display a panoply of architecture, along with antique shops, restaurants, specialty shops and art galleries. More than 200 homes are listed on the National Register of Historic Places, and the 2,000 crape myrtles surrounding them are an at-

traction themselves. Tryon Palace, built by the royal governor in 1770, is open for tours and is the setting for summer re-enactments of historical events.

One of the city's many claims to fame: New Bern is where Pepsi-Cola originated.

Don't plan on too much wild nightlife or fast-paced activities. Just come for some peace and quiet and the appreciation of history, along with watersports and golf.

Historic Edenton is located on Edenton Bay at the head of the Albemarle Sound, and it displays a prestigious collection of 18th-century buildings. A guided tour of the historic district includes St. Paul's Church, the Cupola House, Chowan County Courthouse National Historic Landmark, James Iredell House State Historic Site, Barker House and more outstanding examples of period architecture. Little has changed in this small town while the centuries crawled past; only the new golf courses, shopping boutiques downtown and modern conveniences remind you of the date.

For more information on Eastern North Carolina, pick up a copy of *The Insiders' Guide®* to the *Crystal Coast and New Bern* or *The Insiders' Guide®* to the *Outer Banks* (also available on-line at www.insiders.com/outerbanks).

Note that the area code for all golf courses and other businesses listed in this chapter is 919.

GOLF COURSES IN EASTERN NORTH CAROLINA

Course Name	Type	# Holes	Par	Slope	Yards	Walking	Booking	Cost w/ Cart
Ayden Golf & Country Club	semiprivate	18	72	117	6282	yes	1 day	$12-25
Carolina Pines Golf & Country Club	semiprivate	18	72	111	5845	yes	60 days	$24-28
Chowan Golf & Country Club	semiprivate	18	72	118	5921	yes	1 day	$30
Farmville Country Club	semiprivate	18	71	113	5640	yes	1 day	$18
Harbour Point Golf Links	public	18	72	113	5998	yes	4 days	$24-34
Indian Trails Country Club	public	18	71	118	6172	yes	1 day	$19-24
River Bend Golf & Country Club	semiprivate	18	71	109	6019	yes	5 days	$22-25
Rock Creek Country Club	semiprivate	18	72	110	6233	yes	no	$20-25
The Emerald Golf Club	semiprivate	18	72	124	6451	no	2 days	$37

New Bern, Edenton, and Eastern North Carolina

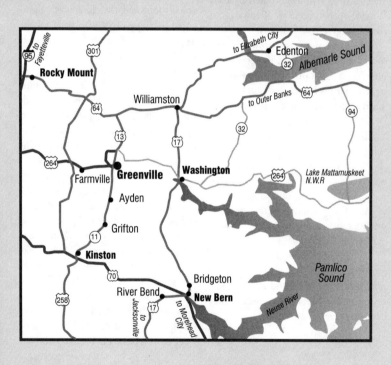

Golf Courses

AYDEN GOLF & COUNTRY CLUB

Golf Club Rd.
Ayden   746-3389
Championship Yardage: 6784
Slope: 117   Par: 72
Men's Yardage: 6282
Slope: 117   Par: 72
Ladies' Yardage: 5057
Slope: 106   Par: 72

This is a straightforward, compact course. It's not extremely demanding. Water only comes into play on four holes. The 18-hole layout, designed by Clay Wright, opened in 1952. Bermudagrass covers the greens and fairways.

The front nine has narrow fairways, so accuracy counts from the beginning. No. 7 is a 515-yard par 5 with an extremely narrow fairway for your tee shot. Then it opens a bit, but the green is small.

The 18th is a long hole — 618 yards — that doglegs slightly right. Bunkers surround the front of the green.

No sand is noticed on this course, which can afford some good practice and raise enthusiasm for your game.

Amenities include practice greens, a driving range, a pro shop, locker room, bar, grill and club rentals.

Walking is allowed. Year-round greens fees are $12 to walk and $20 to ride during the week and $17 and $25, respectively, on weekends. Tee times may be made three days in advance.

CAROLINA PINES GOLF & COUNTRY CLUB

390 Carolina Pines Blvd.
New Bern   444-1000
Championship Yardage: 6270
Slope: 115   Par: 72
Men's Yardage: 5845
Slope: 111   Par: 72
Ladies' Yardage: 4784
Slope: 108   Par: 72

Bermudagrass during the summer and winter rye during colder months grace this 18-hole course designed by Frank Marmarose, Ron Broissoit, Jim Stallings and Joe Hughes. It's not exceptionally long and, therefore, is often preferred by some of us who need all the help we can get to succeed on a course. It wanders among residential areas and over lagoons near the Neuse River.

The signature 15th hole is a medium-distance par 5, reachable in two shots with a good drive. Trouble spots are left and right and behind the green, so the hole requires a decision and some straight shooting.

The course has a pro shop, club rentals, driving range and target greens. Also available are tennis courts, a pool and a clubhouse with lounge and patio.

Year-round greens fees, including cart, are $24 during the week, $28 on weekends. Sometimes a $19 afternoon or senior special is offered. Tee times may be booked a month in advance.

The staff is cordial, which always keeps us coming back, even though Carolina Pines is a bit off our routine path.

Insiders' Tips

Allow faster players to play through. You'll have more fun by observing proper etiquette and not feel rushed by someone waiting for you.

Photo: Carolina Pines Golf & Country Club

The par 5 No. 15 at Carolina Pines overlooks the Neuse River.

CHOWAN GOLF & COUNTRY CLUB

1101 W. Soundshore Dr.
Edenton   482-3606
Championship Yardage: 6392
Slope: 122   *Par: 72*
Men's Yardage: 5921
Slope: 118   *Par: 72*
Ladies' Yardage: 5062
Slope: 112   *Par: 72*

Although this 18-hole course is technically private, the public is welcome.

No. 3 is a par 4 that runs along South Sound Drive, and a stream bisects the fairway 35 yards from the green. If you make it over that, four bunkers are in front of the green. Pine trees are widely spaced along the fairway.

Hole No. 4 is an unusual par 4. You have to play it like two par 3s because of the water that juts out in front of your tee shot and stays on the left and out of bounds on the right; water also juts into the landing area. Then you must hit to an elevated green.

No. 5, originally a par 5, has been changed to a par 4. It's a sharp dogleg right off the tee, with out of bounds to the right and water to the left. The green slants

away from you and is not an easy receptacle for your shot.

Amenities include a practice green, driving range, pro shop, beer and beverage sales, club repair and regripping. Lessons are available.

The cost is $30 for greens fee and cart. Walking is generally allowed but is restricted in the morning weekend hours. This is a first-come, first-served course when it comes to tee times.

Mulberry Hill, a new upscale residential development along the sound, runs along this golf course a few miles outside historic Edenton.

THE EMERALD GOLF CLUB

5000 Clubhouse Dr.
New Bern   633-4440
Championship Yardage: 6824
Slope: 125   *Par: 72*
Men's Yardage: 6451
Slope: 124   *Par: 72*
Other Yardage: 6005
Slope: 119   *Par: 72*
Ladies' Yardage: 5287
Slope: 119   *Par: 72*

Rees Jones designed this course to attract golfers of all skill levels. It is placed among tall pines within a 700-acre residential community. Greens are beautiful bentgrass, and fairways are bermudagrass.

Don't be intimidated by water, because of the four par 3s on this course, three must carry over water. The par 5 No. 5 is a 521-yard hole. The fairway snakes beside the highway up to the green. Water is on the right, and trees are all the way down the left side. A bunker comes into play on any short approaches to the green.

The signature hole is the 18th, a delight for its characteristic rolling mounds on the left side and water surrounding the fairway on the right.

The first round of the PGA qualifying school was conducted here in 1992 and 1993. Also, it's home to the Curtis Strange Shrine Classic.

A pro shop, driving range and lessons are available. Social memberships entitle visitors to use of the tennis, swimming and club facilities as well as to play golf.

The year-round cost Monday through Thursday is $37, including cart; Friday through Sunday and holidays, it's $42. Carts must stay on the path. Members are allowed to walk the course and may make reservations seven days in advance. Nonmembers must use a cart and may make their reservations two days before they plan to tee off.

HARBOUR POINTE GOLF LINKS

750 Broad Creek Rd.

Bridgeton	638-5338
Championship Yardage: 6554	
Slope: 117	Par: 72
Men's Yardage: 5998	
Slope: 113	Par: 72
Ladies' Yardage: 5778	
Slope: 110	Par: 72

Harbour Pointe is one of two 18-hole courses at the Fairfield Harbour resort community that is available to residents and timeshare owners. Occasional overflow from Harbour Pointe is booked at Shoreline, Fairfield Harbour's private club.

Greens at Harbour Pointe are bentgrass, and fairways are bermudagrass. The course was designed by Tom Johnson and D. J. DeVictor. Sand and water combine to provide enjoyable golf for players of every skill level.

The most challenging hole is No. 4. It's a 395-yard par 4, with water from tee to green down the right side and a right dogleg.

The driving range is two-tiered. A pro shop, club rentals, snack bar, lounge, tennis courts and swimming pool round out the amenities.

Walking is allowed after 1 PM. Greens fees and cart range from $24 to $34. Tee times are offered two days in advance.

FARMVILLE COUNTRY CLUB

300 Bynum Dr.

Farmville	753-3660
Championship Yardage: 6206	
Slope: 115	Par: 71
Men's Yardage: 5702	
Slope: 111	Par: 71
Ladies Yardage: 4759	
Slope: 109	Par: 71

Farmville's front nine was built during the 1930s, and the back nine was added during the 1970s. The 18-hole course has bermudagrass greens and fairways. Small greens and tight fairways characterize the front, while wider fairways and larger greens surprise you on the back nine. It's always kept in top condition, with good-quality greens and beautiful fairways.

This course demands accuracy. Every hole is different according to the natural landscape. A ditch runs through most of the front side, except for the par 3s. A creek crosses the 11th and 18th, and ponds add additional hazards on the back side.

Grass is Grass

Photo: NC Travel & Tourism

Courses throughout the Carolinas employ versions of bermudagrass, bentgrass and tifdwarf on their greens and fairways.

As you are reading *The Insiders' Guide® to Golf in the Carolinas*, you may notice that at least two words in this book are spelled and punctuated as you have rarely seen them. Those words are bermudagrass and bentgrass. Most times when these words are used they are spelled and punctuated "Bermuda grass" and "Bent grass." We must admit that we, too, at the beginning of developing this book, used the words in that exact same way. However, when talking to professionals in the field, we found out that we were incorrect in our usage.

Of course, we had to somehow verify this new information that we had come across. After striking out at all attempts to dig up the correct answers, we finally called the USGA in Far Hills, New Jersey. There, we talked to Annette Colbertaldo who assured me that the two words in question were indeed spelled b-e-r-m-u-d-a-g-r-a-s-s and b-e-n-t-g-r-a-s-s with no capitalization. She also expressed thanks for my calling and setting the record straight and said at least some writers were trying to get the right spelling and punctuation of these words.

This question being answered, we went ahead with the task at hand, compiling information for this book. But a deep, burning yearn to know more about bermudagrass and bentgrass kept gnawing inside us. So it was back to research and more calling and asking questions about grass. Our calling and questioning turned out to be mostly hot and cold. Kimberly Erusha at the USGA says that bentgrass is a species of grass mostly used in the northern parts of the United States where the weather is colder. As you may guess, bermudagrass is used mostly in the southern parts of the country where it is warmer year round.

Bentgrass is native to Europe. How it got over here is anyone's guess. Possibly because it was on the first courses, and if it was good enough for the Scots, it's good enough for us. Bermudagrass, contrary to general expectation, is not from Bermuda; it is from the east coast of Africa. Spanish explorers, who used it as food for their horses, introduced it to this country in the 1500s. The horses spread the seed after it had gone through their digestive systems.

Both grasses form a good quality turf for golfing. Bermudagrass in the fairway allows the ball to sit up better. It also can survive long seasons of little rainfall. Bentgrass is an excellent quality turf at low mowing heights and has the toughness to take on the colder weather of the north.

So the next time you are out on the course with your buddies and one of them says, "That tree is blocking your shot, but your ball is really sitting up nice," you can explain why. Plus, you can give the correct spelling of the grass you're playing on.

Except for the par 3s, you must continually contend with a ditch, creek or pond. Bring extra golf balls unless you can keep one in the air.

A practice green, chipping area, pro shop, locker rooms, bar and grill are available. The short driving range is for warm-up purposes only. A cart path is provided for nine holes and planned for the additional nine.

The cost is $18 including cart. Walking is allowed. Only members may book a tee time in advance; for guests it's first-come, first-served.

INDIAN TRAILS COUNTRY CLUB

Country Club Dr.
Grifton   524-5485, (800) 830-4822
Championship Yardage: 6634

Slope: 123	Par: 71
Men's Yardage: 6172	
Slope: 118	Par: 71
Ladies' Yardage: 4796	
Slope: 118	Par: 71

Part of this 18-hole course has been open since the early 1960s, and it has been developed progressively. The small town surprises many travelers with the availability of this course. The public is welcome here, and member programs are under way to encourage junior and women's golf as well as executive networking. It's easily accessible from I-95 to U.S. 11 and is one of the only area courses open to public play. Fairways and greens are bermudagrass.

The course is surrounded by forests on all sides. It's hilly with frequent left or right doglegs and finger lakes wandering through the course that come into play on seven holes. The 1st tee is on the shoreline of what geologists believe was the ocean several million years ago, and the elevation is interesting. The 9th hole is of special note. It's 440 yards from the back tees, has a pond on the right and trees on the right and left. The green is elevated, and the slope is from left to right into trouble.

A putting green, driving range, pro shop, club rentals, snack bar and beer sales are offered. A beverage cart is available occasionally on weekends. A paved cart path complements the course.

Cost is $19 including cart for weekdays; weekend fees increase to $15 plus $9 for cart. Seasonal or twilight specials sometimes are offered, and the Golf Privilege Card is welcomed here on weekdays.

The 18th at The Sound overlooks Albermarle Sound.

Walking is allowed after 3 PM on weekends. You may book weekend tee times a week in advance; weekday tee times are first-come, first-served.

RIVER BEND GOLF & COUNTRY CLUB

94 Shoreline Dr.
River Bend   *638-2819*
Championship Yardage: 6404
Slope: 117   *Par: 71*
Men's Yardage: 5043
Slope: 109   *Par: 71*
Ladies' Yardage: 5012
Slope: 105   *Par: 71*

Greens and fairways are bermudagrass, and fairways are wide open on this Gene Hamm design. This 18-hole course, which was built in 1963, is open to the public and enjoyable by the average golfer.

The signature hole is the 13th, a par 3 across water that plays 184 yards from the back tees. The green slopes away from the left to the right with bunkers on the left and right front. Five holes on the back side have water. The front is tighter, weaving throughout the residential neighborhood. It's a fun layout, referred to as player friendly.

It has a driving range, practice green, club rentals, snack bar, bar, pro shop, tennis courts and an Olympic-size pool.

Cart and greens fees range from $22 to $25. Walking is allowed and the management is very helpful in booking advance tee times for out-of-towners; just call with your request.

ROCK CREEK COUNTRY CLUB

308 Country Club Blvd.
Jacksonville   *324-5151*
Championship Yardage: 7108
Slope: 117   *Par: 72*
Men's Yardage: 6233
Slope: 110   *Par: 72*
Ladies' Yardage: 5389
Slope: 108   *Par: 72*

This 18-hole course is well-kept and playable. It's also off the regular route so it won't be as busy as many others during high season. It was built in 1971.

The signature hole is No. 15 — a par 4. Your tee shot must fly between water and a ditch.

Rental clubs and a restaurant are available here. Walking is allowed. Greens fees, including cart, begin at $20 and increase to $25 on weekends. Advance tee times are not required.

THE SOUND

101 Clubhouse Dr.
Hertford   426-5555, (800) 535-0704
Championship Yardage: 6504
Slope: 124   Par: 72
Men's Yardage: 5836
Slope: 119   Par: 72
Ladies' Yardage: 4665
Slope: 113   Par: 72

The Sound is an 18-hole course in Albemarle Plantation. Albemarle Plantation is a 500-acre world class golfing and boating community outside Hertford. It's tucked away at the tip of Albemarle Sound, and the beautiful new clubhouse looks out over the sound. You have to know about the really good golf courses of the Carolinas to know about this Dan Maples original. Owner and designer Maples stamped his signature here. As with all Maples-designed courses, you get a break on the par 4s and 5s, but the par 3s are extremely difficult. It's a target golf course with a few similarities to a links course.

Fairways are wide, and marsh must be carried frequently. It's critical to hit where you aim. It's a fair course, but tough from the back tees. The pro's advice is, "Don't bite off more than you can chew."

On the 7th and 13th, the landing areas are extremely small. Both are par 4s.

This course is surrounded by undisturbed wetlands and tall pines. You will enjoy the ride from the 16th green to the 17th tee over the wetlands. In fact, you will enjoy all of the cart rides over the bridges. The three finishing holes stretch along the water and provide breathtaking views.

The 12,000-square-foot clubhouse has a pro shop and restaurant. Driving range and putting green are available. The marina is the largest in the area. Amenities for members include a swim and fitness center and a separate recreation center.

Greens fees, including cart range from $30 to $35. Walking is restricted, so call for details. Tee times may be booked up to nine months in advance.

Around New Bern, Edenton and Eastern North Carolina . . .

Fun Things To Do

Antique shopping, historical tours, and of course water sports are major interests for many golfers during their extra time in Eastern Carolina.

New Bern invites you to wear walking shoes or hop on the trolley and enjoy art galleries, gardens in bloom and especially the restored homes, churches and stores reminiscent of the 18th-century architectural influences from many other countries. Sit on a park bench and watch the river, while every care of your 20th century life flows away with it.

Visit the **Croatan National Forest**, where deer, bears, alligators and Venus's flytraps are preserved. You can access the forest at 141 E. Fisher Avenue, just a few miles south of New Bern. Call 638-5628 for more information.

Browse through the **Firemen's Museum** at 410 Hancock Street in New Bern, 636-4087, or the **Civil War Museum** at 301 Metcalf Street, 633-2818. Be sure to leave an afternoon to amble through the **Tryon Palace Historic Site and Gardens** at Pollock and George streets. Call 638-1560 for information about tour options and hours.

You'll want to plan a golfing vacation here each April so you can also attend the **Home and Garden Show**. This event is a must for garden lovers, and the quiet, self-guided stroll through some of the town's most beautiful homes will enchant you while also giving you great decorating ideas for your own home.

Spend some quiet time in this small town. You won't hear the sounds of a big city. Talk to the people here — folks aren't shy about sharing life stories with new friends who are here to enjoy local golf courses.

Visit this area during any festival, and you will absorb some real flavor of the region and its people as well as be entertained and fed like royalty. Call (800) 437-5767 for general tourist information.

Call 482-2637 for information about **Edenton**, and when you arrive here go straight to the **Visitors Center** for a genuine warm welcome by the knowledgeable and courteous staff. You'll want to see the film they offer, then take a guided tour where more than 50 historic buildings populate the tree-lined downtown streets. You might want to visit Edenton during the September shrimp festival or the October peanut festival or any number of other special occasions such as the Christmas candlelight tour of private homes.

The 1730 **Newbold-White House** is located near Hertford, one of the oldest towns in North Carolina. It's the state's oldest surviving home, and it displays medieval English architectural features modified by Colonial touches. Call 426-7567 for information.

Call 923-3971 for information about touring the three restored historic house museums and the state's oldest church in **Bath** which was the state's first town.

The **Albemarle Craftman's Fair** has been celebrated in October for 37 years, and this unique and prestigious showcase of design and workmanship exhibits more different types of craft than you can even name. It's one of the oldest demonstrating shows in the country, and you will remember Elizabeth City for this as well as the walking tour through the historic district. Call the Elizabeth City Area Chamber of Commerce at 335-4365 for information on any events and the nearby attractions.

Lake Mattamuskett National Wildlife Refuge is 50,000 acres of marsh, lake, timber and croplands. The shallow lake is a winter refuge for various waterfowl, including more than 45,000 tundra swan and 150,000 birds. Also, thousands of snow and Canada geese and 22 species of ducks arrive for the season. Fishing and boating are popular here, including herring dipping and blue crab fishing. For information about the refuge, call 926-4021.

Pettigrew State Park outside Creswell has 5 miles of trails through virgin forests and displays Native American culture from the area. Fishing, camping and nature programs are available. Call 797-4475 for information.

The **Great Dismal Swamp Canal** is the oldest continually operating man-made canal in the country. You can view the National Civil Engineering Landmark from the Visitors Center located here. Call 771-8333 for information. Or call 335-3375 for information about the Dismal Swamp Wetlands Boardwalk in North Currituck County.

Somerset Place in Creswell presents hands-on educational programs about the plantation system and daily life during the antebellum period. The main house, a restored early Greek Revival-style coastal plantation home, is furnished with period pieces, and outbuildings include the smoke house, dairy, kitchen and the original Colony House where the family lived while the mansion was being built in the 1830s.

Hope Plantation is the federal plantation home of Governor David Stone, located near **Windsor**, and the tour of the entire complex lends a glimpse of a statesman's life on a self-sustaining plantation in the early 1800s. Call 794-3140 for information.

The small town of **Washington** is the site of some 30 noteworthy structures dating from the late 1700s in its historic district, and this town's restaurants and accommodations will hold your interest for a long time. The self-guided walking tours near the river are a full afternoon's activity, and we'll soon be telling you about new golf courses being constructed nearby. Call the Washington-Beaufort County Chamber of Commerce at 975-9318 for information.

Where to Eat

Fresh seafood is wonderful in eastern North Carolina restaurants. Country cooking is also prevalent, and you won't go home hungry. We believe in eating well when we're on golf trips; actually, we promote eating well all of the time. We recommend a few favorite spots of wide variety, and you will find many others where you can enjoy local specialties and international cuisine. Restaurants accept most major credit cards.

THE HARVEY MANSION

221 Tryon Palace Dr.   638-3205
New Bern
$-$$$

The restaurant and lounge with a water view are in a restored building constructed by John Harvey in the 1790s. Before being turned into a restaurant in 1979, the building served as either a home, a mercantile establishment, a boarding house, military academy or community college during different periods. Pasta buffets and gourmet dinners are served here with seasonal fresh offerings of seafoods either grilled, poached or sauteed. Homemade desserts are delicious. Downstairs the cellar lounge has a copper bar and an inviting atmosphere for before or after dinner.

THE CHELSEA —
A RESTAURANT & PUBLICK HOUSE

Broad and Middle Sts.
New Bern   637-5469
$$-$$$

Shellfish, steaks or sandwiches are good choices for lunch or dinner at The Chelsea. Regional cuisine wears a contemporary flair. You can also learn about Brad's

Insiders' Tips

After you hit, get your clubs and be ready to proceed to your ball.

Drink, the original Pepsi-Cola, where Caleb Bradham first used this building as his drugstore.

MOORE'S BARBECUE
U.S. Hwy. 17 S.
New Bern   638-3937
$

No trip to North Carolina is complete without barbecue, and this is the place to go. Pork, seafood or chicken and all the trimmings make a fine Carolina-style feast to eat in or carry out for lunch or dinner. Call for hours, which vary on weekends. If you ever want to have a big party, talk to these people about catering a pig pickin'. You've not eaten real Southern food until you've done this.

SCALZO'S
415 Broad St.
New Bern   633-9898
$$

A huge variety of pastas and sauces is combined with fresh lamb, seafood, beef, veal or chicken to please any palate. Not a typical Carolina eatery, this is a typical Italian delight. Choose a complementing wine and an Italian dessert and spend a memorable evening here.

POLLOCK STREET DELICATESSEN AND RESTAURANT
208 Pollock St.
New Bern   637-2480
$-$$

If you are visiting and homesick for food from a New York deli, Pollock Street serves breakfast, lunch or dinner to please any northern palate — and Carolinians love it too. Salads, bagels, quiche, pasta, sandwiches and other dinner entrees are delicious and followed by great desserts. Call for hours, which vary daily.

HENDERSON HOUSE RESTAURANT
216 Pollock St.
New Bern   637-4784
$$$

For candlelight dining on a special occasion, choose this award-winning restaurant in a restored historic home. The original art on display is a nice complement to your meal. The selections are exquisite to match the decor. It's open evenings from Tuesday through Sunday.

PG'S CREEKSIDE RESTAURANT
1052 E. Main St.   946-9483
Washington
$-$$

Outside in the gazebo or in your choice of dining rooms (Patty's Porch, The Solarium or Grandpappy's Bedroom) you can enjoy good food and an entertaining menu near the river. Sandwiches include several varieties of Fowl Play, Ham It Up, Beef Encounters and Chicken of the Sea, and dinner entrees are larger creative versions of some of the same foods.

BROAD STREET RESTAURANT & PUB
705 N. Broad St.   482-3902
Edenton
$

Fresh seafood, steaks, ribs and Italian dishes are prepared here. We like the casual and friendly atmosphere as well as the generous helpings.

Where to Stay

The few major hotels located in this part of the state are dependable, and the modest local motels are fine for a quick stop. But, to sample the real flavor of Eastern North Carolina, choose a bed and breakfast inn in a Victorian or Greek Revival-style restored home. If you're here for golf only, you'll want to consider an accommodation that offers a package and helps book you on your choice course.

VACATION RESORTS INTERNATIONAL
Broad Creek Rd.
New Bern   633-1151
Rates vary

Condominiums at Fairfield Harbour overlook one of the golf courses, and rental packages for one- to three-bedroom units will include golf, pool, marina and other amenities.

FAIRFIELD HARBOUR
750 Broad Creek Rd.
New Bern   638-8011
Rates vary

Timeshare units are available for two-somes or several foursomes, and golf privi-leges are offered as well as tennis, pools and other amenities.

HAMPTON INN
200 Hotel Dr.
New Bern   637-2111, (800) 448-8288
$-$$

Golf packages are offered as well as historic district tour packages. This hotel is only a few years old and is clean and comfortable in keeping with its national standards.

THE SHERATON GRAND NEW BERN HOTEL AND MARINA
1 Bicentennial Park
New Bern   638-3585, (800) 326-3745
$$-$$$

Waterfront rooms overlooking the river and marina are comfortable, and packages can include golf at your favorite course.

A bar, lounge, cafe and restaurant make this a one-stop choice if you don't want to venture anywhere farther than the golf course and the hotel.

HARMONY HOUSE INN
215 Pollock St.
New Bern   636-3810, (800) 636-3113
$$-$$$

Enjoy the interesting architecture, the antiques and the hospitality with delicious breakfast and afternoon social hour at this bed and breakfast inn in the downtown historic district. Golf courses and historic tours are easily accessible from here.

ACADIAN HOUSE BED & BREAKFAST
129 Van Norden St.   975-3967
Washington
$

Leonard and Johanna Huber have re-cently renovated this 1902 house fur-nished with antiques and local crafts, some of which may be purchased. It's a block from the Pamlico River and a nice walk to the historic sites. The New Or-leans innkeepers serve Southern Louisi-ana specialties as well as traditional North Carolina food for breakfast.

PAMLICO HOUSE BED & BREAKFAST
400 E. Main St.
Washington   946-7184, (800) 948-8507
$-$$

In the center of the historic district, the large turn-of-the-century home ex-udes the warmth and friendliness found so often in small Southern towns. The Colonial Revival house was the rectory of

St. Peter's Episcopal Church. Period antiques and today's conveniences are delightful. You awake to a delicious breakfast.

Captain's Quarters Inn

202 W. Queen St.   482-8945
Edenton
$$$$

Phyllis Pepper offers a golf-and-snooze or sail-and-snooze two-night package for your really special vacation. Begin this visit with hors d'oeuvres on the first night, have continental breakfast in your room the next morning, then a three-course gourmet breakfast in the dining room. Now, go sailing or golfing for a few hours and hurry back to Captain's Quarters for the two-hour guided tour of Edenton's historic district. Next, enjoy the afternoon refreshments that are served at the inn. And there's more — a four-course gourmet dinner rounds out your evening, and a continental breakfast followed by breakfast buffet is served the next morning. The sailing or golf at Chowan Country Club or The Sound at Albemarle Plantation, all these meals and refreshments are included with a package for two.

Governor Eden Inn

304 N. Broad St.   482-2072
Edenton
$$-$$$

Governor Eden Inn is just a block and a half from the Visitors Center in the historic district and seven blocks from the downtown shopping district. The bed and breakfast inn offers a hearty breakfast as part of its enticement. It's near Chowan Country Club, and The Sound at Albemarle Plantation is about 20 miles away. The old Colonial Victorian inn is a turn of the century home with four rooms including private baths. The wraparound porch and the upstairs balcony invite your relaxation. Ruth Shackelford owns and operates the inn, and you will appreciate her hospitality.

Inside
North Carolina's
Central Coast

North Carolina's Central Coast — known by some people as the Crystal Coast — is halfway between Myrtle Beach, South Carolina, and Norfolk, Virginia or directly below North Carolina's Outer Banks area. It's a 65-mile beach along the southern barrier islands of North Carolina, attached to nothing and similar to little else in this world.

The Crystal Coast includes Atlantic Beach, Beaufort, Down East, Emerald Isle, Morehead City, Pine Knoll Shores, Salter Path and Indian Beach.

Bogue Banks is a 26-mile island stretching from Atlantic Beach (to the east) to Emerald Isle (to the west) and bordered by the Atlantic Ocean (to the south) and Bogue Sound and the Intracoastal Waterway (to the north).

This coast is known for its historic fishing villages and boat-building communities. Seafood festivals provide a background for some enjoyable family-oriented visits.

You wouldn't come here for a golfing vacation per se, but if you find yourself here for some other reason, you can find some nice greens and even golf packages offered by some accommodations.

> Note that the area code for all golf courses and businesses listed in this chapter is 919.

BOGUE BANKS COUNTRY CLUB

MP 5, 152 Oakleaf Dr.
Pine Knoll Shores in Atlantic Beach 726-1034
Championship Yardage: 6008
Slope: 116   *Par: 72*
Men's Yardage: 5757
Slope: 113   *Par: 72*
Ladies' Yardage: 5075
Slope: 116   *Par: 73*

This 18-hole, Morris Bracket-designed course is the only one on Bogue Sound in Atlantic Beach. It features narrow bermudagrass fairways and lush bermudagrass greens.

Although relatively short, this course is deceivingly tough to play. It runs between the sound and the ocean, and the back side includes three holes flanked by the sound; one green and one tee overlook the sound. It's a picturesque layout, and fowl and fauna abound.

The most challenging holes here are the 5th and 16th. No. 5 has a slight dogleg, with trees and bushes on the right and threatening water on the left. On the 16th a slight dogleg leads to the narrow landing area. Water runs along the sides of many holes, patiently waiting for an errant ball.

The course has a pro shop, snack bar and tennis courts. Lessons are offered for golf and tennis.

Greens fees during the summer are $33 for walking or $45 for riding. During the off-season, from September to May, these rates are discounted; rates vary annually. Call up to one week in advance to book your tee time.

GOLF COURSES ON NORTH CAROLINA'S CENTRAL COAST

Course Name	Type	Holes	Par	Slope	Yards	Walking	Booking	Cost w/ Cart
Bogue Banks Country Club	semiprivate	18	72	113	5757	yes	call	$33-45
Brandywine Bay	semiprivate	18	71	115	6150	yes	call	$20-35
Morehead City Country Club	semiprivate	18	72	110	6116	yes	3 days	$30
Silver Creek Golf Club	public	18	73	113	6030	yes	call	$35-40
Star Hill Golf and Country Club								
Lakes Course	semiprivate	9	35	56	2897	yes	365 days	call
Pines Course	semiprivate	9	36	53	2998	yes	365 days	call
Sands Course	semiprivate	9	36	56	2889	yes	365 days	call

North Carolina's Central Coast

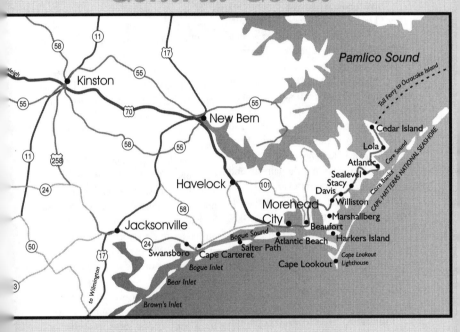

Pamlico Sound

Toll Ferry to Ocracoke Island

Kinston

New Bern

Havelock

Jacksonville

Swansboro

Cape Carteret

Morehead City

Beaufort

Atlantic Beach

Salter Path

Bogue Sound

Bogue Inlet

Bear Inlet

Brown's Inlet

to Wilmington

Cedar Island

Lola

Atlantic

Sealevel

Stacy

Davis

Williston

Marshallberg

Harkers Island

Cape Lookout

Cape Lookout Lighthouse

Core Sound

Core Banks

CAPE HATTERAS NATIONAL SEASHORE

Raleigh

BRANDYWINE BAY

U.S. Hwy. 70
Morehead City   247-2541
Championship Yardage: 6609
Slope: 119   Par: 71
Men's Yardage: 6150
Slope: 115   Par: 71
Other Yardage: 5389
Slope: 113   Par: 71
Ladies' Yardage: 5191
Slope: 113   Par: 71

This 18-hole layout was designed by Bruce Devlin. Its 40 acres of rolling fairways and bentgrass greens are set among tall oaks and private residences. The front nine opened in 1980, and the back nine opened in 1983. It has been revised by Ellis and Don Maples. It's a demanding course where water or woods come into play on every hole. Accurate tee shots and exacting approach shots are needed here.

The 2nd hole is noteworthy, with a winding lake guarding the fairway and green. Your tee shot must carry the lake; your second shot must be of equal accuracy. The 4th hole is a double dogleg right that requires an accurate tee shot followed by a lay-up to a small landing area guarded by water on the left and woods on the right. The green is somewhat elevated and guarded by water on the left. The par 3s are short but not necessarily easy.

Amenities include a pro shop, putting green and snack bar. A pool and two tennis courts are available to members.

Greens fees are $20 for walking or $35 with cart. Call at any time to set your tee time; they're very accommodating here and will try to get you golfing when it's right for you.

Be sure to talk with ever-friendly Coy Brown, former head pro at Bogue Banks for 18½ years — now at Brandywine.

MOREHEAD CITY COUNTRY CLUB

Country Club Rd.
Morehead City   726-4917
Championship Yardage: 6345
Slope: 113   Par: 72
Men's Yardage: 6116
Slope: 110   Par: 72
Ladies' Yardage: 4991
Slope: 105   Par: 72

This 18-hole layout, built in 1952 by C.C. McCuisto, is somewhat flat and easily walkable. The county's oldest course roams along the Newport River. The club is private, but public play is accepted as time permits, particularly during the week. Bermudagrass greens and fairways are well-maintained.

Some holes are tight, and some are more open. The first hole is a good one, albeit tough to start out on. It's a position hole, with a dogleg left of 409 from the back tees requiring you to draw the ball off the tee to get in better position. Several ditches run parallel to the fairways, but otherwise there's not much water to worry about.

The 18th is the signature hole, the only hole where marsh comes into play. It's a par 5 of 509 yards from the back. The tee shot requires you to hit out of a shoot to a fairly wide landing area. Then you have the option of trying to hit over the marsh or laying up short of the marsh, which leaves another 175 yards to the

Insiders' Tips

In hot weather, drink plenty of fluids, especially if you're walking. Beer will only dehydrate you. Drink water *before* you feel thirsty.

The sun sets on another great day of Central Coast golf.

green. It's a beautiful hole with the Newport River running behind the green.

Rental clubs, a driving range, bar and restaurant are offered.

Greens fees are around $35, including cart. Advance tee times aren't really necessary, but they'll happily accommodate you if you call early.

SILVER CREEK GOLF CLUB

U.S. Hwy. 58	
Swansboro	*393-8058*
Championship Yardage: 7005	
Slope: 122	*Par: 73*
Men's Yardage: 6030	
Slope: 113	*Par: 73*
Ladies' Yardage: 5526	
Slope: 110	*Par: 71*

This 18-hole course, with bermudagrass fairways and bentgrass greens, welcomes your play. It was designed by Gene Hamm.

The course is open, flat and easy to walk. Small pines are throughout the course but don't create much of a problem. Twelve holes have ponds coming into play, but some are not extremely difficult. The toughest hole is No. 8, a par 3,

about 185 yards from the back tees, with a pond around the front and the right side.

You will encounter at least seven doglegs. No. 11 is a dogleg right over two ponds. It's a par 5 that requires a lay-up then a long iron over the water. On No. 2 it's also hard to position your drive over the lake, which runs down the hole from right to left. The farther left you go, the longer the carry. Then a trap on the right in the landing area makes it even tougher. No. 14 is a tough straightaway, a par 4 of 460 yards, with the wind usually in your face.

The 16th is another interesting hole, a par 3 of 145 yards, with terracing on the front and back of the green. The 18th is a par 4 of 445 yards with a pond on the right of the green.

The clubhouse is inviting, and amenities include a locker room, driving range, putting greens, pro shop, tennis courts, swimming pool and grill.

Greens fees, including cart, are $35 to $40. Walking is allowed after 2 PM. Advance tee times aren't required, but they'll be happy to book a reservation for you whenever you call.

STAR HILL GOLF & COUNTRY CLUB
Club House Dr.
Cape Carteret 393-8111

The 27 holes of Star Hill run more than 9000 yards. The three nine-hole courses are played as three 18-hole pairs, each set between the Intracoastal Waterway and the Croatan National Forest. They are flat, with narrow tree-lined fairways. All have bermudagrass greens. Russell Burney was the course architect.

Only about five holes have water.

A pro shop, driving range, rental clubs, clubhouse, grill, tennis courts and pool add to the desirability of visiting here. Corporate outings are invited, and a banquet facility is available.

Greens fees, including cart, range from approximately $35 to $45. Walking costs from $25 to $35 and is sometimes restricted. There are no restrictions, however, on how far in advance you can book a tee time.

Lakes Course
Championship Yardage: 3254
Slope: 58   Par: 35
Men's Yardage: 2897
Slope: 56   Par: 35
Other Yardage: 2662
Slope: 52   Par: 35
Ladies' Yardage: 2507
Slope: 52   Par: 36

No. 1 on the Lakes is considered the signature hole of this complex. From the back, it requires a 200-yard carry. You must cross the lake to the landing area, then a creek runs in front of the green.

Pines Course
Championship Yardage: 3194
Slope: 55   Par: 36
Men's Yardage: 2998
Slope: 53   Par: 36
Other Yardage: 2497
Slope: 49   Par: 36
Ladies' Yardage: 2390
Slope: 52   Par: 36

On the Pines, No. 2 is a par 5 where a good tee shot is needed. Then you have to hit two big shots.

Sands Course
Championship Yardage: 3107
Slope: 60   Par: 36
Men's Yardage: 2889
Slope: 56   Par: 36
Other Yardage: 2672
Slope: 52   Par: 36
Ladies' Yardage: 2279
Slope: 56   Par: 36

No. 1 on the Sands requires a good tee shot, or you will need a long iron shot into a slight dogleg left surrounded by trees.

Around the Crystal Coast ...

Fun Things To Do

In addition to playing golf on the few nice courses, fishing, swimming or sunning are among the best things to do here. It's a real getaway from busy resort areas, and you won't find a more beautiful spot for a quiet family vacation and easygoing fun. Eat plenty of seafood and spend

Insiders' Tips

You should buy a yardage book if one is available, especially if you're playing a course for the first time — just don't let it slow your play.

The Changing Face of Golf

Photo: John D. Simmons

The science of club manufacturing has changed through the years.

Ever since a Scot hit that initial ball down the fairway, players have thought of ways to make that little white sphere travel farther and straighter.

One of the first technological innovations happened quite by accident. The Scots first used balls that were smooth all over. They soon noticed that their older balls that had been hit many times — beaten up and bearing a few dimples — traveled much better than those that were newer and smooth. Hence the world saw the beginning of dimpled golf balls.

Players then noticed balls were easier to control when they were hit with somewhat older clubs with check marks on the contact surfaces. Thus, grooves in the club face were created.

Several years ago, Ping produced the square-grooved club. These grooves were a little different from the standard club's beveled grooves and purportedly created greater backspin, thus greater "bite" and control of the ball on the green — essential for difficult approach shots. The USGA declared the club illegal. Ping filed a lawsuit that was later settled out of court (to the satisfaction of both parties). Professionals and duffers still use this type of club today.

In the 1970s, Gary Adams, who founded the Taylor Made company, created the metal wood — an oxymoron that golfers relish. The metal replaced persimmon; as a result, most of today's golfers play with a "wood" that is not made of wood. Adams received the top honor of the International Network of Golf in 1995 for his innovative contributions to the game.

Taylor Made's new Bubble Burner, with its graphite shaft and its theory of weight relocation, has been called the most radical improvement in equipment since the introduction of the metal wood. It was named the top breakthrough product of the year by the International Network of Golf.

Improved ball and club design has not ceased, and golfers can appreciate the nuances that create choices for any player.

Other gadgets make the game easier for those of us who are not on the professional tour. One innovation is the digital caddie system. This addition to the golf cart will give players detailed information about the course and the placement of their ball.

The small computer screen in the golf cart will give information such as the yardages to the front of the green, to the cup and to a water hazard or bunker. The computerized caddy in your cart can give you instant information about fairway slopes and putting greens. It will even give you suggestions on how to play a certain shot on a particular hole.

The cart can also send information back to the clubhouse that can tell the starter every cart's presence on the course, the pace at which a particular cart's golfers are playing, and the predicted finishing time of the twosome in this cart. If you are out on the course and someone just has to get a message to you, the system can do that too.

With midsize and oversized clubs and other technological innovations, golf is getting somewhat easier to play for those of us who can't hit as far as John Daly, shoot with the accuracy of Fred Couples, or putt with the touch of Ben Crenshaw.

sunny days beachcombing and ocean swimming.

The **Golfin' Dolphin** on Manatee Street in Cape Carteret is an enjoyable place to shop for golf equipment or apparel. It' a family entertainment complex, where your big or little children can be entertained with arcade games, miniature golf and bumper boats, while the golfers shop and then break in their new accessories on the 50-tee driving range. Call 393-8131 for information.

Children of all ages will enjoy amusements at **Jungleland** or **The Circle** in Atlantic Beach, **Pirate Island Park** in Salter Path or **Playland** in Emerald Isle. The boardwalks in Emerald Isle and Atlantic Beach also are important stops on any beach trip.

If you crave some educational activity to give your trip a culturally redeeming quality, visit **Fort Macon State Park**. On occasional weekends you can witness militia musket firings and living history in the Civil War fortress at Fort Macon. Call 726-3775 for information.

Check your map to differentiate between Beaufort, North Carolina, and Beaufort, South Carolina, both delightfully historic yet distinctly different cities, including the pronunciation of the names — in North Carolina, say it "Bow-fort"; in South Carolina, say "Beu-ford." **Beaufort Historic Site** (N.C.) provides guided tours including a 21-block historic district featuring homes, buildings and gardens dating from 1732. Call 728-5225 for information. Seasonal celebrations revolve around the architecture and heritage included therein. Also in Beaufort, visit the **North Carolina Maritime Museum**; call 728-7317 for information. And, in Pine Knoll Shores, enjoy the **North Carolina Aquarium**, 247-4004. For a special treat, take a narrated sightseeing cruise on a paddlewheeler.

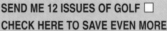

BUSINESS REPLY MAIL

FIRST CLASS   PERMIT NO. 912   BOULDER, COLORADO

POSTAGE WILL BE PAID BY ADDRESSEE

P.O. BOX 51413
BOULDER, CO 80323-1413

NO POSTAGE
NECESSARY
IF MAILED
IN THE
UNITED STATES

BUSINESS REPLY MAIL

FIRST CLASS   PERMIT NO. 912   BOULDER, COLORADO

POSTAGE WILL BE PAID BY ADDRESSEE

P.O. BOX 51413
BOULDER, CO 80323-1413

Outdoor drama is presented at the Crystal Coast Amphitheater on U.S. Highway 58 near Cape Carteret. *Worthy Is The Lamb* is a long-running professional production that draws audiences from far and wide to its June through September performances. Call (800) 662-5960 or 393-8373 for ticket and schedule information.

Regional culture can be enjoyed in Morehead City at the **Carteret County Museum of History**. Examine changing exhibits of American Indian artifacts and memorabilia of the county's settlers from 1722. Call 247-7533.

Small specialty shops dot the villages and tempt shoppers with antiques, art or local crafts. The fresh fare found at prevalent seafood markets will entice you to cook your own deep-sea delights, although world-class local restaurants will be happy to prepare it for you.

Festivals are based on such important leisure activities as kite flying, melon eating, fishing (of course) and the ever-shining convention of bald folks.

One of the year's greatest festivals — bringing entertainment as well as unsurpassed cuisine — is the **North Carolina Seafood Festival** on the first weekend in October on the Morehead City waterfront. It's a three-day celebration of the area's heritage and all that makes life delightful along the Crystal Coast. Call 726-6273 if you want more details. Other events revolve around boats, art, antiques, music or even sandcastle building, and the welcome mat is always rolled out for visitors or newcomers.

Call (800) SUNNY NC or pick up a copy of *The Insiders' Guide® to North Carolina's Crystal Coast & New Bern* for complete Crystal Coast information.

Where to Eat

BEAUFORT GROCERY CO.

117 Queen St.   728-3899
Beaufort
$$-$$$

The restored town grocery store is now famous for its fine cuisine including salads, soups and sandwiches for lunch. Be adventurous and try the gougeres, which are herb pastries stuffed with wonderful salad things like crab, shrimp, chicken or eggs. Then for dinner, try fresh seafood, choice steaks, chicken, duck or lamb with creative sauces. Definitely begin with a Carolina crabcake appetizer and end with a luscious dessert. Sunday brunch is great, and the small bar is well-stocked and invites conversations among locals and visiting golfers who all blend into the relaxed setting.

115 QUEEN STREET

115 Queen   728-3899
Beaufort
$$$$

Next door to Beaufort Grocery Co. you will find the ultimate dining with international cuisine. Each week the menu offers new and different choices to tempt your palate. Four- or five-course

Insiders' Tips

Photo:Carteret County Tourism Development Bureau

Bogue Banks Country Club's course runs between the sound and the ocean.

dinners will transport you away from the Carolinas for an occasional change of pace. Reservations may be made at Beaufort Grocery Co. Don't be in a rush, and don't worry about the cost. Come here when you can relax and enjoy the experience.

NET HOUSE STEAM RESTAURANT & OYSTER BAR

133 Turner St.
Beaufort   *728-2002*
$$-$$$

Conch or clam chowder and every steamed mollusk, plus other dinner choices and delectable desserts (did we mention Key lime pie), are enough to bring any golf group here for lunch or dinner.

RAPSCALLIONS

715 Arendell St.   *240-1213*
Morehead City
$$

Locals and visiting golfers enjoy Raps' bar with its popcorn and wide-screen television. Lunch or dinner are enjoyable in a casual atmosphere. The original Raps Burger is good, or try the ribs and salads.

Steamed clams and crabs are our favorite; they're fresh and provide a great companion to a beer after the golf round.

NIKOLA'S

Fourth and Bridges Sts.
Morehead City   *726-6060*
$$-$$$

Italian fare served in this Victorian house is both creative and delicious. Try the rack of lamb or any pasta or seafood for a delightful treat. The spinach soup is unsurpassed. Reservations are recommended for weekends.

BOGUE'S POCKET CAFE

708 Evans St.
Morehead City   *247-5351*
$$-$$$

Special homemade delicacies include seafood, soups, salads, pasta, chicken, beef and definitely desserts. Hours vary, and the menu changes frequently. The owner also welcomes golfers to the Purple Pelican in Beaufort, (919) 728-2224, overlooking the Intracoastal Waterway.

RUCKER JOHNS
A RESTAURANT & MORE

140 Fairview Dr., MP 19½   354-2413
Emerald Isle
$$

If you find a wonderful beach house to rent in Emerald Isle, you'll love the area so much that you won't want to venture any farther away than a golf course or this restaurant for all the excitement a vacation needs. If you're searching for fried calamari, you've found a home here. It's just one of the special appetizers. Steaks and ribs are great too, but we never tire of the crabcakes, shrimp entrees or seafood pasta choices. The lounge is also a popular nightspot.

FRANK AND CLARA'S
RESTAURANT & LOUNGE

MP 11
Indian Beach   247-2788
$$-$$$

Locals love the crab cakes or anything made with fresh crab. You'll also enjoy other seafood offerings as well as steaks. Relax in the upstairs lounge if there's a wait for a table at dinner, or return to the lounge for a nightcap. Locals and visitors alike feel at home here.

MAZZELLA'S ITALIAN RESTAURANT

N.C. Hwy. 58   393-8787
Cape Carteret
$$

You can't go wrong with this authentic family-owned Italian restaurant where pasta is fresh, sauces are homemade and seafood and pizzas are scrumptious. To add to the positives, it's affordable and convenient to accommodations and golf courses to boot!

Where to Stay

Stay in Beaufort if you're looking for history and variety. You'll certainly find copious amenities and wonderful atmosphere at many Beaufort accommodations, most of which are near golf courses. Some inexpensive local motels also provide standard options both in Beaufort and at the beach if you're comfortable with cut-and-dried lodging. Or stay in one of the islands' super beachfront resorts if you're looking for ocean access and fishing options coupled with close proximity to golf courses.

BEAUFORT INN

101 Ann St.   728-2600
Beaufort   (800) 726-0321
$$$

Head into this historic town and find the Beaufort Inn on Gallant's Channel. Enjoy the rocking chairs on the porch as well as a friendly welcome and the famous breakfast. The 41 guest rooms, all with private porches, feature early American decor created by local artists and craftspeople.

PARKERTON INN

U.S. Hwy. 58 N.
Emerald Isle   393-9000
$$

This somewhat new accommodation (less than 2 years old) is convenient to the golf courses and the Crystal Coast Amphitheater. Room options include kitchenette efficiencies. A complimentary continental breakfast is served daily. Be sure to inquire about golf packages.

CAPTAIN'S QUARTERS BED & BISCUIT

315 Ann St.
Beaufort   728-7711, (800) 659-7111
$$$-$$$$

Complete English-style breakfast featuring Ms. Ruby's famous "Riz" biscuits and the traditional toast to the sunset with complimentary light wines and fresh fruit

Photo: Carteret County Tourism Development Bureau

Some Crystal Coast courses have elevated greens that test your short game.

juices on the veranda or by the parlor fireplace — these are among the reasons you'll enjoy the Captain's Quarters. The family atmosphere in this three-bedroom Victorian home will make you feel . . . well, like part of the family.

It's in the heart of the historic district, a block to the waterfront shops and restaurants. Rated excellent by the American Bed & Breakfast Association, the "home of hospitality with quiet elegance" is furnished with family heirlooms and antiques; yet Ruby and Capt. Dick Collins are as modern as it gets, offering use of computer, modem and facsimile. If you're walking the Information Highway, send them an e-mail at captqtrs@abaco.coastalnet.com.

INLET INN BED & BREAKFAST

601 Front St.
Beaufort   728-3600
$$$-$$$$

Harborfront rooms with sitting areas, bars, refrigerators and ice makers, homemade continental breakfast and afternoon wine are among the amenities at the Inlet Inn, which opened in 1985 on the same block as the 19th-century inn of the same

name. Enjoy the courtyard garden and rooftop lounge.

Impressive views are of the Atlantic Ocean, the Morehead City Harbor, the Cape Lookout Light, Fort Macon, wild ponies on Carrot Island and the Beaufort waterfront. The location in the historic district is also near the North Carolina Maritime Museum and fine restaurants and shops.

SHERATON ATLANTIC BEACH RESORT

Salter Path Rd., MP 4½
Atlantic Beach   240-1155
$$$-$$$$ (800) 624-8875

This full-service beach resort has bar, restaurant, nightclub and pool, and a fishing pier is nearby. All rooms offer private balconies, refrigerators, microwaves and coffee makers, and suites include Jacuzzis.

OCEANANA RESORT MOTEL

E. Fort Macon Rd., MP 1½
Atlantic Beach   726-4111
$$-$$$

This is a basic motel with comfortable standard rooms, oceanfront rooms or suites. Amenities include a pool, children's play area (this place is great for families), fishing pier, picnic tables and grills and more. It's open from spring through fall only. Inquire about golf privileges.

BEST WESTERN BUCCANEER INN

2806 Arendell St.   726-3115
Morehead City   (800) 682-4982
$$

Golf packages are arranged here for two nights or a week, with tee times booked on any area course. A full hot breakfast, nice accommodations, greens fees and cart are included in your price. It's a convenient and comfortable location, also near shopping or historical tours for fun in your spare time.

HOLIDAY INN ON THE OCEAN

Salter Path Rd.   726-2544
Atlantic Beach
$$

On the oceanfront with deep sea fishing, sailing and pier fishing nearby, this is a convenient choice for the golf courses. A pool, restaurant and lounge are nice, too. Golf packages and golf widow packages will be customized for your stay including greens fees, cart, full breakfast daily, golf towel and tees plus your oceanview or poolside room. The best deal is a two-night stay with two days of golf from early November until March.

Photo: NC Travel & Tourism

Wilmington-area courses usually play close to the water.

Inside
Wilmington and The Cape Fear Coast of North Carolina

The Cape Fear Coast of North Carolina is a peninsula that takes its name from the river that flows to the nearby Atlantic Ocean. The area includes Wilmington, Carolina Beach, Wrightsville Beach and Kure Beach. Wrightsville Beach began as Wilmington's upper-class getaway — the quiet, quality vacationer's delight — but now it's often too crowded to lend another spot on the beach. Carolina Beach flashes with more amusements and entertainment and less sophistication but provides more space for parking or beach use. Kure Beach is a peaceful bit of sandy village for the times you don't want to do much of anything except fish.

Topsail Island, a few miles north, is another significant fishing spot and is noted for the protection of sea turtles that regularly nest there.

Wilmington was an important port for its state when it was founded more than two centuries ago, and the Cape Fear River continues to flavor the city and its activities. The past and the present blend on the streets and in the countryside of Wilmington and the Cape Fear Coast. Many annual festivals revolve around the marlin, King mackerel, surf fishing or river-related activities. Jazz and art also are celebrated in the city where cultural events

are surprisingly sophisticated for a seemingly sleepy Southern locale.

A college town and a film capital, Wilmington is a happening place, with shopping, dining, watersports and nightlife to please every modern taste. Also, it's a delight to antique and history lovers for its preservation of the past through extensive renovation efforts.

The Cotton Exchange and Chandler's Wharf are clusters among the 200 city blocks that comprise the state's largest historic district, where shops and restaurants are housed in the restored buildings along the riverfront.

Golf is popular all year, and the moderate, comfortable climate lures travelers from the south during their hot summers and those from the north during their cold winters. We recommend 14 courses that are good quality and fun to play; they are public or semiprivate and will make you welcome if you're a visitor or new resident here.

Courses in parts of the Brunswick Islands, which stretch south from the Southport area, are included in our Grand Strand chapter, as they are about halfway between Wilmington and Myrtle Beach and align themselves with the Myrtle Beach area for ease of identity with a major golf resort.

Contact the Wilmington Golf Association, (800) 545-5494, for information about packages from the leading hotels

GOLF COURSES IN NORTH CAROLINA'S WILMINGTON AREA

Course Name	Type	# Holes	Par	Slope	Yards	Walking	Booking	Cost w/ Cart
Bald Head Island Country Club	semiprivate	18	72	136	6239	yes	7 days	$71
Beau Rivage Plantation	semiprivate	18	72	129	6166	no	30 days	$28-49
Brierwood Golf Club	semiprivate	18	72	121	6170	yes	call	call
Cape Golf & Racquet	semiprivate	18	72	125	6129	no	365 days	$20-40
Duck Haven Country Club	public	18	72	122	6053	yes	none	$20
Echo Farms Golf & Country Club	semiprivate	18	72	126	6073	no	24 days	$25-30
Fox Squirrel Country Club	semiprivate	18	72	123	6208	yes	2 days	$20-29
North Shore Country Club	semiprivate	18	72	123	6358	yes	14 days	$37-50
Oak Island Golf and Country Club	semiprivate	18	72	124	6135	yes	2 days	$35
Old Fort Golf Course	public	18	72	103	5773	yes	none	$20
Olde Point Golf and Country Club	semiprivate	18	72	120	6008	no	7 days	call
Porters Neck Plantation and Country Club	semiprivate	18	72	126	6818	no	60 days	$60-70
Topsail Greens Golf & Country Club	semiprivate	18	71	118	6010	yes	7 days	$22-28
Wilmington Municipal Golf Course	public	18	71	116	6267	yes	7 days	$15-20

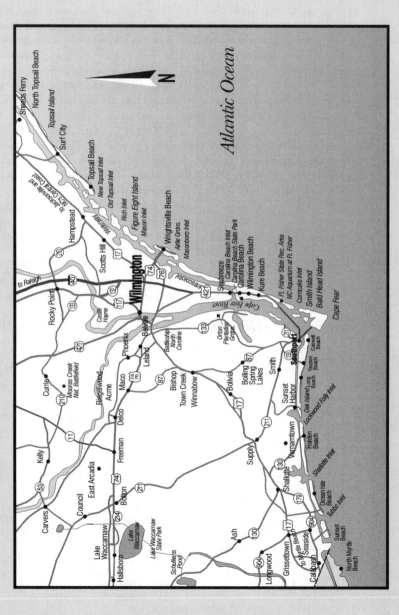

and golf courses. Greens fees vary with the seasons and are usually highest during spring and fall. Several courses in this area are less expensive during the week, and several offer senior or afternoon discounts. Advance booking is recommended, particularly during the peak seasons.

Another good source for package information is the Coastal Golfaway. They can arrange accommodations and tee times, giving you the choice of nearly 100 courses. Breakfast is usually included in their setups. Call 791-8494 or (800) 368-0045 for more information.

> Note that the area code for all golf courses and businesses listed in this chapter is 910.

Wilmington and the Cape Fear Coast Golf Courses

BALD HEAD ISLAND COUNTRY CLUB

Bald Head Is.
Southport   457-7310
Championship Yardage: 6855
Slope: 143   Par: 72
Men's Yardage: 6239
Slope: 136   Par: 72
Other Yardage: 5536
Slope: 124   Par: 72
Ladies' Yardage: 4810
Slope: 132   Par: 72

This George Cobb course opened in 1975. Its bermudagrass fairways and greens provide 18 holes of hard work that is so much fun we call it a game. Exposed greens on the ocean side draw stiff wind to toy with your skill.

The signature hole is No. 16, a par 3 where you can see the ocean and Old Baldy from the elevated tee and remember you are miles away from anywhere.

No. 8 is a par 3 similar to No. 16, although not as elevated. This course is different from any others on the coast, as it lacks a tree line. The maritime forest yields an almost subtropical vegetation not found on most other area courses.

Amenities include a driving range, practice green, pro shop, locker room, bar, rental clubs, beverage cart and snack bar. Restaurants are nearby.

Greens fees average $71, including cart. It's best to stay here if you want to play here. Walking is allowed after noon. Advance tee times are accepted no more than seven days in advance.

A few words about Bald Head Island: It can only be reached by private boat or by passenger ferry from Indigo Plantation in Southport. No vehicles larger than electric golf carts are allowed here. Old Baldy is the 1817 lighthouse, oldest in the state, from whose top you get a view of the 2,000-acre island's dunes, marshes, creeks and beaches — home to abundant wildlife and a few residents.

At the yacht harbor, spend several hours on the restaurant deck at Eb & Flo's — the island's gathering place for the general public. You'll fit right in if you drink your Heineken from cans and play cards while eating fresh seafood from paper plates with your fingers. You can be a yuppie here while biking, golfing or socializing with old or new friends.

BEAU RIVAGE PLANTATION

6230 Carolina Beach Rd.   392-9022
Carolina Beach   (800) 628-7080
Championship Yardage: 6709
Slope: 136   Par: 72
Men's Yardage: 6166
Slope: 129   Par: 72
Other Yardage: 5610
Slope: 126   Par: 72
Ladies' Yardage: 4612
Slope: 114   Par: 72

The first Golf Community in the South Brunswick Islands!

- 18 hole par 72 course
- Fully stocked Pro Shop
- Blue Heron Bar & Grill
- Semi-private
- Pro Shop - (910) 754-4660
- Tee times required

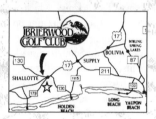

Route 179 at Shallotte City Limits

This 18-hole championship course was built in 1988, designed by Eddie Lewis and features bentgrass greens and bermudagrass tees and fairways. It's considered a difficult course and somewhat resembles a desert around many holes. Except for the tricky sand traps, the course is situated on gently rolling hills populated with Carolina pines and live oaks draped in Spanish moss. It has unusually high elevations (it's the highest point in the city of Wilmington) and a unique character. Water comes into play on eight holes, but the course is playable — not penal. The natural forest between the 3rd, 4th and 5th holes is a conservation area filled with wildlife, including alligators.

The 2nd hole is a 515-yard par 5 dogleg right, with trees flanking the right side. You may want to lay up for your

third shot because the green has an obligatory bunker guarding the front side.

The 18th hole is a par 5 of special interest. It snakes to the right then cuts back to the left. The course on rolling hills holds a number of blind shots among its narrow fairways.

Amenities include chipping and putting greens, a driving range, club rentals and a clubhouse with bar, grill, restaurant, pro shop and locker rooms. Private and group lessons are offered. Pool and tennis courts and gourmet dining are available for lodge guests, and the whole family will enjoy this vacation just a few miles outside Wilmington. Beau Rivage, French for Beautiful Shores, refers to the beaches of the Atlantic, just minutes away from the golf course.

Greens fees range from $28 to $49;

afternoon, group or senior rates are sometimes offered. Walking is not allowed. Tee times are accepted up to 30 days in advance.

BRIERWOOD GOLF CLUB

10 Brierwood Rd.
Shallotte   *754-4660*
Championship Yardage: 6607
Slope: 129   *Par: 72*
Men's Yardage: 6170
Slope: 121   *Par: 72*
Ladies' Yardage: 4812
Slope: 114   *Par: 72*

Dr. Ben Ward designed the first nine holes, now the back nine, which opened in 1976. The second (front) nine opened in 1979, according to staff. This was the first course built in the South Brunswick Islands.

The course is set on flat terrain with houses bordering most holes. You'll find bermudagrass on the greens and in the fairways.

With water on 14 holes, Brierwood offers a challenging but fair test of golf. Even from the back tees, the course is not a backbreaker; however, your wayward drives may find one of the ponds or may end up out of bounds and in the back yard of someone's house. Even with all the water, you won't find many long carries. The emphasis is on accuracy, particularly off the tee. What few bunkers you'll find are around the greens, which are midsize and somewhat flat.

Overall, your shots off the tee need to be sensible and straight. If your approach shot misses the green, you still have a good chance at getting up and down. But, if you reach the green in regulation, a good putt will yield a birdie — you can't ask for more than that!

Amenities include a putting green, bar, snack bar, pro shop, rental clubs and a beverage cart. There are tennis courts adjacent to the course, and we're told that the local fishing is excellent.

Walking is for members only unless you're a guest of a member. You can book a tee time seven days in advance. Approximate cost, including cart, is $36 weekdays and weekends.

THE CAPE GOLF & RACQUET CLUB

535 The Cape Blvd.
Wilmington   *799-3110*
Championship Yardage: 6790
Slope: 133   *Par: 72*
Men's Yardage: 6129
Slope: 125   *Par: 72*
Other Yardage: 5629
Slope: 120   *Par: 72*
Ladies' Yardage: 4948
Slope: 118   *Par: 72*

This 18-hole layout by Gene Hamm sits on the peninsula between the Cape Fear River and the Atlantic Coast. Ponds, marsh and 24 lakes lend character and challenge to this course.

The 3rd hole is a 197-yard par 3. If your tee shot is short, you have a narrow landing area because of the water on the left and right of the hole. Woodland and bunkers back the green. The 13th hole is a notable par 3 (221 yards). You must cross two bodies of water from the championship (blue) tees — a deceptive shot with the wind in your face. The 15th and

Family Golf Trips

Family vacations have not always been synonymous with golf vacations. Times are changing in that respect. Many Carolina resorts that cater to the golfer welcome the non-golfing family members with pools, Lazy Rivers, planned activities akin to children camps, and show or tour packages to attract couples and groups after golfing is done.

Many families find the combination ideal. The golfing parent or couple can enjoy a few hours a day on the greens, while the children enjoy some planned activities away from the folks. Then everyone can join in evening activities without being already tired of unaccustomed togetherness.

Families are also welcome on the many golf courses looking at an investment in their futures — suggesting free golf for children or afternoon programs for the whole family.

International Summer Family Fun Golf Tournaments are popular in the Myrtle Beach area during June, July and August. The one-day tournaments are especially for vacationing families, and 50 or more are played each summer on different golf courses. More than 4,000 golfers participate in these annual events, and many return every year for the same fun.

No minimum age is set for entrants. All winners are based on the Callaway Handicap System, so everyone has a good chance to be a winner. Two-person teams are standard, and Captain's Choice is the format. The cost is $20 per adult and $15 for youths ages 18 and younger, which covers all fees, prizes and cart. Preference is given to entrants who are vacationing with a Myrtle Beach Golf Holiday accommodation member. (Participating accommodations are listed in the *Myrtle Beach Golf Holiday Vacation Planner*.) The accommodation's golf director will make the reservation for family tournament play.

To receive a vacation planner or for additional information, call (800) 845-GOLF.

Family golf vacations in the Carolinas can be easily combined with historical sightseeing tours that reflect the coming of age of the South; many museums are in proximity of golf destinations. From plantation tours in the primitive Lowcountry to state-run sophisticated high-tech aquariums and museums with touch displays and interactive learning, we have no dearth of delights for the young and young at heart.

A festival is happening somewhere in the Carolinas any weekend you want to plan a trip. Festivals are a way of socializing outdoors with food, games, music, entertainment, and they are suitable for every age group: Everyone has fun. Walk around and do nothing more than people-watch or find an activity and sample some delicious food.

Many of the Carolina golf courses are near amusements, arcades — and don't forget the hundreds of miniature golf courses. Any vacation can be planned to include exciting activities for everyone, even if golf remains the central focus for one or two members of your group.

The beaches of the coastal Carolinas and the mountains of the Upcountry provide some of the best reasons for family golf vacations in the Carolinas. Whether you seek quietude and quality (if you're tired of the world's noises) or someplace loud and boisterous (if you crave big city attractions), you'll find what you're looking for either at the beach or in one of our cities. Pick a spot that serves up your kind of family fun: We have year-round championship golf courses here to complement the ideal family vacation.

We recommend that you inquire with the respective chamber of commerce or tourism office, as well as your individual accommodation, for suggestions about nearby attractions as well as children's programs. Review our suggestions in each chapter for specific things to do in every location. Also, ask a local and you might well receive a plethora of ideas for seasonal family activities too numerous to describe in this book.

17th holes are double greens. Sixteen of the holes have water coming into play.

Private lessons and clinics are offered, and custom club fittings are available. A driving range, practice putting and chipping greens, a pro shop, restaurant and lounge are on site. A pool and tennis courts are adjacent to the clubhouse and available to members.

Greens fees range from $20 Monday through Thursday to as much as $40, including cart. Walking is not allowed. Booking is accepted up to a year in advance.

DUCK HAVEN COUNTRY CLUB

1202 Wood Rd.
Wilmington   791-7983
Championship Yardage: 6506
Slope: 125   Par: 72
Men's Yardage: 6053
Slope: 122   Par: 72
Ladies' Yardage: 5361
Slope: 121   Par: 72

Raiford Trask designed this 18-hole course with bermudagrass fairways and greens. Pine trees line the fairways, and only a few are wide open. Accurate tee shots are required, or you'll find yourself punching out from behind trees. The layout features 18 traps — fewer than on the average course.

A new par 5 was recently added to the back side, so if you have previously played this course, note the differences. This 525-yard hole (from the tips) is of special interest. You tee off over marsh, a tight shot requiring extra care and accuracy. Your second shot is over a small ditch to an elevated green.

Another interesting hole is No. 16 — a straightaway par 3 that plays 180 yards from the back tees. The small green is hard to hit.

Practice greens are available but no driving range. A pro shop, locker room, snack bar, beverage cart on weekends and rental clubs are offered.

Year-round cost is $20, including cart. Walking is allowed. Advance booking for tee times is not needed.

ECHO FARMS GOLF & COUNTRY CLUB

4114 Echo Farms Blvd.
Wilmington   791-9318
Championship Yardage: 6708
Slope: 131   Par: 72
Men's Yardage: 6073
Slope: 126   Par: 72
Ladies' Yardage: 5142
Slope: 121   Par: 72

Gene Hamm designed this 18-hole course in 1974 on a former dairy farm. It

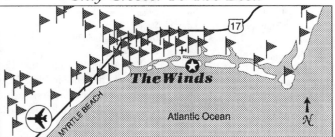

has recently been improved and features bentgrass greens, most of them large, and bermudagrass fairways. Lakes come into play on nine holes.

The 8th hole is a par 5 on which your second shot must account for a dogleg left (you have to lay up); the third shot must carry over a pond to an elevated green. The 16th is a long, straightaway par 5 with three fairway bunkers in the driving area. Play your drive to the right of the bunkers to avoid trouble. Wide fairways, but much water, characterize the course.

This course is well-maintained, and the staff is proud of its quality. Echo Farms is set in a residential community, and a large nature preserve within its boundaries is home to abundant and diverse wildlife.

Amenities include a driving range, prac-tice greens, a pro shop, locker room, club rentals, a bar and restaurant. Lessons and clinics are taught here.

Greens fees range from $25 to $30, including cart. Walking is allowed only with a member. You may book a tee time up to 24 days in advance.

Fox Squirrel Country Club

591 S. Shore Dr.
Boiling Spring Lakes   845-2625
Championship Yardage: 6762
Slope: 125   Par: 72
Men's Yardage: 6208
Slope: 123   Par: 72
Other Yardage: 5485
Slope: 116   Par: 72
Ladies' Yardage: 5349
Slope: 117   Par: 72

Bermudagrass greens and fairways blanket this course that was designed by Ed Riccoboni. Water comes into play on the front nine on almost every hole. Then the fairways tighten on the back nine along corridors of tall longleaf pines.

The 2nd hole is an interesting par 3, 173 yards from the men's tees, and your tee shot must carry the lake. Smart women golfers may play it as a lateral water move.

The 9th hole is a difficult dogleg left with barrier trees that flank the left side and a ditch that runs about 80 yards in front of the green. The hole is 426 from the men's tees, and the prevailing wind is often in your face.

You won't find a single straightaway hole on the back nine, and the numerous doglegs make for interesting shots. Several of the doglegs on the back nine are fun because almost every one provides the chance for birdie or par. The 18th is a par 5, dogleg right, with large centered bunkers in the fairway and natural white sand bunkers on both sides of the green.

Wildlife is prevalent at Fox Squirrel, including (you guessed it!) fox and squirrel as well as deer, alligators and birds. The retirement-community atmosphere is quieter than many resort-type courses, and the friendly staff will help make your visit enjoyable. The course is open and wide.

A practice green, locker rooms, a restaurant and club rentals are on the list of amenities here.

Greens fees range from $20 to $29, including cart. Tee times are accepted two days in advance. Walking is allowed anytime, so take advantage of it.

NORTH SHORE COUNTRY CLUB

Sneads Ferry   327-2410, (800) 828-5035

Championship Yardage: 6866	
Slope: 134	Par: 72
Men's Yardage: 6358	
Slope: 123	Par: 72
Other Yardage: 5636	
Slope: 119	Par: 72
Ladies' Yardage: 5039	
Slope: 122	Par: 72

Bob Moore designed this 18-hole course, which opened in 1988. Relatively wide bermudagrass fairways stretch along extensive mounding, tall pines and lakes. Greens are bentgrass.

Water and wind remind you that you're near the ocean and create a different game every round. Water comes into play on more than half of the holes. The course is scenic, with frequent views of the Intracoastal Waterway. It is always well-maintained.

The finishing holes on both sides are challenging and require a long carry off the tee over water.

The 18th hole puts emphasis on length; it plays 460 yards from the back tees, a slight dogleg left and usually into the prevailing wind. You tee off over water then must clear another pond to a large, slightly elevated green with two bunkers guarding the front. Drive down the right side and forget about those traps, but realize this adds length to the hole.

Amenities include a pro shop, driving range, practice green, rental clubs, a bar and grill.

Greens fees range from $37 to $50,

including cart. Walking is allowed after 3 PM. Advance tee times are not necessary.

This course takes pride in its quality. As you finish each hole, look back and appreciate the magnificent view. Better yet, bring a camera, as photo opportunities abound (just don't let it slow your or anyone else's play). If you take home a photograph of every hole, you can imagine you're still at North Shore.

OAK ISLAND GOLF & COUNTRY CLUB

928 Caswell Beach Rd.

Caswell Beach	278-5275
Championship Yardage: 6608	
Slope: 128	*Par: 72*
Men's Yardage: 6135	
Slope: 124	*Par: 72*
Ladies' Yardage: 5437	
Slope: 121	*Par: 72*

This George Cobb course, completed in 1964, is one of the county's oldest. It was recently improved and is inviting to golfers of all levels who enjoy its bermudagrass fairways and greens.

You'll need all your clubs to play Oak Island. The sea breezes are the challenge here. The wind may help you on one hole then hurt you on the next. Water and sand and open fairways, plus the differences in individual hole layouts, lend character to this course. You won't find adjacent fairways here. If you shoot wide of the fairway, you're in the trees.

One of the notable holes is the par 3 No. 7, which plays 191 yards from the back tees. You must carry over water to an inclined green (up about 35 feet), heavily trapped on both sides.

Both finishing holes are of interest. The 9th is a slight dogleg right with a trap in the corner. It measures 426 yards from the back tees and is played into the head wind; it can be 475 yards on some days.

The 18th is a par 5 that measures 553 yards from the tips. It's a straightaway shot, but you must hit into the same head wind. You must clear water on the third shot which, depending on the wind, may require a 3-wood.

Amenities include a pro shop, rental clubs, a bar, restaurant and lounge, locker rooms, a driving range, putting green and pool.

Cost is $35, including cart. Walking is allowed on weekdays after 1 PM. Tee times are accepted up to two days in advance.

In case you aren't familiar with this area, Caswell Beach is south of Bald Head Island on Rt. 211.

OLD FORT GOLF COURSE

3189 River Rd. S.E.

Winnabow	371-9940
Championship Yardage: 6311	
Slope: 108	*Par: 72*
Men's Yardage: 5773	
Slope: 103	*Par: 72*
Ladies' Yardage: 4580	
Slope: 99	*Par: 72*

This 18-hole course, designed by the Trask Co., opened in 1990. Bermudagrass covers the greens and fairways. This wide-open layout has few trees and few traps. Fairways are wide, and greens are large. Water is a factor on about half of the holes — most of them on the back nine.

The owner's favorite hole, the par 3 196-yard 8th, is a toughie because of its length and small green with surrounding sand trap. The 17th, a par 4 measuring 433 yards from the back tees, requires both the tee and second shots to carry water.

Wind is also a factor on this course near the Intracoastal Waterway.

Practice greens, a driving range and rental clubs are available.

The cost is $20, including cart. Walking is allowed at the same price. The general public is welcome. Advance reservations for tee times are not necessary.

Sea breezes and scenery add to the enjoyment of a round at Bald Head Island.

Photo: NC Travel & Tourism

OLDE POINTE GOLF
AND COUNTRY CLUB

1300 Country Club Dr.
Hampstead   270-2403
Championship Yardage: 6913
Slope: 136   *Par: 72*
Men's Yardage: 6253
Slope: 120   *Par: 72*
Other Yardage: 6008
Slope: 122   *Par: 72*
Ladies' Yardage: 5133
Slope: 115   *Par: 72*

Jerry Turner designed this 18-hole course in 1974. Fairways are bermudagrass, and the spacious greens are bentgrass. The terrain is rolling and scenic, among woods, lakes and streams.

The 12th, 13th and 14th holes are all considered signatures because of their scenic beauty on the lake. Recently added tee-to-green concrete cart paths accommodate Olde Pointe's new fleet of carts.

The 11th hole is famous for its trickiness. It's a narrow par 5 of 589 yards, with a gradual dogleg right and a downward slope into the woods. It's hard to par this one. The wind from the ocean will always affect your game.

A large putting green, driving range, chipping area, practice sand bunker, pro shop, snack bar and club rentals are available. Construction of a large member clubhouse is planned.

Lighted tennis courts and an Olympic-size pool are available to members. A boat ramp on the Intracoastal Waterway invites golfers to arrive by boat and is adjacent to a recreation area where tournaments can conclude with social functions.

Greens fees, including cart, are approximately $32. Walking is allowed for members only. You may book tee times up to two weeks in advance.

PORTERS NECK
PLANTATION AND COUNTRY CLUB

1202 Porters Neck Rd.   686-1177
Wilmington   (800) 423-5695
Championship Yardage: 7209
Slope: 130   *Par: 72*
Men's Yardage: 6818
Slope: 126   *Par: 72*
Other: Yardage: 6323
Slope: 122   *Par: 72*
Ladies' Yardage: 5382
Slope: 115   *Par: 72*

Porters Neck Plantation along the Intracoastal Waterway originated in 1732 when John Porter purchased from Maurice Moore 930 acres of King George II's original land grant. It remained a working plantation until a few years ago. Today it's a private country club community by definition, but the golf course is available for public play. The course, homesites and amenities were carefully placed among the rolling hills and dogwood and pine forests, and the traditional ambiance has been preserved.

The 18-hole bentgrass course was built in 1991 by Tom Fazio. The par 4 14th benefits the right to left player. Water runs the length of the hole on the left side. The second shot must be well-placed on the green. If the pin's up front, aim short of the hole. With the flag to the rear . . . you'll probably want to look ahead to the 15th.

No. 8 favors the straight hitter. It's a par 5 measuring 506 yards. You do have a chance to reach the green in two with very well-played shots. The bunkers on the right side of the green should be avoided at all costs. Also, a fairway bunker on the left could be deadly.

Rental clubs, a driving range and a bar are available. A sports complex includes lighted clay tennis courts, a heated lap pool, an aerobics studio and a fitness room.

Monday through Thursday greens fees are $60 per person, including cart; weekend rates are higher and subject to change. No walking is allowed. You may call as much as 60 days in advance to set your tee time.

TOPSAIL GREENS
GOLF & COUNTRY CLUB

U.S. Hwy. 17 N.
Hampstead   270-2883
Championship Yardage: 6324
Slope: 121   Par: 71
Men's Yardage: 6010
Slope: 118   Par: 71
Ladies' Yardage: 5033
Slope: 113   Par: 71

Topsail Greens is more than 20 years old and was designed by Russell Breeden. This 18-hole course is tight and, as an ocean course, windy. Fairways and greens are bermudagrass. It's considered a shot-making course that requires thinking, not just swinging. Water comes into play on seven holes, and several greens are elevated.

The island green on the par 3 No. 8, the signature hole, plays 159 yards from the men's tees. It's a test of accuracy as well as being a scenic beauty.

The 11th has a water hazard about 220 yards from the tee, which still leaves some 180 yards over a large lake to the green. It's a solid par 4.

The staff here is friendly and the course is kept in quality condition. A new large practice green, a driving range, pro shop, bar and restaurant, beverage cart and club rentals are available.

Greens fees range from $22 to $28, including cart. Twilight specials are offered for $10 to $12. Walking is allowed after 3 PM. Individuals may call seven

Lift and clean your ball only when necessary.

Insiders' Tips

days in advance to book a tee time; if you have a big group, just call and they'll do whatever they can to accommodate you.

WILMINGTON MUNICIPAL GOLF COURSE
311 S. Wallace Ave.
Wilmington   *791-0558*
Championship Yardage: 6564
Slope: 118   *Par: 71*
Men's Yardage: 6267
Slope: 116   *Par: 71*
Ladies' Yardage: 4978
Slope: 114   *Par: 72*

This 18-hole Donald Ross design has fewer water hazards and more flat terrain than most area courses. Fairways and greens are bermudagrass. Generally, fairways are relatively wide, and water hazards are not extreme.

A favorite hole is the 4th, a par 3 of 160 yards, with an elevated tee to an elevated green. A big valley in between leads to a big hill afterward if you shoot too long. To the right and left are woods. To the far right is a pond.

A nice feature here is the practice fairway left of the 9th hole. The clubhouse has showers and lockers for men. Practice greens, pro shop, locker room, rental clubs and beer sales add to the pleasure of the course.

Greens fees are inexpensive for residents, $7 to $8, as well as for nonresidents, $11 to $12. The cart fee is an additional $8. Walking is allowed, and you may set a tee time seven days in advance.

Around Wilmington and the Cape Fear Coast...

Fun Things To Do

The city of **Wilmington** is surrounded by attractions, and every day dishes up something to do. The Riverwalk is open for strolling, and here you can appreciate the historic area, with its shopping and dining, as well as the waterfront, with its leisure and commercial activities. Walking, boat or horse and carriage tours are pleasant ways to see the sights.

The USS *North Carolina* Battleship Memorial, across the river from downtown, is dedicated to veterans of World War II. The ship was the first modern U.S. battleship. It's open for tours every day and is a summer evening host to a spectacular sound and light show. Call 251-5797 for schedules.

Enjoy live entertainment at **Thalian Hall**, home of the country's oldest community theater and current host to national touring companies as well as numerous local theater companies. For more information, call 343-3664. Art is also at its best with permanent collections of 19th- and 20th-century North Carolina artists in the **St. John's Museum of Art**, 763-0281.

Wilmington Railroad Museum includes exhibits from the important rail era of the city's history. The railway system was once the largest in the world and an important contributor to Wilmington's economic development in the mid-1800s. For more information, call 763-2634.

The **Cape Fear Museum**, 341-7413, displays an interesting nautical exhibit and provides information about the social and natural history of the region. The *Henrietta II* riverboat is available for a cruise along the waterfront. It's a replica of an 18th-century steamboat.

Airlie Gardens on Wrightsville Sound offers a walking tour or a 5-mile scenic drive. It's open to the public from March through October, and the 20-acre garden is enchanting for its grand display of azaleas, camellias among the live oaks and tall pines. Call 763-9991 for information.

Poplar Grove Plantation is on U.S.

Talk about a water hazard!

Photo: NC Travel & Tourism

17 outside Wilmington. It showcases an 1850 Greek Revival house on a 628-acre plantation. Costumed guides and a number of events depict the history of the period. Call 686-9989 for information about prices and schedules.

Take the family to **Treasure Island Family Fun Park** in Sneads Ferry for go-cart racing, bumper boats, kiddie rides and miniature golf. It's a few minutes north of Topsail Island. Call 327-2700 for information.

One of the best summer activities is a 90-minute narrated tour of the Intracoastal Waterway. Climb aboard the *Endless Summer* pontoon boat and enjoy learning about the wildlife and the landscape of the famous waterway. Call 350-BOAT for information.

Fishing, boating and sailing are always popular, and the Cape Fear River and the Atlantic Ocean welcome visitors year round. For serious beach or fishing time, visit any of the coastal villages.

For more information, contact the **Cape Fear Convention and Visitors Bureau** at (800) 222-4757 or 341-4030 or pick up a copy of *The Insiders' Guide® to Wilmington & the Cape Fear Coast.*

Where to Eat

Food is a Southern experience enjoyed by visitors, and locals use mealtimes as gathering times, especially during sunny spring or fall days, for outdoor socializing along the downtown riverfront. Seafood is abundant and fresh, and other offerings reflect regional as well as international flair. Restaurants accept most major credit cards. We recommend that you call for hours of operation, as varying schedules are common during different seasons.

THE PILOT HOUSE

2 Ann St.
Wilmington   343-0200
$$$

The historic Craig House is home to a riverfront restaurant which serves good seafood and pasta with many regional recipes and frequently changing specials. Try a huge burger or sandwich for lunch, and note the wine list to accompany your dinner selection. Lunch and dinner are served daily except Sunday. The atmosphere is casual for lunch and a bit dressier for dinner.

CAFFE PHOENIX
9 S. Front St.
Wilmington   343-1395
$$

Don't complain about a short wait in line to dine here — it's worth it. Italian by nature, the restaurant's seasonal specials are always tasty, and this downtown luncheon or dinner spot provides atmosphere as well as delicious food. The decor is attractive, the staff attentive, and from appetizer to dessert it's a treat.

TRAILS END STEAK HOUSE
Trails End Rd.
Wilmington   791-2034
$$$

Beef and history are served here in equal portions. The view of the Intracoastal Waterway adds to the interest of the old restaurant with many stories to tell. You'll want to call for reservations and directions if you are ready for authentic broiled steak, salad and appetizers.

HIRO JAPANESE STEAK & SEAFOOD HOUSE
419 S. College Rd.
Wilmington   452-3097
$$$

Japanese steakhouses are fun dining destinations if you can take your time and enjoy the show of preparation as well as share some laughs with new friends. Your own chef cooks dinner on your teppan table. The food is delicious and plentiful (expect more than just steaks here), and the entertainment rounds out an evening. Soup, salad, sauces, fried rice, green tea

and of course sake or plum wine add to a great entree.

INDIA MAHAL
4610 Maple St.
Wilmington   799-2089
$

Indian food usually features lamb, curry, rice, chutney, good vegetarian dishes and breads. Our favorites are the tandoori dishes of chicken or lamb from the fired clay oven. As with many Indian restaurants, you should specify the degree of spicy-hot you like. This is an authentic restaurant with inexpensive and plentiful lunches and genuine-article dinners.

FRANKO'S CAFFE & TRATTORIA
10 Market St.
Wilmington   763-8100
$$$-$$$$

Authentic Italian dishes are prepared with fresh seafood and complemented by Italian wines. Prime rib and lobster are touted here, along with daily specials of risotto or pasta. Breads and desserts also are homemade, and so tempting. We sample Italian in every city and critique the choices of wines, and this trattoria certainly measures up with the best.

THE BRIDGE TENDER RESTAURANT
1414 Airlie Rd.   256-3419
Wrightsville Beach
$$$

The view is of the Wrightsville Beach drawbridge over the Intracoastal Waterway. The decor is enhanced by lamplight and high-raftered ceilings. The food includes frequent specials of seafood or beef. The wine list is excellent and has been nationally recognized frequently. Our favorites are seafoods that are Cajun-spiced. Locals frequent this restaurant, and the atmosphere is welcoming to visitors.

Photo: NC Travel & Toursim

Accuracy is the name of the game here if you don't want big numbers.

GARDENIAS

7105 Wrightsville Ave.   256-2421
Wrightsville Beach
$$$

Fresh pasta, fresh-baked bread, local seafood, Angus beef, vegetarian dishes and delectable desserts are well matched by fine wines at Gardenias. It's west of the Waterway and presents a dinner experience to suit any budget or taste. If you like wine and enjoy learning, the wine dinner specials are for you. Wine makers and chefs create complementary blends for each course and add commentary. Reservations are accepted but are only necessary for the wine dinners.

BIG DADDY'S SEAFOOD RESTAURANT

202 K. Ave.   458-8622
Kure Beach
$$$

A trip to the beach isn't complete without a seafood platter, and this is one of the great places to enjoy it. Choose broiled, fried, grilled, steamed or however you like. Steaks and chicken also are available in this casual setting. If you're really hungry, get the all-you-can-eat buffet. This is a huge restaurant that has been dishing it out for many years, and we keep coming back.

SOUNDSIDE

209 N. New River Dr.   328-0803
Surf City
$$$

Soundside is literally on the sound, where the views are enchanting. Seafoods predominate of course, but prime rib, chicken, soups and salads are good too. Good wines accompany fabulous dinners creatively prepared and properly served. Reservations are suggested. The Market, next door to Soundside, serves many of the same items, except entrees, with wine and followed by dessert.

Where to Stay

You'll probably want to stay near your favorite golf course. We recommend a few special accommodations here that are convenient, and most offer golf packages.

BALD HEAD ISLAND RESORT

Bald Head Is.   457-5002
Southport   (800) 234-1666
$$$$

The management group handles cottage, condo and villa rentals. This might be the farthest away from the real world you'll ever get, and it's no more than a 20-minute ferry ride. Golf carts and bikes are the only modes of transportation here faster than your feet, so imagine the noise and pollution levels dropping accordingly. Not the least expensive of resorts, this exclusive residential and vacation island will lure you into its luxurious golf course and yuppie-like atmosphere, and you can be part of it for a vacation or a lifetime. Golf packages include the round-trip ferry ride, cart and greens fees. Weekday fees are more affordable than weekend rates.

BEAU RIVAGE PLANTATION

6230 Carolina Beach Rd.   392-9021
Wilmington   (800) 628-7080
$$$-$$$$

Luxurious suites with balconies overlooking the golf practice facility, a pool and restaurant welcome you into the true plantation life, while you enjoy a golf vacation. Golf packages are available.

WILMINGTON HILTON

301 N. Water St.   763-5900
Wilmington   (800) HILTONS
$$-$$$$

Overlooking the Cape Fear River, the restored downtown district and the USS *North Carolina* battleship, this hotel is ideally situated for shopping, dining and a short drive to golf courses. Almost every amenity you could want is available, including a pool, restaurant, lounge, fitness center, conference space and courtesy van. You can also choose the concierge level for extra amenities such as beverages and continental breakfast.

BLOCKADE RUNNER RESORT HOTEL

275 Waynick Blvd.   256-2251
Wrightsville Beach   (800) 541-1161
$$$-$$$$

Golf, sailing and children's packages are offered at this fine oceanfront resort. A bar, restaurant, health center, pool and beach and comedy club provide choices of things to do during your visit, especially useful if you're traveling with a family.

THE WINE HOUSE

311 Cottage Ln.
Wilmington   763-0511
$$

The tiniest-ever bed and breakfast inn is a two-room cottage replicating an 1860s wine house. It's tastefully furnished with antiques, completely private and comfortable and located downtown, providing easy access to just about anything you'd need.

Golf Equipment

Tee Smith Custom Golf Clubs at 1047 S. Kerr Avenue, Wilmington, 395-4008, is one place you will want to visit for the serious purchase of new clubs.

Regripping service and various brands are available. Nearby at 914 S. Kerr Avenue is **Pro Golf Discount**, 392-9405, offering a variety of equipment and accessories as well as providing repair and regripping services on site. **The Golf Bag**, U.S. Highway 17 S., Hampstead, 270-2980, has a good selection of items, with emphasis on equipment and accessories for ladies.

Photo: Pinehurst Resort and Country Club

*The magnificent hotel at Pinehurst Resort and Country Club
is a destination for visitors from all over the world.*

Inside
Pinehurst and The Sandhills of North Carolina

Pinehurst is to golf what Aspen is to skiing, London is to fog, and the Sahara is to sand. If there's a finer, better, more fun, *endroit de golf* than the Pinehurst area, please tell us, and we'll go there (at your expense) to see if you know what you're talking about. There are probably a few golf destinations that offer more courses, amenities, direct flights, restaurants or driving ranges with more balls, but nobody comes close to Pinehurst when it comes to tradition, history, ambiance, character and quality of golf. And don't geographically limit this zone: In the surrounding counties, there are plenty of excellent but lesser-known courses — so much so that you could easily play 36 holes a day for about a month and never play a poor track. One aspect of this area that's often overlooked is that there's something here for every budget; there are courses, restaurants and accommodations for the millionaire as well as those of more limited means.

But the epicenter of it all is Pinehurst Resort and Country Club. This, after all, is the house that Donald built. "The Donald" is Donald Ross, the greatest golf course architect of all time. At least that's the opinion of the Donald Ross Society, a group of Ross fanatics. Pinehurst is where Ross settled and lived after a brief stint in the Northeast. This is also where he created his greatest course (Pinehurst #2) and based his design business. He owned and operated a small hotel, restaurant and bar: the Pine Crest Inn. Of course, other great

architects have been active in the area; you'll find courses by Ellis Maples, Dan Maples, Tom Jackson, Russell Breeden, Arnold Palmer, Gene Hamm, Jack Nicklaus, Jack Nicklaus II (yes, they're related), Tom Fazio, Rees Jones, J. Porter Gibson and a few others of whom you may not have heard.

You could take any course in the Pinehurst vicinity, place it in any metropolitan area in the United States or Canada, and that course would instantly be one of the top two or three courses in that given area. After seeing so many Pinehurst courses, you'll be numbed and spoiled. Golf just is not the same anywhere else.

Also special is the fact that just about every course here is accessible to the public in one way or another. Out of approximately 35 courses within 30 minutes of the traffic circle at the junction of U.S. highways 211 and 15/501, all but three or four are open to the public golfer. Some are more public than others. In other words, some courses are resort-oriented, and your chances of getting a choice tee time at a famous course are better if you're staying in a room that's just a few feet from the first tee. But, local knowledge includes the fact that, season permitting, you'll be able to play on almost every course.

The key here is getting to know the professional staff at a local club or, better still, at the resort where you're based. In the Pinehurst area, everyone in the business knows each other. The pro at resort

GOLF COURSES IN NORTH CAROLINA'S PINEHURST AREA

Name	Type	# Holes	Par	Slope	Yards	Walking	Booking	Cost
Beacon Ridge	semiprivate	18	72	123	6143	restricted	anytime	$39-52
CC of Whispering Pines								
West Course	semiprivate	18	71	125	6007	restricted	anytime	$39-49
East Course	semiprivate	18	72	124	6406	restricted	anytime	$39-49
Cypress Lakes	public	18	72	118	6585	anytime	anytime	$25-27
Foxfire								
East Course	semiprivate/resort	18	72	123	6286	restricted	anytime	$45-64
West Course	semiprivate/resort	18	72	123	6333	restricted	anytime	$45-64
Hyland Hills	public	18	72	113	6111	restricted	anytime	$30-40
Keith Hills	public	18	72	124	6129	anytime	anytime	$29-34
King's Grant	semiprivate	18	72	118	6222	anytime	3 days	$29-36
Knollwood Fairways (9 holes)	semiprivate	18	72	121	5218	anytime	anytime	$22
Legacy	public	18	72	124	6505	no	anytime	$45-75
Longleaf Country Club	semiprivate	18	71	110	6073	restricted	anytime	$42-67
Midland Country Club (9 holes)	semiprivate	18	70	n/r	5714	restricted	anytime	$25
Mid Pines Golf resort	resort	18	72	122	6121	restricted	anytime	$58-90
Pine Needles	resort	18	71	126	6318	restricted	anytime	$68-98
Pinehurst								
#1	resort	18	70	114	5873	caddies	anytime	$59-94
#2	resort	18	72	127	6354	caddies	anytime	$134-170
#3	resort	18	70	117	5593	caddies	anytime	$59-94
#4	resort	18	72	117	6396	caddies	anytime	$59-94
#5	resort	18	72	123	6357	caddies	anytime	$59-94
#6	resort	18	72	132	6603	restricted	anytime	$59-94
#7	resort	18	72	114	6692	restricted	anytime	$104-139
#8	resort	n/a	n/a	n/a	n/a	n/a	n/a	n/a
The Pit	public	18	71	128	6138	anytime	anytime	$45-80
Seven Lakes	semiprivate	18	72	122	6151	restricted	anytime	$45-60
Talamore at Pinehurst	public	18	71	134	6393	llamas	anytime	$42-82
Whispering Woods	semiprivate	18	70	n/a	6334	no	anytime	$30-42
Woodlake Country Club	semiprivate	18	72	129	6584	restricted	3 days	$45-70

The Sandhills

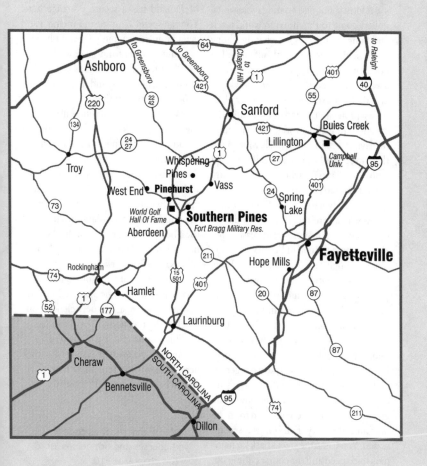

#1 knows the pro at resort #2 who can get a tee time at #2 because he knows the guy in the starting tower who, in turn, plays golf with the guy who used to caddie on tour for the friend of the pro at course #4 where the greenskeeper is friendly with the bartender at bar "A," which also happens to be Wayne Gretzky's favorite watering hole when he's down with family, friends and Marty McSorley for a week of 36 holes a day. You get the picture.

A lot of young and aspiring professional golfers come to Pinehurst to work, teach and hone their games for what they hope will be a life of professional golf on the big boys' tour. There are plenty of professionals and directors of golf whose knowledge and skills are excellent. What better place to be a professional than in Pinehurst, the capital of the golfing world. When it comes to playing certain courses, ask. More often than not, pro #1 can make a call to pro #3 who can call pro #9 who picked up Laura Davies' bar tab the last time she was here and owes a favor to pro #3 — and so on.

As with any resort area, seasons dictate operations. The first major "in-season" period begins at the end of February and extends through late May and early June. You'll find plenty of fine sunny days with perfect temperatures interspersed with days of rain and gloom. The summer months are primarily quiet on most of the courses. The intensity of the summer heat and humidity makes golf a chore, and the frequent late-day thunderstorms make it dangerous and wet. In deep summer the fairways are excellent, but the greens will be slow as the greenskeepers fight to save them from the heat and humidity. Fall brings a second season: You'll find the greens back to championship speed and the courses filling up. The fall season ends around Thanksgiving. The winter season is somewhat dead, but the courses are playable (unless the course has overseeded with rye, fairways will be brown and dull), and the rates can be at their lowest. Still, there can be plenty of wonderful and comfortable days in the winter season, and most of the courses offer outstanding rates.

Overall, Pinehurst offers some great values in any season; there's a course for nearly every budget. Low-cost but comfortable lodging options abound, and if you're on an eating budget, Ronald McDonald has a secure presence here. You can spend a fortune in Pinehurst and get a lot in return, but you won't have to take out a second mortgage to have an excellent time here. Still, it's fun to have a couple of blowouts, and there are plenty of opportunities for that.

Whatever the size of your wallet or golfing desires, the key is to book and plan ahead as much as possible. Many, many courses host large outings and leagues, and there's nothing more depressing than showing up at a course only to find that you've arrived (without a tee time) smack dab in the middle of the annual tournament of the Mid-Atlantic Chapter of the Association of Undertakers and Mortuary Professionals (UMP). After your hour wait as the pro struggles to fit your foursome in, the pace of play will best be described as funereal. Just remember, the desk clerk at your hotel or the pro at your resort can be incredibly resourceful if you're polite.

Anyway, get to know people who work here, have fun and remember that it's always a beautiful day in Pinehurst.

Note that the area code for all golf courses and businesses listed in this chapter is 910.

Profile: Donald Ross

Photo: The Architects of Golf

Donald J. Ross

Donald Ross is to golf course architecture what Elvis is to rock 'n' roll. No, that doesn't work. Donald Ross is to golf course architecture what Mozart is to opera. No, that doesn't work either. Donald Ross is to golf course architecture what Stradivarius is to violin making. That's it. That should give you the picture. And Pinehurst was his home for most of his life.

It's impossible to quantify Ross's influence on golf and golf course design. The first ever biography about Ross is currently being written, although we were unable to discover when the book is due on the shelves or who will publish it. W. Pete Jones of Raleigh is the author.

Born in 1872 in Dornoch, Scotland, Ross was the first son of Mundo and Lily Campbell Ross. At age 10, he began work as a caddie at Royal Dornoch Golf Club. He traveled to St. Andrews where he apprenticed as a clubmaker and professional under Old Tom Morris. It was here that he developed a love for golf and the understanding of what made a good golf hole. In 1899, Ross emmigrated to Boston and became head professional and greenskeeper at Oakley Country Club where he improved the somewhat basic layout. It was at Oakley that he met members of the Tufts family. The Tufts were building Pinehurst, and they urged the young Ross to become the winter professional at their new resort.

At Pinehurst, Ross started to build his first great golf courses. Those courses — Pinehurst #1, #2, #3 and #4 — firmly placed Ross as the preeminent golf course architect in America, a country whose population was just beginning its love affair with the game. From 1912 until his death in 1948, Ross was the busiest and arguably the best golf course architect in the United States. In 1925, more than 3,000 men were building courses designed by Donald J. Ross and Associates. The firm had winter offices in Pinehurst, summer offices in Rhode Island plus offices in North Amherst, Massachusetts and Wynnewood, Pennsylvania.

Ross formed the American Society of Golf Course Architects. The society's jacket is Ross tartan. The award for contributions for furthering public understanding of golf is called the Donald Ross Award. There can't be a golf course architect in America who has visited Ross's best-known and least-known courses and come away without learning something.

Original and untouched Donald Ross courses incorporate a number of links touches from his native Dornoch and St. Andrews. He built fairway and greenside bunkers with steep faces and gave his greens a series of difficult undulations. Even though a Ross course always seems to play tougher than it looks, Ross never tricked up a course; he always made it playable and fair for all levels of golfer. The best place to see the finest original Donald Ross work is at Pinehurst's #1, #2 and #3.

A large number of Donald Ross courses were changed by other architects, yet many clubs are finding ways to restore their courses to original Ross form. A couple of architects are even making a good living in this line of work. As we've already mentioned, you'll see Ross's best efforts in the Pinehurst area, but examples of his work abound, from some of the most exclusive clubs in the country to munis where greens fees are $6 a round.

The list of fine Donald Ross courses is endless, and you'll find a number of them in anyone's ranking of the top 100 courses in the country.

By the way, Ross fans might consider joining the Donald Ross Society. For more information, write to P.O. Box 403, Bloomfield, Connecticut 06002.

This portrait of Donald J. Ross, legendary golf course designer, was painted in oil by artist Anthony Franklin Weddington of Apex, N.C.,and is part of the Pinehurst resort and Country Club collection.

Artist: Anthony Franklin Weddington

Golf Courses In and Around Pinehurst

BEACON RIDGE
GOLF AND COUNTRY CLUB

Seven Lakes W.	
West End	673-2950
Championship Yardage: 6414	
Slope: 125	Par: 72
Men's Yardage: 6143	
Slope: 123	Par: 72
Other Yardage: 5354	
Slope: 114	Par: 72
Ladies' Yardage: 4730	
Slope: 115	Par: 72

Beacon Ridge Golf and Country Club, a Gene Hamm design on rolling, wooded terrain, opened in 1988. This well-maintained course has bermudagrass fairways and bentgrass greens.

Located about 10 minutes outside the main Pinehurst area, Beacon Ridge offers some fine golf in a relaxed environment. It's part of a housing development, but houses don't interfere too much, if at all.

You'll find that the back nine is less undulating than the front and, therefore, a little less difficult by comparison. But overall, the course is challenging without

Photo: Pinehurst Resort and Country Club

Pinehurst #2 is consistently rated as one of the best and most challenging courses in the world. In 1999 it will host the U.S. Open.

being impossible — a happy medium that will satisfy golfers of all levels. Perhaps what sets Beacon Ridge apart from a number of other courses in the area is its variety. Just about every hole has its own character. There isn't too much water to contend with, but when it comes into play, it will definitely affect your thinking. There are plenty of bunkers lurking to distract you as well, most of which are large and flat, with no face. The greens are mostly large and sloped. You'll find decent room off the tee, but if you miss the fairway, you'll end up in deep rough and pine trees and might not find your ball. Keep it in play and your score should be sensible.

Amenities include a practice green, range, chipping green, locker room, bar, restaurant, rental clubs and a pro shop.

The course is walkable for the extremely fit, but you'll be better off with a cart. You can book a tee time anytime you choose. Approximate cost, including cart, is $52 high, $39 low.

COUNTRY CLUB OF WHISPERING PINES
2 Clubhouse Blvd.
Whispering Pines   949-2311

The Country Club of Whispering Pines opened the East Course in 1959 and the West Course in 1970 — both Ellis Maples designs. The West Course is relatively flat; the East Course is set on rolling terrain. In the fairways, you'll find bermudagrass; on the greens, bentgrass.

The housing around the course is mostly owned by retirees who purchased the club from the developers a few years ago. There's a big membership push going on, so don't be surprised if the club goes private within three to five years. The club offers a limited number of condos for rent.

Amenities include a practice green, range, chipping green, locker room, restaurant, rental clubs and a pro shop.

Both courses are walkable, but you must take a cart if you're not a member. You can book a tee time anytime. Approximate cost, including cart, is $49 high, $43 medium and $39 low.

West Course

Championship Yardage: 6340
Slope: 128 — Par: 71
Men's Yardage: 6007
Slope: 125 — Par: 71
Other Yardage: 5525
Slope: 118 — Par: 71
Ladies' Yardage: 5135
Slope: 121 — Par: 71

Let's start with the West Course — newer, shorter and tighter than its sister track. There's also plenty of water to negotiate on the back nine, thus this course demands accuracy and sound judgment. There's a great variety of interesting holes and relatively few homes — the course is mature enough so that tall pines tend to obscure the back porch of Ted and Millie Morris's place.

The key from the tee is to keep the ball in play on the tight fairways; the key to scoring from there is to avoid the many and mostly large bunkers that protect the large greens. If you miss the green and the rough is deep, then you're bound to have some scoring difficulties.

The back nine is definitely challenging, and just about every hole brings water into play. You'll really enjoy your good shots on the two par 3s. Overall, this is a fun course that will suit the player whose strength is accuracy, not distance.

East Course

Championship Yardage: 7110
Slope: 125 — Par: 72
Men's Yardage: 6406
Slope: 124 — Par: 72
Other Yardage: 5943
Slope: 117 — Par: 72
Ladies' Yardage: 5542
Slope: 123 — Par: 72

Perhaps the opposite could be said of the East Course, a track that's more than 7000 yards from the back tees. Of course, you don't have to play from the tips. The course will be somewhat more friendly from other tees. The fairways are mostly wide, and there seem to be quite a few of the epic and sweeping doglegs that made Ellis Maples famous. The track is really extremely fair and somewhat challenging, and most holes offer difficulties without gimmicks.

On the back nine, you'll find a couple of holes where water comes into play, but it's not as abundant as on the West Course. Still, it helps to be somewhat straight off the tee. You'll have plenty of chances to risk aiming for a certain segment of the fairway — the reward for a well-placed shot will be an easier approach. The greens are large, sloped and protected primarily by large bunkers. Once again, if the rough is grown up around the green, you'll have a difficult time finding your ball as well as getting up and down. There are also quite a few fairway bunkers. This fun and challenging course will test even the scratch golfer (from the back tees).

CYPRESS LAKES GOLF CLUB

Cypress Lake Dr.
Hope Mills — 483-0359
Championship Yardage: 7217
Slope: 126 — Par: 72
Men's Yardage: 6585
Slope: 118 — Par: 72
Ladies' Yardage: 5060
Slope: 116 — Par: 74

Insiders' Tips

If you're going to play several golf courses and stay at a local hotel, go for the golf packages. This will save you the hassle of making telephone calls to several different courses and will often save you money off the advertised walk-up rates; plus you're more likely to get a preferred tee time.

You can cruise around the village of Pinehurst in a horse-drawn carriage.

We were told that Cypress Lakes opened in 1968, although we think (and we'll tell you why later) that it's much older. L.B. Floyd designed the course on rolling, wooded terrain, with bermudagrass fairways and bentgrass greens.

There are probably better golf courses in the greater Fayetteville metropolitan area, but this one stands out because it was previously owned by L.B. Floyd, father of golfing greats Raymond and Marlene Floyd. If you've ever read Ray Floyd's *From Sixty Yards In*, you know about the young Raymond splashing about in the bunkers on his father's course. This is where we believe that the younger Floyd learned how to get the ball up and down so impressively — and so lucratively. And this is why we think the course is older than 1968. The scorecard describes this as an "Open, Championship Course."

The course itself has been under new ownership for quite some time, and a renovation is currently under way. The layout is somewhat straightforward, and the obvious hazards or difficulties that need to be negotiated are easily visible from wherever you are. Still, it's a fun track that's well worth a visit if you're into finding out where the Floyds originally played golf.

Amenities include a practice green, range, chipping green, locker room, bar, restaurant, rental clubs and a pro shop.

You can walk your round and book a tee time anytime. Approximate cost, including cart, is $25 on weekdays and $27 on weekends.

FOXFIRE RESORT AND COUNTRY CLUB
Hoffman Rd.
Pinehurst   295-5555

First, a note about the resort and accommodations. Plenty of people live all year at Foxfire, but many visit for a conference or just for golf. There are plenty of condominiums for rent, each with various bedroom/bathroom configurations. Call (800) 736-9347 for a brochure with all the details. Foxfire also specializes in conferences and golf tournaments/outings.

Once you've completed all your business, spend some quality time on the golf course. Then check out the restaurant, snack bar and bar, which we're told will stay open pretty much until you're ready to stop imbibing. Everyone here is warm and friendly; if you're looking for a relaxed setting for whatever sort of golf outing suits your fancy, you can't go wrong at Foxfire. With an advance call to the pro shop, the public can get a tee time on either course.

Now, about the golf courses. Both were designed by Gene Hamm. The East Course opened in 1968 and the West Course, in 1973. Both are set in rolling terrain, with pine forest bordering the bermudagrass fairways. Greens are covered with bentgrass.

Amenities include a practice green, range, chipping green, locker room, bar, restaurant, rental clubs and a pro shop.

Both courses are walkable for the fit, but you'll be encouraged to take a cart. You can book a tee time anytime. Approximate cost, including cart, is $64 high, $55 medium and $45 low.

East Course

Championship Yardage: 6851	
Slope: 130	Par: 72
Men's Yardage: 6286	
Slope: 123	Par: 72
Other Yardage: 5864	
Slope: 114	Par: 72
Ladies' Yardage: 5256	
Slope: 119	Par: 72

Let's start with the East Course. You'll begin with the No. 1 handicap hole, a medium-length par 5. There's plenty of length from the back tees and plenty of width on most of the fairways. If you spray it a little off the tee, you'll find either deep rough or a nasty bunker, heavily infiltrated with love grass. You'll find some of those same bunkers around many of the greens. (By the way, the greenskeeper here is called Sandy Greens.) The greens are primarily large and sloped. You can push the ball a little, be pin high and still have a long putt for birdie.

Water could prove irritating if you miss a shot badly. You might enjoy the back nine a little more than the front: It's completely undeveloped, and you really feel like you're away from it all. Some of the finest holes are on the back nine and require your best form and behavior.

West Course

Championship Yardage: 6742	
Slope: 128	Par: 72
Men's Yardage: 6333	
Slope: 123	Par: 72
Ladies' Yardage: 5273	
Slope: 115	Par: 72

The West Course is fun, well-designed and perhaps a little easier in places than its counterpart, although it's plenty difficult in other places. Water comes into play on a few holes but shouldn't pose much of a problem unless you're particularly wayward. The greens are large and mostly flat, as are the bunkers. The challenges are evident; there's nothing tricked-up or artificial. If we had to choose between the two courses, we'd probably pick the East, but you'll be just as satisfied with the West. Foxfire is fortunate to have two good golf courses at its disposal.

HYLAND HILLS GOLF CLUB

4100 U.S. Hwy. 1 N.	
Southern Pines	692-3752
Championship Yardage: 6726	
Slope: 120	Par: 72
Men's Yardage: 6111	
Slope: 113	Par: 72
Ladies' Yardage: 4677	
Slope: 109	Par: 72

Hyland Hills Golf Club opened in 1973. Tom Jackson designed the course on rolling, wooded terrain bordered by houses and pine forest. Fairways are bermudagrass; greens, bentgrass.

Located just north of Southern Pines, Hyland Hills offers a fine and fun golf course in a pleasant, primarily open setting. It's one of Tom Jackson's earlier designs and lacks some of the excesses of the modern Jackson era, such as huge mounds. But as you might expect from Jackson, this course offers well-designed holes. You won't find too much trouble off the tee. If you spray it, you may find the deep rough in the summer, some nasty bunkers or the occasional small mound. Around the large and interestingly shaped greens are bunkers, more mounds and some greens with considerable slope and undulation. The greens pose the most difficulty, so bring your best putting game.

Overall, Hyland Hills provides outstanding variety. It's a good example of what made Tom Jackson such a sought-after designer. Mid- to low-handicappers should play the course from the back tees for the full effect and the most challenge. The course is an excellent value and justifiably popular.

Amenities include a practice green, range, chipping green, locker room, bar, restaurant, rental clubs and a pro shop.

The course is walkable for the extremely fit, but walking is restricted. You can book a tee time anytime you choose. Approximate cost, including cart, is from $40 down to $30.

KEITH HILLS COUNTRY CLUB
Keith Hills Rd.

Buies Creek	893-1371
Championship Yardage: 6660	
Slope: 129	Par: 72
Men's Yardage: 6129	
Slope: 124	Par: 72
Ladies' Yardage: 5535	
Slope: 120	Par: 72

Keith Hills opened in 1977. Ellis Maples designed the course and Dan Maples grabbed the assist. The course is set in primarily rolling, wooded terrain bordered with houses, with bermudagrass fairways and bentgrass greens.

Keith Hills is a well-regarded course that's owned and operated by Campbell University, so if you see a Camel wandering across the first fairway, you'll understand why (and if you don't understand — the university's mascot is a camel). The course is so well-regarded that it's often difficult to get a tee time during peak seasons. You can book a tee time just about anytime, but, in 1995 the month of October was fully booked by mid-September.

This beautiful course has the reputation for being kept in excellent condition. The fairways are wide, but the rough can get thick. The greens are large and sloped. A couple of elevated tees make for some dramatic tee shots. There's a reason why a course that's a little off the beaten track is so popular . . . it's not necessarily the hot dogs in the snack bar.

In October 1995, Keith Hills opened the largest practice facility in North Carolina, designed by Dan Maples. There's also an indoor teaching center. If you're in the Buies Creek or sandhills area, check out Keith Hills.

Amenities include a practice green, range, chipping green, locker room, snack bar, rental clubs and a pro shop.

The course is walkable, and you can walk anytime, although in the busy seasons you will be charged a cart fee whether

Plan now for a trip to the 1999 U.S. Open that will be held at Pinehurst #2. This should be a very special event, and if you enjoy golf tournaments, you'll love this one: See the greatest golfers on the greatest Donald Ross course.

Insiders' Tips

you ride or not. You can book a tee time anytime but make sure you call ahead; the course is very popular, as we've mentioned. Approximate cost, including cart, is $29 weekdays and $34 on the weekend.

KING'S GRANT
GOLF AND COUNTRY CLUB

198 Shawcroft Rd.
Fayetteville   630-1114
Championship Yardage: 6634
Slope: 125   Par: 72
Men's Yardage: 6222
Slope: 118   Par: 72
Other Yardage: 5814
Slope: 113   Par: 72
Ladies' Yardage: 5060
Slope: 115   Par: 72

Jim Holmes designed King's Grant Golf and Country Club, which opened in 1990. The course is set in rolling, wooded terrain bordered with houses. In the fairways, you'll find bermudagrass; on the greens, bentgrass.

Fayetteville is best known throughout the world as home to one of the largest army bases in the United States: Fort Bragg. This is where you'll find paratroopers and red berets. You'll also find King's Grant, a housing development course that's quite a challenge, particularly from the back tees. Many of the holes are extremely close to the houses, but if you ignore the back tees and the out-of-bounds markers, you'll find some fine, well-designed holes offering lots of challenge and interest.

Amenities include a practice green, range, chipping green, locker room, snack bar and a pro shop.

You can walk anytime. Book a tee time three days in advance. Approximate cost, including cart, is $29 on weekdays and $36 on weekends.

KNOLLWOOD FAIRWAYS GOLF CLUB

1470 Midland Rd.
Southern Pines   692-3572
Championship Yardage: 5398
Slope: 123   Par: 70
Men's Yardage: 5218
Slope: 121   Par: 70
Ladies' Yardage: 4730
Slope: 120   Par: 70

C.A. Pitts designed Knollwood Fairways, although we were told that the great Bobby Jones designed the track (hmmm...). The course is set on flat terrain bordered by pine trees and condos. In the fairways, you'll find bermudagrass; on the greens, bentgrass.

Knollwood Fairways is a fun, short and entertaining layout that's great for a practice round or for the beginning or seasoned golfer who doesn't want to play a huge course. You start off with a short par 3 over water followed by a longer par 3 over land. Then you begin a series of short, tight par 4s. A local pro told us that he and his friends play the course with

Profile: Peggy Kirk Bell

Born and raised in Findlay, Ohio, Peggy Kirk Bell excelled at sports and graduated from Rollins College in Winter Park, Florida, with a degree in physical education. Today she lives in Pinehurst, owns Pine Needles and is part of an ownership group that recently purchased Mid Pines.

Ms. Bell enjoyed an outstanding professional and amateur career. She was a charter member of the LPGA and was the first female professional to fly from event to event in her own plane. In 1953, she married Warren "Bullet" Bell and, in the same year, they purchased Pine Needles with Julius Boros and the Cosgrove family. In two years they bought out the partners and began developing the buildings around the course and the resort.

Today, Ms. Bell has developed the course into one of the foremost resorts and teaching centers in the country. She was a consultant with the Spalding Golf Company for 44 years. In 1950, she represented her country as a member of the Curtis Cup Team.

The Pinehurst area owes a great debt to Ms. Bell for bringing so many great tournaments to Pine Needles and for making the area friendly to women golfers of all levels. It must be exciting for her that the best in the world will come to her home for the 1996 U.S. Women's Open.

---

one rule: You must use your driver on every par 4. You might not have that same degree of control with your big stick, so take a little less club with you. There are a couple of full-length holes in the middle of the course. The massive driving range is popular with locals. Knollwood Fairways is a great place for an after-work practice round.

You can walk anytime (and you should walk here). You can book a tee time anytime you choose. Approximate cost, including cart, is $22 for 18 holes.

LEGACY GOLF LINKS

U.S. Hwy. 15/501 S.	
Aberdeen	944-8825
Championship Yardage: 7008	
Slope: 133	Par: 72
Men's Yardage: 6505	
Slope: 124	Par: 72
Other Yardage: 594	
Slope: 122	Par: 72
Ladies' Yardage: 5080	
Slope: 128	Par: 72

Legacy Golf Links opened in 1992. Jack Nicklaus II, son of the Golden Bear, designed the course on rolling, wooded terrain, with bermudagrass fairways and bentgrass greens.

Jack Nicklaus II is perhaps best known

as his father's son, but don't underestimate the design skill of the "second edition." Don't underestimate his golfing skill either: The younger bear won the North and South Amateur Championship in 1985. After graduating from the University of North Carolina, Jack II tried various pro circuits but soon decided to concentrate on working with his father's golf architecture business. His other efforts include Ibis Golf and Country Club in Florida and Hanbury Manor in England.

At Legacy, Jack II created a course that's extremely well-respected among locals who will not hesitate to recommend that their out-of-town friends visit this course. Legacy is a totally public course with an upper-market atmosphere. At the bag drop, an attendant takes care of placing your bag on the cart, and there's a shoe shine waiting for you after your round.

The course itself is outstanding — one of the best tests in the area, in fact — particularly from the back tees. Jack II and his design team built challenging, fun and playable holes. Water comes into play frequently and could lead to a big score if you're not careful. Off the tee, stick to the middle of the fairway; however, balls struck to the left and right sometimes come back to the middle due to favorable mounding. It's not death to miss the fairway, but you may find a bad lie or your view of the green obstructed by a pine tree. The course is not heavily bunkered. The greens are large and mostly sloped.

Golf Digest praised the layout and the course's value — a true rarity. If you like sensible and playable modern tracks, you'll enjoy Legacy. Play it and you'll understand why locals give it well-deserved kudos.

Amenities include a practice green, range, chipping green, locker room, bar, restaurant, rental clubs, a beverage cart, shoe shine and a pro shop.

Carts are required. Book a tee time anytime. Approximate cost, including cart, is $75 high, $50 medium and $45 low.

LONGLEAF COUNTRY CLUB

1010 Midland Rd.
Southern Pines   692-2114
Championship Yardage: 6,600
Slope: 117   *Par: 71*
Men's Yardage: 6,073
Slope: 110   *Par: 71*
Ladies' Yardage: 4,719
Slope: 108   *Par: 71*

Dan Maples designed the golf course at Longleaf Country Club, which opened in 1988. The back nine is set in rolling, wooded terrain bordered with houses; the front is generally open. Fairways are bermudagrass, and greens are bentgrass.

As you drive down Midland Road for the first time, likely awed by the sheer number of golf courses concentrated on one road, you may pass Longleaf thinking it's a horse farm. Actually, the front nine is built on a former horse-training facility, and Dan Maples kept many of the old fences and hedges intact. The 100-, 150- and 200-yard markers are takeoffs on furlong markers. In case you're wondering why Dan Maples was chosen as the designer (aside from the fact that he's a darn good architect): He's part of the partnership that's developing this course. Ah, that explains it.

The front and back nines at Longleaf are quite different. It's sort of like Kyle Petty's hair: short in the front, long in the back. The front is so open, you would be excused for thinking it a links layout. The back is wooded and somewhat tight in places due to the intrusion of homes. There's a bit of water on the back nine, and one hole includes a tree right in the middle of the fairway — a Dan Maples eccentricity. There's plenty of room off the tee, and you should have lots of fun driv-

Mid Pines Golf Resort has been improved since its purchase by Peggy Kirk Bell and other investors.

ing the ball. The greens are predominantly large, subtly undulating and well-guarded in places. The fairways feature some mounds and the occasional bunker. Overall, this fun course is suitable for all golfers.

Amenities include a practice green, range, chipping green, locker room, bar, restaurant, rental clubs and a pro shop.

The front nine is very walkable, and the back nine is walkable for the fit; you can walk anytime but still must pay a cart fee. You can book a tee time three months in advance. Approximate cost, including cart, is $67 high, $55 medium and $42 low.

MIDLAND COUNTRY CLUB

2205 Midland Rd.
Southern Pines   295-3241
Championship Yardage: 6186
Slope: 119   Par: 70
Men's Yardage: 5714
Slope: No rating   Par: 70
Ladies' Yardage: 5066
Slope: 113   Par: 70

Tom Jackson designed this nine-hole course on flat terrain bordered by houses. In the fairways, you'll find bermudagrass; on the greens, you'll find bentgrass.

Midland is owned by the same crew that's in charge of Knollwood, and you'll find the same ambiance and similar characteristics: fun, walkable, decently challenging, tight in places and excellent value. While this is not one of Jackson's extravaganzas, the course is wonderfully playable and well worth the approximately $20 per round. Before and/or after your round, challenge the Dunes Restaurant, just a lob wedge from the pro shop.

Amenities include a practice green, restaurant and rental clubs.

The course is extremely walkable, so walk if you can. Book a tee time whenever you choose. Approximate cost, including cart, is $25 for 18 holes.

MID PINES GOLF RESORT

1010 Midland Rd.
Southern Pines   692-2114
Championship Yardage: 6515
Slope: 127   Par: 72
Men's Yardage: 6121
Slope: 122   Par: 72
Ladies' Yardage: 5592
Slope: 128   Par: 72

The golf course at Mid Pines Golf Resort, a Donald Ross design, opened in 1921. The course is set in rolling, wooded terrain, with bermudagrass fairways and bentgrass greens.

First, a word or two about the resort: Mid Pines is well-known in the Carolinas as a great place for corporate meetings and conferences. Adjacent to the course are numerous houses available for rent; these wonderful old homes are a pleasant change from the typical hotel setting.

Should you want more of a hotel atmosphere, Mid Pines offers one of the most attractive and well-run facilities in the area. The rooms are traditionally appointed, many with antiques. We can't think of a more wonderful setting for a conference or weekend getaway. There's also some wonderful food and drink. Other amenities include a lounge, outdoor deck, bikes, indoor game room, volleyball, babysitting services, outdoor swimming pool, tennis courts, children's play area and shuffleboard. You can also organize or be part of a golf clinic.

Until recently, word was that the course was not in the best condition. That's all changed since Peggy Kirk Bell and some investors purchased Mid Pines in 1994. Mrs. Bell also owns Pine Needles, and you can read more about her in the Pine Needles review. The end result is that the same superintendent who keeps Pine Needles in such great shape has been at work at Mid Pines. The result of this union: A great Donald Ross layout is enjoying a well-deserved renaissance.

Mid Pines offers classic, wonderful Ross resort golf. You'll find all the characteristics that made Ross so great: plenty of room off the tee, wonderful landscaping and tough greens and green complexes. It's exciting that such an excellent design is back on the map. And although you're more likely to get a good tee time if you stay at the resort, the track is open to public play.

If you're a fan of Donald Ross layouts and you enjoy a more traditional course, you'll really enjoy Mid Pines. And make sure you visit the locker room — one of the oldest, most traditional and untouched in the area; it's like stepping back into the 1920s.

Amenities include a practice green, range, chipping green, locker room, bar, restaurant, rental clubs, a beverage cart and a pro shop.

You must take a cart. We suggest you book a tee time with your reservation. The public can book up to a week in advance in-season and anytime out-of-season. Approximate cost, including cart, is $90 high, $68 medium and $58 low.

PINE NEEDLES RESORT

Midland Rd.

Southern Pines	*692-7111*
Championship Yardage: 6708	
Slope: 131	*Par: 71*
Men's Yardage: 6318	
Slope: 126	*Par: 71*
Other Yardage: 6003	
Slope: 124	*Par: 71*
Ladies' Yardage: 5039	
Slope: 118	*Par: 71*

Hyland Hills proves that you can play a great golf course in the Pinehurst area without having to pay a huge sum.

The golf course at Pine Needles Resort opened in 1927. Donald Ross designed the course on rolling, wooded terrain, with bermudagrass fairways and bentgrass greens. The course has hosted numerous significant tournaments and in 1996 will be the site of the U.S. Women's Open.

Speaking of the resort, you'll need to stay here if you want to play Pine Needles. Like its new relative, Mid Pines, Pine Needles is an excellent corporate retreat or weekend getaway. There are villas and apartments for rent, and you'll find the accommodations welcoming and well-appointed. Instruction is big here at Pine Needles: One of the finest teaching facilities in the Southeast is just seconds from the accommodations and is staffed by some fine instructors, including one of the most famous in the country: Peggy Kirk Bell. The course is also home to touring professional Pat McGowan. Pat's married to the former Bonnie Bell, a relative of Mrs. Bell. A family atmosphere predominates; you'll feel right at home at Pine Needles. The place exudes golf, relaxation and Southern hospitality.

The golf course is magnificent. Like many Ross courses, the layout will not blow you away or drop your jaw; it will provide a stern but playable test. It's such a fair, fun and picturesque track, you'll be tempted to play it over and over again. Keep your ball out of the deep rough adjacent to the fairways and greens and play your approach shots to the right part of the greens. The rough isn't always grown up, and the greens aren't always fast, but you'll still find plenty of challenge. There's ample room off the tee on most holes, and a couple of water hazards come into play if you're not careful. Fairway bunkers on a few holes may envelop your ball. The greens are large and protected by a series of bunkers and small mounds and are somewhat more consistent than the putting surfaces on other Ross courses.

All potential problems are readily apparent, so keep your eyes open and you'll be OK. The layout features some extremely reachable par 5s, some long par 4s and some exciting par 3s where club selection is critical. But overall, there's no trickery, just pure golf in a wonderful setting — a true championship course with minimal death or glory shots.

It should be extremely interesting to watch the U.S. Women's Open when it comes to Pine Needles. It's exciting that the resort has made the effort to host such an important event. We would rank Pine Needles as a must-play in the Pinehurst area.

Amenities include a practice green, range, chipping green, locker room, bar, restaurant, rental clubs and a pro shop.

Walking is restricted primarily to the off-season. Book a tee time with your reservation. Approximate cost, including cart, is $98 high, $72 medium and $68 low.

PINEHURST
RESORT AND COUNTRY CLUB

Carolina Vista Dr.
Pinehurst   *(800) 487-4653*

Here it is — the golf resort of golf resorts. If there's a resort that's more golf than Pinehurst, please show us. If there's a resort where golf is more celebrated and important, please take us there. If there's a resort with more high-quality courses, we'd love to see it. If there's a course with more history and prestige than Pinehurst, show us the book.

People come to the Pinehurst Resort and Country Club from the world over, and they're not coming for the logo golf towels in the golf shop or the gin martini (shaken not stirred) in the Ryder Cup Lounge. In fact, there's even a book about Pinehurst, by Lee Pace, entitled *Pinehurst Stories*. Even if you're not a golf history buff, pick up this volume; it's interesting reading.

The actual resort dates back to 1895 when Boston soda fountain magnate James Walker Tufts bought about 5,500 acres of former timberland in the middle of North Carolina. Tufts hired Frederick

Olmstead to design and plan the resort and accompanying village. Olmstead designed New York City's famed Central Park as well as the grounds of the Biltmore Estate in Asheville, North Carolina (see our Mountains of North Carolina chapter).

The first golf course opened in 1897. Donald Ross was hired as the professional and greenskeeper in 1900, and it was from here that he built his reputation as the finest golf course architect ever.

The hotel that now dominates the scenery opened in 1901. The resort flourished and even stayed open during the Great Depression, when staff were compensated in coupons redeemable for merchandise in the Pinehurst Village General Store.

In 1943, the Holly Inn, the first hotel in Pinehurst, began year-round operations for the first time. In 1970, the Tufts family sold the resort to the Diamondhead Corporation, which in turn sold it in 1984 to present owners ClubCorp, Inc. For a better picture of the history of the course, take a stroll down the hallway on the first floor of the hotel where the staff have intelligently laid out the story behind the Pinehurst resort. There's more history in the clubhouse where the stories and pictures are more golf-oriented.

As soon as Donald Ross began sculpting great golf courses here, great golfers followed — coming here for tournaments and other events or just for pleasure. You'll see the names in the clubhouse. Palmer, Nicklaus, Snead, Hogan, Pavin, Love, Bobby Jones, Miller, Watson and Faldo are just a few of the greatest of the great who have come for the challenge, usually on course #2 — in Ross's opinion the greatest test of championship golf he designed. Others must think so too: Pinehurst #2 is consistently ranked in the top 10 of all golf courses throughout the country.

The 1996 U.S. Women's Open at Pine Needles

The par 5 10th hole at Pine Needles.

Women's professional golf continues to increase in popularity, and we think you'll see it increase even more when it comes to Pine Needles in 1996. The championship will take place from May 27 through June 2, 1996.

Pine Needles, as you've probably read in this chapter, is an outstanding course. With the rough grown up to neck-level and the greens at superfast speeds, you'll see some great moments and some despair. It should be an opportunity to watch some excellent golf as well. A portion of the proceeds from the tournament will go towards wellness programs in North Carolina to aid in early detection of breast cancer. The tournament offers a great value as well. You can watch a Monday practice round for just $8 with an advance ticket purchase, and you can watch the final round for just $15, again with an advance purchase. For a ticket order form or more information, write to the 1996 U.S. Women's Open, P.O. Box 5369, Pinehurst, North Carolina 28374.

Remember, this is the one major all the participants want to win. You'll see some great golf. If you're an avid golfer and live in the area, don't miss this event.

Pinehurst #2 has hosted what has to be the most prestigious amateur tournament outside the U.S. Amateur: the North and South Championship. Some of the greatest names in the sport have won this tournament on their way to stardom as professionals. Once a professional tournament, it was Ben Hogan's first win. Other tournaments hosted by Pinehurst include the PGA Tour Championship, the PGA Championship, the Ryder Cup, the U.S. Senior Open, the PGA Junior

Championship and the U.S. Amateur. In 1999, Pinehurst #2 will host the U.S. Open.

As part of Pinehurst's centennial celebration, the resort opened a new Tom Fazio-designed course, Pinehurst #8, in the fall of 1995.

Golf amenities at Pinehurst include a range (called Maniac Hill), chipping and putting greens galore, a full golf school with some wonderful packages, restaurants, a bar called the 91st hole, locker rooms, shoe shine, rental clubs and pro shops. On course #1 through course #5, you can book ahead for a caddie. The cost will range from $25 to $50, depending on tip and the number of bags carried.

Unless you're a member of Pinehurst Country Club, you need to stay at the Pinehurst Hotel to play here. That's the official word. Some local hotels and some other resorts in the area offer access to Pinehurst courses, but you didn't hear that from us — OK? But why not get the full experience and stay at the hotel anyway: It's the centerpiece of Pinehurst hospitality, and it's well worth the price of admission, which fluctuates seasonally. The hotel offers several packages, many of which are good values, especially in the evergreen season (winter).

Pinehurst Hotel has 310 rooms in all. The Manor Inn, which is closer to the village, offers 49 rooms. And golf course condominiums are available as well.

The hotel provides ample meeting and exhibition space. In addition to the golf courses, which we promise to get to soon, there are 24 tennis courts, a lake for sailing and other watersports, swimming pools, a croquet court and a bowls lawn. A shuttle service can whisk you around the resort. And, of course, the hotel offers a full range of dining and drinking options, all serviced by staff dressed in

britches. We think you'll love the hotel and we're certain you'll love the golf courses. It's expensive but a great value if you believe in the tradition and excellence of a truly world-class resort. Go ahead! Get out the credit card, close your eyes, think of Donald Ross and have a great time. You won't regret it.

Pinehurst #1
Championship Yardage: 6102
Slope: 117 — Par: 70
Men's Yardage: 5873
Slope: 114 — Par: 70
Ladies' Yardage: 5307
Slope: 117 — Par: 73

Pinehurst #1 opened with nine holes in 1899; a second nine opened in 1901. Dr. D. Leroy Culver, an amateur architect, designed the first nine. Donald Ross revised the first nine, added a second nine and made major changes to the course in 1913, 1937, 1940 and 1946. This rolling, wooded track has bermudagrass fairways and bentgrass greens.

As the number implies, #1 was the first course built at the Pinehurst resort and probably the first course that Donald Ross designed — unless you count the work he completed at Oakley Country Club near Boston. For Donald Ross fans, #1 is a shrine of sorts and a great example of his work. Although the course is not long by modern standards, it's still a fine test of golf: narrow fairways and tough, small greens. A couple of holes offer decent length off the tee. The fairways reveal examples of devilish Ross bunkers with steep grass faces — a true hazard for any golfer. Around the greens you'll see more grass-faced bunkers, and if you have a bad day with your short game, your score is likely to become larger than you'd care to admit. If you're a low handicapper, this course will provide a good tune-up for some of the other challenges that await you. If you're a mid- or high handicapper, you'll find this course pleasantly manageable if you keep the ball straight and putt well.

You must take a cart unless you take a caddie. You can book a tee time with your reservation at the hotel. Approximate cost, including cart, is $94 high, $72 medium and $59 low.

Pinehurst #2

Championship Yardage: 7053

Slope: 131   *Par: 72*

Men's Yardage: 6354

Slope: 127   *Par: 72*

Ladies' Yardage: 5863

Slope: 135   *Par: 74*

Pinehurst #2 opened with nine holes in 1901; an additional nine was completed in 1906. Donald Ross designed the course and made major changes in 1922, 1933, 1934, 1935 and 1946, although he constantly made minor improvements. Changes were made after Ross's death in 1948, but descendants of the Tufts family and others have brought the course back to its original form and shape.

So much has been said and written about #2 that it's somewhat unfair to summarize the course and the experience in just a few paragraphs. It's easily the finest golf course in the Carolinas as well as one of the best public-access courses in the world. And it's the reason why many golfers come to the Pinehurst. It's hosted several major and professional tournaments and is home to the top amateur tournament in the country (behind the U.S. Amateur) — the North and South. For many professional golfers, this is the finest course anywhere.

So what makes #2 No. 1? At first, you might wonder. There are courses with better scenery and better views. There are courses with bigger clubhouses. And there are courses that will make your jaw drop more, that are more difficult. Yet for any apparent "shortcomings," Pinehurst #2 remains at the top of the list of the greatest golf courses. And in 1999, it will host the U.S. Open. Even with a somewhat moderate slope rating, par or worse will probably win the tournament. So, still, what's the big deal?

Two things. First, this is the course that Donald Ross built and nurtured to what he thought was perfection. He eventually built a house next to the 3rd green near the confluence of the 3rd, 4th, 5th and 6th holes. He deemed Pinehurst #2 the greatest test of championship golf that he designed — that the person who won a championship here would be a golfer who had come as near as possible to all-around competence.

The terms "championship course" and "you'll have to use every club in your bag" have become well-worn clichés, but they apply at #2 perhaps more than anywhere in the Carolinas. Donald Ross built more than 400 courses in his lifetime — and this was his best.

Second, and perhaps more importantly, #2 is a golf purist's dream. Pinehurst #2 is a stunning example of what makes a great golf course: a designer who understands that a course is defined by the variety and fairness of the test.

Each hole here has its own set of difficulties and problems. Lose your con-

---

Several private courses offer tee times in tandem with golf packages. These courses include (designers in parentheses): Pinehurst Plantation (Ed Seay and Arnold Palmer), Pinehurst National (Jack Nicklaus), Pinewild (Gene Hamm) and Southern Pines Elks Club (Donald Ross).

Insiders' Tips

Photo: Foxfire Resort and Country Club

Foxfire Resort and Country Club is just one of the many fine golf
resorts in the Pinehurst area.

centration and your score will mushroom. In fact, it's a course where even the low to mid-handicapper will find that the score has somehow reached levels that mirror the national debt. From the back tees, we were humbled to the point of tears by the end of the round. Thankfully, on a second non-golfing visit, we spent two hours in the company of legendary starter and ranger Americus "Max" Lamberti, former curator of the PGA Hall of Fame.

Mr. Lamberti pointed out that many great golfers have been similarly humbled by #2. They may drive the ball well (you must) and hit their fair share of greens (you must), but it's the golfer with the creative and wizard-like short game who will ultimately prevail here. The fairways are generous, but it helps to be in the right place — and where you want to be often is where Ross placed a bunker or love grass. From there, your approach shot (often with a long iron) needs to hit the right portion of the green for a birdie putt. Often, the route to the correct portion of the green is well-guarded by deep grass-faced bunkers or rough-infested

hollows or a swale. And more often than not, the green plays smaller, and the less than perfect iron shot will roll off the edge. This is where the fun begins — and where the wizard of the short game will prevail. To get up and down requires such a masterful touch that if you do so with relative ease you'll feel ready to give a short game clinic or write a book. But the severely undulating greens will give you nightmares. No putt is a gimme. And this is without all the gimmicks of modern golf course architecture. If you play to the top of your game, you'll be rewarded; but if you're "off," you'll be in for a long, frustrating round. What could be closer to the true spirit and challenge of the game?

Low handicappers will love the constant challenge and should play from the back tees. Mid-handicappers should play from the middle tees and hold on to their hats. High handicappers: Try to play within yourself, take in the experience, ignore the score and try not to impede the progress of the group behind you. Pinehurst #2 is a course you should play before you pass away. Despite the fee, you'll want to come back time and time again, constantly drawn by the addiction and timelessness of the greatest of all Donald Ross courses.

You must take a cart unless you take a caddie. Go ahead and take a caddie to experience the full effect and to keep you loose and limber. You can book a tee time with your reservation at the hotel. Approximate cost, including cart, is $170 high, $147 medium and $134 low.

Pinehurst #3

Championship Yardage: 5593

Slope: 117	Par: 70

Ladies' Yardage: 5307

Slope: 117	Par: 71

Pinehurst #3 opened in 1907. An additional nine was added in 1910. Donald Ross designed the course and made major changes in 1936 and 1946. The course is set on rolling, wooded terrain, with bermudagrass fairways and bentgrass greens.

Pinehurst #3 is similar to #1: short and tight. And, like #1, it should not be discounted as too short to be interesting. It's a course where you must be straight off the tee and sharp with your short game to score well. The greens are small and crowned; there's plenty of trouble lurking off the tee in the form of deep grass-faced bunkers and irritating swales and hollows. Pinehurst #3 will be appreciated by those whose strength is accuracy, not distance. Many of the holes on #3 have been praised by avid Donald Ross fan Ben Crenshaw.

You must take a cart unless you take a caddie. You can book a tee time with your reservation at the hotel. Approximate cost, including cart, is $94 high, $72 medium and $59 low.

Pinehurst #4

Championship Yardage: 6919

Slope: 126	Par: 72

Men's Yardage: 6396

Slope: 117	Par: 72

Ladies' Yardage: 5696

Slope: 119	Par: 73

Pinehurst #4 opened nine holes in 1912 and nine more in 1919. Donald Ross designed the course and Robert Trent Jones revised the layout in 1973, lengthening it and adding water. Rees Jones revised the layout once more in 1982. The course is set in rolling, wooded terrain. In the fairways, you'll find bermudagrass; on the greens, bentgrass.

Ross designed Pinehurst #4 as a short course well-suited to the high handicapper. The course was toughened to complement #2 in time for the World Open.

Enter the Jones clan.

Robert Trent and son Rees designed a muscular track from the back tees. You can't help but be impressed with how the Joneses turned the course into a playable track for golfers of all levels. While #2 justifiably gets all the attention, #4 is well-deserving of its popularity. Gone are the grass-faced bunkers of the Ross era, which have been replaced and flattened. The result is a more aesthetically pleasing layout — but one just as challenging. Overall, it's a super track.

You guessed it; you must take a cart unless you take a caddie. You can book a tee time with your reservation at the hotel. Approximate cost, including cart, is $94 high, $72 medium and $59 low.

Pinehurst #5

Championship Yardage: 6929

Slope: 130	Par: 72

Men's Yardage: 6357

Slope: 123	Par: 72

Ladies' Yardage: 5720

Slope: 131	Par: 73

Pinehurst #5, an Ellis Maples design, opened in 1961 on rolling, wooded terrain. Fairways are bermudagrass; greens, bentgrass.

This one of the lesser-known courses in the Pinehurst crown — and, perhaps, the most underrated. Maples lived in the Pinehurst area and supervised construction on Donald Ross's final design at Raleigh Country Club. Maples was a fine golfer who once shot 62. But he was also a teacher of the game and understood the needs and desires of the average golfer. Maples became one of the most sought-after architects in the Southeast. It's fitting that Pinehurst tapped Maples to design a course; he provided the resort with one of his finest efforts.

This course plays long from the back tees. But it's still fair and fun — though it will be more so for the average player from the forward tees. Ironically, although Maples is sometimes considered the master of the long, sweeping and majestic dogleg, you won't find much of that here. Instead, you'll find some wonderful straightaway holes that demand accuracy. There's plenty of variety, from long and short par 4s to par 5s where the long-hitter will feel somewhat inclined to gamble. Pinehurst #5 is a tremendously playable course as well as being just plain fun to play.

As is typical at Pinehurst, you must take a cart unless you take a caddie. You can book a tee time with your reservation at the hotel. Approximate cost, including cart, is $94 high, $72 medium and $59 low.

Pinehurst #6
Championship Yardage: 7157
Slope: 139   Par: 72
Men's Yardage: 6603
Slope: 132   Par: 72
Ladies' Yardage: 5430
Slope: 125   Par: 72

Pinehurst #6 opened in 1979. George Fazio and nephew Tom Fazio tag-teamed the design here. The course is set in rolling, wooded terrain, with bermudagrass fairways and bentgrass greens.

Although it has been ranked as one of North Carolina's better golf courses, Pinehurst #6, like #5, is underrated. This course is "off-campus," and you'll have to drive or take the shuttle bus to get here.

It's away from the main bulk of the Pinehurst courses, and its topography is more undulating. Fazio did not want to compete with the Ross designs, thus you'll find that #6 is quite different from the other courses. The site is more dramatic, and there are some significant elevation changes.

When #6 opened, many felt Fazio had created the most difficult Pinehurst course. You have to keep the ball in play here; if you miss the course, you'll end up in thick vegetation or water or on steep fall-offs, and you may have to negotiate some mounds and swales. It doesn't look difficult, but as we all know, looks can be deceiving. Better golfers will have all they can handle from the back tees.

Tom Fazio returned to the course in 1991 to soften some of the green contours, but it's still possible to shoot some big numbers on this course. For a kinder, gentler ride, shoot from the forward tees; it's still an exciting track from there.

The course is walkable for the fit, but walking is restricted. You can book a tee time with your reservation at the hotel. Approximate cost, including cart, is $94 high, $72 medium and $59 low.

Pinehurst #7
Championship Yardage: 7152
Slope: 117   Par: 72
Men's Yardage: 6692
Slope: 114   Par: 72
Ladies' Yardage: 4996
Slope: 117   Par: 72

Pinehurst #7 opened in 1986. Rees Jones designed this lengthy course on rolling, wooded terrain, with homes bordering some of the holes. In the fairways, you'll find bermudagrass; on the greens, bentgrass.

Pinehurst #7, like #6, is another off-campus golf course. It's been consistently rated as one of the top 10 golf courses in North Carolina and as one of the best

Photo: Pinehurst Area Convention & Visitors Bureau

When you visit the Pinehurst area, stop by the Pinehurst Area Visitor Information Center on U.S. 15/501.

resort courses in the country since it opened.

Rees Jones is one of the most in-demand golf course architects in the nation, and he's created a significant course here. Some golfers are not excited about Jones's work, and a few locals feel there are too many uphill or blind shots. Still, it's impossible to describe the course without being positive. There's simply too much variety, interest and natural beauty to ignore.

Pinehurst #7 blends elements of links golf with elements of Pine Valley (as if we will ever play at Pine Valley!). There are lots of downhill tee shots, mounds and severely tiered, undulating greens to make life extra-interesting. There's also quite a bit of water as well as bunkers of all shapes and sizes. Some truly challenging holes are laid out in a "come get me" fashion.

If you're a traditionalist, perhaps you'll enjoy some of the older Pinehurst courses. But if you're a fan of Rees Jones and modern architecture, you'll absolutely love #7. We found Pinehurst #7 to be a spectacular course, deserving of its high ranking.

It's worth a visit if you're in the Pinehurst area. It will certainly challenge you.

You must take a cart, although efforts are being made to introduce walking on the course. You can book a tee time with your reservation at the hotel. Approximate cost, including cart, is $139 high, $117 medium and $104 low.

Pinehurst #8

To celebrate Pinehurst's centennial, the resort is opening a new course to be designed and built by Tom Fazio. At the time this book went to press, the course was not yet developed to the point that it could be reviewed. But we'll pass along the few things we were told.

The course was scheduled to open in fall 1995. Needless to say, the combination of Fazio and Pinehurst is one that should produce some excellent results. The course will be set in rolling terrain with a variety of vegetation. And there is no development on adjacent property.

The local golfing community is quite excited about Pinehurst #8. It should be interesting to hear what people think about what promises to be another great course in the Pinehurst crown.

THE PIT GOLF LINKS

N.C. Hwy. 5
Pinehurst   944-1600
Championship Yardage: 6600
Slope: 139   *Par: 71*
Men's Yardage: 6138
Slope: 128   *Par: 71*
Other Yardage: 5690
Slope: 120   *Par: 71*
Ladies' Yardage: 4759
Slope: 121   *Par: 72*

Dan Maples designed The Pit Golf Links, which opened in 1984. The course is set in pine barrens, with bermudagrass fairways and bentgrass greens.

Ask locals, even good golfers, what they think about the Pit and there's a sudden moment of silence . . . followed by a slightly glazed look and punctuated with "I hate that course," "It's quite a track" or "It's awesome." You'll either love or hate The Pit.

Oddly, The Pit has its devotees among the mid- to high handicappers. We say "odd" because The Pit, in addition to being one of the most daring golf courses in the area, is the most penal. If you miss the fairway, that's it. Lost ball. Game over. As soon as a foursome of duffers arrives and pays the greens fee, you can see Titleist's stock shoot up. You're going to lose a lot of balls if you're not hitting it straight, so be prepared.

You know something's wrong when the back tees are called the screw tees. You know something is wrong, or different, when you drive up to the course through the rear end of Southern Pines past industrial plants. Word is The Pit was an excavation site for sand eventually used to build roads in the Great North State.

The result is a true test of target golf.

Maples shows you the landing area (in most cases) and says "hit this or else." It's a truly penal course in an area known for it's less-than-penal tracks. Some compare it to Pine Valley. The Pit isn't a beautiful track by any stretch of the imagination. In fact, it might be the least attractive course in the Pinehurst area. But it's great and exciting golf.

There are some truly unbelievable golf holes where par seems almost impossible. Take the par 5 15th, for example — the No. 1 handicap hole. From the back tees, at 550 yards, it demands that you bang it straight down the middle. Your approach shot to the small green must tumble through two massive mounds. The next hole, a 100-yard par 3 from the middle tees, features a green where there is no such thing as a flat pin placement.

But by far the most goofy hole is the par 5 No. 8. It's just 480 yards from the back, and it plays from an elevated tee. Keep it dead straight or you'll lose your ball. (A recurring theme.) A solid 3-wood will leave you just 200 yards from the green. However, the green is nearly 20 yards deep, and a tree on the left of the green makes the hole completely inaccessible if the pin is on the left-hand side. It must be the most puzzling golf hole anywhere. Yet the course begs repeat visit after repeat visit; there is simply nothing like it.

Amenities include a practice green, range, chipping green, locker room, bar and a pro shop.

The course is not very walkable, but you can walk anytime. You can book a tee time anytime too. Approximate cost, including cart, is $80 high, $50 medium and $45 low.

SEVEN LAKES COUNTRY CLUB

Seven Lakes Dr.
West End   673-1092
Championship Yardage: 6927
Slope: 133   Par: 72
Men's Yardage: 6151
Slope: 122   Par: 72
Ladies' Yardage: 5186
Slope: 128   Par: 73

Seven Lakes opened in the early 1970s. Peter Vail Tufts designed the course on rolling, wooded terrain flanked with houses. In the fairways, you'll find bermudagrass; on the greens, bentgrass.

You won't find seven lakes, but you will find a sound course designed by Donald Ross's godson. When the Tufts family decided to sell the Pinehurst resort, Peter Vail established Seven Lakes as a housing development built around a golf course. It should come as no surprise that someone so close to Donald Ross produced such a fine golf course. We didn't see a rip-off of a Ross design. Rather, we saw a well-conceived, challenging, yet playable course, with a good reputation among local golfers.

Some water comes into play here and there. The fairways are relatively wide, but it will help to play your shot carefully. A few bunkers lurk in the fairways, ready to create trouble. There are also some greens that require daring shots over water from uneven lies. Overall, this fun and thoroughly worthwhile course probably would have made Mr. Tufts' godfather proud.

Amenities include a practice green, range, chipping green, locker room, bar, restaurant, rental clubs and a pro shop.

The course is walkable for the fit, but walking is restricted; call for details. You can book a tee time anytime. Approximate cost, including cart, is $60 high, $50 medium and $45 low.

TALAMORE AT PINEHURST

1595 Midland Rd.
Southern Pines   692-5884
Championship Yardage: 7020
Slope: 142   Par: 71
Men's Yardage: 6393
Slope: 134   Par: 71
Other Yardage: 6058
Slope: 126   Par: 71
Ladies' Yardage: 4995
Slope: 125   Par: 72

Talamore at Pinehurst, a Rees Jones design, opened in 1991. The course is set in rolling, wooded terrain. Fairways are bermudagrass, and greens are bentgrass.

Yes, this is where you'll find the llama caddies. Perhaps this is a publicity stunt, but so what; it's a fun addition to a course, and it means that some people are out there walking. And golf needs more walking. The llamas go out about 30 times year, and it will set you back an additional $100 per person for the luxury of having one of the beasts carry your bag for you. The service is only available in the late fall, winter and early spring. Llamas are social creatures, so you must bring them out in pairs or not at all. Book well ahead for llama service and make sure that you are quite fit: Talamore is not a particularly walkable course, and you'll have to negotiate about 6 miles of undulating terrain.

Let's meet the llama caddies. Dollie Llama (no relation) is the first known llama caddie in the world; her hobbies include tree pruning and mud wrestling. Jack began caddying in August 1993 and is the quiet and somewhat reserved type. Sir Hogan (no relation) is fond of apples and carrots and takes the game fairly seriously. Freddie loves kids and prefers a bad day on the golf course to a good day at the office. Reg the Wonder Llama is still in the opening credits of *Monty Python and the Holy Grail* and is unable to caddie at this time.

Photo: Talamore Golf Partners Ltd.

If these llama caddies won't encourage your walking game, nothing will.

We've heard about the llamas, now what about the golf course? It's been highly rated and touted and is a fine example of Rees Jones's work. Rees apparently wanted to make this a thinker's course rather than a muscle layout. Well, he made the course a par 71 that plays more than 7000 yards from the back tees. Of course, you won't have to play the track from there, but you will find plenty of length, even from the front; the course seems to play a bit longer than the card.

As you might expect with a Rees Jones layout, the course is very picturesque. The bunkers and mounds are attractively shaped and visually appealing — unless your ball happens to be in the bunker or on top of the mound. The greens are undulating and can be particularly difficult if fast. Plenty of trouble lurks, and you'll find that Talamore offers a serious challenge, whatever your ability.

Amenities include a practice green, range, chipping green, locker room, bar, restaurant, rental clubs, a beverage cart and a pro shop.

The course is not walkable (without a llama) so you'll want to take a cart (if you're not taking a llama). You can book a tee time anytime. Approximate cost, including cart, is $82 high, $55 medium and $42 low.

WHISPERING WOODS GOLF CLUB

26 Sandpiper Dr.

Whispering Pines	949-4653
Championship Yardage: 6334	
Slope: 122	Par: 70
Men's Yardage: 6006	
Slope: Not available	Par: 70
Ladies' Yardage: 4924	
Slope: Not available	Par: 70

Whispering Woods opened in 1974. Ellis Maples designed the course on rolling, wooded terrain bordered with houses.

In the fairways, you'll find bermudagrass; on the greens, bentgrass.

This fine and relatively mature design is going through somewhat of a renaissance. Whispering Woods has sometimes been confused with the Country Club of Whispering Pines, just a few doors down the way. The new owners of Whispering Woods have pumped a lot of cash into the course, and the result is consistent conditioning and improved play.

Don't let the lack of length fool you. There's plenty of heft from the back tees, particularly if the course is wet. Whispering Woods is more difficult than it looks — and it looks plenty difficult in places. It's probably one of the area's most underestimated courses; and its final hole, one of the most interesting in the area. If you're looking to play a good course in the Pinehurst area at a very affordable price, Whispering Woods is an excellent venue.

Amenities include a practice green, locker room, snack bar, rental clubs and a pro shop.

You must take a cart but may book a tee time anytime. Approximate cost, including cart, is $42 high, $38 medium and $30 low.

WOODLAKE COUNTRY CLUB

150 Woodlake Blvd.

Vass	245-4686
Championship Yardage: 7012	
Slope: 134	Par: 72
Men's Yardage: 6584	
Slope: 129	Par: 72
Other Yardage: 6144	
Slope: 120	Par: 72
Ladies' Yardage: 5080	
Slope: 128	Par: 72

The golf course at Woodlake Country Club opened in 1969. We bet you didn't know the course was originally called Lake Surf Country Club. Dan and Ellis Maples tag-teamed the design on mostly flat terrain next to a lake. Fairways are bermudagrass; greens, bentgrass.

Actually, there are 27 holes at Woodlake. The most recent nine opened in 1992 and was exclusively designed by Dan Maples. That nine is being blown up, and the owners have hired the Arnold Palmer design firm to rework the Dan Maples nine and add an additional nine. This new course should be open in 1996.

The original nine, designed by Maples and Maples, is an outstanding course and well worth the short drive from Pinehurst. Its reputation among Pinehurst golfers is excellent. The first few holes border a lake, and you'll have to be accurate. The lake is not a large man-made pond but a seriously grand lake that generates significant wind on occasion. Thus the first few holes can be very difficult, and the wind will play havoc with shot selection and shot making.

After this potentially brutal introduction to Woodlake, the course leaves the lake and heads for the woods where the wind is not quite as much a factor. In the woods you'll find plenty of sweeping doglegs the likes of which gained Maples notoriety. There's decent room off the tee, but your ball might find a tree or two if you're not careful. The greens are well bunkered and large. These "inland" holes offer great variety and challenge, but you'll be glad to know that the course returns to its lakeside location for the final three holes.

The 18th, a wonderful par 5, begs you to go for glory with a second shot over water to a small, well-protected green. Are you gutsy enough? This course is certainly worth the price of admission. We look forward to the new course too.

One notable item here is an aquatic driving range. You actually hit balls into the water, and a large subsurface net shags them.

Amenities include a practice green, range, chipping green, locker room, bar, restaurant, rental clubs and a pro shop.

The course is walkable for the fit, although walking is restricted. You can book a tee time three days in advance. Approximate cost, including cart, is $ 70 high, $50 medium and $45 low.

Around Pinehurst and Southern Pines...

Fun Things To Do

So you're in **Pinehurst** and you're not playing golf. What's wrong? It must be raining to the point where even the Japanese golfers are off the courses. Or perhaps it's snowing. Or dark. That's it. It's dark and raining, and even the Japanese are looking for other entertainment.

The village of Pinehurst, built by the original owner of Pinehurst and laid out by Frederick Law Olmstead, is quaint and picturesque with its New England feel. Even the owner of the local bookstore has a New England accent, but she's become Southern enough to greet you with a smile as you walk in. **The Library** is worth a visit for the Tufts Archives as well as for the exhibition that will show you the history of Pinehurst and give you some insight into Donald Ross.

The village offers some excellent shopping and dining. If you're looking for a unique golf-oriented gift, take a few minutes to visit **Burchfield's Gallery**, (800) 358-4066. Take away a chess set made of golf figurines, a map of Pinehurst #2 in a solid frame, a personalized golf ball, framed golf cartoons, a hole-in-one memento, Pebble Beach bookends — even a ball drying rack.

Perhaps what you'll find most amusing are some of the framed sayings, including "I once gave up golf; it was the most terrifying weekend of my life." If you're looking for a great gift for the golfer who has just about everything, then you'll love Burchfield's.

If you must play something, and it can't be golf, **Sandhill's Bowling Center** recently opened on N.C. Highway 5, just five minutes from Pinehurst Village. There are no fewer than 32 state-of-the-art computerized scoring lanes. For those of you who are more culturally inclined, check out the **Performing Arts Center**, 692-3611, in Southern Pines; call for information about upcoming events.

For comprehensive information about Pinehurst, contact the **Pinehurst Area Convention and Visitors Bureau**, P.O. Box 2270, Southern Pines, North Carolina 28388, (800) 346-5362.

Where to Eat

You'll find plenty of great places to eat in the Pinehurst vicinity. And you'll find that most of the better hotels still believe in the importance of matching the quality of the accommodations with the restaurant — somewhat of a rarity these days. Anyway, there's a better variety of cuisine than you might expect in Pinehurst, and we've included but a few of the many fine establishments. We also give you a couple of good choices in the Fayetteville area.

THE SQUIRE'S PUB
1720 U.S. Hwy. 1 S.
Southern Pines   695-1161
$$

Squire's is a fun watering hole and restaurant that's popular with locals and out-of-town golfers. The ambiance approaches that of an English pub, and you'll certainly find the same sort of friendliness. When the professional tours are in town, Squire's is a magnet. For instance, when the LPGA cruised through, long-hitting Laura Davies arrived with an entourage of 10 and proceeded to fill up the bar. The manager quantified the final bill as "plenty." If you're going to see a famous golfer enjoying a drink and meal, this is a place where this might happen.

Squires is a fantastic place to enjoy a drink. There are more than 40 beers available, most of them from England, and if you're in the mood for something stronger, how about a martini? (Two of these, and your handicap is five strokes less; three, and you'll be telling everyone that you just took £20 off Laura Davies.)

BEEFEATER'S
672 W. Broad St.
Southern Pines   692-5550
$$

As the name implies, Beefeater's is an outstanding place for beef, from filet mignon to prime rib. There's more, however, in the form of seafood, chicken and lamb chops, the latter being somewhat of a rarity in these parts; serve it up with mint jelly and a big baked potato and you're in fine fettle. The ambiance is low ceilinged and white tableclothed but not stuffy and more casual than you might think. Get dressed up if you want, but feel free to visit the lounge after a round still dressed in shorts.

According to our waitress, Beefeater's is popular with those who hail from climes north of the Mason-Dixon line. Evidently, the bartender is just a little rude to those folks, but no one seems to mind too much: He's not particularly conservative when it comes to pouring mixed drinks.

The restaurant is busy on most nights, particularly so on the weekends and during the season. It's the type of restaurant where golfers in the area for a week come over and over again.

THAI ORCHID
1404 Sandhills Blvd.
Aberdeen   944-9299
$$

And now for something completely different. Thai Orchid is the only restaurant that serves good Thai food in an unpretentious setting. You won't be coming here for the atmosphere necessarily, but if you're a devotee of Thai food and you need a fix while in Pinehurst, you'll want to come here.

Try the Thai grilled steak, Bangkok duck or spicy and sour fish. Start with koong da bog (shrimp roll) and wash the whole meal down with a cool Singha beer from Thailand. You can have your food prepared Thai hot, extra hot, medium or mild. The restaurant also offers excellent lunch specials: You'll leave with change from a $5 bill.

THE LOBSTER HOUSE
448 Person St.
Fayetteville   485-8866
$$$

The Lobster House is so well known that it's almost a landmark. As the name implies, the Lobster House is the place to go for live Maine lobster — if you're into that sort of thing. If lobster is not your game, sample other fresh seafood entrees. If beef is your taste, try the prime rib or charcoal steaks. It's closed on Mondays and is only open for dinner.

ROMA GOURMET ITALIAN RESTAURANT
3729 Sycamore Dairy Rd.
Fayetteville   864-1313
$$

At Roma Gourmet you'll find a menu

including live lobster, steaks, seafood and Roma's brand of Italian cuisine. With advance notice, Giovanni Giannone will prepare anything your stomach desires. In addition to cooking, Giovanni will sing any of your old Italian favorites — although he doesn't necessarily need advance warning for this. For your information, Giovanni came to America from Sicily, Italy, more than 25 years ago, jumped ship and ended up in Fayetteville.

RAFFAELE'S
U.S. Hwy. 1
Southern Pines   692-1952
$$

Raffaele's is situated at the northern end of the main business district in Southern Pines. The cuisine is Italian, and you'll find a real attention to detail in the preparation of the food.

Raffaele's is a local favorite, so much so that one local told us not to write about it so it won't become too full of tourists. That's probably as good a recommendation as you can find in the Pinehurst area.

Begin your meal with stuffed mushrooms; move on to spaghetti with Italian sausage; and complement everything with a beefy bottle of Valpolicella. The menu isn't massively extensive, but we feel confident that you'll find something you really enjoy.

THE COVES
Market Square
Pinehurst   295-3400
$-$$

Just opposite the Holly Inn and right in the thick of the "village" of Pinehurst is The Coves, an eatery and drinkery with two distinct characters.

Upstairs, you'll find a restaurant where the atmosphere is on the casual side of formal; and downstairs, you'll find a subterranean bar that looks like it could become

The village of Pinehurst is a great place to shop, dine and relax. The Coves Restaurant is just one of the many good eateries in the area.

a touch raucous in the later hours of the evening.

The restaurant is open for lunch and dinner.

For lunch, go downstairs and ask the bartendress to pull you a pint of Bass ale; then order a hamburger — one of the best around. For dinner, impress your better half with the varied menu and the better-than-average selection of wine. And then head downstairs for a game of Putt-Putt, another Bass ale, a shag on the dance floor and a game of darts.

The Coves is a locally owned gem that's, dare we say it, not quite as stuffy as some of the other eateries in and around the village. Perhaps that's why it's so popular.

Where to Stay

As we've mentioned, one of the attractions of Pinehurst is the fact that there's something here for everyone's budget. You can spend a lot of money here on places to play, or you can spend a lot less on your hotel room and spend what you save to play on the better golf courses. If you want tradition, service and amenities, you'll find it here (for a price); if all you want is a basic room with Clint Eastwood movies and a shower, you'll find that here as well.

It should be noted that most of the following hotels have excellent restaurants and wonderful dining rooms. They are all worth visiting for their restaurants, even if you are not staying there as a guest.

PRINCE CHARLES HOTEL
AND CONFERENCE CENTER

450 Hay St.
Fayetteville   433-4444
$$$

In historic downtown Fayetteville, the Prince Charles Hotel and Conference Center is an elegantly restored 105-room hotel that's one of the finest in the region. Luxurious suites with wet bars are available. You'll also find conference space for up to 350 people, and corporate rates are available. Chloe's restaurant features continental cuisine and is a great place to indulge in Sunday brunch. The

Prince Charles is also home to Babe's, a nostalgic sports bar that serves an express lunch.

FAIRFIELD INN BY MARRIOTT
562 Cross Creek Mall
Fayetteville   487-1400
$$

Fayetteville's Fairfield Inn by Marriott is located by the All-American Freeway at U.S. Highway 401 — one of the city's busiest intersections. The inn offers clean and comfortable rooms at reasonable rates. You'll get free cable TV and local calls plus access to an outdoor pool. Children 17 and younger stay for free.

HAMPTON INN
1675 U.S. Hwy. I
Southern Pines   692-9266
$$

The Hampton Inn is a modern motel-style accommodation that's always popular with golfers and visitors. There are 126 newly renovated guest rooms. The price of admission includes free continental breakfast. Amenities include a pool, cable TV (with HBO), meeting room, guest laundry room and fax service. Local phone calls are free. There are golf packages with access to 18 local golf courses. The Hampton Inn's location could not be better.

THE HOLIDAY INN
U.S. Hwy. I Bypass and Morganton Rd.
Southern Pines   692-8585
$$

As you enter Southern Pines from the north, you can't help but notice the Holiday Inn — it will be on your right just before you enter the "main drag." For years the Holiday Inn has been a local stalwart and a popular place to stay among the golfing public. The hotel offers more than 160 guest rooms and suites. Enjoy the pool, room service, cable TV (with HBO) and four tennis courts plus a game room and fitness center. Golf packages are available, and most packages include free breakfast. Meeting and exhibit space is available as well. Hennings restaurant offers three meals a day and serves a surprising variety of dishes plus a sizeable breakfast buffet. But most importantly, there's TAMS lounge, where, a couple of years ago, *The Insiders' Guides® to Golf in the Carolinas* coauthor Scott Martin served notice of his karaoke prowess with his show-stopping rendition of "All My Ex's Live in Texas."

THE PINEHURST HOTEL
AT PINEHURST RESORT
AND COUNTRY CLUB
Carolina Vista   (800) 487-4653
Pinehurst   295-6811
$$$-$$$$

We've already gone through what makes the golf courses at Pinehurst so special, and golf is what Pinehurst is all about — so read about the courses before you read about the hotel. Driving through the Village of Pinehurst, you will surely stumble across the grand and magnificent Pinehurst Hotel. It has hosted all the great golfers in addition to some of the most famous people in the universe. And it's been an award-winning accommodation 12 years in a row.

As soon as you enter the hotel, your bags will be handled by a bell hop in plus fours. Enjoy this new and wonderful experience as you're taken care of in 1920s fashion. The rooms are traditionally appointed but offer all modern conveniences. In addition to the golf courses, the hotel offers children's programs, a swimming pool, a lake, tennis courts, croquet, lawn bowls and historical tours. You'll find a variety of restaurants as well as the Ryder Cup Lounge, where you can have a drink and discuss whether Lanny should have picked Curtis as the wild-card choice (he shouldn't have). It's a place for a blowout, so get out the Osmium credit card. . . . You'll enjoy every second of it.

THE PINE CREST INN
Dogwood Rd.
Pinehurst   295-6121
$$-$$$

Donald Ross purchased the Pine Crest Inn in 1921 and owned it until his death in 1948. Thus, for the golfing purist, the Pine Crest Inn is a special place — almost hallowed territory.

Today's Pine Crest Inn is known as one of the most popular and famous places to stay, eat and drink in Pinehurst. It's also one of the most fun and, at time, rambunctious — but in a polite way.

The rooms are wonderfully appointed and offer all modern amenities. The atmosphere is like being at home. The inn's excellent restaurant serves traditional cuisine. But perhaps the most famous part of the Pine Crest is Mrs. B's Bar where, since the inn's inception, golfers have come to recount their day of adventure and calamity on the links. The bartender, in addition to dispensing adult beverages, also flows with wit and wisdom about golf. And did we mention the occasional well-directed barb? One employee has said: "We have no featured or specialty drinks as such, but whatever the golfers drink, they usually end up singing."

There's nothing pretentious about the Pine Crest; it's pure fun and pure golf. If there's a hotel with better access to local golf courses, please let us know. In addition to all the Pinehurst Courses (including #2), the folks at the Pine Crest can get you on just about anywhere, often at a special rate.

THE HOLLY INN
Cherokee Rd.
Pinehurst   295-2300
$$-$$$

The Holly Inn was the first hotel in Pinehurst, and it lives on today as one of its finest. There's a wonderful and understated charm to the place that's both relaxing and timeless. You'll feel like you're stepping back in time as soon as you pass through the doors.

The restaurant is worth mentioning because it's one of the best in Pinehurst. The dining room, with its cupola roof, is like a scene out of *The Great Gatsby*; check out the intricate molding. Feast on duck with a smoked salmon appetizer; wash it down with a robust claret.

The rooms are all quite different: wonderful and traditionally appointed. The inn offers a number of golf packages and the golf course access is excellent. Once you've finished your round, relax with a gin and tonic in the garden, under a shade tree or on the veranda. The inn is part of the Historic Hotels of America and the National Trust for Historic Preservation.

FOXFIRE RESORT AND COUNTRY CLUB
Hoffman Rd.
Foxfire Village, Pinehurst   295-5555
$-$$$

We've already told you that Foxfire has two fine Gene Hamm golf courses, but you should also consider staying at Foxfire, particularly if you're looking for great value in a setting that's relaxed and secluded. Foxfire is also well suited for conferences.

At Foxfire, you'll stay in a condominium where you can cook for yourself. Or wander over to the lodge for breakfast or dinner. There's also a lounge where the bartender will stay as late as you do.

Play at other fine courses in the area can be arranged by the courteous and

PINEHURST AND THE SANDHILLS

well-connected staff. You'll really enjoy the hospitality and value at Foxfire.

MID PINES INN AND GOLF CLUB
1010 Midland Rd.
Southern Pines   692-2114
$$-$$$

If you've read the description of the course at Mid Pines, you'll know that the inn has always been a popular spot for meetings — and for good reason. Pinehurst Hotel notwithstanding, there might not be a more charming and stately building in the area.

All 118 guest rooms are graciously furnished with period antiques. The inn actually dates back to 1921. The cuisine is wonderful, and you'll feel like you're getting away from it all in the traditional atmosphere.

Golf packages are available, and the staff will work to get you a tee time at a course of your choosing other than Mid Pines or its sister course, Pine Needles.

PINE NEEDLES
Ridge Rd.
Southern Pines   692-7111
$$-$$$

For a full description of the magnificent course at Pine Needles, see the description earlier in this chapter. The course is reserved for hotel guests only. There are 71 sleeping rooms in Swiss-style lodges. Guest services include a heated pool, grass tennis courts, sauna, dining rooms, a lounge and learning center. The golf packages include unlimited greens fees on the Pine Needles course. The staff can arrange tee times for you at other courses in the area as well.

Golf Equipment

A number of courses have excellent golf shops where you'll find just about every-

thing you'll need. And it's here that a number of PGA pros have been trained in the art of personal club fitting. Three prominent golf shops are in Southern Pines near the junction of U.S. Highways 1 and 15/501. **Spoon and Mashie,** 944-1982, on U.S. Highway 1 is one the largest and best-equipped golf stores in the Carolinas and carries just about every type of club made. The store can custom fit clubs and offers full repair services as well. **Robert's Golf and Tennis,** 944-2757, offers a full range of gear and clubs in a friendly atmosphere; it's also located on U.S. 1 in Aberdeen. And at **Carolina Custom Golf,** 695-1670, you'll find a massive store as well as a range with mats where you can pay $5 and hit balls all day.

Golf Schools

As you might expect, Pinehurst is a great place to learn how to play or to improve your technique. Just about every course has excellent practice facilities, many of which have been specially designed by well-known architects. And most courses have PGA professionals who are qualified to help you with your game. A couple of courses boast teaching professionals who are sought after by the better golfers in the Sandhills and the Carolinas. Probably the two best-known golf schools are at Pinehurst and Pine Needles.

The Golf Advantage School at Pinehurst is designed to help golfers of all skill levels improve their games. The school is supervised by former PGA president Don Padgett. The maximum student/teacher ratio is 5-to-1, and you'll get a chance to test your improved game on any of the seven great Pinehurst courses. If you really want to get serious, you can stay for a week's worth of school. Or, if you haven't got the time, stay for the weekend. Either way,

the program includes lodging for the entire stay, three meals a day, daily greens fees and carts, unlimited range balls, personal video analysis, personalized club fitting, access to all the amenities and a graduation cocktail party. Quite a gig! Call Pinehurst at (800) 795-4653 for the brochure and rates. Junior programs are also available.

At Pine Needles, Peggy Kirk Bell and her staff will lead you on a **Golfari**. Either Ms. Bell or PGA touring pro Pat McGowan will begin your day with an instructional session before helping you on an individual basis with your swing.

After lunch, play golf all afternoon on the great Pine Needles course. The facilities at Pine Needles are excellent, and there aren't many instructors with a better reputation than Peggy Kirk Bell. For more information about instruction at Pine Needles, call (800) 747-7272.

Taking a slightly different approach is the **Woodlake Total Performance Golf School** at Woodlake Country Club in Vass. In addition to a full instructional program and access to a wonderful golf course, your fee includes fitness and nutrition evaluations. Call (800) 334-1126 for more information.

Photo: Carolinas Golf Group, LLC

Hole #2 at The Neuse Golf Club in Clayton.

Inside
The Triangle
of North Carolina

Raleigh/Durham/Chapel Hill

The Triangle is best known for three major institutions of higher learning: the University of North Carolina at Chapel Hill, North Carolina State in Raleigh and Duke in Durham. The area is also well known nationally for the Research Triangle Park, a collection of research facilities owned and run by large industrials like IBM and Glaxo. The concentration of individuals with a Ph.D. to their name is greater here than in any other place in the country. Thus it can be safely said that your chances of a mind-bending conversation of massive intelligence is greater here than in just about any part of the Carolinas. We can't decide if that means golfers here have better thought processes or course management prowess.

In the counties that surround Raleigh, Durham and Chapel Hill, life is less high-tech and less academically oriented. The plentiful fields of Eastern Carolina are overflowing with a crop that's been the mainstay of agriculture in the great north state for centuries: tobacco. In these rural areas, a few golf courses have been built where the golden-leafed plant once grew. You'll be able to smoke wherever you feel like it in these outlying areas. Ask the people what they think about Californian-style thou shalt not smoke anywhere laws and you'll probably receive a answer that we would not dare print in a family-style book like this one.

In the heart of the Triangle it's diffi-

cult, but not impossible, to avoid the influence of the universities. This is particularly true in Chapel Hill, less so in Durham, and even less so in Raleigh — a city perhaps more dominated by the state government than by N.C. State.

The Triangle has figured prominently in a number of "best places to live" surveys, and the number of people moving to the area seems to increase each and every year. Many come for the high-tech jobs, others to service those with the high-tech jobs, and others are here due to the wonderfully rich and diverse cultural life, inspired in part by the universities. Like other spots in North Carolina, the Triangle is increasingly home to retirees who want to relocate anywhere but Florida.

All this growth has meant that a number of new and very modern courses have sprung up in the area and that other older tracks are popular, successful and well-maintained. In the past few years, the weather has been unkind to many area courses. A big freeze burned many a bermudagrass fairway a couple of years ago, and several courses are still recovering from that shock. When we visited the area for our course inspections, the area had just hosted three straight weeks of solid rain. Oh, to be a greenskeeper!

Meteorology aside, you'll find an excellent variety of public courses in the area. There's plenty of old traditional designs plus some ultramodern moundfests that will test the patience of every golfer

GOLF COURSES IN THE TRIANGLE OF NORTH CAROLINA

Name	Type	# Holes	Par	Slope	Yards	Walking	Booking	Cost w/ Cart
Caswell Pines	public	18	72	114	6270	restricted	5 days	$20-25
Cheviot Hills	semiprivate	18	71	107	5975	restricted	anytime	$24-30
Crooked Creek	public	18	72	116	6028	restricted	7 days	$28-36
Devil's Ridge	semiprivate	18	72	127	6430	restricted	7 days	$34-44
Eagle Crest	public	18	72	n/r	6038	anytime	anytime	$23-30
Finley Golf Course (UNC)	public	18	72	117	6102	anytime	2 days	$26-32
Hedingham Golf Club	semiprivate	18	72	116	6276	restricted	anytime	$29-38
Hillandale Golf Club	public	18	71	118	6100	restricted	anytime	$25-29
Kerr Lake	semiprivate	18	72	118	6185	anytime	2 days	$23-28
Lake Winds Golf Course	semiprivate	18	72	n/r	6008	anytime	anytime	$22-26
Lochmere Golf Club	semiprivate	18	72	116	6156	restricted	7 days	$30-40
The Neuse Golf Club	semiprivate	18	72	129	6626	restricted	7 days	$32-38
Occoneechee Golf Club	semiprivate	18	71	119	5692	anytime	3-4 days	$24-26
The River	semiprivate	18	72	n/a	6116	anytime	14 days	$20-30
Roxboro Country Club	semiprivate	18	70	113	5364	anytime	2 days	$22-28
Sourwood Golf Club	public	18	72	112	6285	anytime	anytime	$16-20
Wake Forest Country Club	semiprivate	18	72	129	6525	restricted	7 days	$25-38
Washington Duke Golf & CC	semiprivate	18	72	129	6721	restricted	anytime	$50-60
Willowhaven	semiprivate	18	72	117	6342	anytime	3-5 days	$31.50-37.50

The Triangle Area

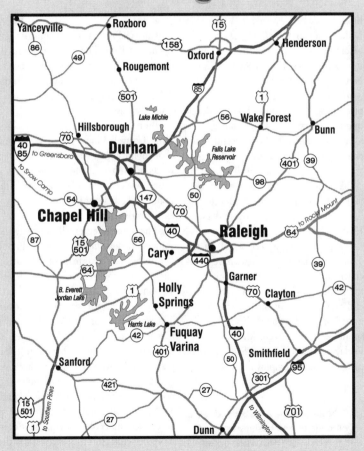

from scratch to 36. A couple of courses are family-owned and maintained, and there are some fine courses designed by architects no one has ever heard of.

Although it pains true-blue Tarheels to say it, the golf course at the Washington Duke Golf and Country Club, after its recent renovation by Rees Jones, might be one of the most magnificent in the Southeast. We believe the golfing world will soon discover this course as one of the best public-access tracks in the Carolinas. Don't be surprised if Washington Duke slides into *Golf Digest's* top 100 before the end of the century. Two ultra-modern courses, Devil's Ridge and The Neuse, were recognized by *Golf Digest* as top new courses. These are show-stopping tracks built around housing developments. A couple of golf course management companies have recently purchased or developed courses in the area.

A number of fine and well-known architects have been at work in the area, including George Cobb, Russell Breeden, Ellis Maples, John LaFoy and Gene Hamm.

One annoying aspect of golf in the Triangle is that many courses have a special Friday greens fee that's more than the weekday rate but less than the weekend rate. Most of us have to play hooky from work to play golf on Friday, so why should we be penalized? Makes no sense: Friday is still a school day. Sadly, most of the good courses employ this policy.

Note that the area code for all golf courses and businesses listed in this chapter (with a few exceptions noted) is 919.

Golf Courses in the Triangle

CASWELL PINES GOLF CLUB

2380 County Home Rd.	(910) 694-2255
Yanceyville	(800) 694-1888

Championship Yardage: 6651

Slope: 120	Par: 72
Men's Yardage: 6270	
Slope: 114	Par: 72
Other Yardage: 5720	
Slope: 108	Par: 72
Ladies' Yardage: 5145	
Slope: 111	Par: 72

Caswell Pines, a Gene Hamm design, opened in 1993. The course is primarily open, but woods and homesites border some holes. In the fairways, you'll find 419 bermudagrass; on the greens, you'll find bentgrass.

Built on what was previously a tobacco farm, Caswell Pines is an exciting and challenging course with a fine design in a pleasant setting. The Gene Hamm courses we've seen tend toward the traditional; this one leans toward the modern: earth-worked and mounded.

The course offers excellent variety and some truly outstanding holes, including a number with significant elevation changes. Off the tee, you'll have a decent amount of room: Big hitters will want to play from the back tees and use the driver. The great thing about Caswell Pines is that it makes you think. You'll need to keep your golfing wits about you if you plan to score well. The greens here are typically large, with plenty of subtle and not so subtle breaks; two putting is quite a feat on many holes. Large bunkers around a number of greens make life even more difficult. And did we mention the significant amount of water? . . . Anyway, it's well worth the visit to Yanceyville to play this course. Just plan to stay well clear of all the trouble spots.

Designer Profile: Gene Hamm

Photo: The Architects of Golf

Hamm served in the U.S. Navy during World War II. Using the GI bill, Hamm studied golf management in Pinehurst. He worked with Ellis Maples before Maples took up architecture full time. In the mid 1950s, Hamm left his professional job to supervise the construction of the original Duke course designed by Robert Trent Jones. After this project, Hamm started his own design firm and was active in the Carolinas and Virginia.

An excellent golfer, Hamm won the 1978 and 1979 Carolinas Seniors on courses he designed. How 'bout that for fairness!

Gene Hamm

Amenities include a practice green, range, snack bar, restaurant, rental clubs and a beverage cart.

The course is walkable for the very fit but is restricted; call for daily details. You can book a tee time five days in advance. Approximate cost, including cart, is $20 weekdays and $25 on weekends.

CHEVIOT HILLS GOLF CLUB

7301 Capital Blvd.
Raleigh   876-9920
Championship Yardage: 6475
Slope: 116   Par: 71
Men's Yardage: 5975
Slope: 107   Par: 71
Ladies' Yardage: 4965
Slope: 114   Par: 71

Cheviot Hills Golf Club opened in 1930. *Architects of Golf* lists Harold Long as the original designer. Gene Hamm came along later to remodel and probably redesign. The course is set in rolling wooded terrain without a house in sight. In the fairways, you'll find bermudagrass; on the greens, bentgrass.

As you walk up to the 19th-century clubhouse, you'll be greeted by the pro-shop attendant who expertly combines friendliness with brusqueness (somehow). You'll feel like you're at a country club, standing among people who have been friends for 50 years. The course itself is a masterpiece of understatement and traditionalism. There's nothing tricked up, nothing silly. Mounds are few and far between, and the only house you might see belongs to the man and wife who own the course. The only thing missing here is a knowledgeable caddie to carry and clean your clubs and help you read putts. The staff here at Cheviot Hills is justifiably proud of the course — and woe betide you should your cart stray from the path. The aforementioned pro-shop attendant, equipped with binoculars and a sound system that can be heard in Cary, will let you know that "CARTS MUST BE KEPT ON PATHS AT ALL TIMES," (caps for CLEAR emphasis) please.

Interestingly, you'll find some short par 5s and some long par 4s, with plenty of room off the tee. The staff informs us that you'll be using all your clubs and hitting all your shots. The course offers particularly good value if you walk. Which you should. You need the exercise.

If you're thinking about skipping Sunday morning services at your chosen house of worship and sneaking onto the course, think again. It doesn't open until 12:30 PM on Sundays.

Amenities include a practice green, range, chipping green, locker room, snack bar, rental clubs and a pro shop.

The course is walkable and you can walk almost anytime (two cheers!). You can book a tee time whenever you choose. Approximate cost, including cart, is $24 Monday to Thursday, $26 on Friday and $30 on weekends.

Chuck Smith designed Crooked Creek, slated to open in late 1995. Fairways are 419 bermudagrass, and greens are bentgrass.

We visited this course while it was still under construction. We were informed that it will offer a traditional design that will demand accuracy off the tee. The greens will be midsize and undulating, with a few bunkers. You'll also find plenty of doglegs. The back nine will provide more in the way of rolling greens, but you'll find a number of mounds on the front nine. From all appearances, Crooked Creek (have you ever seen a straight one?) will be a good addition to courses in the eastern section of the Triangle and will be worth an reconnaissance mission if you're in Raleigh and are interested in surveying a new course.

Amenities include a practice green, range, chipping green, locker room, snack bar, rental clubs and a pro shop.

Walking is permitted Monday through Friday. You can book a tee time seven days in advance. Approximate cost, including cart, is $28 Monday through Thursday, $30 on Friday and $36 on weekends.

CROOKED CREEK
4621 Shady Greens Dr.
Fuquay-Varina 557-7529
Championship Yardage: 6704
Slope: 120 Par: 72
Men's Yardage: 6028
Slope: 116 Par: 72
Other Yardage: 5296
Slope: 112 Par: 72
Ladies' Yardage: 4978
Slope: 114 Par: 72

DEVIL'S RIDGE GOLF CLUB
5107 Linksland Dr.
Holly Springs 557-6100
Championship Yardage: 7002
Slope: 138 Par: 72
Men's Yardage: 6430
Slope: 127 Par: 72
Other Yardage: 5852
Slope: 120 Par: 72

If you're playing a course for the first time, or if you're on a particularly difficult course, don't be afraid to play from the mid-front tees. You won't have to use your driver quite as often and you'll probably enjoy your day a lot more.

Insiders' Tips

Photo: Carolinas Golf Group, LLC

Devil's Ridge — a must-play course in the Raleigh area.

Ladies' Yardage: 5244
Slope: 121 *Par: 72*

The golf course at Devil's Ridge opened in 1991. This John LaFoy design is set on undulating terrain, and many holes are bordered by woods or houses. In the fairways, you'll find bermudagrass; on the greens, you'll find bentgrass.

John LaFoy is a well-known architect and former associate of George Cobb. LaFoy made frequent trips to Augusta National with Cobb, and when Cobb was slowed by illness in his later years, LaFoy took over a number of the design responsibilities; in fact, he was most responsible for Linville Ridge Country Club in the mountains of North Carolina. LaFoy began his own design business in 1986.

Here at Devil's Ridge, LaFoy created a somewhat demonic track with all the trappings of a modern course: mounds, wild greens, tough tee shots, extensive bunkering, elevation changes, mounds, backbreaking length from the back tees and more mounds. It's interesting to see how different this course is from many Cobb designs. You'll certainly want to spend a couple of dollars for the excellent

yardage book, especially if you're playing this course for the first time. Keep your cart speed down on the front nine, as a state trooper lives next to one of the greens.

Excess velocity aside, the course is well-designed, greatly varied and interesting. However, if you're not a fan of modern courses, steer toward a more traditional course. A good score requires hitting just about every club in your bag. Particularly interesting are the shapes of the greens: Many look like amoebae on steroids.

Devil's Ridge is a must-play course in the Raleigh area, even if you only play it once. Perhaps this description of the 17th hole from the yardage book best describes the course:

"This is the hole for which Devil's Ridge got its name. Not too long, not too narrow, not too hard. However, don't miss any shot or you'll post a BIG (their caps) number. Favor the left on your tee shot. If you miss the green to the right and look for your ball, you may never be heard from again." Enough said.

Amenities include a practice green,

range, chipping green, snack bar, rental clubs, a beverage cart and a pro shop.

Walking is restricted, although we wouldn't recommend it anyway. You can book a tee time seven days in advance. Approximate cost, including cart, is $34 Monday to Thursday, $38 on Fridays and $44 on weekends.

EAGLE CREST

4400 Auburn Church Rd.
Garner   772-6104
Championship Yardage: 6514
Slope: No rating   Par: 72
Men's Yardage: 6038
Slope: No rating   Par: 72
Ladies' Yardage: 4875
Slope: No rating   Par: 72

Eagle Crest opened in 1968. This John Baucom design is set in rolling primarily open terrain, with bermudagrass fairways and bentgrass greens.

We found a fun, straightforward, relaxing and soundly designed country course at Eagle Crest. You won't find any sand traps, so if you hate the beach, you'll love it here all the more. Water comes into play on four holes. Fairways are predominantly wide, although approach shots must hit small greens, some of which are crowned. If the ground is hard, you might be able to run the ball up to the hole with a low running hook. Feel free to use your Texas wedge. You'll find some mounds, swales and grass bunkers around some of the greens. If you enjoy no-frills courses with a minimum of fuss and tricks, you'll enjoy the laid-back setting we found here.

Amenities include a range, snack bar and rental clubs.

You can walk this course anytime; book a tee time whenever you choose as well. Approximate cost, including cart, is $23 weekdays and $30 on weekends.

FINLEY GOLF COURSE

Finley Golf Course Rd.
Chapel Hill   962-2349
Championship Yardage: 6580
Slope: 122   Par: 72
Men's Yardage: 6102
Slope: 117   Par: 72
Ladies' Yardage: 5277
Slope: 118   Par: 73

The University of North Carolina's Finley Golf Course, designed by George Cobb, opened in 1950. It's a mostly flat track with some minor undulations on the back nine. In the fairways, you'll find bermudagrass; on the greens, bentgrass.

Quite a few well-known students, professors and coaches have graced this course. Michael Jordan started to play the game here under the tutelage of Davis Love III, a member of the golf team. And you might run into Dean Smith here too. Yes, there's strong level of stardom and tradition at this course adjacent to Siler's Bog.

The course itself is a fine and mature George Cobb design and one of the better courses in the Triangle area. The front nine is flat and its fairways are bordered by woods, especially pine. The back nine is just as wooded but features a few holes on undulating terrain. There's plenty of variety here, and the difficulties on this course come from the bunkering, trees and subtly undulating putting surfaces. If the bermudagrass rough is grown up around the greens, finesse recovery shots will be difficult. If you're a fan of well-designed traditional-style golf courses, play at Finley.

Amenities include a practice green, range, chipping green, snack bar, rental clubs and a pro shop.

You can walk anytime and can book a tee time two days in advance. Approximate cost, including cart, is $26 weekdays (same for Friday) and $32 on weekends.

HEDINGHAM GOLF CLUB

4801 Harbour Town Dr.
Raleigh   250-3030
Championship Yardage: 6675
Slope: 121   Par: 72
Men's Yardage: 6276
Slope: 116   Par: 72
Other Yardage: 5565
Slope: 107   Par: 72
Ladies' Yardage: 4845
Slope: 107   Par: 72

Hedingham Golf Club opened in 1992. David Postlethwait designed the primarily open track, although the course is part of a residential community, and houses border some holes. Fairways are bermudagrass, and greens are bentgrass.

We're not familiar with David Postlethwait, but based on the evidence here at this popular Raleigh course, he is in the modern-architecture camp. Locals tell us that the course is fair and not overly demanding. It's tight off the tee, with out-of-bounds lurking on many holes. So keep the ball in play. Let's say that again. Keep the ball in play.

The greens are medium-size to large, are not overly undulating and boast some potentially difficult subtleties. A few small changes are being made to the course to make it more playable. And as with most modern courses, you'll find plenty of mounds in the fairways and around the green complexes.

Amenities include a practice green, range, chipping green, locker room, snack bar, rental clubs and a pro shop.

You can only walk at the end of the day. You can book a tee time six days in advance. Approximate cost, including cart, is $29 Monday through Thursday, $32 on Friday and $38 on weekends.

HILLANDALE GOLF COURSE

Hillandale Rd.
Durham   286-4211
Championship Yardage: 6445
Slope: 122   Par: 71
Men's Yardage: 6100
Slope: 118   Par: 71
Ladies' Yardage: 5555
Slope: 113   Par: 74

Hillandale opened in the early 1900s. *Architects of Golf* lists Donald Ross as the original designer and Perry Maxwell and George Cobb as redesigners. You'll find information about Ross and Cobb throughout this book. Maxwell was a former banker who took to golf course architecture after World War I. He built the first grass greens in the state of Oklahoma. He was known for designing wildly undulating greens and he has rebuilt the putting surfaces at such mega-famous courses as Augusta National, Pine Valley and the National Golf Links. Maxwell eventually designed about 70 courses and remodeled 50 others. Thus Hillandale boasts a fine architectural heritage. The terrain varies between flat and rolling. Bermudagrass covers the fairways, and bentgrass, the greens.

With more than 50,000 rounds of golf played here every year, Hillandale is probably one of the most popular golf courses in North Carolina. The track is owned and operated by The Durham Foundation, Durham's Community Trust and

At least once a year, spend a day at a golf tournament. You might want to follow a golfer whose play you enjoy. Or, camp out next to a reachable par 5 and watch the pros demonstrate their short game prowess.

Insiders' Tips

Golf for Women in the Carolinas

It's different from probably anywhere else in the world.

Those of us who live and play in the Carolinas are accustomed to the absolute fact that women are present, allowed and, yes, welcome . . . the same as male golfers. Women golfers here possibly take this acceptance for granted until they are asked about it by visitors, usually from northeastern states, who are not accustomed to women being allowed on private courses every day, let alone every time of day. Women are welcome on all of the public or semiprivate golf courses that we researched for *The Insiders' Guide® to Golf in the Carolinas.*

Val Skinner, Katie Peterson-Parker and Nancy Lopez exemplify the talent and grace of today's women golfers.

More than five million women in America play golf, and social acceptance has changed dramatically since the 16th century, when Mary Queen of Scots was criticized for taking a liking to the sport of the male nobility.

A recent book by Marcia Chambers, *The Unplayable Lie,* tells of the discrimination that exists in American golf today and of options that help both men and women understand how and why rules can change. The Carolinas, thankfully, are not the setting for any of the cases cited in Chambers's book.

Our differences probably stem from the fact that the vast majority of Carolina courses are public or semiprivate and not country clubs of the type found in many other locations. Also, with a plethora of courses — including more than 90 on the Grand Strand — everyone's business is wanted and needed.

Many clubs do not have women's locker rooms, which may be somewhat annoying, but equal access has been considered for all of the newer clubhouses.

The Executive Women's Golf League has chapters in several cities throughout the Carolinas. It's part of a national movement including nearly 10,000 members in more than 100 chapters. The league intends to promote golf by providing a nurturing atmosphere for women who will not be intimidated while learning the game. It also emphasizes familiarizing women with the business etiquette of using golf as part of professional networking. In fact, the organization pushes the etiquette and the training to such a point that women may be more conscious of their proper manners, and even of some rules of golf, than many men.

The camaraderie, including business and social networking, is spoken about among the league's members as an important part of their association. Women new to the area find immediate acceptance among a group with common interests, and those new to golfing find encouragement to learn how to buy clubs and get on a real course.

The leagues in any city welcome visitors from other chapters and invite new members — whether beginning or experienced golfers. For more informaton, call any of the Executive Women's Golf League Carolina chapters.

In North Carolina:

Charlotte	(704) 892-9274
Pinehurst	(910) 245-3270
Raleigh	(800) 326-3418
	(919) 781-5552
Wilmington	(910) 799-0132

In South Carolina:

Charleston	(803) 881-2014
Hilton Head	(803) 689-1300, Ext.223
Myrtle Beach	(803) 448-5942, Ext. 21

the Central Carolina Bank and Trust Company. So you might refer to Hillandale as Durham's muni.

The course is fun and relatively straightforward and has the ambiance of an Old World course. Maxwell didn't get too wild with the greens — crowned and midsize to large. On the back nine, three holes have dual greens due to the sheer volume of play. The fairways are relatively wide and open, but water comes into play on a few holes. The course is not overly bunkered, but chipping areas are mowed around the greens, so your ball may roll off if it hits the edge.

The golf shop at Hillandale is one of the best-stocked and largest of any golf course in North Carolina. In 1993, the golf shop was voted the Nation's Most Outstanding by the PGA of America.

Amenities include a practice green, range, chipping green, locker room, snack bar, rental clubs and a pro shop.

You can — and should — walk anytime; same for booking a tee time. Approximate cost, including cart, is $25

Monday through Thursday, $27 on Friday and $29 on weekends.

KERR LAKE COUNTRY CLUB

N.C. Rt. 3
Henderson   492-1895
Championship Yardage: 6430
Slope: 122   Par: 72
Men's Yardage: 6185
Slope: 118   Par: 72
Ladies' Yardage: 4799
Slope: 111   Par: 72

The golf course at Kerr Lake Country Club opened in the 1960s. A group of agricultural types designed this open layout, with bermudagrass fairways and bentgrass greens.

Here at Kerr Lake you'll find a fun, entertaining and relaxed course. This well-designed track follows the lay of the land faithfully, and its challenge is due in part to the decent length from the back tees. Locals feel Kerr Lake appears easier than it plays. There isn't a great deal of trouble off the tee, but you'll rarely have an even lie in the fairway. The recent installation of a sprinkler system increased the length of the course. The greens are medium-size and undulating, and their designs mandate good club selection.

Kerr Lake added its first-ever bunker in the spring of 1995! Curiously, the clubhouse at this good and popular country course resembles a bomb shelter. But, so what? You don't play golf in the snack bar, right?

Amenities include a practice green, range, snack bar, rental clubs and a pro shop.

The course is walkable and you can walk anytime. Call on Thursday for a weekend tee time. Approximate cost, including cart, is $23 weekdays and $28 on weekends.

LAKE WINDS GOLF COURSE

1807 Moores Mill Rd.
Rougemont   471-GOLF
Championship Yardage: 6365
Slope: 120   Par: 72
Men's Yardage: 6088
Slope: No rating   Par: 72
Ladies' Yardage: 5388
Slope: No rating   Par: 72

Lake Winds opened in 1982. Don Mason designed the course on rolling terrain, with bermudagrass fairways and bentgrass greens.

A few miles north of Durham, Lake Winds is an example of how good a family-owned, operated and maintained country course can be. The layout winds around and through tranquil, rolling wooded terrain. The fairways offer decent width, and the greens vary in size and shape. There are some fun tee shots. Most of the greens are protected by bunkers whose influence will vary greatly depending on pin placement. You'll find some surprisingly wonderful golf holes here. Senior PGA Tour professional Jim Thorpe holds his annual charity golf tournament at Lake Winds. Mr. Thorpe also holds the course record: 61. The closing three holes are exciting — perfect for those who like to wager while they play. The amount of postgame money ex-

Insiders' Tips

Many professional golfers are very happy to score par on a hole. They shoot for the middle of the fairways and greens to avoid trouble and big numbers.

changed will be greatly influenced by these three holes.

Amenities include a practice green, rental clubs and a pro shop.

The course is walkable, and you can walk anytime. You can book a tee time whenever you choose. Approximate cost, including cart, is $22 weekdays and $26 on weekends.

LOCHMERE GOLF CLUB

2511 Kildaire Farms Rd.

Cary	851-0611
Championship Yardage: 6867	
Slope: 124	Par: 72
Men's Yardage: 6156	
Slope: 116	Par: 72
Ladies' Yardage: 5052	
Slope: 113	Par: 74

The golf course at Lochmere Golf Club is predominantly flat and laid out in woodlands, with 419 bermudagrass fairways and bentgrass greens. This Gene Hamm-designed track opened in 1985.

Lochmere offers a fun and challenging round in a picturesque setting, even though some holes are bordered by homes. For a modern course, the track is a little short; but don't think that makes it any easier. Many holes are tight off the tee, particularly if the rough is up. Once you've banged your ball down the middle of the fairway, you'll have to deal with water, bunkers, mounds, embankments and swales. And once you've hit the green, you'll be faced with a sloping putt with all sorts of subtle breaks. Lochmere definitely will test your accuracy and short-game prowess.

Cary, North Carolina, is a booming and trendy suburb of Raleigh and is quite busy with traffic and construction. Amid the trendiness and bustle Lochmere is amazingly peaceful and relaxed — part of what makes it so attractive. It's a chal-

lenging but fair track that we recommend you try.

Amenities include a practice green, range, locker room, snack bar, rental clubs, beverage cart and pro shop.

The course is walkable for the dedicated, and you can walk anytime except before 2 PM on weekends. You can book a tee time seven days in advance. Approximate cost, including cart, is $30 Monday to Thursday, $34 on Friday and $40 on weekends.

THE NEUSE GOLF CLUB

918 Birkdale Dr.

Clayton	550-0550
Championship Yardage: 7010	
Slope: 136	Par: 72
Men's Yardage: 6626	
Slope: 129	Par: 72
Other Yardage: 6027	
Slope: 123	Par: 72
Ladies' Yardage: 5478	
Slope: 126	Par: 72

John LaFoy designed the Neuse Golf Club, which opened in 1994. The course is set in rolling terrain, with houses bordering the fairways. In the fairways, you'll find 419 bermudagrass; on the greens, bentgrass.

The Neuse is a sister club to Devil's Ridge and, like its sister, is owned by Carolinas Golf Group. You can read about LaFoy in the Devil's Ridge write-up. *Golf Digest* rated the course as one of the best new tracks in the country when it opened.

Yes, you might want to think about this course as The Noose — and after a round here, you might want to bind, gag and tie Mr. LaFoy to the nearest flagstick. This course appears to be more difficult than Devil's Ridge. Maybe it was a bad-eyesight day when we visited, but the mounds seemed bigger here, the elevation changes bigger, the undulations on the

Photo: © 1995 Mike Klemme/Golfoto/Carolinas Golf Group, LLC

The lush greens of Lochmere Golf Club entice players from far and wide.

green bigger, the bunkers steeper and deeper and the green complexes more menacing. The Neuse River flanks the course and comes into play on the 4th and 17th holes. The difficulties are easily viewed from the tee boxes and fairways. The most amazing hole is, in fact, called "The Noose," a tortuous 192-yard par 3, with water and bunkers to the right of the green and a large rock on the left. It's quite unlike any golf hole in the Triangle.

Other holes offer just as much challenge and difficulty. Here's what could happen: Your slightly pushed tee shot ricochets off a mound and ends up out-of-bounds — next to the Smiths' gas grill on their large back deck. Or it might land in one of the deep bunkers. Plop your ball in the middle of the fairway and you might have a lengthy walk from the cart path down a slope only to find that your lie is a foot above your feet. Your approach shot might hit a mound next to the green and bounce into a grass swale or down

an embankment or into a pot bunker. Your first putt might have a three-foot break — or it might end up rolling down a slope to the base of the green. Or you might bang it down the middle of the fairway, hit the middle of the green, one-putt and tell your friends that the course is not as difficult as it looks. Just remember that throwing clubs or smashing them on the cart path won't improve your score.

The Neuse provides an excellent example of an architect strutting his heroic and penal stuff. It's certainly a statement: "I'm going to make this course as difficult as I can. But if you have a good round here and you conquer the challenge, you should feel extremely pleased with yourself."

And that's the point of a modern and challenging golf course. Like Devil's Ridge, you should play this course for the experience — even if just once.

Amenities include a practice green, range, chipping green, locker room, snack bar, rental clubs, a beverage cart and pro shop.

The course is not walkable. You can book a tee time seven days in advance. Approximate cost, including cart, is $32 Monday through Thursday, $34 on Friday and $38 on weekends.

OCCONEECHEE GOLF CLUB

1500 Lawrence Rd.
Hillsborough 732-3435
Championship Yardage: 6062
Slope: 124 Par: 71
Men's Yardage: 5692
Slope: 119 Par: 71
Other Yardage: 4936
Slope: 106 Par: 71
Ladies' Yardage: 4681
Slope: 113 Par: 71

Occoneechee Golf Club opened in 1963. Marvin Ray designed the course, and James Ray, whom we believe is related to Marvin, renovated it. Set in rolling terrain, you'll find bermudagrass fairways and bentgrass greens.

What a great name for a golf course! Too many tracks have mundane natural or town-oriented names. Nomenclature aside, Occoneechee is a fine and fair track laid out in a pleasant country setting. Frankly, there are more challenging courses out there, but there are less challenging courses as well. This one is set up to provide some interest to the big hitting flat-belly but is best suited for the mid-level golfer who wants to play on a good course without losing numerous balls in the woods, without having to hit it 275 yards over water, or without carrying it over a morass of bunkers and/or mounds.

The fairways are medium in width, although out-of-bounds areas make a couple of holes play a bit narrower. The greens are slightly raised and crowned — thus, harder to hit than they appear. There

are plenty of pretty trees, some of which may come into play — especially if you're wayward off the tee. Water comes into play on some holes and will affect your golfing thought process if not your shot — ample proof that you don't have to hire a big-name architect to produce a fine and playable golf course. Might we dare to say that the course has an Ellis Maples feel to it? An ongoing course renovation is under way. Occoneechee provides good value for your golfing dollar.

Amenities include practice green, range, chipping green, locker room, bar, snack bar, a beverage cart and pro shop.

The course is walkable, you should walk, and you can walk anytime (hooray!). You can book a tee time three to four days in advance. Approximate cost, including cart, is $24 weekdays and $26 on weekends.

THE RIVER GOLF AND COUNTRY CLUB

Sledge Rd.
Bunn 478-3832
Championship Yardage: 6407
Slope: 122 Par: 72
Men's Yardage: 6116
Slope: Not available Par: 72
Other Yardage: 5870
Slope: Not available Par: 72
Ladies' Yardage: 4483
Slope: Not available Par: 72

The golf course at the River Golf and Country Club opened in 1990. We tried to find out who designed the course, but no one knows. Most of the holes are bordered by woods. Fairways are bermudagrass; greens, bentgrass.

The River Golf and Country Club is a serious "find." Bunn, North Carolina, is a little remote, but the course is well worth the drive. For our money, this is one of the best courses in the Triangle. Each hole is well-designed and thought out. The setting is both peaceful and magnificent.

The fairways vary in width, and there are some fun tee shots from a couple of the elevated tees. The green complexes feature bunkers of various size and shape and large undulating greens. There's a double green on the back nine. Water comes into play on a number of holes in the form of streams and ponds. There's a distinct lack of housing — rare for a newer course.

Although recently built, River possesses a traditional feel well beyond its years. Students of golf course architecture may leave wondering who is responsible for this outstanding track. The course is also a good value.

Amenities include a practice green, range, snack bar and pro shop.

Walk anytime except weekends before 2 PM. You can book a tee time two weeks in advance. Approximate cost, including cart, is $20 weekdays and $30 on weekends.

ROXBORO COUNTRY CLUB

260 Club House Dr.
Roxboro   (910) 599-2332
Championship Yardage: 5663
Slope: 114   Par: 70
Men's Yardage: 5364
Slope: 113   Par: 70
Ladies' Yardage: 4425
Slope: 113   Par: 70

Roxboro Country Club opened in 1945. Ellis Maples rerouted the course (we think) and added nine holes in 1969. The course is set in rolling, slightly wooded terrain, with fairways of bermudagrass and greens of bentgrass.

Roxboro Country Club is a fine country club course. It's not the longest in the world, but it might rate as one of the prettiest in the area. There are plenty of super holes, although those around the turn, which may have been part of the original nine, are not as pretty as the others. As

with many Ellis Maples courses, you'll find beautiful sweeping doglegs, excellent use of the land, plenty of room off the tee, deep undulating greens and large bunkers protecting half or two-thirds of the green. You'll find plenty of examples of how Maples matches design elements with the length and pitch of the hole: Long holes have big greens; short holes have smaller greens with more protection. Water comes into play on a few holes and adds a great deal visually to the course.

Amenities include a practice green, range, snack bar and pro shop.

You can walk anytime. You won't need a tee time during the week; call Thursday for a weekend tee time. Approximate cost, including cart, is $22 weekdays and $28 on weekends.

SOURWOOD GOLF CLUB

8055 Pleasant Hill Church Rd.
Snow Camp   (910) 376-8166
Championship Yardage: 6862
Slope: 117   Par: 72
Men's Yardage: 6285
Slope: 112   Par: 72
Ladies' Yardage: 5017
Slope: 106   Par: 72

Sourwood Golf Course was designed by Elmo Cobb and opened in 1991, with a mix of open and wooded terrain. In the fairways, you'll find bermudagrass; on the greens, bentgrass.

We found Sourwood to be a fine owner-designed country course; Cobb could easily have made a good golf course architect based on the soundness of this layout. The course is named after the sourwood tree that still shows up in places but is sadly disappearing. Most holes are relatively straightforward – neither too easy nor overly difficult, just very playable. There's decent enough room off the tee,

Photo: NC Travel and Tourism

Many Triangle-area courses require accurate placement.
Expect unhappy consequences if you miss your mark.

so use your driver liberally. The greens are sloped and midsize.

Even though the course is somewhat remote, it's worth the drive for a break from the city and a fun round of golf in a pleasant country setting on a playable track.

Amenities include a practice green and snack bar.

You can walk anytime except before 1 PM on weekends. Book a tee time whenever you choose. Approximate cost, including cart, is $16 weekdays and $20 on weekends.

WAKE FOREST COUNTRY CLUB

13239 Capitol Blvd.
Wake Forest   556-3416
Championship Yardage: 6956
Slope: 135   *Par: 72*
Men's Yardage: 6525
Slope: 129   *Par: 72*
Other Yardage: 6109
Slope: 126   *Par: 72*
Ladies' Yardage: 5124
Slope: 122   *Par: 72*

Wake Forest Country Club opened in 1968. Gene Hamm designed this course on undulating wooded terrain, with bermudagrass fairways and bentgrass greens.

Wake Forest Country Club is unrelated to Wake Forest University, which is more than an hour's drive to the west. The course is well-known for the "world's longest par 5," a 711-yard behemoth on which you'll be happy to reach the ladies' tees on your first shot. If you don't reach the ladies' tees, the normal penalty (whatever *yours* is) does not apply: Please, just keep it in. Play it from the white tees and it's an ample 526 yards. And to make matters more difficult, there's a stream that bisects the hole close to the green that could easily destroy your confidence if you're not careful.

The course was recently purchased by GolfSouth, and improvements are being made to the track and its adjoining facilities. The absurd length of the first hole aside, Wake Forest should be better known for the quality of the layout. You'll find an excellent example here of a fine and playable traditional track that provides plenty of visual attraction and challenge. Attack this course and you'll be rewarded for sound execution, but realize that you'll be penalized proportionally for poor and wayward shots. Occasional trouble off the tee is augmented if the rough has grown up above an inch or two. The greens vary in size, shape, slope and waviness, but we're told that they are true and can get wonderfully fast. Water provides a hazard on a few holes. If you prefer mature, challenging courses, make the trip to Wake Forest Country Club.

Amenities include a practice green, range, chipping green, locker room, bar, snack bar, rental clubs, a beverage cart and pro shop.

Walking is restricted to after 2 PM on weekends. You can book a tee time seven days in advance. Approximate cost, including cart, is $25 Monday through Thursday, $29 on Friday and $38 on weekends.

WASHINGTON DUKE GOLF AND COUNTRY CLUB

N.C. Rte. 751 and Science Dr.
Durham   681-2288
Championship Yardage: 7045
Slope: 137   *Par: 72*
Men's Yardage: 6721
Slope: 129   *Par: 72*
Other Yardage: 6207
Slope: 119   *Par: 72*
Ladies' Yardage: 5505
Slope: 124   *Par: 72*

The golf course at Washington Duke Golf and Country Club opened in 1957.

Robert Trent Jones designed the original course; Rees Jones redesigned the course in 1993. This picturesque track has 419 bermudagrass fairways and bentgrass greens.

This is Duke University's golf course, and it's the most magnificent course in the Triangle — and one of the finest courses in North Carolina. Robert Trent Jones cut the original course out of Duke Forest, thus just about every hole is bordered by wonderfully pretty woods replete with towering trees. Rees Jones must have kept the original routing; however, he blew up the tee boxes and green complexes, and the result is nothing short of stunning. The targets are wonderfully defined and some of the holes are breathtaking. A lot of money was pumped into this course and it shows.

There's subtle mounding in the fairways and quite a few gaping fairway bunkers. You won't always have an even stance in the fairway. And water comes into play on a few holes. But it's the attention to detail around the green complexes that makes the course so spectacular. You'll see large, tiered greens, undulations and obvious slopes. Two-putting any green on this course is an achievement. Many greens are flanked by embankments; but, more importantly, each features a dizzying array of bunkers — some large, some small, but all potentially difficult and score-destroying. And as if the challenge wasn't great enough, the course finishes with two long and difficult uphill par 4s; you'll have to bust the ball off the tee if you want any chance of reaching the green in regulation. Make sure you play this course before you lose your swing.

You can also spend a night at the well-appointed inn adjacent to the course.

Amenities include a practice green, range, chipping green, locker room, bar, snack bar, restaurant, rental clubs, a beverage cart and a pro shop.

The course is walkable for the physically fit, but walking is restricted; call ahead for daily details. You can book a tee time whenever you choose. Approximate cost, including cart, is $50 weekdays and $60 on weekends.

WILLOWHAVEN COUNTRY CLUB

253 Country Club Dr.
Durham   383-1022

Championship Yardage: 6655	
Slope: 120	Par: 72
Men's Yardage: 6342	
Slope: 117	Par: 72
Other Yardage: 5721	
Slope: 111	Par: 72
Ladies' Yardage: 5436	
Slope: 117	Par: 75

The golf course at Willowhaven Country Club opened in 1957. George Cobb designed the course on rolling wooded terrain. In the fairways, you'll find bermudagrass; on the greens, you'll find bentgrass.

During our visit to Willowhaven, we were informed of the unfortunate fact that public play may soon end at this fine course. It's difficult to blame the members for wanting to keep the course to themselves.

The course is approaching its 40th birthday, so it's definitely a mature track. It's one of Cobb's earlier efforts, one that clearly shows his skill in taking a pretty piece of land and turning it into a playable and attractive course. Of course, there are plenty of the long and subtly dramatic Cobb courses too. But at Willowhaven Cobb gives us variety and challenge without anything tricked-up or fancy.

There isn't a lot of trouble off the tee, although it helps to be in the right sector on many of the doglegs. Trouble around the greens comes in the form of large sloped putting surfaces, swales, embankments and basic bunkers. The better golfer won't think that the course offers a huge amount of challenge, but there's easily enough from the back tees. If you're fond of traditional courses, you should make your way to Willowhaven while you still can.

Amenities include a practice green, range, snack bar, rental clubs and a pro shop.

Walk anytime; you can book a tee time three days prior to a weekday, five days prior to the weekend. Approximate cost, including cart, is $31.50 weekdays and $36.50 on weekends.

Around the Triangle...

Fun Things To Do

Raleigh is North Carolina's state capital as well as home to St. Mary's College, Peace College, Meredith College, St. Augustine's College, Shaw University and the North Carolina State University. Take the time to visit the **Executive Mansion**, home to Gov. James B. Hunt. It's an outstanding example of Queen Anne Cottage Victorian architecture. Call 733-3456 for tour information. You can also tour the State Capitol building in downtown Raleigh; call 733-4994.

North Carolina State University Arboretum is worth a visit, especially in the fall and spring; call 737-3132. The **North Carolina Symphony** is based in Raleigh and plays several concerts here; call 733-2750 for upcoming concerts.

Durham is perhaps best known for tobacco processing and as the location of the best movie ever about minor-league baseball: *Bull Durham*. The movie starred Kevin Costner, Tim Robbins and Susan Sarandon. Sadly, the ball park where the movie was filmed is no longer used.

If you're not in the mood for baseball or golf, then start with a visit to **Duke University**. You can take in the Gothic architecture in addition to the **Sarah P. Duke Gardens**, a 55-acre bouquet of daffodils, pansies, roses and other flora; call the Duke Gardens Office at 684-3698. You might also want to visit the **Duke Homestead and Tobacco Museum**. This attraction is housed in the former home of Washington Duke, father of the tobacco trade; you'll learn a lot about the influence of tobacco on the local economy. Call 477-5498.

West Point on the Eno is part of the Eno River City Park and is a pleasant and quiet retreat from the city. The park covers 400 acres and is full of wildlife. You can enjoy camping, fishing, rafting, picnicking, hiking and general solitude. Call 471-1623. Another excellent museum is the **North Carolina Museum of Life and Science** where you'll find hands-on exhibits, live experiments and wildlife. Call 220-5429.

Durham is also a major center for medicine; naturally, we hope that you've come to Durham for golf and not for a visit to one of the area's healthcare facilities.

Chapel Hill is where author Scott Martin spent four extremely studious and serious years at the University of North Carolina, flagship institution of the University of North Carolina system. You should visit **The Morehead Planetarium**, one of the finest in the country; call 549-6863. While you're there, you might cruise down Franklin Street to take in the general ambiance of one of the prettiest and most eclectic college towns in America. If you

A beautiful fall day is the perfect backdrop for a day of golf in the Triangle.

want to tour the campus of the University of North Carolina, call 962-2211.

Where to Eat

As far as urban areas go in North Carolina, it's probably tough to beat the Triangle for flair and variety. There's plenty of down-home Southern cooking to go around, but the diverse tastes brought here by the universities mean that food-lovers are well taken care of here. You'll find plenty of the chain-style eateries you might find at home, but while you're here, why not try something different: There's plenty to sample.

ANGUS BARN
U.S. Hwy. 70 at Airport Rd.
Raleigh   781-2444
$$$$

OK, so we'll start with something a little more traditional. Something that will stick to your ribs. This is one of the busiest and most popular steak houses in North Carolina and has been — in the same location — for more than 30 years.

The restaurant is popular with business people. Bring a big appetite and leave room for a desert. Don't even think about the word "diet."

MARGAUX'S
8111 Creedmore Rd.
Raleigh   846-9846
$$$

French cuisine in northern Raleigh? In the land of new houses and shopping centers? Two well-educated chefs turned a sporting goods store into a restaurant that's been acclaimed in print and by word-of-mouth. Check it out and be sure to ask about the specials, which may range from Carolina quail to crab casserole.

EST EST EST TRATORIA
19 W. Hargett St.
Raleigh   832-8899
$$

Enter on Salisbury Street. The restaurant is popular at lunch and has become even more so in the evenings. This place is perfect for the romantic in you, and, hopefully, your current or prospective better half too. Pasta is made on the premises. Choose a fine bottle of house wine to wash down your meal. You'll find a variety of entrees that change daily, but the basic menu components include pasta, seafood and lighter meats.

GREENSHIELD'S BREWERY AND PUB
214 E. Martin St.
Raleigh   829-0214
$$

For fine hand-crafted beer, you can't go wrong here. The pub is so authentic, it's frequented by Anglophiles, real English people (who only drink real beer), rugby players and darts-throwers. When hunger replaces thirst, try the fish and chips or pot pies.

ANOTHERTHYME
109 N. Gregson St.
Durham   682-5225
$$

We know locals who call this place home. The menu is varied — French, Italian, Spanish, Chinese — so you never get bored. And besides, all your friends are here, so how could you have anything but a good time. The food is prepared with always-fresh ingredients. Count this one in for lunch or dinner, or even for a late-night snack. You'll have a great meal at a great price.

DARRYL'S 1890
4603 Chapel Hill Blvd.
Durham   489-1890
$$

Part of the Darryl's chain, this version offers plenty of ambiance and plenty

of food. The multi-page menu offers everything from seafood to chicken to prime rib to massive desserts and liver-threatening frozen drinks. The restaurant is significantly popular after football games and other events in Chapel Hill or Durham. Note that there is also a Raleigh location on U.S. 70, just a few miles west of Crabtree Valley Mall.

BULLOCK'S BAR-B-CUE
3330 Wortham St.
Durham   383-3211
$

There just had to be an establishment with the word "Bull" in it, and this is it. Don't come here for the decor or to be coddled and "waited-on." Do come for the variety and quality of the barbecue, the hush puppies and tea so sweet that your spoon stands at attention.

MAGNOLIA GRILL
1002 Ninth St.
Durham   286-3609
$$$$

When you just had your best golf day ever and it's time to celebrate, do so at the Magnolia Grill. This is one of the area's best restaurants, and it has the loyal customers to prove it. Your dining pleasure will depend on what's fresh and what's on the chef's ever-changing, always-innovative menu. You should definitely leave room for dessert.

Make reservations here so you won't miss the opportunity to see why the Triangle is raving about this fine establishment.

AURORA

200 N. Greensboro St.
Chapel Hill   942-2400
$$$

Trendy, and justifiably so, Aurora is not a place to be seen, because you can't be — it's very dimly lit, especially at night. You'll find some of the most-acclaimed Italian food in the Triangle. Complement your veal, lamb, poultry or seafood with fresh pasta and dizzying sauces. Match it all with a hearty Italian wine and you're in for a great evening. Make a reservation here.

CROOK'S CORNER

610 W. Franklin St.
Chapel Hill   929-7643
$$$

Crook's offers one of the most unique and subtly intense dining experiences anywhere. The restaurant itself, which looks like a cross between a hair salon and a former service station, is crowned with a statue of a pig. Wooden animal statuary rounds out the decor. The menu changes so rapidly, you'll never be disappointed. It might be something South American; it might be something like shrimp 'n' grits. It's always praiseworthy — and usually loud and fun. Crook's Corner is a great place for reunions of sorts.

PYEWACKET

431 W. Franklin St.
Chapel Hill   929-0291
$$

Pyewacket has been a Chapel Hill fixture with the old Volvo and tweed jacket academic crowd for years. Or at least that's how it's reputed. Actually, its popularity base has increased to include sorority women on "girls' night out" to businessmen in town to close

a deal. The food is the key. Somehow, it seems light and hearty at the same time. The wine list is excellent, and you'll find many fine vegetarian dishes here.

THE RATHSKELLER

157-A Franklin St.
Chapel Hill   942-5158
$

"The Rat," in its own subterranean fashion, exudes fumes of Chapel Hill past and present. It's a major student hangout, with a major and passionate following among alumni who line up after football games for spaghetti and tea. It's not a place for the claustrophobic but it is a place for those whose blood runs Tarheel blue. A must.

Where to Stay

COURTYARD BY MARRIOTT

1041 Wakestowne Dr.
Raleigh   821-3400
$$

The Courtyard by Marriott concept is popping up all over the country and is popular with business travelers. This version may look like some of the others you've seen, but there are some important amenities to note, including an on-site gym, whirlpool room and outdoor pool. Guests also have free access to a full-scale gym with extensive facilities across the road. When you're through working out, drop by the restaurant, serving breakfast and light dinners, and the bar. Staff members are quite friendly here. Due to the large volume of business travelers in the area, you should definitely book ahead for a room.

From the mountains to the beaches, courses in the Carolinas
typically feature plenty of water hazards.

HILTON CONVENTION CENTER
3415 Wake Forest Rd.
Raleigh 872-2323
$$$-$$$$

Convenient to Raleigh Community Hospital, and very near the Beltline, this popular and glitzy hotel boasts 338 rooms and quite a few large-scale political parties.

On the special executive floor you'll have access to a private cocktail bar; your room will be a little larger than a regular room plus you'll have an ironing board and a few other bells and whistles at your disposal. The standard rooms are comfortable as well, and all are equipped with coffee makers. Guests receive a free copy of *USA Today* daily.

Other amenities include a workout room, an indoor pool and a whirlpool. If you're in the mood for a boogie, venture forth unto Bowties night club, where the price of admission is free if you're staying at the hotel. Enjoy the full-service restaurant; otherwise try one of the 30 restaurants within an hour of the hotel.

ARROWHEAD INN
106 Mason Rd.
Durham 477-8430
$$$

This wonderful bed and breakfast inn features eight guest rooms and is convenient to everywhere in Durham. Relax in the parlor with a game or some light TV. You'll also get a hearty breakfast when you awaken from a peaceful slumber.

WASHINGTON DUKE INN AND GOLF CLUB
3001 Cameron Blvd.
Durham 490-0999
$$$

This 171-room hotel cost roughly $16 million to build, so it had better be nice, right? Well this is one of the finest places in Durham. We've already raved about the golf course, so why not rave about the hotel that dominates the 9th hole, a dangerous par 5.

Service is a key at Washington Duke — room service, turndown service and just the right touches of white-glove style to keep you content. You can relax in their four-star restaurant, The Fairview, and enjoy an after-dinner drink in the Bull Durham Lounge. If golf is not your game, there's tennis and Duke Forest jogging trails or a swimming pool.

THE CAROLINA INN
W. Cameron Ave.
Chapel Hill   933-2001
$$$

Venerable and storied, this is the inn of the University of North Carolina. In 1995 this accommodation underwent a series of changes and improvements, to equip it for latter part of the 20th century and prepare it for the 21st. The inn opened in 1924, so it needed some work. You'll love the architecture as well as being within walking distance of downtown Chapel Hill and all of its attractions.

HOLIDAY INN OF CHAPEL HILL
U.S. 15/501 Bypass
Chapel Hill   929-2171
$$

Looking for a clean, comfortable hotel that won't take up all your golf money? This is a great choice. It's near a shopping mall and the UNC campus, and this location offers easy access to I-40, so scooting around the Triangle is convenient.

Teddy's restaurant is on-site, and plenty of other good eateries are also nearby. There's also an outdoor pool.

FEARRINGTON HOUSE COUNTRY INN
Fearrington Village
Pittsboro   542-2121
$$$$

OK, we know this inn isn't in Chapel Hill proper, but it's less than 10 minutes away, and the experience you'll have at this charming spot is more than worth the drive. The 15 suites at Fearrington House are the definition of luxury but are presented without any of the highbrow attitude that too often accompanies an accommodation of this quality. Each room is unique, with beautiful antiques collected by the owners on trips to Europe. And the surrounding landscaping takes full advantage of the relaxing countryside that once was home to a dairy farm.

You'll also enjoy afternoon teas and a complimentary breakfast served in the on-site restaurant that has been commended by both *Gourmet* and *Food and Wine* magazines. Dinner here is an experience you'll want to add to your list.

Photo: Mark Sluder

PGA SENIOR TOUR competitor Jimmy Powell blasts out of a sand trap at the TPC at Piper Glen. The Senior Tour stops in Charlotte, Winston-Salem and Myrtle Beach.

Inside
The Triad of North Carolina

The Greensboro, Winston-Salem, Burlington and High Point areas are best known in the Carolinas for their industrial base. R.J. Reynolds, Sara Lee and Guilford Mills have large manufacturing plants and administrative offices in the area. Wachovia Bank, one of the nation's largest financial institutions, is based in Winston-Salem and is building a brand spanking-new headquarters (it looks like a brown candle) right in downtown. There are numerous fine cultural organizations and four well-known universities: North Carolina A&T, Winston-Salem State, UNC-Greensboro and Wake Forest. There's also plenty of minor-league ice hockey in the area. Winston-Salem began play in the fall of 1995, and the Greensboro Monarchs have played in Greensboro for a number of years. So if it's too cold outside for golf, take solace in the fact that hot dogs, beer and glove-dropping fisticuffs are close at hand.

Golf-wise, there's more public golf in the Triad than you can shake a 4-iron at. There might be more public golf here than in any other non-resort area in the Carolinas. And more courses are on the way. When we visited the area for our reviews, one new course had just opened and three or four more were about to celebrate their first-ever tee time. One course owner complained that there were too many public tracks!

Can you have too many public courses in a given geographic zone? We noticed that the excess supply means that prices are generally lower in the Triad than in other urban areas. This means less money for the owners; it can also mean less money for maintenance and, on many tracks, it showed. Given favorable climatic conditions, many course will be fine. Given poor natural conditions, you won't always find magnificent greens and fairways. It's difficult enough to grow anything on all this Piedmont clay, let alone lush bermudagrass. We should stress that in 1995 the courses had been hit with a winter freeze-out of the fairways and a summer that began with floods and ended with baking heat. No, Mother Nature was not kind to these courses in '95.

But economics and conditioning aside, the Triad is stacked with good public courses. The municipal governments have, with the help of significant donations of free land, invested heavily in fine golf facilities with national reputations. Tanglewood, in Clemmons, hosts a PGA SENIOR TOUR event and in 1974 hosted the PGA Championship won by Lee Trevino. Bryan Park's Champions Course in Brown Summit is probably a good enough layout to host a significant professional event. And each year, two weeks after the Masters, the big boys of the PGA Tour come to the area for the Greater Greensboro Open (see our Tournaments in the Carolinas chapter). In addition to these professional events, the area is host to a number of top-quality amateur tour-

GOLF COURSES IN THE TRIAD OF NORTH CAROLINA

Name	Type	# Holes	Par	Slope	Yards	Walking	Booking	Cost w/ Cart
Bryan Park								
Champions Course	public	18	72	125	6622	restricted	30 days	$30-32
Players Course	public	18	72	120	6499	anytime	30 days	$30-32
Hickory Hill Country Club	semiprivate	18	70	110	5902	restricted	3 days	$22-28
Holly Ridge Golf Links	public	18	72	127	6121	restricted	anytime	$21-27
Jamestown Park	public	18	72	122	6186	restricted	7 days	$22-24
Lexington Golf and Country Club	public	18	70	116	5703	anytime	7 days	$18-20
Lynrock Golf Club	public	18	70	109	5538	anytime	2 days	$19-21
Maple Leaf	public	18	71	n/r	5655	restricted	7 days	$21-24
Mill Creek	public	18	72	127	6387	n/a	n/a	n/a
Monroeton Golf Club	public	18	70	103	5428	anytime	anytime	$11-16
Oak Hollow Golf Course	public	18	72	118	6090	anytime	2 days	$23-26
Pine Knolls	semiprivate	18	72	110	5923	restricted	anytime	$22-28
Pine Tree	semiprivate	18	71	107	6046	restricted	10 days	$24-28
Pudding Ridge	semiprivate	18	70	123	6234	restricted	7 days	$24-28
Reynolds Park	public	18	71	118	5923	restricted	7 day	$22-28
Sandy Ridge Golf Course	semiprivate	18	72	n/r	5645	restricted	5 days	$21-25
Southwick Golf Course	public	18	70	111	5431	restricted	anytime	$12-20
Stoney Creek Golf Club	semiprivate	18	72	132	6573	restricted	7 days	$30-35
Tanglewood Park								
Championship Course	public	18	72	135	6638	restricted	7 days	$45-63
Reynolds Course	public	18	72	120	6061	anytime	7 days	$30

The Triad Area

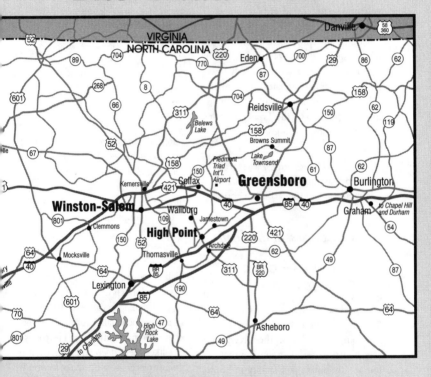

naments. Wake Forest University has one of the most successful golf programs in the country; its alumni include Jay Haas, Arnold Palmer and Curtis Strange. Notable architects whose work graces this area include Robert Trent Jones, Rees Jones, Pete Dye, Gene Hamm and Tom Jackson. Plus there are numerous courses designed by "no-name" architects: Their efforts are worthwhile and interesting. If you live in the Triad area, count your blessings. If you're visiting the Triad, schedule some time to visit some of the tracks listed in this chapter.

Triad Golf, an excellent monthly newspaper, gives timely updates on course developments, tournaments and other pertinent information for the Triad golfer. It's available in most pro shops.

> Note: Unless otherwise stated, all courses and businesses in this chapter are in the 910 area code.

Golf Courses in the Triad

BRYAN PARK AND GOLF CLUB
6275 Bryan Park Rd.
Brown Summit   375-2200

The Triad area is fortunate that most of its municipalities have invested in fine golf complexes. Here in the Greensboro area, it's Bryan Park — a complex that's as fine as any public golf facility in North Carolina. Each of the two courses was designed by a fine architect. A state-of-the-art practice facility is slated for completion in January 1996.

If you're looking for a couple of public courses with real difficulty and serious challenge, visit Bryan Park; you won't be disappointed on either track and you'll be rewarded if you travel a decent distance to play here. Both

courses also provide excellent value for your golfing dollar.

Amenities include a practice green, range, chipping green, snack bar, rental clubs and a pro shop.

Both courses are walkable for the fit; you can walk anytime on the Players and after 4 PM on the Champions. You can book a tee time one month in advance. Approximate cost, including cart, is $30 weekdays and $32 on weekends.

Champions Course
Championship Yardage: 7135

Slope: 130	*Par: 72*
Men's Yardage: 6622	
Slope: 125	*Par: 72*
Other Yardage: 5977	
Slope: 118	*Par: 72*
Ladies' Yardage: 5395	
Slope: 123	*Par: 72*

Rees Jones designed the Champions Course, which opened in 1990 and is set in open terrain bordered by woods on some holes. Fairways are bermudagrass; greens, bentgrass.

The Champions Course offers some wonderful and difficult holes. Jones made good use of the natural landscape, including several acres bordering Lake Townsend, which comes into play on a number of holes. Rees Jones is the son of Robert Trent Jones, and both father and son demonstrate an annoying penchant (from a players perspective) for mass bunkering. The younger Jones likes them deep and somewhat irregularly placed — some make us wonder whose ball would ever find these traps, they're so out of the way. Perhaps these bunkers exist solely for your viewing pleasure.

There's usually plenty of room off the tee. Wayward drives may end up in woods or bouncing around the many large mounds. You might find a bunker. Water comes into play a lot here in the form of the lake, ponds and streams. The greens are large and sloped and flanked by many bunkers and a few embankments. You'll have trouble getting to most of the greens and just as much trouble getting up and down.

Players Course
Championship Yardage: 7076
Slope: 128   Par: 72
Men's Yardage: 6499
Slope: 120   Par: 72
Other Yardage: 5925
Slope: 115   Par: 72
Ladies' Yardage: 5260
Slope: 120   Par: 72

The Players Course at Bryan Park, designed by George Cobb, opened in 1974. The bermudagrass fairways and bentgrass greens are set in open terrain, with woods flanking some holes. Rees Jones made some changes to the Players Course when he built the Champions Course.

Even from the front tees, the Players Course is difficult; as the scorecard reads, it's "recognized as one of the best public tests of golf."

The Players Course is the more mature of the two, and if you're familiar with the work of George Cobb, you'll recognize this as one of his signature efforts. Rees Jones's modifications likely account for the addition of mounds and some new bunkering. But don't think that the Players Course is an easier version of its sister. From the back, there's still more than 7000 yards of tough golf ahead of you. There isn't nearly as much water, but you'll still find difficult greens and extensive bunkering. If the Champions Course

looks crowded, think about trying the Players; it's still an excellent challenge.

HICKORY HILL COUNTRY CLUB
U.S. Hwy. 64 E.
Mocksville   998-8746
Championship Yardage: 6537
Slope: 116   Par: 70
Men's Yardage: 5902
Slope: 110   Par: 70
Ladies' Yardage: 4973
Slope: 109   Par: 70

The Golf Course at Hickory Hill Country Club, a Russell McMillan design, opened in 1970. Typical of courses in the Triad, Hickory Hill is primarily open and bordered by woods on some holes. In the fairways, you'll find bermudagrass; on the greens, you'll find bentgrass.

Although Hickory Hill is not a terribly old course, it has what might be described as a pre-war design. The layout is an excellent example of minimalist architecture in a pretty, relaxed setting. You'll find mostly wide fairways and a few lonely grass or sand bunkers. Most of the green complexes are not raised — you can play all the run-up shots you want — and the greens are mostly flat. There's no irrigation system in the fairways, so from 50 yards in, one of your options may be the putter.

A new pro and course manager recently came on board here, and he is in the process of improving the club, in general, and its golf facilities, in particular. If you're looking for an ultra-modern moundfest with greens from hell, look

---

When the course you're playing is busy, spend a maximum of two or three minutes looking for your ball. Or, better still, take a little less club off the tee and concentrate on hitting it straight.

Insiders' Tips

Days like this are rare in the Carolinas, where you can usually play golf comfortably all year.

elsewhere. Hickory Hill harkens back to the early days of golf when every good player knew how to run the ball up to the green from almost anywhere.

Amenities include a practice green, range, chipping green, locker room, snack bar, rental clubs and a pro shop.

This course is a good one to walk, and you may walk anytime during the week and before 2 PM on weekends. You can book a tee time three days in advance. Approximate cost, including cart, is $22 weekdays and $28 on weekends.

HOLLY RIDGE GOLF LINKS

7727 U.S. Hwy. 311
Archdale   861-GOLF
Championship Yardage: 6579
Slope: 135   *Par: 72*
Men's Yardage: 6121
Slope: 127   *Par: 72*
Other Yardage: 5727
Slope: 121   *Par: 72*
Ladies' Yardage: 4754
Slope: No rating   *Par: 72*

Holly Ridge Golf Course opened in 1994. Jim Bevins designed the course on rolling and open terrain, with bermudagrass fairways and bentgrass greens.

Holly Ridge offers an interesting addition to the Triad golf scene. The course is predominantly open, but some holes are bordered by woods and cow pasture. A lake comes into play on several holes and poses quite a challenge in places. Jim Bevins may not be a big name, but he's provided a golfing test that demands intelligence to conquer. Like many modern courses, you'll find a lot of mounds at Holly Ridge — but you won't find any holly. You'll also find some tough driving tests, large bunkers and sloped greens and decent variety from hole to hole. Many greens are flanked by potentially nasty embankments. Perhaps the back nine is prettier for the moment than the front. Grow-in went well here; in time Holly Ridge will be a good course for all levels of golfer. The course wins the prize for the most rakes per sand trap.

Amenities include a practice green, range and chipping green.

Walking is permitted on weekdays only. You can book a tee time whenever you choose. Approximate cost, including cart, is $21 weekdays and $27 on weekends.

JAMESTOWN PARK GOLF COURSE
200 E. Fork Rd.

Jamestown	454-4912
Championship Yardage: 6665	
Slope: 126	Par: 72
Men's Yardage: 6186	
Slope: 122	Par: 72
Ladies' Yardage: 5298	
Slope: 118	Par: 72

No one is sure when the golf course at Jamestown Park opened, but it is known that John V. Townsend designed it. The course is set in rolling terrain and flanked by woods. In the fairways, you'll find bermudagrass; on the greens, bentgrass.

We're not sure what the "V" in John V. Townsend stands for. In fact, no one is sure who Townsend is. However, he may have had the makings of a fine golf course architect. The course here is pleasant, challenging, sensible and thoroughly well-designed. You won't find a lot of trouble off the tee. The fairways are relatively wide. The greens are large to huge, with the occasional bunker providing a challenge. Three of the par 3s are fronted by gaping bunkers running the entire length of the putting complex. On other greens, you'll be able to run the ball up to the hole. A bit of water comes into play on the back nine, though it's nothing to lose sleep over.

The front nine is pretty enough, but the back nine is more interesting, varied and fun. Dare we say it, but John V. Townsend may have been a fan and imitator of Ellis Maples, for a couple of holes would have made Mr. Maples seek a copyright-infringement suit. Perhaps. We'll let you decide.

The course here at Jamestown Park is well worth a visit if you're looking for something relaxed yet challenging. And it's a good value.

Amenities include a practice green, range, chipping green, locker room, snack bar and pro shop.

You can walk anytime except before 12:30 PM on weekends. You can book a tee time seven days in advance for the week and on Thursday for the weekend. Approximate cost, including cart, is $22 weekdays and $24 on weekends.

LEXINGTON GOLF AND COUNTRY CLUB
200 Country Club Blvd.

Lexington	246-3950
Championship Yardage: 5703	
Slope: 116	Par: 70

Dugan Aycock designed Lexington Golf and Country Club, which opened in 1936. Set on rolling terrain and flanked by houses, Lexington boasts bermudagrass fairways and bentgrass greens.

You may not have heard of Dugan Aycock, which is a shame ... he was quite a character. Aycock played on the U.S. Army golf team during World War II, was friends with the likes of Trevino, Nicklaus and Palmer, encouraged the great Bobby Locke to come to America from South Africa, raised enormous sums of money for charity and was a golfing partner with Bill "Earthquake" Smith, an officer of the law, former football player at the University of North Carolina and an excellent golfer. You can read the full story about Aycock in the men's locker room. Ladies, please ask before you enter.

If times had been different, perhaps Aycock would have been a designer. His product here in Lexington is a quirky and fascinating track, with enormous character and variety. The course is set on what must be fewer than 100 acres, thus the course is somewhat tight and short. This makes for quite a test of shotmaking and accuracy. Big numbers await the even slightly wayward. There aren't a large number of bunkers, but they are to be avoided at all costs. The greens are flat and smallish, and you'll be able to run the ball up on a few holes — just like in the 1930s. There are more than a couple of holes that would catch the attention of almost any golf course architect. Play this one if you're in the area and, after your round, devour some Lexington-style barbecue for a real treat.

Amenities include a practice green, locker room, rental clubs and a pro shop.

Walk anytime and book a tee time seven days in advance for the weekend and anytime for the week. Approximate cost, including cart, is $18 weekdays and $20 on weekends.

LYNROCK GOLF CLUB
636 Valley Dr.
Eden   623-6110
Championship Yardage: 6046
Slope: 114   Par: 70
Men's Yardage: 5538
Slope: 109   Par: 70
Ladies' Yardage: 4913
Slope: 109   Par: 70

Jim Wilson designed Lynrock Golf Club, which opened in 1959. The course is set on mostly flat terrain, with bermudagrass fairways and bentgrass greens.

Lynrock offers fun and reasonably demanding country golf on a pretty track that winds around the valley floor immediately adjacent to the confluence of the Dan and Smith rivers. The river here is remarkably wide and comes into play on a couple of holes. This is most noticeable on the par 3 No. 2, which plays 150 yards from the tips. You tee off on one side of the river to a shallow green on the other side. Park it on the dance floor and you have to cross one of the most picturesque and longest bridges on any golf course in the area — perhaps in the Carolinas. A wonderful start to your round.

The rest of the course will not disappoint. The fairways are not overly wide, although they are fairly open. The greens

are large and sloped; some are crowned and, thus, will play a little smaller if the greens are firm. Many of the green complexes include a series of medium-size bunkers, and you'll have to fly some of them. On other holes, you'll be able to run the ball up to the pin with a well-executed half-shot or some creative use of your Texas wedge.

Amenities include a practice green and rental clubs.

The course is walkable, you should walk and you can walk anytime. You can book up to two days in advance. Approximate cost, including cart, is $19 weekdays and $21 on weekends.

MAPLE LEAF GOLF CLUB
4070 Hastings Rd.
Kernersville   769-9122
Championship Yardage: 6028
Slope: No rating   Par: 71
Men's Yardage: 5655
Slope: No rating   Par: 71
Ladies' Yardage: 4643
Slope: No rating   Par: 71

Maple Leaf Golf Club opened a front nine in 1981, designed by Ellis Maples, and a back nine in 1988, designed by Don Charles. The course is set in rolling wooded terrain, with bermudagrass fairways and bentgrass greens.

You won't find many Canadians here, but you will find a fine secluded course with an outstanding design pedigree. Anyone who has played golf in the Carolinas has heard of the great Ellis Maples. Charles is lesser-known, although he assisted with the renowned Legends complex in the Myrtle Beach area.

The result is a course with great interest and variety. It's not long from the back, but the narrowness of the fairways, in places, makes up for it. On the front nine, the 5th is a fun hole. Hit a decent drive downhill and you'll have a short iron over water to a small green set on a peninsula. But don't let this hole make you think the course is overly penal. On most holes you can recover from slightly errant shots. Extremely errant shots will have you dipping into your pocket for an extra ball.

You'll find a variety of options off the tee as well as in the size, shape and structure of the green complexes. With its challenge, picturesque setting, subtleties and sensible pricing, Maple Leaf offers one of the best low-cost golfing venues in the Triad.

Amenities include a practice green and snack bar.

You can walk anytime during the week and after 4 PM on weekends. You can book a tee time seven days in advance. Approximate cost, including cart, is $21 weekdays and $24 on weekends.

MILL CREEK GOLF CLUB

1700 St. Andrews Dr.
Mebane   (919) 563-4653
Championship Yardage: 7004
Slope: 141   Par: 72
Men's Yardage: 6387
Slope: 127   Par: 72
Other Yardage: 5711
Slope: 122   Par: 72
Ladies' Yardage: 4884
Slope: 113   Par: 72

Mill Creek Golf Course was scheduled to open in the fall 1995. Rick Robbins, Gary Koch and Brian Lussier designed the course. We visited Mill Creek while it was still under construction. However, we picked up a brochure, and the plans look tremendous. Robbins and Lussier were

both formerly associated with the design of Jack Nicklaus courses, and Koch was formerly a tour player.

The course was being built in tandem with an upscale housing community. Based on the initial scorecard, there will be some amazing and treacherous golf holes that will test the stamina of even the finest golfers (check out the slope rating from the tips!). There will be four sets of tees (as noted). The course may turn private after the housing is established, so play this one while you can.

MONROETON GOLF CLUB

213 Monroeton Golf Course Rd.
Reidsville   342-1043
Championship Yardage: 5729
Slope: 106   Par: 70
Men's Yardage: 5428
Slope: 103   Par: 70
Other Yardage: 4955
Slope: No rating   Par: 70
Ladies' Yardage: 4282
Slope: 105   Par: 70

According to local legend, there was a golf course here when golfers still played on sand greens. Estimates of the date of origin indicate sometime in the 1940s, but the real date play began here might be even earlier. No one is sure who designed this course, which is bordered by woods and houses amidst a rolling landscape. In the fairways, you'll find a combination of bermudagrass and native grasses; on the greens, you'll find bentgrass.

You might think that Monroeton Golf Club is a bit of an anachronism . . . it is. This classic country track probably has been

Take the time to learn something about golf course architects and architecture. Many fine books have been written on the subject, and you'll enjoy a course more if you're familiar with the architect's style.

Insiders' Tips

untouched since the first golfer teed off here. The fairways are wide and somewhat undefined. The course has no bunkers. The greens are sloped, crowned and large. If the ground is hard, you'll have to run the ball up to the green because it's unlikely your shot will hold. If you want to see what it was like playing golf before earth was moved and sands shifted, you need to play here. Is there a lower cost for 18 holes, including cart, in the Triad? No way. Now you know why you bought this book!

If you're having some sort of legal dispute either on or off the golf course, you'll be pleased to know that the firm of Griffin and Crapse, with offices adjacent to the 3rd tee, will be more than willing to help you (for a fee, of course). If you call and the secretary says Mr. Crapse is on the golf course and he'll be back in a minute, it's probably true.

Amenities include a practice green, range, locker room and snack bar.

You can walk this course anytime. You won't need a tee time during the week; call on Tuesday for your weekend slot. Approximate cost, including cart, is $11 weekdays and $16 on weekends.

OAK HOLLOW GOLF COURSE

1400 Oak View
High Point   *883-3260*
Championship Yardage: 6483
Slope: 124   *Par: 72*
Men's Yardage: 6090
Slope: 118   *Par: 72*
Ladies' Yardage: 4796
Slope: 114   *Par: 72*

Oak Hollow Golf Course opened in 1972. Pete Dye designed the course on rolling, primarily open terrain, with a lake bordering many holes on the front nine, bermudagrass fairways and bentgrass greens.

Yes, *the* Pete Dye designed the course. And what a course it is, especially for a pub-

lic track. After the Robert Trent Jones era of golf course architecture came the Pete Dye era, and you'll see many of the features that made Dye (and his sons) some of the most in-demand architects in the universe. Dye began life as a successful life insurance salesman, and there must be many a befuddled golfer who wishes that he had stuck to explaining the difference between term and life. During the '60s, Dye and his wife, Alice, herself an accomplished course designer, toured Scotland in between designing moderate-cost courses in the Midwest. Oak Hollow was built before Dye's career really took off and Japanese investors began lining up with bunkers full of cash just to have a Dye course. Oak Hollow is the only Pete Dye course in North Carolina that's open to the public.

Although Dye incorporated a number of Scottish features into his work, this is not a links course. There isn't a great deal of trouble off the tee on most holes. The real work begins around the green complexes, which feature bizarre slopes, bunkers and shapes. It's quite possible to hit a green and still work extremely hard for a par. One of us hit the green on the perilous 6th hole — a 420-yard par 4 — found a grassy mound between the ball and the hole and had to get up to the pin with a wedge. On many holes, Dye brings Oak Hollow Lake into play in spectacular fashion, particularly on the aforementioned 6th hole where the tee box sits seemingly in the middle of the lake. Other golf course architects spend time creating subtle shapes and nuances in an effort to create aesthetically pleasing layouts. Dye uses his imagination to create golf holes that are bizarre, penal at times, wonderful and somewhat mind-bending. His goal is to get you thinking; of course, that's when the trouble begins. If you're a student of golf course architecture, make the

Photo: NC Travel & Tourism

Thousands of golf enthusiasts attend the Greater Greensboro Open.

effort to play this course. It's quite an experience. And at less than $30, it's a Dye course that won't increase your overdraft.

Amenities include a practice green, range, chipping green, locker room, snack bar, rental clubs and a pro shop.

The course is walkable (can you believe it?) and you can walk anytime (also hard to believe). You can book a tee time two days in advance. Approximate cost, including cart, is $23 weekdays and $26 on weekends.

PINE KNOLLS GOLF COURSE

1100 Quail Hollow Rd.	
Kernersville	*993-5478*
Championship Yardage: 6287	
Slope: 121	*Par: 72*
Men's Yardage: 5923	
Slope: 110	*Par: 72*
Ladies' Yardage: 4480	
Slope: 92	*Par: 72*

Pine Knolls Golf Course opened in 1969. Most holes are open, and others are bordered by woods or houses. Bermudagrass blankets the fairways; bentgrass, the greens.

Yet another Triad golf course with the word "Pine" in its name, Pine Knolls offers a fun and mostly straightforward golf outing. The setting is pleasant and relaxed. You won't find a lot of bunkers, but you will find plenty of variety and a decent amount of challenge. The layout is sensible and not overly penal, although really bad shots will yield really bad results. Off the tee, you must think about and choose the correct weapon; use the driver wisely. Around the medium-size greens, you'll find slope and some undulation. A few greens allow you to run the ball up from the fairway. One touch we especially liked was the path cut through the rough from the tee boxes to the fairways. It's a statement from the management that says: "yes, we like walkers." Pine Knolls is clearly popular; it's also a good value.

Amenities include a practice green, range, chipping green, locker room, snack bar, rental clubs and a pro shop.

Walk Pine Knolls anytime during the week and after 1:30 PM on weekends. You can book a tee time whenever you choose. Approximate cost, including cart, is $22 weekdays and $28 on weekends.

PINE TREE GOLF CLUB

1680 Pine Tree Ln.
Kernersville   (919) 993-5598
Championship Yardage: 6604
Slope: 113   Par: 71
Men's Yardage: 6046
Slope: 107   Par: 71
Ladies' Yardage: 4897
Slope: 110   Par: 71

Pine Tree Golf Club opened in 1971. Gene Hamm designed the course on rolling, wooded terrain. In the fairways, you'll find bermudagrass; on the greens, bentgrass.

Pine Tree is a course with challenge, scenic beauty and excellent variety. There are virtually no houses, so you'll feel far away from the hassles of urbanic civilization.

You'll find a great deal of room off the tee on most holes. Feel free to take out the big stick — you'll need it on many of the longer par 4s. The greens are large and sloped. The green complexes boast an abundance of large and flat bunkers: Avoid them. Quite a few greens are flush with the fairway; they're not built up in any way. So, despite all the bunkers, you can run the ball up to the pin on a few holes if you choose. Water comes into play here and there but should not cause too much of a problem. Occasional trees near or in the fairways will make you think twice about your next shot.

The general feeling of being away from it all is what we liked best about Pine Tree. Combine the peaceful setting with a challenging and varied course and you should be in for a good round. It's definitely a good value.

Amenities include a practice green, range, chipping green, locker room, snack bar, restaurant and pro shop.

You can walk Pine Tree only on weekdays. You can book a tee time up to 10 days in advance. Approximate cost, including cart, is $24 weekdays and $28 on weekends.

PUDDING RIDGE GOLF CLUB

224 Cornwallis Dr.
Mocksville   940-4653
Championship Yardage: 6750
Slope: 128   Par: 70
Men's Yardage: 6234
Slope: 123   Par: 70
Ladies' Yardage: 4709
Slope: 111   Par: 70

Pudding Ridge Golf Club opened in 1994. The course is set in open, rolling terrain, with bermudagrass fairways and bentgrass greens. Mark Charles and Don Bowles teamed up on the design.

Pudding Ridge takes the cake for the most intriguing golf course name. According to local experts, the area was named Pudding Ridge by General Cornwallis's troops during the American Revolutionary War. The troops thought that the soil looked like pudding, which, as you may know, is the British word for dessert.

Nomenclature aside, Pudding Ridge is a brand-new course with an interesting design. The owners of the property took the architectural duties upon themselves, and their work is admirable. Pudding Ridge needs some maturity to reach its aesthetic peak, but its openness is unique and in stark contrast to the Triad's many wooded courses. The openness also gives the course a links feel.

You'll find a lot of room off the tee, some sloping medium to large-size greens and assorted sizes of bunkers that come into play in varying degrees based on pin placement. One of the great aspects of Pudding Ridge is that, unlike many modern courses, there's a dearth of mounds. You'll like the abandoned grain silo in the 5th fairway — a unique hazard. The question of what happens if the ball falls in the silo is best left to the rules gurus in Far Hills, New Jersey (at USGA headquarters). Pudding Ridge is a welcome addition to the already bulging portfolio of courses in the Triad.

Amenities include a practice green, chipping green, locker room, snack bar, restaurant, rental clubs and a pro shop.

The course is walkable for the physically fit, and you can walk anytime during the week and after 3 PM on weekends. You can book a tee time seven days in advance. Approximate cost, including cart, is $24 weekdays and $28 on weekends.

REYNOLDS PARK GOLF COURSE

2391 Reynolds Park Rd.
Winston-Salem   650-7660
Championship Yardage: 6320
Slope: No rating   Par: 71
Men's Yardage: 5923
Slope: 118   Par: 71
Ladies' Yardage: 5538
Slope: No rating   Par: 75

Reynolds Park Golf Course opened in 1940. Perry Maxwell designed the original layout, and Ellis Maples revised the track in 1966. The course is primarily open, although woods border a few holes. Fairways are bermudagrass; greens, bentgrass.

Here at Reynolds Park, you'll find a fine old municipal course that's justifiably popular. Maxwell is not a big name in North Carolina, but he is best known for another popular municipal course: Hillandale in Durham. He was quite a character, and you can read about him in the Hillandale review in our Triangle chapter.

The course is laid out on a relatively small tract of land, thus some of the fairways are pretty tight. But the course is open, so you won't be out of bounds very often even if your drive strays somewhat. It's certainly an entertaining course. There are some holes where it seems like Maples

left well enough alone. These holes are somewhat featureless and bunkerless but challenging. Other holes reveal Maples' influence; these feature large bunkers and sloped greens. The result is a lot of variety and a need for accuracy with approach shots. You'll also see some fine views of downtown Winston-Salem.

Amenities include a practice green, range, locker room, snack bar, rental clubs and a pro shop.

You can walk the course anytime during the week and after 1 PM on weekends. Book a tee time seven days in advance for a weekday and on Thursday for the weekend. Approximate cost, including cart, is $22 weekdays and $28 on weekends.

SANDY RIDGE GOLF COURSE

2055 Sandy Ridge Rd.
Colfax   668-0408
Championship Yardage: 6021
Slope: No rating   Par: 72
Men's Yardage: 5645
Slope: No rating   Par: 72
Ladies' Yardage: 5175
Slope: No rating   Par: 72

Sandy Ridge Golf Course opened in 1972. Gene Hamm designed the course. The course is set in rolling wooded terrain. In the fairways, you'll find bermudagrass; on the greens, you'll find bentgrass.

Just to the south and west of Greensboro near Piedmont Triad International Airport sits the tiny town of Colfax and its one golf course — Sandy Ridge. You're greeted by a docile and somewhat geriatric dog of mixed breed who sniffs at your golf shoes with comforting approval.

Just before our visit, a new greenskeeper had been hired, and we heard distinct murmurs of approval from golfers with whom we spoke. The design is interesting and varied. Most of the time you'll find plenty of room off the tee, although the back nine seems a little tighter.

The greens vary in size, are only slightly sloped and, on some holes, are surrounded by small mounds. There are no bunkers, thus you'll be able to play some run-up shots if you're a long way away from the green and don't want to land your shot like a well-thrown dart. The terrain is pretty, the golf is relaxed and the dog is well-fed and amenable.

Amenities include a practice green, locker room and snack bar.

You may walk this course anytime during the week or after noon on weekends. You can book a tee time whenever you choose for the week and on Monday for the weekend. Approximate cost, including cart, is $21 weekdays and $25 on weekends.

SOUTHWICK GOLF COURSE

3136 Southwick Dr.
Graham   227-2582
Championship Yardage: 5778
Slope: 116   *Par: 70*
Men's Yardage: 5431
Slope: 111   *Par: 70*
Ladies' Yardage: 4413
Slope: 108   *Par: 70*

Southwick Golf Course opened in 1991. Elmo Cobb designed this well-maintained course on predominantly open land, with woods bordering a few holes. In the fairways, you'll find bermudagrass; on the greens, bentgrass.

Don't let the yardage fool you. Let's just call Southwick a Dudley Moore course: short yet entertaining. Truly, it can be plenty tough from the back tees, especially considering the need to play it

straight with the driver. The rolling terrain may cause some difficulty with club selection on your approach shots. Call it the "Witches of Southwick" effect. You won't find Cher here, nor will you find Jack Nicholson, but you will find greens that vary in size, shape and slope, quite a few bunkers and some water.

Overall, Southwick offers good variety, plenty of doglegs and plenty of entertainment. A section of the county amateur tournament is held here, and the staff in the pro shop tells us that scores for that event are always highest here.

Amenities include a practice green, range, snack bar, rental clubs and a pro shop.

You can walk anytime, save weekends before 3 PM in the summer. You can book a tee time anytime. Approximate cost, including cart, is $12 weekdays and $20 on weekends.

STONEY CREEK GOLF CLUB

911 Golf House Rd. E.
Burlington   449-5688
Championship Yardage: 7063
Slope: 144   *Par: 72*
Men's Regular Yardage: 6573
Slope: 132   *Par: 72*
Men's Yardage: 6179
Slope: 129   *Par: 72*
Other Yardage: 5546
Slope: 109   *Par: 72*
Ladies' Yardage: 4737
Slope: 123   *Par: 72*

Stoney Creek Golf Club opened in 1992. Tom Jackson designed the course, which is set in rolling terrain and bordered by woods and houses. Fairways are bermudagrass; greens, bentgrass.

The slope of 144 from the back tees is as high a slope rating as you'll find most anywhere in North and South Carolina. Consider that the rating from the back tees for the Ocean Course at Kiawah (South Carolina) is about 149. According to the staff in the pro shop, Stoney Creek from the tips is every bit as difficult as its muscular slope rating. If you're not a scratch golfer and you're not up for more than 7000 yards of Tom Jackson, consider the other more forgiving tees: There are four sets for your golfing enjoyment.

Ask Tom Jackson about some of his favorite self-designs, and Stoney Creek makes the list. Perhaps this is because Jackson was allowed to lay out the course before the housing development was initiated. If you're going to have houses around a golf course, Stoney Creek is an example of the proper way to do it.

You won't find the large numbers of mounds that you might find on other Jackson courses, but you will find plenty of bunkering off the tee and around the green complexes. Many of the bunkers are of the large cloverleaf-shaped variety; others are a little smaller but no less penal. Many of the greens are flanked by steep embankments. Stoney Creek — the creek itself — is not as much a factor as it might seem. The putting surfaces are mostly sloped and large, although some are quite undulating.

Perhaps what separates this Jackson course from others is the excellent variety. Jackson manages to incorporate a number of different looks in most of his courses, but at Stoney Creek he offers increased interest and mental challenge on a playable and not overly penal design. The setting is also remarkably peaceful — given the proximity of houses to many holes.

Just five minutes from I-40/85 between Burlington and Greensboro, Stoney Creek is an accessible course; it's also an excellent value.

Amenities include a practice green, range, chipping green, snack bar, restaurant and pro shop.

The course is walkable for the physically fit, and you may walk anytime during the week and after 3:30 PM on weekends. You can book a tee time seven days in advance. Approximate cost, including cart, is $30 weekdays and $35 on weekends.

TANGLEWOOD PARK
U.S. Hwy. 158 W.
Clemmons   766-5082

Tanglewood Park boasts two formidable Robert Trent Jones courses: the Championship, which opened in 1959 and was redesigned in 1973, and the Reynolds, which opened nine holes in 1965 and was completed in 1970. Both tracks are set in rolling wooded terrain, although the Championship Course is slightly more open, and both offer bermudagrass fairways and bentgrass greens.

But let's talk about Tanglewood Park. Just west of Winston-Salem, in bucolic and ancient woodlands, sits this magnificent park. The land, once part of the Reynolds estate, was donated by the Reynolds family. You may have heard of their company: R.J. Reynolds. In a day at Tanglewood, you could play golf, attend a corporate picnic, get married in the wedding chapel, go horseback riding, attend a steeplechase, play tennis, jog, go camping and then be buried in the graveyard adjacent to the 18th green on the Championship Course. There can't be many park complexes like Tanglewood.

But we're here to talk about golf. There are two wonderful and nationally recognized courses here, both of which have been ranked in *Golf Digest's* list of the Top 100 Public Courses. In 1974, the Championship hosted the PGA Championship — won by Lee Trevino. Each fall, members of the PGA SENIOR TOUR gather here for one of the richest event of the year, the Vantage Championship. The $1.5 million purse typically brings out the best players on the tour, including Palmer, Trevino, Charles, Rodriguez and Floyd.

During the rest of the year, the course brings out people from all over North and South Carolina who feel motivated to attack one of the least vulnerable golf courses anywhere. Estimates vary, but Tanglewood "boasts" somewhere between 120 and 140 bunkers. It just depends on who you ask. You could ask the maintenance supervisor, but he's probably too busy maintaining the sand to notice your query. We'll get to the bunkers later.

The only problem here, in our minds, is the architecture of the clubhouse, which looks more like a large-scale chiropractic clinic than a structure befitting two of the prettiest and finest public golf courses in North and South Carolina. Anyway, who cares what the clubhouse looks like — as long as the burgers and hot dogs are worth their mustard (and they are).

Amenities include a practice green, range, chipping green, locker room, snack bar/grill, rental clubs, a wedding chapel and a pro shop.

The Championship Course is more walkable than the Reynolds; ironically, you can walk the Reynolds Course anytime but may only walk the Championship Course in December, January, July and August. You can book a tee time seven days in advance. Approximate cost, including cart, is $45 weekdays and $48 on weekends for the Championship and $30 for the Reynolds.

If you live outside North Carolina, the cost for the Championship Course is upwards of $63.

Championship Course

Championship Yardage: 7022	
Slope: 140	Par: 72
Men's Yardage: 6638	
Slope: 135	Par: 72
Other Yardage: 6014	
Slope: 130	Par: 72
Ladies' Yardage: 5119	
Slope: 130	Par: 74

This might be the prettiest and most challenging public course in the Southeast. If it's not No. 1, then it's got to be in the top three. The course is long and plays even longer. The fairways are as wide as the rough will allow, meaning it can play both narrow and long at times. The greens are large and undulating to the point where a two-putt is an accomplishment. But it's the excessive bunkering that makes this course so difficult. It's Bunkers R Us. Just about every shot you play from the tee, and certainly every approach shot, will be influenced by the beach. If you're shooting for a green, it's safest to aim for the middle and hope for the best. Adding insult to injury is the inconsistent condition of the bunkers: Some are full of sand; others are concrete-hard at the bottom. No course will test your bunker play and patience like Championship at Tanglewood.

Even if your ball is finding the bunkers more than the greens, you can't help appreciating the wonderful setting and ambiance. With its pristine ponds and lakes, its large and mature trees, its chutes and its tranquility, this outstanding layout feels like an exclusive country club. In fact, there are probably plenty of country clubs that would gladly trade courses with Tanglewood. You'll find magnificent hole after magnificent hole. It's a must-play course in North Carolina even if the weather preceding your visit has made course maintenance difficult. Play here before you pass on to the great sand trap in the sky.

Reynolds Course

Championship Yardage: 6469
Slope: 125   Par: 72
Men's Yardage: 6061
Slope: 120   Par: 72
Ladies' Yardage: 5432
Slope: 120   Par: 72

Don't think of the Reynolds Course as the poor sister of the Championship Course. Robert Trent Jones, bless his heart, blessed Reynolds with far less bunkering. The challenge here comes from the dense woods surrounding many of the holes. From the back tees, all the trees make driving the ball a serious challenge. Even if you avoid the trees, you may end up in the deep rough. The greens on this course are predominantly massive, so note the pin's position and feel free to fire at it. Even if you miss the green, you'll have a good chance at par if you chip well out of three-inch-deep rough. Water comes into play in the most awkward places, such as right in front of the green on a 214-yard par 3. Thanks, Mr. Jones. While some of the greens are slightly sloped, others offer dramatic elevation changes, making putting all the more difficult.

When we visited the course, several greens were in need of serious help, although this may have been caused by the inclement weather preceding our inspection. The course is undergoing a long-term renovation supervised by the head of maintenance. If you can't get on the Championship Course, or if you're in the mood for slightly less bunkering and difficulty, try the Reynolds Course. It would be walkable except for the fact that the distance between the 9th green and the 10th tee is nearly a mile. Again, it's a wonderfully pretty and peaceful course, just like its sister.

New Courses in the Triad

Numerous new courses are about to open in the Triad area — as if there weren't enough good ones already! These courses opened after this edition went to press, so look for more detail in the next edition of *The Insiders' Guide® to Golf in the Carolinas*.

Greensboro National is being built north of Greensboro. This course is scheduled to open in late 1995. Call 643-GOLF for more information.

Oak Valley, near Tanglewood and Bermuda Run, is scheduled to open in December 1995. The course is being designed by Arnold Palmer. For more information, write to the club at 261 Oak Valley, Advance, North Carolina 27006, or call 940-2000.

Jack Nicklaus and PGA Tour player Glen Day (a.k.a. Glen "All" Day, for his slow play) are teaming up to design the **Salem Glen Golf Club** near Winston-Salem and just south of Tanglewood.

Silo Run Golf Club in Boonville opened in fall of 1995; you can contact the course at 367-3133.

Meadowlands, in Wallburg, opened in late summer, 1995; call 769-1011 for more information.

In and Around the Triad...

Fun Things To Do

After you've played the courses, you will find plenty of opportunities for fun in the Triad. For sunny days, which are plentiful, outdoor entertainment abounds. The natural beauty of the Triad lends itself to many green city parks, perfect spots for picnics, and beautiful gardens. The Triad is also home to historical sites and several battlegrounds. If its rain that's keeping you off the course, visit one of the numerous museums or shopping establishments in the area. Greensboro and Winston-Salem have several shopping malls; Burlington is home to a large number of factory outlet stores; and High Point is a renowned furniture mecca.

Reynolda Gardens of Wake Forest University, 100 Reynolda Village, Winston-Salem, 759-5325, was made possible by tobacco magnate R.J. Reynolds who gave this wonderful land to the city; it's now home to some of the most magnificent gardens in the Triad. Reynolda Gardens is a must-visit for anyone interested in flora.

If you've never been on a brewery tour, you'll definitely want to tour the **Stroh Brewery**, 4791 Schlitz Avenue, Winston-Salem, 788-6710. This is one of the largest breweries in the United States. You'll be able to see all that goes into producing a can or bottle of beer; at the end of the tour, you can sit down and enjoy a cold one.

By American standards, **Old Salem**, Old Salem Road, Winston-Salem, 721-7300, offers a slice of history. This Moravian village dates back to the 18th century. More than 80 buildings from the original village have been restored. Re-enactors dressed in period costume act out the daily events of the 18th century in museums and shops along the streets of Old Salem. Don't leave without trying the Moravian sugarcake.

After a hot summer day of golfing, or if you have the kids with you, a trip to **Emerald Point Waterpark**, 3910 Holden Road, Greensboro, 852-9721, may be in order. The 45-acre waterpark features 30 rides and attractions including a wavepool, several waterslides and bodyslides, and kiddie pools. For the adventurous, the Skycoaster offers an airborne thrill: It's a huge swing, attached to an arch by steel cables, that launches you, secure in your body harness, horizontally 115 feet into the air and swings you back and forth under the arch like Superman.

Greensboro Historical Museum, 130 Summit Avenue, Greensboro, 373-2043, is housed in a former church that dates back to the turn of the century. Exhibits trace the many and varied religious and racial groups that built the city of Greensboro into what it is today. Learn about military history, early transportation and decorative arts.

Those interested in American military history may want to visit the American Revolution battleground sites located in Greensboro and Burlington. The **Guilford Courthouse National Military Battleground Park**, 2332 New Garden Road, Greensboro, 288-1776, was the site of a 1781 battle in the American Revolution. The site features a museum, walking trails, 28 monuments, musket demonstrations, and guided tours. The **Alamance Battleground**, 5803 N.C. Highway 62 S., Burlington (Exit 143 off I-85), 227-4785, was the site of a 1771 battle that preceded, but was an early part of the Revolutionary War. Re-enactments of the battle, which was between Regulators (country farmers) and the troops of Royal Gov. William Tryon, are held periodically at the battleground. An audio-visual program and tours of the battlefield, monuments and the historic 1780 Allen House make for an interesting day of learning about the 18th-century battle.

High Point touts itself as "the furniture capital of the world," so if you need furnishings, you might as well check out the bargains. Don't worry about lugging a settee around for the rest of your visit to the Triad; the store will ship it home for you. More than 50 furniture stores, including Rose, the Atrium, Furniture Land South and Young's, are scattered around the city;

call the High Point Convention and Visitors Bureau at 889-5151 for information. The **Furniture Discovery Center**, 101 W. Green Drive, High Point, 887-3876, is a museum dedicated to the art of furniture making.

Places to Eat

LONGHORN STEAKS
RESTAURANT AND SALOON

2925 Battleground Ave.
Greensboro   545-3200
$$$

Longhorn was one of the pioneers in the introduction of Texas-style steakhouses in the Carolinas. You'll find a large yet friendly environment, with a rustic Western-looking decor. There's a bar, and you may have to wait a few minutes here while a table is readied for your appetite. Once you sit down, indulge in a big steak — washed down with a couple of beers. Or try the salmon if you're not a steak person. The atmosphere is relaxed, and it's almost essential to wear jeans. You can wear a cowboy hat if you like, but there's no discount for this type of behavior.

SUNSET CAFE

4608 W. Market St.
Greensboro   855-0349
$$$

The Sunset Cafe offers a solid alternative to the chain-style restaurants that dominate the local scene. The Sunset Cafe specializes in vegetarian, seafood, poultry and lamb dishes served in a warm, cozy atmosphere.

J. BUTLER'S BAR AND GRILLE

3709 Battleground Ave.
Greensboro   282-8080
$$

Located across from Brassfield Cinema and Brassfield Shopping Center, J. Butler's offers a feast of sandwiches, gourmet burgers, salads and entrees to enjoy before or after taking in a movie or tackling a shopping expedition. Couple this with a fully stocked bar and you also have a really fun and relaxed place to unwind after a rough day on the links.

KYOTO FANTASY

1200 S. Holden Rd.
Greensboro   299-1003
$$

There's always something fun, funny and bizarre about going to an authentic Japanese steakhouse. The chef comes to your table, and you bear witness to his wizardry as he slices and dices with knives of surgical sharpness. You'll get the full treatment here at Kyoto Fantasy: Take your shoes off and sit down for your session. Make sure you change your socks before you go. There's also a sushi bar for raw fish fans or the extremely trendy.

VINCENZO'S

3449 Robin Hood Rd.
Winston-Salem   765-3176
$$

Vincenzo's is one of those great institutions where you feel right at home the second you walk in the door. The restaurant has been serving up Italian dishes since 1964. There's veal parmigiana, spaghetti,

The newly opened Oak Valley Golf Club in Advance.

eggplant parmigiana, lasagna, veal marsala, a delightful clam sauce and steamed clams. Plus there's lots of Italian vino to help you wash down all that great pasta.

TWIN CITY DINER
1425A W. First St.
Winston-Salem   724-4203
$$

Twin City Diner is a relaxed and fun neighborhood restaurant where locals meet and mingle. There's a well-stocked bar where you can swap stories or watch a sports event on the discreetly placed televisions. The menu is extensive. The wings, served in multiples of five, are excellent. Sample some traditional pub fare — hamburgers and sandwiches — or delve into some more substantial entrees like Cajun salmon.

SZECHWAN PALACE
3040 Healy Dr.
Winston-Salem   768-7123
$$

Tucked away in a somewhat innocuous strip mall in the Hanes Mall area is one of Winston-Salem's best Chinese restaurants. The decor is somewhat predictable, with a dominant theme of meandering scenes of the Great Wall of China interspersed with red dragons. The menu, however, is less predictable, and you'll find some unique creations that go well beyond your typical sweet and sour fare — even the name implies some hot and spicy entrees. You can also sip a Chinese beer, although the Chinese are not especially renowned as world leaders in the production of quality adult malt beverages.

Places to Stay

COURTYARD BY MARRIOTT
4400 W. Wendover Rd.
Greensboro   294-3800
$$

If you've seen a Courtyard by Marriott before, then you won't be surprised to find this clean, well-kept hotel in a convenient location and run by an efficient staff. Suites have two TVs and a separate second bedroom with a pullout couch. Amenities include an outdoor pool, an indoor whirlpool and an exercise room. A restaurant on the premises serves breakfast daily.

BEST WESTERN WINDSOR SUITES
2006 Veasley St.
Greensboro   294-9100
$$$

Best Westerns are best known for providing a clean and pleasant but basic motel-type environment in good locations. The Windsor Suites is a step-up from the usual — it's feels more like a fine hotel. Rooms are elegantly decorated and there's lots of faux wood paneling. Unlike many hotels, you can actually open the window to the outside world. You'll find plenty of restaurants just around the corner and easy access to I-40.

HOLIDAY INN FOUR SEASONS
3121 High Point Rd.
Greensboro   292-9161
$$$$

With 522 rooms, the Holiday Inn Four Seasons is one of the largest and most impressive hotels in Greensboro. As you drive by on I-40, you can't miss the place — it's about 30 stories tall. This hotel offers meeting and convention facilities in addition to a nightclub with live entertainment, a weight room and other amenities, including an indoor/outdoor pool to keep you active. You'll also find four restaurants on site, including Stinger's Bar & Grill and Joseph's — serving Italian cuisine. Shoppers will enjoy the nearby mall as well.

HAMPTON INN
1990 Hampton Inn Ct.
Winston-Salem   760-1660
$$$

This Hampton Inn exemplifies the trademark quality that has gained this chain a reputation for clean, well-appointed

rooms and friendly service. We recommend the Jacuzzi suites on the third floor as a pleasant and slightly more spacious version of the standard rooms. There's nothing better than a hot bath with swirling jets of water to relax you after a hard day on the links. And once the muscles are loosened up, head for the work-out room to tighten them again. Business travelers will appreciate the meeting facilities as well. The hotel is convenient to I-40.

STOUFFER WINSTON PLAZA
425 N. Cherry St.
Winston-Salem   725-3500
$$$

One of Winston-Salem's biggest hotels, the Stouffer Winston Plaza offers all the amenities you might expect from a top hotel, including an indoor pool, an outdoor sun deck, 24-hour room service, two restaurants, a lounge and a gift shop.

BEST WESTERN REGENCY INN
128 N. Cherry St.
Winston-Salem   723-8861
$$

You've seen plenty of Best Westerns around the country on your travels, and this one is a little different from others in that it's not the typical motel-style that defines most Best Westerns. The Regency Inn is a downtown hotel that offers a great place to stay at a sensible price with color cable TVs in every room and a full range of amenities. Enjoy the outdoor pool when the weather is right, and don't miss the complimentary continental breakfast.

Reservations staff inform us that this Best Western is about to undergo renovations as this book goes to press. Plans include a restaurant and exercise facilities, so call for updates.

Inside
The Charlotte Region
of North Carolina

Charlotte is one of the most talked-about cities in the country — and usually for all the right reasons. Economic success in the Queen City of the South has been strong and steady. Drive past downtown Charlotte (locals call it Uptown) and you'll see visible signs of prosperity in the form of grandiose skyscrapers normally reserved for larger cities like New York, Los Angeles and Chicago. Much of the success has been created by NationsBank, First Union and the other smaller yet significant financial institutions that employ a lot of men in heavily starched white shirts and a lot of women in blue suits. Depending on whose figures you use, Charlotte is the number two financial center in the United States, surpassing cities like Chicago, Los Angeles, San Francisco and Atlanta. So stuff that in your safe deposit box and smoke it!

The big banks have grown in part through the acquisition of other banks, but much of their success is the result of the strong economy in Charlotte and its surrounding counties. Charlotte is also a major distribution and trucking center. Surrounding towns like Gastonia, Kannapolis and Concord are home to some massive and not so massive textile mills. But perhaps the most visible sign of the arrival of the Charlotte area is the construction of the Charlotte Panthers' stadium next to the Charlotte Observer building. Soon the stadium will be home to one of the two new franchises in the ever-burgeoning National Football League. Talk about an economic boost!

All this success has meant that the Charlotte region has seen an influx of new residents from all over the country and all over the world. (Believe it or not, Charlotte even boasts a strong cricket team!) Sadly, the public golfing scene in the Charlotte region has been languishing behind Charlotte's success. As recently as 1990, if you were an avid golfer, you would have to travel a good 45 minutes to an hour to find a course worthy of your weekend golfing investment. But, with apologies to Bob Dylan, the times, they are a-changin' — and golfers region wide have plenty of reasons to sing. In fall 1995, eight public courses were under construction. Since 1990, a number of public courses have opened with rave reviews and have hosted a lot of play (perhaps too much).

Looking into the crystal Titleist, we see the increased competition creating the following conditions for the Charlotte golfer: Greens fees should come down a little. You'll have to drive less for more and better golf options. Outlying courses that used to receive a lot of play from Charlotte will receive less play and may suffer financially. There will be more golf courses than golfers to play them, thus the courses with the best value for money, conditioning and marketing creativity will prosper.

GOLF COURSES IN NORTH CAROLINA'S CHARLOTTE REGION

Name	Type	# Holes	Par	Slope	Yards	Walking	Booking	Cost w/ Cart
Charlotte Golf Links	public	18	71	121	6220	restricted	anytime	$35-44
Eagle Chase Golf Club	semiprivate	18	72	122	6103	anytime	5 days	$28-33
Fort Mill Golf Club	semiprivate	18	72	118	6373	restricted	3 days	$29-32
Gastonia Municipal	public	18	71	110	5671	anytime	7 days	$25-27
Glen Oaks Country Club	semiprivate	18	70	n/r	6026	restricted	7 days	$24-34
Highland Creek Golf Club	semiprivate	18	72	124	6505	no	3 days	$42-48
King's Mountain	semiprivate	18	72	118	6143	anytime	3-4 days	$23-30
Lincoln Country Club	semiprivate	18	72	121	6017	anytime	anytime	$25-31
Mallard Head	semiprivate	18	72	116	6442	restricted	2-3 days	$23-28
Monroe Country Club	semiprivate	18	72	116	6310	restricted	5 days	21-26
Mooresville Golf Course	public	18	72	121	6102	anytime	3 days	$18.50-21.50
Regent Park Golf Club	public	18	72	n/r	6478	no	4-7 days	$37-43
Renaissance Park	public	18	72	121	6880	anytime	7 days	call
River Bend Golf Club	semiprivate	18	72	117	5956	restricted	3 days	$25-32
Rock Barn Club of Golf	semiprivate	18	72	128	6318	anytime	6 days	$36-40
Westport Golf Course	semiprivate	18	72	118	6291	restricted	3 days	$20-26
Woodbridge Golf Links	semiprivate	18	72	121	6156	restricted	5-7 days	$26-35

The Charlotte Area

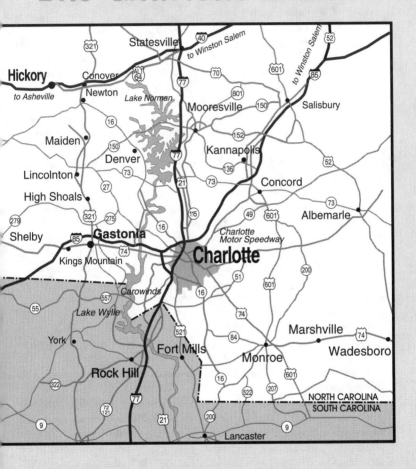

Courses with a reputation for slow play will lose golfers to courses known for fast play. A course that emphasizes walking, tradition and a lack of adjacent housing will also find a niche and be successful.

Charlotte has always had a significant number of outstanding private courses like Myers Park, Charlotte Country Club and Quail Hollow. But now things are looking bright for the daily-fee golfer. Look for complete reviews of new courses-in-progress in the next edition of *The Insiders' Guide® to Golf in the Carolinas.* The next five years should prove interesting for the public golfer in Charlotte.

The Charlotte area is excellent territory for the golf course architect. There's an abundance of wonderful hardwood trees in addition to numerous streams, ponds and other natural hazards. The sticky red clay makes life difficult at times for grasses, but modern turf maintenance and construction methods mean that good clubs can maintain their courses to high standards all year. Golfing weather is best in fall and spring. But there are plenty of good days for golf in the winter. Summer can be exceedingly hot at times, and the greens can be exceedingly slow as a result. But it's still bearable if you avoid the midday sun, the mad dogs and the Englishmen.

For month-to-month local golf information, pick up a copy of *Metrolina Golfer* at any area golf course. You'll find tips about golfers, tournaments, equipment and courses.

Except where noted, all golf courses and businesses appearing in this chapter are in the 704 area code.

Charlotte Region Golf Courses

CHARLOTTE GOLF LINKS

11500 Providence Rd.
Charlotte   846-7990
Championship Yardage: 6700
Slope: 127   Par: 71
Men's Yardage: 6220
Slope: 121   Par: 71
Ladies' Yardage: 5279
Slope: 117   Par: 72

Charlotte Golf Links, designed by Tom Doak, opened in 1992. The course is mostly flat and open. Fairways are bermudagrass; greens are bentgrass.

Doak is a young architect who, after graduating from Cornell University, spent several months touring Scottish links courses and even spent some time as a caddy at venerable St. Andrews. He currently writes for *Golf Magazine* and has authored two books about golf courses. Doak's *Anatomy of a Golf Course,* in particular, is a must-read for anyone interested in golf course architecture and design. Doak is also an expert golf course photographer. He apprenticed himself to notable architect Pete Dye. Doak is quite opinionated about design and is, not surprisingly, at his most positive when discussing his favorite type of course: the links (his passion and specialty).

Charlotte Golf Links is a challenging course and a must-play for the golfing purist. Much of the land here is open. With the wind blowing and a light rain coating the course, you're going to feel like you're in Scotland — or at least that's the idea. The fairways are wide in places, narrow in others, but they boast a number of subtle slopes and undulations just like the genuine article. Each hole has been designed to reward the successful risk-taker more than the conservative. However, with risk comes the potential

for poor results, and there's always a chance that your ball might find the long native grass that borders many holes. Locals have a name for this "stuff" — it's a scatological word that we can't publish in this book.

The green complexes feature a number of small pot bunkers with grass faces and coarse sand. The greens don't pitch or roll much, but you'll find that some of the shortest putts are some of the most difficult. In really hot weather, be prepared to bang the ball toward the hole with a degree of authority.

Charlotte Golf Links, along with Highland Creek, marked the beginning of a new era in public golf in Charlotte, and it's exciting that one of the newest courses is also one of the most traditional and walkable. Todd Smith and his staff run a tight ship here, and the course is well-organized.

The best time to see and play Charlotte Golf Links is late in the day when the shadows bring out all the subtle shaping in the fairways and the grass faces of the bunkers are dark and menacing. It's a special place. And it's very accessible to southeast Charlotte.

Amenities include a practice green, driving range, chipping green, locker room, snack bar, rental clubs, a beverage cart and pro shop.

You can walk this course anytime during the week and on weekend afternoons. You can book a tee time whenever you choose. Approximate cost, including cart, is $35 Monday through Thursday, $39 on Friday and $44 on weekends.

THE DIVIDE GOLF LINKS

2200 Divide Dr.
Matthews   882-8088
Championship Yardage: 6973
Slope: 137   Par: 72
Men's Yardage: 6587
Slope: 127   Par: 72
Other Yardage: 6145
Slope: 121   Par: 72
Ladies' Yardage: 5213
Slope: 121   Par: 72

The Divide opened in the fall of 1995. John Cassell designed the course, which is set on gently undulating terrain and is currently surrounded by woods, although houses will eventually border some holes. Fairways are 419 bermudagrass, and the greens are pennlinks bentgrass.

The Divide is brought to you by the same group who built Charlotte Golf Links, one of Charlotte's premier public courses. Thus it comes as no surprise that the Divide, despite its youth, is already shaping up as a fine public golf facility. The Divide marks John Cassell's entry into the noble profession of golf course architecture. Judging by The Divide, there should be plenty of other public golf course owners who will want to use his services. Cassell designed the track with the help of Todd Smith and the staff and ownership of the course and thus there's an emphasis on playability. If you're an average public golfer, then you'll find that the course has been built with you in mind. However, if you're a stronger player, this course should give you a stern test from the back tees (note the 137 slope from the tips).

The fairways are mostly wide and there's the occasional bunker lurking although these fairway bunkers tend to be on the small side. On many holes, your wayward drive may find the woods. The green complexes feature mildly undulating greens that tend to be on the large side, pot bunkers, flat bunkers and embankments. Thus, you'll need to bring a strong short game to get up and down successfully. A brook wanders through some of the layout.

Perhaps what we liked most about the Divide is that it's straightforward while still being interesting: It lacks the excesses that make too many public courses too difficult and time consuming. The course has clearly been designed to keep your round less than 4½ hours, and most importantly, it's clearly been designed to put the fun back into public golf. We think that The Divide will ultimately become one of Charlotte's most popular public golf courses. You'll also find that it's one of the prettiest.

Amenities include a first-class driving range, putting green, chipping green, bar, restaurant, snack bar, pro shop and beverage cart.

With 8 miles of cart path, you'll need to take a cart. You can book a tee time three days in advance. Approximate cost, including cart, is $33 weekdays and $39 weekends.

EAGLE CHASE GOLF CLUB

3215 Brantley Rd.
Marshville   385-9000
Championship Yardage: 6723
Slope: 128   Par: 72
Men's Yardage: 6103
Slope: 122   Par: 72
Ladies' Yardage: 5139
Slope: 121   Par: 72

Eagle Chase Golf Course opened in 1994. Tom Jackson designed this rolling course. Bermudagrass covers the fairways, and bentgrass covers the greens.

To most Charlotteans, Marshville is well known as a town you pass through on the way to the beach. Doze off for a few minutes and you've missed it. It's also the home of Randy Travis and numerous poultry processing plants: These two facts

Charlotte's Renaissance course is one of the more popular public courses in the region. Extensive changes are planned in 1996.

are not necessarily related, though. Marshville is also home to this outstanding new course designed by Tom Jackson. For a new course, it's not overly mounded (as is typical of most Jackson courses). It is, however, visually appealing, challenging and playable. It's also a great thinking course. Each hole requires a plan of attack. But if the plan goes awry, you'll still be in the hole with a chance for redemption. On the front nine you'll think, at least for a few holes, that you're in the North Carolina mountains — such is the drama created by the elevation changes. During our visit, the course had apparently grown in successfully and most of the greens were in good shape. Give the course a couple of years to establish itself and it could be one of the best maintained courses in the Charlotte area.

Anyway, back to the course. There's usually a decent amount of room off the tee. There's also quite a bit of water lurking in potentially awkward places. The greens are large and sloped, and you'll find a number of bunkers surrounding many of the greens. The bunkers are well-placed and will alter your strategy. Overall, Eagle Chase is a welcome and exciting addition to the Charlotte golfing scene, and you should definitely play it if you're in Charlotte or if you're in Marshville visiting a poultry plant or seeking out Randy Travis.

Amenities include a practice green, driving range, locker room, bar, rental clubs and a pro shop.

We do not recommend walking this course, but you're allowed to anytime. You can book a tee time five days in advance. Approximate cost, including cart, is $28 weekdays and $33 on weekends.

Ed. note: The following course is in South Carolina. While you might expect to find it in our Midlands chapter, we've included it in the Charlotte Region because of its proximity to the Queen's City and the volume of Charlotte-area golfers that play here.

FORT MILL GOLF CLUB

101 Country Club Dr.
Fort Mill, S.C.   (803) 547-2044
Championship Yardage: 6865
Slope: 133   Par: 72
Men's Yardage: 6373
Slope: 118   Par: 72
Ladies' Yardage: 5448
Slope: 123   Par: 72

The front nine at Fort Mill Golf Club opened in the 1930s. The back nine opened in the 1970s. Donald Ross designed the front nine, and George Cobb, the back. The front nine is open, and the back is set in rolling terrain. In the fairways, you'll find bermudagrass; on the greens, you'll find bentgrass.

Fort Mill has long been a well-known favorite of Charlotte golfers. The club is part of a triumvirate of Springs Industries-owned courses, all of which are popular and well-run; the others are in Chester and Lancaster, and each is well worth a visit. You'll find write-ups in our Midlands chapter.

It's difficult to find a golf course that has enlisted two better architects than Ross and Cobb. The result is a fine and mature course that's more challenging than it looks. This is a country-club caliber design.

The front nine, designed by Ross, offers plenty of room off the tee. If you're wayward with your driver, the most significant hazards are posed by the large trees. As you might expect with a Ross course, the trouble begins on and around the greens, where there are plenty of small bunkers and difficult putts. If you're playing for money, never give your opponent a gimme on this nine — make 'em drop it in the hole. Watch as a two-foot putt is rammed three feet past or ends up two inches short. (Hit it, Alice.) It's part of what makes Ross's designs so timeless (and irritating).

The back nine is a genuine Cobb championship-caliber test. Many of the holes are truly long and seem to play even longer. The greens are large and not quite as undulating as the Ross greens, but no less difficult. The bunkers are larger and the fairways are wider on this nine. Water is sparse, but you'll discover that wayward shots will find the hazard if you're not sensible. Have fun here and buy textiles made by Springs Industries out of gratitude for their excellent contributions to public golf in South Carolina.

Amenities include a practice green, snack bar and pro shop.

You can walk anytime on weekdays and after 2 PM on weekends. You can book a tee time three days in advance. Approximate cost, including cart, is $29 weekdays and $32 on weekends.

GASTONIA MUNICIPAL GOLF COURSE

Niblick Dr.
Gastonia   866-6945
Championship Yardage: 6474
Slope: 115   Par: 71
Men's Yardage: 5671
Slope: 110   Par: 71
Ladies' Yardage: 4344
Slope: 110   Par: 71

Gastonia Municipal Golf Course opened in the 1930s. The course is set on open and rolling terrain. Fairways and greens are covered with bermudagrass.

Gastonia Muni offers a fun and playable track that's a great value for Gastonia residents. If you live in this lovely town just west of Charlotte, you can walk as many holes as you're able on a weekday for just $8. You can't beat that deal anywhere.

Muni courses have a charm and quality that's somewhat hard to define or describe. Many munis were built on land that was once open countryside. Thus the golf course often becomes an oasis of green in the middle of urban sprawl. This is the case here. A couple of power lines traverse the

course in a few places, but for the most part you still feel like you're out in the country.

The front nine is open, and the fairways are a little tight in places. The greens are small and sloped, and you can run the ball up to the pin on quite a few holes. You'll find an average of one bunker per green on both the back and front nines. A stream wanders through the track in a couple of places.

The back nine offers a bit more room, and many of the holes are more strategic — especially around the green complexes. Still, the setting is pleasant and relaxed, and the course provides a fun and potentially rewarding challenge for all levels of golfer. The more than 40,000 rounds of golf per annum prove that the course has something going for it besides its sensible pricing. There's a bit of a debate as to who designed

the course. We might venture to guess that our old friend Russell Breeden had a hand in part of the redesign.

Amenities include a practice green, chipping green, locker room, restaurant, beverage cart and pro shop.

The course is walkable anytime. You can book a tee time seven days in advance. Approximate cost, including cart, is $25 weekdays and $27 on weekends. As we mentioned before, the rates are less if you're a resident of Gastonia.

GLEN OAKS COUNTRY CLUB
245 Golf Course Rd.
Maiden   428-2451
Championship Yardage: 6430
Slope: 116   *Par: 70*
Men's Yardage: 6026
Slope: No rating   *Par: 70*
Ladies' Yardage: 4953
Slope: No rating   *Par: 70*

The golf course at Glen Oaks Country Club opened in 1967. This Bill McRee design is set on flat terrain with many open holes. Bermudagrass covers the fairways, and bentgrass covers the greens.

Glen Oaks presents a remarkably interesting and challenging course in a country setting. The strength of the course is its variety, although the routing of the holes is a little bizarre. The course is intelligently bunkered. The front nine tends to be a little more wooded than the back and, thus, is a little tighter off the tee. The greens are mostly flat and midsize, and many are flush with the fairway, making run-up shots possible and advisable if the fairways are hard. There's quite a bit of water on the back nine, and you'll find your golfing skills tested by a number of approach shots requiring accurate club selection and shot execution. There's even an island green — perhaps a tip of the hat to Pete Dye. You might arrive at the 18th with your best score ever only to find the closing hole one of the most difficult on the course. Clearly, Glen Oaks is popular with the local population — for good reason.

Amenities include a practice green, driving range, locker room, bar, snack bar, restaurant, rental clubs and a pro shop.

The course is walkable for the fit and dedicated, and you can walk on weekdays. You can book a tee time seven days in advance. Approximate cost, including cart, is $24 weekdays and $34 on weekends.

HIGHLAND CREEK GOLF CLUB

7001 Highland Creek Blvd.
Charlotte   *875-9000*
Championship Yardage: 7008
Slope: 133   *Par: 72*
Men's Yardage: 6505
Slope: 124   *Par: 72*
Other Yardage: 5947
Slope: 122   *Par: 72*
Ladies' Yardage: 5080
Slope: 128   *Par: 72*

Highland Creek Golf Club opened in 1993. Lloyd Clifton and Ken Ezell designed the course, which is set in rolling wooded terrain bordered with houses. In the fairways, you'll find bermudagrass; on the greens, you'll find bentgrass.

When it opened Highland Creek was almost universally acclaimed as the greatest thing for public golf in the Charlotte area since the invention of public golf. Along with Charlotte Golf Links, it certainly marked the end of a drought for Charlotte's public golfer. Here, at last, was a modern and well-designed course, well-kept and within sensible driving distance of Charlotte. Since then, the course has maintained its popularity and is one of the most played tracks in the area.

The Clifton-Ezell team hasn't completed a lot of work in North and South Carolina — Highland Creek is their only course in the Carolinas, but the firm has been active for years in Florida. At Highland Creek they produced one of the most challenging and demanding public golf courses in the western section of the Carolinas. In places, it's also one of the prettiest and most varied.

Photo: Regent Park Golf Club

The large green at the difficult par 4 8th hole at Regent Park Golf Club just south of Charlotte. The course opened in 1995.

On quite a few holes, the course is tight off the tee. The locals will tell you that it's essential to be in just the right place in the fairway; thus, you need to be accurate with whatever you like to use off the tee. Should you spray your shots around somewhat, you'll find your ball in Highland Creek, someone's back yard or the woods. If it seems like Highland Creek comes into play on just about every hole, it's not an illusion. The creek poses quite a hazard, and it's no fun having to fish for your ball.

Once you've navigated the hazards off the tee, you must play an accurate approach shot. The greens are predominantly large — as are the bunkers and embankments that flank many of the green complexes. You'll certainly leave here with memories of many holes — and with an opinion about the layout. We think you'll want to come back and challenge this exciting course again and again.

You'll find a fun and friendly staff here at Highland Creek. Coauthor Scott Martin took golf lessons here from Mark McLaughlan, the head pro and a man of great patience whom we highly recommend as an instructor. A new clubhouse is scheduled for completion in 1996 and will feature all sorts of amenities, including many geared towards accommodating tournaments and corporate outings.

Current amenities include a practice green, driving range, chipping green, locker room, bar, restaurant, rental clubs, a beverage cart and pro shop.

Walking is not allowed. You can book a tee time three days in advance. Approximate cost, including cart, is $42 weekdays and $48 on weekends.

KING'S MOUNTAIN COUNTRY CLUB
Country Club Dr.
Kings Mountain   739-5871
Championship Yardage: 6483
Slope: 121   Par: 72
Men's Yardage: 6143
Slope: 118   Par: 72
Ladies' Yardage: 5019
Slope: 119   Par: 72

King's Mountain Golf Course opened its first nine holes in the 1940s; the second nine opened in the 1970s. The course is set on rolling wooded terrain. In the fairwaysy, you'll find bermudagrass; on the greens, you'll find bentgrass.

King's Mountain offers a couple of varied and thoroughly interesting nines. The front is the original nine and is built much like many courses of its day. The greens are somewhat small and sloped, and there's plenty of room for run-up shots from just about anywhere. Your chipping game will be seriously tested. There are a few bunkers — enough to wreck a potentially good score. Many of the greens are flanked by steep embankments. What you'll probably notice most about the front nine are the towering pine trees that delineate the fairways. They create quite a frame for many of the holes.

On the back nine, there's a little more room off the tee. Many of the holes are bordered by thick woods that create quite a hazard. The greens are still relatively flat and somewhat small. It's still possible to run the ball up to many of the holes due to the lack of bunkers fronting the greens. There are also some fun tee placements on a few holes. Overall, it's a relaxed yet challenging course, exhibiting a maturity rarely seen on many modern courses.

Amenities include a practice green and snack bar.

The course is walkable anytime. You can book a tee time whenever you choose for the weekdays and on Wednesday for the weekend. Approximate cost, including cart, is $23 weekdays and $30 on weekends.

LINCOLN COUNTRY CLUB

2108 Country Club Rd.
Lincolnton   735-1382
Championship Yardage: 6467
Slope: 125   Par: 72
Men's Yardage: 6017
Slope: 121   Par: 72
Ladies' Yardage: 5011
Slope: 118   Par: 72

The current back nine at Lincoln Country Club opened in 1949, and the front nine opened in 1993. Peter Tufts is credited with Lincoln's recent design. The course is set on rolling wooded terrain. Lincoln has bermudagrass fairways and bentgrass greens.

There are two distinct nines here. The front is newer, though not particularly modern or penal in design; it's not a tricked-up course. You'll find some mounds, but they're not of the massive variety. The terrain is somewhat flat, and many holes are bordered by trees. Thankfully, there's decent width off the tee. You'll find a number of tough but short par 4s, each with an interesting and unique feature. The greens are midsize and sloped.

The back nine is older and more traditional in design. If the fairways become hard, you'll be able to play a variety of run-up shots to the greens, which are flush with the fairways. You'll also find a fair amount of sensible bunkering. All in all, it's a fun and playable track that's justifiably popular with the local population.

Amenities include a practice green, driving range, chipping green, locker room, snack bar and pro shop.

Rock Hill: Charlotte's Bedroom Community

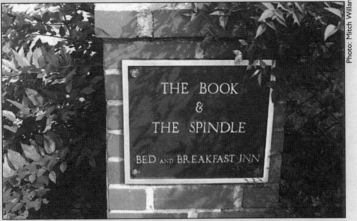

Photo: Mitch Willard

The Book & The Spindle offers grace and charm in Rock Hill, South Carolina.

While you're in the Charlotte area for golf, you may want to forget about staying in the usual big hotels downtown and instead stay in the bedroom community of Charlotte: Rock Hill, South Carolina. It's not like you will be blazing any trails. Both of Charlotte's professional teams, the football Carolina Panthers and the basketball Charlotte Hornets, have training facilities in the area.

Two bed and breakfast inns in Rock Hill are second-to-none when it comes to comfort, accessibility and convenience. **The Book and The Spindle** at 626 Oakland Avenue is a lovely, luxurious 1930s home restored by Pam and Warren Bowen. Each of the two suites has its own breakfast nook. Two additional rooms are smaller but still comfortable. All have private baths. Our favorite spot in the whole house is the piazza in the Charleston suite. The Bowens call it a porch dummy. It's a bright little sunroom where you can read, work or relax in a wicker chair while communing with the redbirds perched on a branch outside the window. The Camden suite features its own private canopied rooftop patio. With the proper weather, this could be another favorite spot. Each room has a different theme at this charming English-style inn with modern amenities.

Before you go to bed, leave a message with Pam as to what time you want your breakfast served — as long as it's before 10 AM. Promptly at the time you ordered, your breakfast is brought upstairs on a tray. This may be a welcome change from inns where breakfast is served at the dining room table, especially if you like to linger in the morning with your significant other. The suites also have full kitchens if you'd prefer to stay in and prepare a meal.

You will feel right at home at the Park Avenue Inn in Rock Hill, South Carolina.

Book and Spindle has myriad antiques and fine reproductions about the house. Rooms overlook the beautiful campus of Winthrop University.

Just a few blocks away at 347 Park Avenue is **Park Avenue Inn**. Sharon and Donny Neely will make you feel right at home with their Southern hospitality; they open their hearts and home to the fullest. Their tons of knickknacks include antique toys and glass. Also, collections of family memorabilia hang on the walls, creating a homey atmosphere. Breakfast is served between 7 and 9 AM at the diningroom table. We think you'll appreciate both the breakfast and the table: It's a 10-foot-long primitive piece of furniture made from four large boards. The house includes three guest rooms and three baths, and the rooms are quite comfortable.

Rates at both of these inns are no more than you would pay for one of the nationally recognized hotels in the city. For reservations, call the Book and Spindle at 328-1913 or the Park Avenue Inn at 325-1764.

Walk this course anytime and book a tee time whenever you choose during the week and two days before the weekend. Approximate cost, including cart, is $25 weekdays and $31 on weekends.

MALLARD HEAD COUNTRY CLUB

Brawley School Rd.
Mooresville   664-7031
Championship Yardage: 6904
Slope: 121   Par: 72
Men's Yardage: 6442

Slope: 116   Par: 72
Other Yardage: 6233
Slope: 113   Par: 72
Ladies' Yardage: 5469
Slope: 121   Par: 72

The Golf Course at Mallard Head Country Club opened in 1979. J. Porter Gibson designed this course, which is set on rolling terrain with houses bordering some of the holes. Fairways are bermudagrass, and greens are bentgrass.

Mallard Head is a popular and reasonably priced golf course that has long attracted golfers from Charlotte and the eastern shores of Lake Norman. There are some interesting and diverse golf holes with plenty of challenge, particularly from the back tees. The greens are large- to medium-size and flanked by bunkers and the occasional embankment. The front nine is more wooded than the back. Water comes into play on a few holes, and its influence varies in intensity. On most holes you'll find enough room off the tee to allow you to pull out the big stick and take a big whack. Overall, Mallard Head is a fun course that's popular with the locals and well worth a visit if you're in the area.

Amenities include a practice green, locker room, snack bar, rental clubs and a pro shop.

The course is walkable for the physically fit, and you can walk anytime during the week. You can book a tee time whenever you choose for weekdays and on Thursday for the weekend. Approximate cost, including cart, is $23 weekdays and $28 on weekends.

MONROE COUNTRY CLUB

U.S. Hwy. 601 S.
Monroe   282-4661
Championship Yardage: 6759
Slope: 118   Par: 72
Men's Yardage: 6310
Slope: 116   Par: 72
Ladies' Yardage: 4964
Slope: 117   Par: 73

The golf course at Monroe Country Club opened in 1936 with nine holes, and a second nine was added in 1984. Tom Jackson designed the front nine, and Donald Ross, the back. The course is set on rolling wooded terrain. You'll find bermudagrass on the greens and fairways.

There can't be many better Carolina-based architectural combinations than Donald Ross and Tom Jackson. Both have worked extensively in the area, and their efforts here at Monroe Country Club make the course well worth a visit. It's also an excellent value.

The Jackson nine is tight and challenging. Those who have seen many of Jackson's designs will marvel at how little work took place — apparently, at least. There are very few mounds. The greens are large and somewhat flat. The bunkers aren't quite as demonic as those on other Jackson layouts. Anyway, the length from the back and the tight fairways will give you all the challenge you want — and then some. Particularly remarkable is the maturity of this front nine: It looks like it's been there as long as the original nine.

We're constantly awestruck by the quality and timelessness of a Donald Ross track; this back nine is no exception. The simple yet sensible layout might lead you to believe that you'll run away with a low score. But the intelligent placement of bunkers and the small crowned greens make the course more difficult to play than it looks. There's no such thing as a gimme on a Ross course, and with the added element of those grainy bermudagrass greens, you'll be praying that your two- and three-footers for bogey somehow find the bottom of the cup. The setting is pretty, and many of the holes have an Ellis Maples-like sweeping quality. This nine is wider off the tee. If you're a fan of good golf course architecture, take some time to visit Monroe.

Amenities include a practice green, driving range (opening in spring 1996), snack bar, restaurant and pro shop.

You can walk anytime during the week and after 2 PM on weekends. You can book a tee time five days in advance. Approximate cost, including cart, is $21 weekdays and $26 on weekends.

Arnold Palmer sizes up a putt.

MOORESVILLE GOLF CLUB

W. Wilson Ave.
Mooresville   663-2539
Championship Yardage: 6528
Slope: 124   Par: 72
Men's Yardage: 6102
Slope: 121   Par: 72
Ladies' Yardage: 4976
Slope: 115   Par: 72

The front nine at Mooresville Golf Club, designed by Donald Ross, opened in the 1940s. The back nine, designed by Porter Gibson, opened in 1978. The front nine is open and the back is set on rolling terrain. In the fairways, you'll find bermudagrass; on the greens, bentgrass.

There aren't many low-cost public-access Donald Ross courses in the Carolinas, but Mooresville Golf Club is one of them. As with many Ross courses, the layout is excellent. There's plenty of room off the tee. The difficulties include some awkward bunkers and mounding around small greens with numerous minute and irritating undulations. Donald Ross perfected the art of the heart-attack-inducing two-foot putt, and you'll see many examples of that here. Each hole has a character and challenge all its own. All the subtle shaping and innuendoes become magnificently apparent late in the day.

The back nine is no less interesting. It's tight in places and some of the holes require a decent thump off the tee if you're going to score well. The greens are larger, as are the bunkers and the embankments that flank some of the greens. Mooresville is a fun and challenging course, a great value and one of our favorites. Some of the older greens get a bit beaten up during the summer, but you won't find better fairways anywhere — especially for the investment.

Amenities include a practice green, driving range, snack bar and pro shop.

Walk anytime you wish. You can book a tee time three days in advance. Approximate cost, including cart, is $18.50 weekdays and $21.50 on weekends.

Ed. note: The following is a South Carolina course; however, its proximity to Charlotte and the fact that it is frequented by Charlotte golfers makes it a natural addition to this Charlotte Region chapter.

REGENT PARK GOLF CLUB

3000 Heritage Pkwy.
Fort Mill, S.C.   (803) 547-1300
Championship Yardage: 6861
Slope: No rating   Par: 72
Men's Yardage: 6478
Slope: No rating   Par: 72
Other Yardage: 6083
Slope: No rating   Par: 72
Ladies' Yardage: 5258
Slope: No rating   Par: 72

Ron Garl designed Regent Park Golf Club, which opened in 1995. The course is set on rolling wooded terrain. In the fairways, you'll find bermudagrass; on the greens, bentgrass.

Regent Park has risen from the ashes of what used to be Jim and Tammy Bakker's PTL empire just south of Charlotte in Fort Mill. Close to the clubhouse, you'll find all sorts of evangelical theme park items that are well worth a quick look — if you're fascinated by that sort of thing.

If your group is one of the first on the course, it's all the more important to practice fast play.

Insiders' Tips

The new owners of Regent Park, a group of Malaysian money-magnates, have created a stunning golf course as the centerpiece of what will eventually be a large housing development. They have also built a top-quality, state-of-the-art practice facility with lights, action and a place to practice the uphill and sidehill shots you'll need on this course.

Playing at Regent Park, you can't help being staggered by and impressed with the money that must have been poured into its construction and design. It's a golfing extravaganza the likes of which you won't find on any public course in the immediate area. The result is a number of beautiful golf holes flanked by serious hazards and difficulties. You'll find large bunkers, mounds, water, swamp, tricky lies in the fairway and the type of problems normally reserved for professional and low-handicap golfers. It's as stern a test of golfing skill and patience as you'll find on any top-quality public or private course. Many of the greens are sensible and sloped, while others make you feel like you've landed on a Putt-Putt course with a few too many under your belt. You'll see what we mean when you visit this course — something you definitely should do.

There's a serious emphasis at Regent Park to make this a top-quality public facility. Tee times are spread out at 15 minute intervals, and your tee time is secured by a Visa card (preferably your own). So show up for your tee time whatever the weather. As you leave the course, your clubs are cleaned and carried to your car . . . talk about service!

You won't find a larger testament to modern golf anywhere in the Charlotte region than at Regent Park. You must use a cart at Regent Park, and it must stay on the cart path. At times, you'll walk halfway across the golf course to your ball — only

to discover that you've brought the wrong club. Such is the state of golf in the 1990s.

Amenities include a practice green, driving range, chipping green, snack bar, rental clubs, a beverage cart and pro shop.

You can book a tee time four to seven days in advance for an $8 service charge; otherwise it's three days in advance. Approximate cost, including cart, is $37 weekdays and $43 on weekends.

RENAISSANCE PARK GOLF COURSE

1525 Tyvola Rd. W.

Charlotte	357-3373
Championship Yardage: 7525	
Slope: 126	Par: 72
Men's Yardage: 6880	
Slope: 121	Par: 72
Other Yardage: 6270	
Slope: 115	Par: 72
Ladies' Yardage: 4606	
Slope: No rating	Par: 72

Renaissance Park Golf Course opened in 1987. Michael Hurdzan, a well-respected architect and agronomy expert, designed the course on a mix of open and wooded terrain on what used to be a landfill. In the fairways, you'll find bermudagrass; on the greens, you'll find bentgrass.

A host of Charlotte golfers tee it up at Renaissance, and in the past many complained about the funereal pace of play as well as the seven or eight holes that are virtually impossible for the average golfer. Thankfully, someone was listening, and the course is planning a number of major changes; it will close for up to nine months for this purpose.

Almost $1 million is being spent to renovate the track. The main focus of attention at Renaissance will be on the 1st, 8th, 15th, 16th, 17th and 18th holes — those deemed most in need of help. The therapy will make the course more playable and ostensibly will speed up play. Twenty-two thousand cubic yards of dirt

Photo: Dick Van Halsema

Former PGA SENIOR TOUR player Gordon Jones practices for the annual
Paine-Webber Seniors at the TPC at Piper Glen.

will be imported for the project, and if all goes according to plan, Renaissance's re-design should be complete by late summer 1996.

One reason for Renaissance's popularity is its proximity to Charlotte-Douglas International Airport and the Charlotte Coliseum, each just a five-minute drive away, as well as Uptown Charlotte (10 minutes).

RIVER BEND GOLF CLUB

Longwood Dr.
Shelby 482-4286
Championship Yardage: 6555
Slope: 130 Par: 72
Men's Yardage: 5956
Slope: 117 Par: 72
Ladies' Yardage: 4920
Slope: 102 Par: 72

River Bend opened in 1965. Russell Breeden designed the course, which is open and set on rolling terrain. In the fairways, you'll find bermudagrass; on the greens, bentgrass.

River Bend has a local reputation as a playable track that's usually in good condition. It's exactly what you'd expect from a Russell Breeden course. You won't find a ton of trouble off the tee, and your approach shot will be hit to a medium-size green flanked by a series of bunkers that are not too penal. The owner of the course talks wistfully about Russell Breeden cruising around, building the course with the help of an earth mover. He also talks proudly about the conditioning. The course is definitely worth a visit.

Amenities include a practice green, driving range, chipping green, snack bar and pro shop.

The course is walkable on weekdays. You can book a tee time three days in advance. Approximate cost, including cart, is $25 weekdays and $32 on weekends.

ROCK BARN CLUB OF GOLF

Rock Barn Rd.
Conover 459-9279
Championship Yardage: 6778
Slope: 132 Par: 72
Men's Yardage: 6318
Slope: 128 Par: 72
Other Yardage: 5921
Slope: 122 Par: 72
Ladies' Yardage: 4812
Slope: 117 Par: 72

Rock Barn Club of Golf opened in 1968. Russell Breeden designed the course. The club recently added an additional nine holes, designed by Tom Jackson. The course, which is convenient to I-40, is set on rolling terrain, with woods bordering many of the holes. In the fairways, you'll find bermudagrass; on the greens, bentgrass.

In the northern reaches of the Charlotte region, Rock Barn Club of Golf has long had an excellent reputation for its sound design and great conditioning. We found this to be true. Rock Barn Club of Golf is, perhaps, one of Breeden's finest efforts — a course with outstanding variety and playability and laid out in a peaceful setting. Should anyone accuse Breeden of being a cookie cutter architect, bring them here: There are some wonderful and imaginative holes on this excellent layout.

Insiders' Tips

A driver with more loft (at least 11 degrees) is better for the average golfer.

You'll find decent room off the tee, though it helps to keep to the right part of the fairway. The greens are large and sloped. Three putts are an annoying possibility. There's just enough slope and undulation to make even the shortest putt an adventure. As with many Breeden courses, the large bunkers vary in intensity, depending upon pin placement. You should definitely take time to play here.

Jackson's nine is new — and modern in design. The architect unleashed some of his most venomous features, and you'll find plenty of major elevation changes, large mounds, nasty bunkers and severely undulating greens. It's certainly a stunning and entertaining track — a strong contrast to Breeden's more mature and less penal 18. The Jackson nine would benefit from a touch of maturity, but after your round on the main course, take a few beers to the new nine and you'll have had all the golf you could possibly want, and more.

Amenities include a practice green, driving range, locker room, snack bar, rental clubs and a pro shop.

The original course is walkable for the fit, and you can walk anytime, but we don't recommend you walk the Jackson nine. You can book a tee time six days in advance. Approximate cost, including cart, is $36 weekdays and $40 on weekends.

WESTPORT GOLF COURSE

7494 Golf Course Dr.
Denver   *483-5604*
Championship Yardage: 6805
Slope: 123   *Par: 72*
Men's Yardage: 6291
Slope: 118   *Par: 72*
Ladies' Yardage: 5597
Slope: 118   *Par: 72*

Photo: The Charlotte Observer

LPGA Golfer Terrie Foote.

Westport Golf Course opened in 1968. Charlotte resident J. Porter Gibson designed the course, which is set on rolling wooded terrain. Bermudagrass blankets the fairways, and bentgrass covers the greens.

Westport has long been popular with the droves of Charlotte golfers, us included, who would gladly make the trek to the western shores of Lake Norman in search of a fun round at a sensible price on a well-designed course.

Even though Lake Norman is close by, it does not come into play, and water is a

Woodbridge Golf Links has long been one of the better courses in the Charlotte region. The 600-yard par 5 13th is a difficult but picturesque hole.

factor on only a few holes. What makes Westport a popular course is its pretty setting combined with the variety and challenge. There's decent room off the tee on most holes, and the greens are medium-size, predominantly sloped and not excessively bunkered. Gibson placed some light mounding around the green complexes as well. For many years, the course was famous (or infamous) for its 4th hole, a 424-yard par 4 where you had to lay up with a mid-iron off the tee; you then had to hit a long-iron or fairway wood off a tight downhill lie over a lake and uphill to a large green, where three-putting was a distinct probability. The most popular score on the hole was "X." The State of North Carolina recently forced the course to dredge part of the lake (why, we're not sure), and the result was that the hole evened out, making it slightly less difficult.

With all the new courses under construction closer to Charlotte, it will be interesting to see how Westport fares. If courses like Westport are going to prosper, it will be important to maintain the track to consistently high standards year round. Still, Westport is well worth a visit.

Amenities include a practice green, driving range, locker room, snack bar, rental clubs and a pro shop.

You can walk the course anytime during the week and after 2 PM on weekends. You can book a tee time whenever you choose for the weekdays and on Wednesday for the upcoming weekend. Approximate cost, including cart, is $20 weekdays and $26 on weekends.

WOODBRIDGE GOLF LINKS

1007 New Camp Creek Church Rd.

Kings Mountain	482-0353
In Charlotte	338-9024
Championship Yardage: 6743	
Slope: 131	*Par: 72*
Men's Yardage: 6156	
Slope: 121	*Par: 72*
Ladies' Yardage: 5054	
Slope: 127	*Par: 73*

Woodbridge Golf Links opened in 1971. Porter Gibson and Bob Toski designed the course, which is set on rolling, partially wooded terrain. The fairways are blanketed with bermudagrass; on the greens, you'll find bentgrass.

J. Porter Gibson is a well-known and respected Charlotte-based golf course architect. He has worked with the likes of Sam Snead and, for a while, with Bob Toski, the renowned instructor who still plays in the Paine Webber Seniors Tournament at Piper Glen. Gibson was a leader in the development of wastewater irrigation systems for golf courses. Bet you didn't know that!

Woodbridge is owned by the same people who own the Beck Mercedes Dealership in Charlotte. The solid ownership has meant that the course has developed a reputation for good maintenance. This reputation has in turn meant that the course has attracted numerous golfers from the Charlotte and Gastonia areas. It's always been a popular and challenging course with a sound design. Woodbridge has been host to a women's collegiate golf tournament.

The front nine is set in open terrain and features a number of holes where water comes into play. The course is at its prettiest on the back nine where several holes dip into woodland next to a rivulet. A wooden bridge crosses the rivulet after the 600 yard par 5 No. 13 (hence the course's name). The greens are large enough that club selection becomes a significant issue on many holes. There's plenty of room off the tee, so you'll be fine taking the big stick out and giving the ball a good thump. Water comes into play in a number of instances and could really irritate you and lead to some big numbers.

Woodbridge is a fun and playable course that stands a good chance of remaining popular in the face of all the competition from the new courses coming on line in the Charlotte area.

Amenities include a practice green, driving range, locker room, snack bar, rental clubs, a beverage cart and pro shop.

The course is walkable for the fit, and you can walk anytime during the week. You can book a tee time seven days in advance for the week and on Monday for the weekend. Approximate cost, including cart, is $26 weekdays and $35 on weekends.

New Courses in the Charlotte Region

Here we go! The new-course scene in Charlotte is about to explode. No fewer than eight courses are coming on line in the next two years, and all of them promise to be upscale public courses with excellent facilities. Here's a brief look at what's on the horizon. (Look for detailed reviews in subsequent editions of *The Insiders' Guide® to Golf in the Carolinas*.)

The Tradition is slated to open in late 1996 and will be located on city-owned land near UNC-Charlotte. John Cassell is designing this course as well. As the name implies, the design will be more traditional in nature, and you'll be able to walk here. There will be no housing on the course.

Charlotte real estate magnate B.V. Belk (no relation to the retailers) is building a new course east of Charlotte to be named either Old Creek or Sycamore Creek. Tom Jackson is the architect.

The Harris Group, a Charlotte-based real estate firm, is developing **Birkdale**, a golf course community north of Charlotte in Huntersville. Arnold Palmer is involved in the project as design consultant. Ed Seay, an associate of Palmer's, is also involved in the project. This is the same team that designed the TPC at Piper Glen.

Charlotte National is slated for completion in June 1996 and is being designed by Russell Breeden. As this book entered production, Breeden was out at the Charlotte National site with his bulldozer, shaping the course. It should be very interesting to see what type of product the venerable octogenarian delivers to the Charlotte golfing public.

Charlotte is well known as a hub of NASCAR activity. Charlotte Motor Speedway is the engine that drives much of this activity, and the Speedway is slated to build and develop a golf course, although final details were not available as this book went to press.

The same can be said of **Waterford** and **Crystal Lakes**, two courses that are also scheduled for completion in 1996 or 1997.

Fox Den near Statesville promises to be an accessible course to Charlotte golfers. It's just 45 minutes from uptown on I-77. The course is being built in tandem with a housing development. Clyde Johnston is designing the course, and it's scheduled to open in May 1996. Johnston is well-known as a former associate of Willard Byrd — one of the finest architects in the Carolinas. According to owners, Fox Den promises excellent variety. Some holes will remind you of mountain golf, others will remind you of beach-type courses.

The next few years are going to be great ones for the long-suffering Charlotte public golfer. Stay tuned for details.

In and Around the Charlotte Area . . .

Fun Things To Do

Charlotte is a working town, so you're not going to find a large number of really touristy things to do and see. You will, however, discover some major attractions that draw people from all over the city and surrounding counties.

As Charlotte is retailing epicenter of the Carolinas, **SouthPark Mall**, 4400 Sharon Road, Charlotte, 364-4411, is the retailing epicenter of Charlotte. In addition to Belk, Hecht's and Dillard's, there are more than 100 retail stores, including a Warner Brothers Store, two Victoria's Secret shops, Pea in the Pod, the Nature Conservancy and Brooks Brothers. The mall is well-run, clean and an excellent place for those who love to shop. Amid the myriad retail stores, you'll find a number of interesting eateries. Besides SouthPark, there are three other malls in this area offering a fine collection of specialty shops: Specialty Shops on The Park, Morrocroft Village and Sharon Corners.

Discovery Place, 301 N. Tryon Street, Charlotte, 845-3882, is a nationally known state-of-the-art science museum. It's a hands-on type of place that will fascinate children of all ages. Wander around the numerous displays and well-designed exhibits. Learn about subjects such as the rain forest, electricity, weather and moon exploration. This is a great place to spend hours discovering the nature of the world around you.

Once you've finished your museum tour, step over to the Charlotte Observer Omnimax theater. Watch a movie in a special surround-sound environment that truly has to be seen to be believed — it's like watching a movie on all four walls of the theater.

Charlotte is successfully on the map as sports town. The **Charlotte Hornets** of the National Basketball Association's Eastern Conference play in the Charlotte Coliseum and come close to selling out each and every home game. NBA action Hornets-style is a never-ending barrage of noise and off-court entertainment. If you're a fan of excellent dancing, you'll enjoy the cheerleading squad, affection-

ately known as the Honeybees. For ticket information, call 357-0252.

The **Carolina Panthers** franchise is one of two new entrants in the National Football League. As this book goes to press, the Panthers are playing their inaugural season in Clemson, South Carolina, while their Charlotte home is being built. The team has been quite competitive, already setting a record for the most consecutive wins by an expansion franchise (four in a row at press time — and counting). For the 1996-97 campaign, the Panthers will take the field in brand-new Panthers Stadium. Single-game tickets are available for each home game. Call 358-1644 for more information.

The 1995-96 season marks the **Charlotte Checkers** third ice-hockey campaign at Independence Arena, 2700 Independence Boulevard, Charlotte, 342-4423 — known to locals as the "Big I." The Checkers play in the East Coast Hockey League — the hockey equivalent of Class AA baseball. The team is affiliated with the Boston Bruins and New York Rangers of the NHL and the Chicago Wolves of the IHL. The season starts in October and lasts until mid-April.

There's nothing quite like minor league ice hockey. The Checkers were popular in the 1950s, '60s and early '70s until their league folded. The revamped Checkers features youthful players who hope that their stay in Charlotte lasts but a season. ECHL teams can only have three players with three or more years of professional experience on the roster. Plenty of players are eager to prove themselves worthy of a better league, so the action is always fast, furious and hard-hitting. And, yes, there is the occasional incident where players drop their gloves and engage in fist-to-fist combat. In the Checkers' first season the team mascot, a seven foot bear

named Chubby, got into a fight with player Sebastien LaPlante of the Greensboro squad over the use of a water pistol.

There's never a dull moment at a Checkers game. Plenty of home games sell out. As you enter the Big I, turn left and say hello to the ticket-taker named Betty.

Opened in 1992 in tandem with the tallest building in the Carolinas — the NationsBank Corporate Center — the **Blumenthal Performing Arts Center**, 130 N. Tryon Street, Charlotte, 372-1000, is a testament to Charlotte's commitment to quality entertainment. The Blumenthal Center is home to the Charlotte Symphony Orchestra, Opera Carolina and numerous other arts groups. The main performing hall seats about 2,000 patrons.

In the course of a recent year, you could take in an opera, a symphony, a rock 'n' roll performance, Carol Channing in *Hello Dolly*, and a major dance production. The adjacent state-of-the-art Belk Theater seats about 400 in a warm and intimate setting. Consult a copy of the *Charlotte Observer* to see what's playing.

Charlotte Motor Speedway, N.C. Highway 49 N., Concord, 455-2121, is the place to go for stock-car racing, or NASCAR as it is more commonly known. It's a major industry in the Charlotte region, and many of the top racing teams are headquartered just a smooth 3-wood shot from the speedway. There are three major races at CMS — the Winston Select and the Coca-Cola 600 in May and the Mello-Yellow 500 in the fall. Both races are about to change sponsors as this book goes to press, so they may have new names soon. Actually, it shouldn't matter to race fans who is sponsoring a race — each is exciting.

Each race event is replete with "extra-curricular activities," so come prepared for long days in the sun — the local population provides much of the entertainment. During the year, there are many ancillary events including auto fairs, demonstrations, non-NASCAR races and exhibitions. Call to arrange a tour of the facility. For motorsports fans, a trip to Charlotte is not complete without a stop at CMS.

Paramount's Carowinds, south of Charlotte just off I-77 on Carowinds Boulevard, Fort Mill, South Carolina, 588-2600, has been one of the Charlotte region's biggest attractions for years. It was called simply "Carowinds" until corporate giant Paramount bought the theme park.

It must be one of the most entertaining places in the Carolinas: from long, screaming roller coasters and water rides to smaller-scale carousels designed for smaller-scale people. The larger, more involved roller coasters are some of the most radical in the Southeast. You'll be turned upside-down at high speeds on The Vortex, a stand-up roller coaster. In addition to the rides, Carowinds' Palladium is a great place to see pop-music concerts in the summer months.

The Mint Museum of Art, 3730 Randolph Road, Charlotte, 337-2000, is housed in the city's former 19th-century federal mint, a fact that in part explains why the town is such a banking center today.

For an art museum nestled in one of Charlotte's oldest neighborhoods, the Mint is a pretty hopping place. The various auxiliaries and affiliated organizations spend a lot of time and energy keeping the museum alive and funded, so it's quite a social center as well. There's always at least one exhibit going on in addition to the regular collection, including one of the world's best accumulations of pre-Columbian art.

The museum is closed on Mondays.

Where to Eat

DILWORTH BREWING COMPANY
1301 East Blvd.
Charlotte   377-2739
$

Dilworth Brewing Company, or Dilworth Brewery as it's better known, has been a stalwart on the Charlotte restaurant scene for a number of years. All the beer is brewed on the premises — and it's all excellent. There's nothing like good fresh beer, and the brewmaster at this wonderful establishment has been improving his ales for some time. The place has been open for a while — it has a wonderful lived-in feel and coziness usually reserved for an old pub. The food has also improved over the years to the point where you can complement your pint with anything from chicken wings to a burger or a fresh fish entree. It's also an excellent value.

LA BIBLIOTHEQUE
1901 Rexford Rd.
Charlotte   365-5000
$$$

La Bibliotheque has become one of Charlotte's best fine restaurants. You'll want to wear a coat and tie for dinner at this award-winning establishment. Owner Adam Kantback runs the restaurant as if it's his home, and he greets you with a hospitality and grace that you won't find in many places. Although located in an office building, its ambiance is that of a fine French restaurant. The service is impeccable and the menu is diverse and exciting but rooted in French cuisine.

Both kids and adults enjoy the Discovery Place.

La Bibliotheque is open for a remarkably reasonable lunch, but things are at their best during dinner. This place is best suited to the full-course type of meal, and you need to take your time, have an appetizer, clear the palate, order a good bottle of wine and then indulge in some dessert. Round out the meal with a glass of port and you'll be in heaven until you wake up. Don't leave without trying the marinated salmon.

LA PAZ

523 Fenton Pl.
Charlotte   372-4168
$$

La Paz is located off Providence Road in Eastover — one of Charlotte's oldest and most venerable neighborhoods. The restaurant is situated in what used to be a house, thus the ambiance steers well away from the cookie-cutter type of restaurant so prevalent today. The drinks are generous and the large selection of Mexican beers is always kept ice-cold. You'll probably find a greater diversity of imaginative Mexican dishes at La Paz than at most Mexican establishments. It's a lot of fun and always popular with old-money locals.

MANZETTI'S

6401 Morrison Blvd.
Charlotte   364-9334
$$

Located in the SouthPark area in Specialty Shops on the Park, Manzetti's has long been a popular stop on the drinking and dining scene. It's a pretty trendy place, so come expecting to see a number of slightly aging yuppie-types dressed up for the kill. The atmosphere is definitely fern-bar-like, with bright brass rails and dark wood predominating. The food is outstanding; menu items include fun appetizers and a number of traditional American entrees. There's plenty to drink at the bar, and it's always crowded with fun people. A great place for a relaxed outing with friends.

PROVIDENCE CAFE

110 Perrin Pl.
Charlotte   376-2008
$$

If you're looking for excellence for your dollar value, then look no further than Providence Cafe, just off Providence Road near the intersection of Providence and Queens. If you get lost in this area of Charlotte, don't worry — you're not the first and certainly not the last. As you enter Providence Cafe, you might be fooled into thinking that you're going to spend a lot of "cashola," but don't worry — your bill for a big session will be less than you think. In addition to a fine array of beverages, the mildly eclectic menu features a number of interesting selections that won't increase your overdraft.

HILLBILLYS BARBEQUE AND STEAKS

930 E. Garrison Blvd.
Gastonia   861-8787
$$

Yer invited for supper here at Hillbillys, which describes itself as a "cook-out inside." You'll find some of the best pit barbeque in town, in addition to hickory-cooked ribeye and New York strip steaks. Also enjoy ribs, chicken, pork, beef, sizeable hot dogs, hamburgers and a pretty extensive kid's menu as well. Hillbillys will also cater anything from family reunions to shotgun weddings.

EL CANCUN

516 E. Garrison St.
Gastonia   853-2855
$

Take a tasty trip to Mexico at one of the Charlotte region's greatest venues. If you like Mexican food but don't want to spend a fortune on it, head for El Cancun. Your waiter or waitress (always Mexican) will bring you chips with excellent salsa. After that, you should skip reading the menu and indulge in the cream burritos. But all the choices on this extensive menu are wonderful. Wash it all down with a Dos Equis or two.

Where to Stay

THE PARK HOTEL
2200 Rexford Rd.
Charlotte   364-8220
$$$

In the heart of SouthPark, with some of the best shopping in the Southeast just a short walk away, the Park offers great location and excellent service. The Park is well-known in Charlotte as one of the best hotels in the city. In fact, it's where the players in the Paine Webber Senior PGA tournament stay. With nearly 200 rooms, the Park boasts a European feel. Morrocroft's Restaurant, on the first floor, is an outstanding place to eat.

Amenities at The Park Hotel include several meeting rooms, an outdoor swimming pool with a whirlpool, two ballrooms and a newsstand plus full meeting and banquet facilities. Wayne Shusko is one of the friendliest, most helpful and most experienced hotel managers in Charlotte. The Park enjoys tremendous repeat business — with good reason.

THE DUNHILL HOTEL
237 N. Tryon St.
Charlotte   332-4141
$$$

The Dunhill is located in Uptown Charlotte near the new NationsBank tower. It's in an old building with an old-world bed and breakfast inn ambiance that makes it a great alternative to the larger chain-style hotels. Yet it's extremely convenient

to the central business district, library and Discovery Place. You'll find a restaurant on the ground floor, in addition to services tailored to the business traveler.

RADISSON PLAZA HOTEL
2 NationsBank Plaza
Charlotte   377-0400
$$$

The Radisson Plaza in Uptown Charlotte was one of the city's first large hotels with connections to a large chain. It's a magnificent accommodation, with close to 400 rooms and a bunch of meeting rooms and entertainment suites. If you're in Uptown and you're looking for a first-class large hotel with every amenity under the sun, then you won't go wrong here.

HILTON AT UNIVERSITY PLACE
6929 JM Keynes Dr.
Charlotte   547-7444
$$-$$$

Located just off I-85 near the University of North Carolina at Charlotte, the Hilton at University Place is a fully-appointed 240-room hotel. The Hilton is convenient to the university area (hence its name), but it's also near Charlotte Motor Speedway, all the new office developments in the area, a couple of fine golf courses (including Highland Creek) and the new hospital. So should you be suddenly hit by a flying golf ball and need some stitches to your head, the Hilton will be a convenient location for you.

HOLIDAY INN LAKE NORMAN
I-77 & N.C. Hwy. 73
Cornelius   892-9120
$$

On the east side of Lake Norman, the Holiday Inn is convenient not only to the lake but to the entire Charlotte region. The hotel has 119 guest rooms, offers a free breakfast buffet, a restaurant and lounge, a pool and a fitness room as well as meeting and banquet facilities. If you're someone who can't survive the day without a cup of coffee, rest easy here: You'll find an in-room coffee maker at your disposal.

ECONO LODGE

I-85 & N.C. Hwy. 274
Gastonia   *867-1821*
$$

Just seconds from the always bustling I-85, Gastonia's Econo Lodge offers a swimming pool, free cable TV (with HBO), free local calls, continental breakfast and meeting rooms. Inquire about seniors' and other discounts.

Golf Equipment

One of the leaders in golf retailing in Charlotte is **Pro Golf Discount**. The three stores in Charlotte offer an outstanding variety of equipment for all levels of player. If you want the latest state-of-the-art clubs custom fitted to your swing, you can find that here as well. If your golfing budget is limited, Pro Golf offers playable clubs perfect for those who are just starting the game. Pro Golf stocks a wide range of putters and utility clubs that you won't find anywhere else. You'll also find a wide selection of name-brand accessories from gloves to shoes to shirts, balls and bags. Stop by any of the three locations in Charlotte: Central Avenue, 536-9021; South Boulevard, 523-7262; and Pineville, 541-6950.

Photo:The Grove Park Inn Resort

The Grove Park Inn Resort's course, at nearly a century old,
is one of the most magnificent in the country.

Inside
The Mountains
of North Carolina

Stretching from the deep valleys around Murphy to the foothills around Hendersonville and North Wilkesboro, the North Carolina mountains offer some spectacular scenery and excellent opportunities for rest and relaxation. For more than a century and a half, the North Carolina mountains have been a year-round haven for vacationers from all over the eastern seaboard. Many bring their golf clubs. In the early part of the century, golf was mostly limited to the resorts and their wealthy guests. Slowly but surely, a number of purely public and semiprivate courses opened and were immediately popular. Today, due in part to the lack of population in the mountains, many courses don't appear quite as crowded as their counterparts to the east.

The steep wooded hillsides of the mountains and the lush verdant valleys have provided magnificent canvases for some of the world's greatest architects. Donald Ross, Jack Nicklaus, Tom Fazio (who lives in Hendersonville), Fred Hawtree, Martin Hawtree, Tom Jackson, George Cobb and Ellis Maples have produced fine work in the mountains, although many of their courses are private.

The line between public and private courses is somewhat ill-defined in the mountains. At quite a few private courses, you can play if you rent a condo or apartment for a week. In our minds, that still means they're private, so those courses have not been reviewed. However, we've included a number of courses where you can get a tee time if you stay at an accompanying hotel or inn. But if a tent or motor home is more your style, we've included a number of courses where you can strap on your golf shoes in the parking lot, plunk down some cash in the pro shop and play to your heart's content.

It's interesting to see how designers have adapted their styles to the mountainous terrain. For example, if your home course is designed by George Cobb, then it's probably a difficult layout, lengthy and trying. Here in the mountains, Cobb may have realized that many if not most golfers are probably on vacation, so he turned down the difficulty meter and produced tracks that are a little more user-friendly. The key to a good course in the mountains is a good layout, and the better designers make use of the hazards and difficulties produced by Mother Nature. Thus, you'll find plenty of elevation changes on many courses in addition to potentially annoying small streams. Not much earth has been shifted here — it isn't necessary.

One of the great golfing difficulties in the mountains is judging distance. You'll be faced with plenty of shots where you're shooting straight uphill or downhill. A decent rule of thumb is to take two extra clubs for an uphill shot and take one less if it's seriously downhill. Avoid the steep embankments that you'll find on many courses.

GOLF COURSES IN NORTH CAROLINA MOUNTAINS

Name	Type	# Holes	Par	Slope	Yards	Walking	Booking	Cost w/ Cart
Apple Valley Golf Club	public	18	72	130	6297	no	30 days	$40
Bald Mountain	public/resort	18	72	121	6125	restricted	30 days	$40
Black Mountain Golf Course	semiprivate	18	71	n/r	5780	restricted	6 dats	$25-30
Boone Golf Club	semiprivate	18	71	112	5859	restricted	7 days	$40-45
Buncome County Muni	public	18	72	107	5929	anytime	3 days	$23
Chatuge Shores	public	18	72	118	6269	restricted	3 days	$24
Cleghorn Plantation	public	18	72	126	6313	no	anytime	$22-30
Crooked Creek Golf Club	public	18	72	n/r	6267	restricted	2 days	$25
Cummings Cove Golf and CC	semiprivate	18	70	n/r	5720	restricted	anytime	$25
Etowah Valley Country Club								
South/West Course	resort	18	72	123	6880	restricted	anytime	$43
West/North Course	resort	18	73	122	6700	restricted	anytime	$43
North/South Course	resort	18	73	121	6604	restricted	anytime	$43
French Broad Golf Center	public	18	72	115	6313	restricted	7 days	$36-38
Glen Cannon	semiprivate	18	72	121	6272	no	3 days	$50
Granada Farms	semiprivate	18	72	112	5835	restricted	anytime	$20-23
Grassy Creek Golf and CC	public	18	72	116	5774	restricted	7 days	$32-35
Great Smokies Hilton	public/resort	18	70	117	5131	restricted	anytime	$26-32
Grove Park Inn	semiprivate/resort	18	71	119	6033	restricted	anytime	$60
Hawksnest Ski and Golf	semiprivate	18	72	110	5953	restricted	7 days	$32-36
High Hampton Inn	semiprivate/resort	18	71	120	6012	anytime	1 day	$37-48
Hound Ears Club	resort	18	72	120	6036	restricted	anytime	$48
Jefferson Landing	semiprivate/resort	18	72	115	6424	no	anytime	$39-49
Lake Junaluska Golf Course	public	18	68	n/r	4579	anytime	anytime	$21

Name	Type	# Holes	Par	Slope	Yards	Walking	Booking	Cost w/ Cart
Lake Toxaway	resort	18	71	116	5594	anytime	anytime	$62
Lenoir Golf Course	semiprivate	18	71	106	5886	anytime	anytime	$22
Maggie Valley Resort and CC	resort	18	72	118	6031	restricted	anytime	$48
Marion Lake Club	semiprivate	18	70	n/r	5710	anytime	anytime	$39-49
Meadowbrook Golf Club	public	18	72	105	5850	anytime	anytime	$20-25
Mill Creek	semiprivate	18	72	113	5775	restricted	2 days	$38
Mountain Glen Golf Club	semiprivate	18	72	119	6195	anytime	7 days	$35
Mount Mitchell Golf Club	public	18	72	116	6110	restricted	14 days	$40-45
Olde Beau Golf Club	semiprivate	18	72	129	6264	no	14 days	$40-50
Orchard Hills Golf Club	semiprivate	18	72	106	5673	restricted	4 days	$22-26
Quaker Meadows Golf Course	public	18	71	108	6133	restricted	anytime	$20-24
Red Fox Country Club	semiprivate	18	72	124	6393	no	anytime	$30-35
Reems Creek Golf Course	semiprivate	18	72	127	6106	no	anytime	$38-42
Sapphire Mountain Golf Club	public	18	70	118	5690	no	30 days	$25
Springdale Country Club	semiprivate/resort	18	72	121	6437	anytime	anytime	$35
Village of Sugar Mountain GC	public	18	64	91	4198	yes	5 days	$29-30
Waynesville Country Club Inn								
Carolina/Dogwood Course	semiprivate/resort	18	70	100	5395	restricted	anytime	$41
Dogwood/Blue Ridge Course	semiprivate/resort	18	70	100	5258	restricted	anytime	$41
Blue Ridge/Carolina Course	semiprivate/resort	18	70	100	5493	restricted	anytime	$41

The Mountains of North Carolina

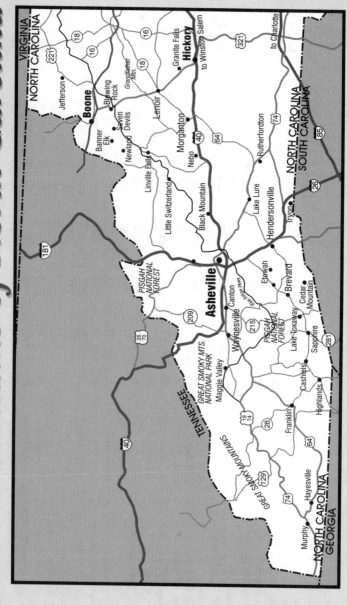

The most noticeable difference between the older and newer courses is the layout. Older courses tend to meander around valley floors, while the modern ones venture forth into the hills and, with the help of your golf cart, you'll be able to smack the ball from mountaintop to mountaintop. Almost.

The seasons and climate are quite different from the plains of North and South Carolina. Summers can be warm or even hot. Spring and fall boast temperate days where you might need a sweater or rain gear, while winter life can include snow, sleet, wind, rain, crisp temperatures and bright sun. Some courses choose to stay open all year, while others close up shop. Thus, in winter it's essential to call a course before you leave the driveway or hotel parking lot. The cooler summer temperatures mean that courses can use bentgrass or bluegrass in the fairways. Is there a prettier sight on a golf course than a crosscut bentgrass fairway on a bright autumn day in the North Carolina mountains? On the greens, you'll find bentgrass greens almost exclusively. In the spring and fall, the greens can become unbelievably fast.

Fall and spring bring a fair share of visitors to the mountains, but no season is quite like summer, when it seems that most of Florida transplants here for at least three months. Many of these migratory birds are part of the older generation of Americans, and they live to play golf. They venture forth onto the course with no other agenda for the day apart from having a great time and perhaps a vodka and tonic at cocktail time (ahhh — what a life!).

Enjoy golf in the mountains and don't let the terrain bother you too much. Remember that most people are playing golf as part of a getaway from the real world, so take the leisurely pace in stride, enjoy the fine views, the relaxing ambiance and the fine and varied challenges that some of the greatest golf architects in the world have planned for your pleasure.

Note that we've divided this chapter geographically into three sections: the Asheville area west, the Boone/Blowing Rock area and the Hickory/Lenoir area. We realize the tourism bureaus probably wouldn't divide things this way. But the Mountains region is widespread enough that we thought it helpful to write about the courses that are in your general vicinity, no matter where in the mountains you may be.

> Unless otherwise noted, all courses and businesses in this chapter are in the 704 area code.

Golf Courses in North Carolina's Mountains

Asheville Area West

APPLE VALLEY GOLF CLUB

201 Boulevard of the Mountains
Lake Lure   652-2888
Championship Yardage: 6726
Slope: 138   Par: 72
Men's Yardage: 6297
Slope: 130   Par: 72
Other Yardage: 5511
Slope: 118   Par: 72
Ladies' Yardage: 4661
Slope: 114   Par: 72

Apple Valley opened in 1985. Like its sister course, Bald Mountain, Apple Valley is part of the Fairfield Mountain Golf Resort. Dan Maples, son of Ellis Maples, designed the course. Some holes are flat; others are set in rolling terrain. Fairways are bermudagrass, and greens are bentgrass.

Apple Valley is a fine mountain course. Interestingly, you'll be hard pressed to understand why the slope rating is so high from the back tees. We must assume that the course is a lot tougher than it looks. Play it from the middle or front tees for a more sensible approach.

The course boasts a number of interesting holes. We particularly enjoyed the par 4 12th that plays 369 yards from the back tees. A mountain stream bisects the hole. From the tee, you'll have to decide whether to lay up or go for it. Go for it successfully, and the approach shot is less fraught with difficulty. Many of the holes are bordered by woods. The greens are fairly large and sloped, with the occasional buried elephant in the green complex: Like father, like son. A couple of holes feature interesting blind shots where local knowledge might result in a big reward. Water frequently comes into play. Overall, Apple Valley is a fun and interesting course designed by one of the finest and most respected architects in the Carolinas. We'd play this one over Bald Mountain, although if you're at the resort for two days, play both courses.

Amenities include a practice green, range, locker room, snack bar, rental clubs and a pro shop.

You must take a cart here. You can book a tee time 30 days in advance. Approximate cost, including cart, is $40 weekdays and weekends.

BALD MOUNTAIN

201 Boulevard of the Mountains
Lake Lure   625-3040
Championship Yardage: 6575

Slope: 125	*Par: 72*
Men's Yardage: 6125	
Slope: 121	*Par: 72*
Other Yardage: 5208	
Slope: 108	*Par: 72*
Ladies' Yardage: 4808	
Slope: 112	*Par: 72*

200 •

Bald Mountain, a Willie B. Lewis design, opened in 1974. Most of the holes are bordered by woods. The rolling fairways are covered with bermudagrass; the greens, bentgrass.

Bald Mountain is part of the Fairfield Mountain Golf Resort. We found a genuine and challenging mountain track that's fun from any of the tees. If you're a movie buff or a fan of Patrick Swayze, you'll enjoy the 16th green, where part of the cinematic masterpiece *Dirty Dancing* was filmed. (Hmmm . . .) In fact, a good bit of the movie was filmed in and around the resort town of Lake Lure. Cinematography aside, the course is worth playing, particularly in tandem with Apple Valley, its sister course. We're not quite sure why the course is called Bald Mountain.

You'll need to keep the ball straight off the tee and away from the hazards, including several bunkers and a mountain stream.

Amenities include a practice green, range, locker room, bar, snack bar, restaurant, rental clubs, a beverage cart and a pro shop.

The course is walkable for the physically fit, and you can walk after 2 PM. You can book a tee time 30 days in advance. Approximate cost, including cart, is $40 weekdays and weekends.

BLACK MOUNTAIN GOLF COURSE

17 Ross Dr.
Black Mountain   669-2710
Championship Yardage: 6181

Slope: 129	*Par: 71*
Men's Yardage: 5780	
Slope: No rating	*Par: 71*
Ladies' Yardage: 4959	
Slope: No rating	*Par: 71*

The front nine at Black Mountain opened in the 1930s, and a back nine opened in the 1960s. Ross Taylor designed the course, which mixes open holes with those bordered and framed with woods.

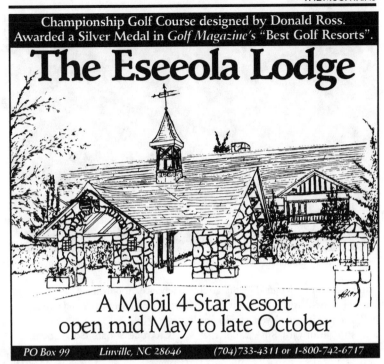

Championship Golf Course designed by Donald Ross.
Awarded a Silver Medal in *Golf Magazine's* "Best Golf Resorts".

The Eseeola Lodge

A Mobil 4-Star Resort
open mid May to late October

PO Box 99   Linville, NC 28646   (704)733-4311 or 1-800-742-6717

In the fairways, you'll find an interesting combination of bluegrass and bentgrass; on the greens, you'll find bentgrass.

Here at Black Mountain, we found a playable and justifiably popular course, with good variety and interest. Locals inform us that the back nine is more difficult than the front. The front provides significant difficulties in the form of streams, small greens, small mounds, bunkers and narrow fairways. Difficulties on the back come from some longer par 4s, plenty of creeks, undulating greens plus the world's longest par 6 — the 747-yard 17th. With the small greens here, you'll need to plan your approach shots and manage your short game with a degree of precision.

Amenities include a practice green, snack bar, rental clubs and a pro shop.

The course is walkable for the fit and you can walk anytime except weekend mornings. You can book a tee time six days in advance. Approximate cost, including cart, is $25 weekdays and $30 weekends.

BUNCOME COUNTY MUNICIPAL GOLF COURSE

226 Fairway Dr.
Asheville   298-1867
Championship Yardage: 6356
Slope: 115   Par: 72
Men's Yardage: 5929
Slope: 107   Par: 72
Ladies' Yardage: 4897
Slope: 109   Par: 72

Buncome County Municipal Golf Course opened in 1927. Donald Ross designed the course. Fairways are bermudagrass, and greens are bentgrass. The front nine is flat and open, while the back nine is wooded, tighter and much more rolling.

Quick, how many counties have a

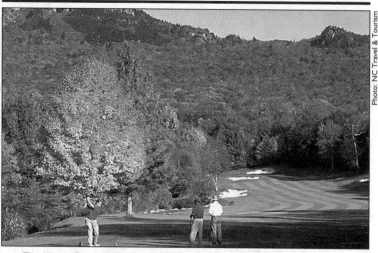

Photo: NC Travel & Tourism

The North Carolina Mountains area is known for its many quality courses.

municipal course designed by the great Donald Ross? Answer, not many. Here at Buncome Municipal, you'll find a fine and straightforward Ross layout that hasn't been touched since it opened, or at least that's how it appears. We found a sensible layout, with small and flat bunkers fronting large crowned greens. The significant difference in layout between the back and the front nines makes the course all the more interesting. We were told that the course is host to close to 50,000 rounds a year. If you've got a twenty spot burning a hole in your pocket, and if you've never played a Donald Ross course, then you should stop by for a round. Just be careful on the 9th hole: If you airmail your approach shot, you'll hit a car in the parking lot . . . no free drop from the front seat of a Subaru.

Amenities include a practice green, snack bar, rental clubs and a pro shop.

The course is walkable, you can walk anytime, and you should walk (it's great!). You'll only need a tee time on weekends and holidays, and you can book three days in advance. Approximate cost, including cart, is $23 on weekends and weekdays.

CHATUGE SHORES GOLF COURSE

Myers Chapel Rd.
Hayesville   389-8940
Championship Yardage: 6687
Slope: 123   *Par: 72*
Men's Yardage: 6269
Slope: 118   *Par: 72*
Ladies' Yardage: 4950
Slope: 120   *Par: 72*

Chatuge Shores Golf Course, designed by J. Townsend, opened in 1969. Some holes are flat, but most feature some undulation. In the fairways, you'll find bermudagrass; on the greens, you'll find bentgrass. Water comes into play on some of the holes.

Chatuge Shores offers a fun and friendly mature course, offering challenges for golfers of all levels. The layout is fairly straightforward. Some of the fairways are wide, some are on the narrow side. Trees delineate the fairways. The greens are primarily small and slightly rolling. Bunkers will make you think about the safest approach shot on a number of holes. The main interest comes from the variety in the shape and size of the greens. There aren't many public courses in the immediate area, so Chatuge Shores is definitely worth a visit. It's clearly a popular track, so you won't be alone.

Amenities include a practice green, range, chipping green, snack bar, rental clubs and a pro shop.

The course is walkable. You can book a tee time three days in advance. Approximate cost, including cart, is $24.

CLEGHORN PLANTATION
GOLF AND COUNTRY CLUB

200 Golf Cir.
Rutherfordton   286-9117
Championship Yardage: 6903
Slope: 134   Par: 72
Men's Yardage: 6313
Slope: 126   Par: 72
Other Yardage: 5679
Slope: 115   Par: 72
Ladies' Yardage: 4751
Slope: 111   Par: 73

The golf course at Cleghorn Plantation, a George Cobb design, opened in 1969. The course is set amid rolling terrain, and many holes are bordered by homes or woods. In the fairways, you'll find bermudagrass; on the greens, bentgrass.

Cleghorn Plantation is a real find. The course may originally have been planned as a private track, but financial hard times in the 1980s likely necessitated the course to open to the public. A number of recent improvements have been made, and it looked to us like the course is shaping up to be one of the finest in the North Carolina foothills. Many of Cobb's resort/vacation courses are less demanding than his more serious efforts. Cleghorn is not a vacation course.

Play the tips and you're in for a long day, unless you can hit the ball a country mile off the tee. Play it from the Men's or Other tees for a more sensible outing. The course features a number of epic sweeping holes, including elevated tee shots followed by uphill approach shots to large and heavily bunkered greens, which pitch and roll significantly.

The attraction of the course is its excellent layout, great variety, playability and sensible combination of natural and man-made hazards. It's excellent news for area golfers that this outstanding golf course is on the way up in the world. If you're visiting the area, this is the course to play. If you live in western North Carolina and you're up for a serious challenge, Cleghorn is a must-play for you too. And it's an excellent value as well.

Amenities include a practice green, range, snack bar, and pro shop.

A cart is required to play Cleghorn, but you may book a tee time whenever you choose. Approximate cost, including cart, is $22 weekdays and $30 on weekends.

CROOKED CREEK GOLF CLUB

764 Crooked Creek Rd.
Hendersonville   692-2011
Championship Yardage: 6652
Slope: No rating   Par: 72
Men's Yardage: 6267
Slope: No rating   Par: 72
Ladies' Yardage: 5546
Slope: No rating   Par: 72

Alex Guin and Stewart Goodin designed Crooked Creek Golf Club, which opened in 1968. The course has a wide-open feel; many of the holes are flat and others are set in rolling terrain. Fairways are bermudagrass; greens are bentgrass.

First, a note about the clubhouse. It was built by Warner Brothers executives, afraid that Japanese investor-types would invade California, necessitating a move to the East Coast. So if Bugs Bunny says

"What's up, Doc?" right in the middle of your backswing, you'll know why.

This is one of the earliest examples of a course set in a housing development. Homes and out-of-bounds provide potential threats on many holes. You'll find good variety on this course. Some of your tee shots must negotiate narrow fairways. Some of the greens are small, others are midsize to large. Most of the greens are crowned and sloped, others offer significant undulations. There isn't a lot of water on the course. The most omnipresent hazards are the bunkers around the green complexes; they come in an interesting variety of shapes and sizes. Overall, it's a fun and straightforward track that will provide a decent challenge from the back tees.

Amenities include a practice green, range, snack bar and pro shop.

The course is walkable, although walking is restricted. You can book a tee time two days in advance. Approximate cost, including cart, is $25.

CUMMINGS COVE
GOLF AND COUNTRY CLUB

3000 Cummings Rd.
Hendersonville   *891-9412*
Championship Yardage: 6008
Slope: No rating   *Par: 70*
Men's Yardage: 5720
Slope: No rating   *Par: 70*

Cummings Cove Golf and Country Club, which originally may have been called Horseshoe Country Club, opened in 1986. Robert Cupp, a man with an interesting background, designed the course. Cupp is certainly a prolific architect, having designed courses in almost every state in the Union. In the North Carolina mountains, he assisted Jack Nicklaus in the design of Elk River, one of the state's best private courses. Cupp's resume includes a Master's of Fine Arts degree from the University of Alaska, advertising ex-

perience, pro shop management, an associate's degree in agronomy and a significant stint as an associate in the Jack Nicklaus design firm. He has worked with a variety of touring pros, including Tom Kite and Fuzzy Zoeller.

Cupp produced a challenging course here at Cummings Cove. Your tee shots need to be precise though not always very long. Your approach shots must hit small and undulating greens with little or no bail-out potential. Many of the greens are flanked by embankments. The course is bordered by woods and homes.

You'll probably remember two holes in particular. The 10th, a 370-yard par 4 flanked by a lake, provides one of the smallest landing areas of any course around. And the green on the par 5 No. 5 is horseshoe-shaped; hit the ball to the wrong level and you may have to bring out the lob wedge to get it close to the hole.

Take the challenge of this course if you get the chance. It's target golf for the most part, so keep it straight and you'll have a good round.

Amenities include a practice green and snack bar.

The course is not easy to walk, but you may anytime during the week and after 2 PM on weekends. You can book a tee time whenever you choose. Approximate cost, including cart, is $25.

ETOWAH VALLEY COUNTRY CLUB

Brickyard Rd., Etowah
Resort   *891-7022*
Golf shop   *891-9412*
South/West Course
Championship Yardage: 7108
Slope: 125   *Par: 72*
Men's Yardage: 6880
Slope: 123   *Par: 72*
Other Yardage: 6287
Slope: 118   *Par: 72*
Ladies' Yardage: 5480
Slope: 119   *Par: 72*

West/North Course
Championship Yardage: 7003
Slope: 124 — Par: 73
Men's Yardage: 6700
Slope: 122 — Par: 73
Other Yardage: 6215
Slope: 121 — Par: 73
Ladies' Yardage: 5319
Slope: 117 — Par: 73

North/South Course
Championship Yardage: 6909
Slope: 124 — Par: 73
Men's Yardage: 6604
Slope: 121 — Par: 73
Other Yardage: 6156
Slope: 118 — Par: 73
Ladies' Yardage: 5391
Slope: 115 — Par: 73

The South and West courses at Etowah Valley opened in 1967. The North course opened in 1988. Edmund B. Ault designed all three courses. Ault's credits include only two courses in North Carolina and one full 18-hole course in South Carolina. However, he was a prolific designer who built and redesigned more than 100 courses, primarily in Maryland, Arkansas, Pennsylvania and Virginia. He was a scratch golfer at one stage and played in the national amateur championship. (Bet you didn't know that!) He died in 1989 at age 81.

These well-maintained courses have bentgrass fairways and greens. Overall, all three courses are playable, fun and laid out in a picturesque setting. All of your approach shots will be influenced by large bunkers of varied shapes. On the longer par 4s, you'll often have a chance to run the ball up to the green. All of the green complexes offer bailout areas; if you're a good chipper, then head for these areas and avoid the bunkers.

The South Course is primarily flat and somewhat narrow. Water comes into play on quite a few holes in the form of a large pond or mountain stream. The greens are primarily midsize and sloped. Play from the back tees and you'll have a long course to negotiate. If you want a more sensible outing and you're not a long hitter, play from the other (white) tees.

The West Course is also primarily flat, although three holes offer elevation change. From the tips, the course is even longer than the south course. The greens might be a little larger, but so are the bunkers!

The newest nine is the North Course. The terrain is more rolling, giving the course a more open feel. A stream will come into play on most of the holes. The greens are large and undulating. Once again, bunkers will make you think about the most sensible approach to the green.

There's a lodge where you should stay if you definitely want to play Etowah Valley. If you don't stay here, you may be able to get on this course if you call in advance, although resort guest and member play take priority. So there will be times when you'll be told "Sorry, members and guests only." Your chances of playing here if you're not staying here are best out of season.

Amenities include three practice greens, a range, bar, snack bar, restaurant, beverage gazebo, rental clubs and a pro shop.

Walking is restricted, although the first two nines are walkable, and you should walk. You can book a tee time with your reservation or two days in advance. Approximate cost for 18 holes, including cart, is $43.

FRENCH BROAD GOLF CENTER

5 French Broad Ave.
Asheville   687-8545
Championship Yardage: 6857
Slope: 120   *Par: 72*
Men's Yardage: 6313
Slope: 115   *Par: 72*
Other Yardage: 5881
Slope: 111   *Par: 72*
Ladies' Yardage: 5082
Slope: 113   *Par: 72*

The golf course at French Broad Golf Center opened in 1993. Karl Litten designed the course. The layout is about as flat as a pancake and wide open, with woods bordering the course. In the fairways, you'll find rye; on the greens, you'll find bentgrass.

Okay, so who is this Karl Litten guy? Apart from the fact that he's a graduate of Steubenville College, he's an accomplished architect who apprenticed under the flamboyant Robert von Hagge, surely the greatest and most prolific architect who never designed a course in South Carolina. Litten formed his own firm in 1979 and, like his teacher, was very busy in Florida in the 1980s. Litten formed a design partnership with Gary Player in 1987 that continued through 1989. His design here, just south of Asheville, is remarkable in that the ground is almost totally flat and treeless. Trees have been planted, but they shouldn't come into play for years. The result is an interesting and subtly varied links design. Play the course in a fresh wind and you might feel like you're in Scotland.

Off the tee, the fairways are relatively wide, with mounds presenting most of the

---

Profile: Ellis Maples

Ellis Maples is one of North Carolina's greatest golf course architects. In fact, he may be one of the greatest in the country. Maples' father, Frank, was a construction superintendent for Donald Ross and the greenskeeper at Pinehurst Country Club.

Photo: The Architects of Golf

Ellis Maples

Ellis attended Lenoir-Rhyne College and spent two years as assistant greenskeeper at Mid Pines and Pine Needles. In 1937, Ellis helped build a course in Plymouth, North Carolina. He remained at the course as greenskeeper and spent the war years as an engineer. In 1947, he redesigned the course at New Bern where he was the pro and the manager. After this, he remodeled and planned a number of layouts.

In 1948, he supervised the building of the last Donald Ross layout — at Raleigh Country Club. He stayed on as superintendent until 1953 when he opened a design firm. From 1953 until his death in 1984, Maples built close to 70 golf courses, including Forest Oaks Country Club and Grandfather Golf and Country Club, both top tracks in North Carolina. Forest Oaks is home of the Greater Greensboro Open. Maples hired Ed Seay who eventually became top designer in the firm of Arnold Palmer design. Son Dan joined Ellis's firm. Son Joe was the head pro at Boone Golf Club, and son David built courses.

Ellis Maples courses include Country Club of North Carolina, Country Club of South Carolina, Midland Country Club near Aiken (a favorite of this author), Boone Country Club, Greensboro Country Club, Pinehurst #5, Red Fox Country Club and Devil's Knob. Ellis Maples completed courses in Alabama, Georgia, Tennessee, Virginia and North and South Carolina.

trouble. Upon initial inspection, you might be tempted to think that the green complexes have a certain similarity. But upon closer inspection, you'll find that Litten has used the flatness to produce approach shots that require a great deal of thought and strategy. On some holes, for instance, a low, running bounce-up shot is possible — even advisable — if the course is dry and there's a hearty wind. The greens are typically medium-size and mostly flat or slightly sloped. Bunkers provide most of the problems around the green. Water comes into play on the majority of holes on the front nine and is a factor on the back nine on a few holes. Interestingly, the final three holes provide excellent scoring opportunities for the better player. Overall, French Broad is a fine course that you should make an effort to play.

Amenities include a practice green, range, chipping green, snack bar, bar and restaurant, rental clubs, a beverage cart and a pro shop.

The course is walkable after 1 PM on weekdays, and you should walk here. You can book a tee time seven days in advance. Approximate cost, including cart, is $36 weekdays and $38 on weekends.

GLEN CANNON COUNTRY CLUB

Wilson Rd.
Pisgah Forest   884-9160
Championship Yardage: 6548
Slope: 124   Par: 72
Men's Yardage: 6272
Slope: 121   Par: 72
Ladies' Yardage: 5172
Slope: 117   Par: 72

Glen Cannon Country Club opened in 1966. According to *Architects of Golf*, Willie B. Lewis of Greenville designed the course. Lewis used to be an associate of George Cobb. For a mountain track, this course has a remarkably wide-open feel; also remarkable is its flatness. Fairways are bermudagrass; greens are bentgrass.

Locals tell us that Glen Cannon is one of the more private semiprivate courses in the area, so make sure you call for a tee time.

Glen Cannon offers a fine, playable and relatively straightforward mountain course that winds around a lush and wide valley floor. The fairways are mostly spacious and delineated by trees and shrubs. The greens are medium-size to large. The grass around the greens is mostly bentgrass: If it's a couple of inches deep,

plan to avoid it at all costs. Most of the greens are sloped and not overly rolling. Water hazards come in the form of several branches of a mountain stream; watch out for it. Bunkers provide frequent hazards, and many are grass-faced; some are in the fairway, others are around the greens. The back nine is a little hillier and offers fine views from some tee boxes. Particularly pretty is a small but beautiful waterfall that complements the 2nd hole.

If you're looking for a good course in the Brevard area with a sound design and plenty of variety, try Glen Cannon. You'll likely have an enjoyable round. Just make sure you ring the bell before venturing towards the 17th hole.

Amenities include a practice green, range, chipping green, locker room, bar, snack bar, restaurant, rental clubs, a beverage cart and pro shop.

The course is walkable, but you must use a cart if you're not a member. You can book a tee time three days in advance. Approximate cost, including cart, is $50.

GREAT SMOKIES RESORT

1 Hilton Inn Dr.
Asheville   254-3211
Championship Yardage: 5600
Slope: 118   Par: 70
Men's Yardage: 5131
Slope: 117   Par: 70
Ladies' Yardage: 4502
Slope: 112   Par: 70

The golf course at Great Smokies Resort opened in 1975. According to *Architects of Golf*, Willie B. Lewis designed the

---

course. The course is somewhat tight, particularly on the front nine, with woods bordering many of the holes. You'll find bluegrass and fescue in the fairways and bentgrass on the greens.

Corporate takeovers and changes have affected, if not the course, at least the name of the hotel attached to this interesting mountain track. The course was opened as Great Smokies Hilton, but the Holiday Inn chain took over and renamed the complex as the Great Smokies Resort. It's actually a Sunspree Resort, for what it's worth. Improvements to the hotel complex were under way during our visit.

The golf course is a truly challenging mountain layout with a solid design. While cruising around the course, we sensed that someone has redesigned the layout and perhaps some of the holes. You'll find plenty of elevation changes. Hazards come in the form of well-placed bunkers and potentially pesky mountain streams. You'll need to keep it straight off the tee and think about your approach shots. The course is not long, but don't think that this makes it easy. The greens are predominantly large and sloped. The first four or five holes seem particularly tight. When you arrive on the 5th tee, you're confronted with your mortality as you tee off next to a small graveyard. Hello! The course is also dotted with octagonal holiday chalets, and certain holes are dominated by the 279-room hotel whose aspects lie firmly in the East German school of architecture.

Amenities include a practice green, bar, snack bar, restaurant, rental clubs and a pro shop.

The course is walkable for the fit and dedicated, and you can walk after 1 PM from Monday through Thursday. You can book a tee time with your hotel or octagonal holiday chalet, although you don't need

to stay here to play here. Approximate cost, including cart, is $26 weekdays and $32 on weekends (including Fridays).

THE GROVE PARK INN RESORT

230 Macon Ave.	252-2711
Asheville	(800) 438-5800
Championship Yardage: 6520	
Slope: 125	Par: 71
Blue Yardage: 6033	
Slope: 119	Par: 71
Ladies' Yardage: 4987	
Slope: 111	Par: 71

The golf course at The Grove Park Inn opened in February 1899. *Architects of Golf* lists Willie Park Jr., Herbert Barker, Donald Ross and Russell Breeden as architects who have worked on or influenced the course. Ask the staff here who has had the biggest influence and they'll tell you it was Donald Ross. The course is laid out on the hillside beneath the magnificent and storied Grove Park Inn. You'll find Vamont bermudagrass in the fairways and Pencross bentgrass greens.

Nearly a century old, the golf course at The Grove Park Inn is steeped in history — the likes of which would fill a book with stories. But, first, let's investigate the Grove Park Inn. There's a book about this veritable lodge, and it's worth the small investment. Few resorts can rival the Grove Park Inn's legacy and physical appearance. From F. Scott Fitzgerald to George Bush to Beau Bridges to Tammy Wynette, the Grove Park Inn's list of guest luminaries is unsurpassed in its depth and variety. There's something extremely special about staying in a room just a corridor away from where Fitzgerald wrote short stories and articles. Today, guests come to The Grove Park Inn from all over the world to relax in the well-appointed rooms, eat in the fine restaurants, dance in the nightclub or relax with a drink on the balcony overlooking Asheville.

But this is a book about golf, not hotels, right? So let's talk about this wonderful course. If you're an architecture fan, the first thing you'll notice is that this track was built in a remarkably tight area — covering just 80 acres. Just as remarkable is the fact that very few of the holes are noticeably tight. The front nine is predominantly flat, while the back nine, which is closer to the hotel, makes greater use of the slope beneath the inn. The greens vary in shape, size and slope. Errant tee and approach shots risk landing in bunkers, but the course is not overly penal. Water comes into play mostly on the front nine. The yardage book is a useful guide if you're playing the course for the first time.

As you might expect from a course touched by Donald Ross's hand, it provides tremendous variety and interest. Every hole has its own character and charm, including the 9th, supposedly one of Bobby Jones's favorites. It's a lengthy, tight par 3 with a long green fronted by three flat bunkers — a great way to finish the front nine.

But the layout is only a part of the story here. Golfers who have played here include such greats as (the aforementioned) Bobby Jones, Ben Hogan, Jack Nicklaus, Arnold Palmer, Fuzzy Zoeller and Walter Hagen. There's a wonderful story about Ben Hogan scoring 11 on the par 3 7th and 4 on the par 5 8th; fable has it that his expression never changed.

From about the mid-'20s to the mid-'50s, the course was a stop on the PGA Tour. During that period, many of the pros would come to the inn for the summer and play for big bucks with the wealthy guests here to escape the heat of the cities. So when you play at The Grove Park Inn, you're walking in the footsteps of giants.

Finally, let's not forget that the course is closing in on 100 years; there are few courses with such magnificent views and maturity. One of the magnificent views will be you as you putt on the 17th green in full view of the guests in the Sammons Wing. You can play at the Grove Park Inn without staying at the hotel; but that's a lot like visiting the Metropolitan Museum of Art without taking a look at the Renoirs.

Amenities include a practice green, rental clubs, a locker room, bar, snack bar, restaurant, beverage cart and pro shop.

You can walk after 3 PM . . . if you're fit. You can book a tee time whenever you choose. Approximate cost, including cart, is $60 weekdays and weekends.

HIGH HAMPTON
INN AND COUNTRY CLUB

N.C. Hwy. 107 S., Cashiers

Inn	*(800) 334-2551*
Pro Shop	*743-2450*
Blue Yardage: 6012	
Slope: 120	*Par: 71*

The golf course at High Hampton Inn and Country Club opened in 1923. According to *Architects of Golf*, J. Victor East designed the original layout. However, the course has been redesigned twice by George Cobb; once in 1958 and again in 1980 with the help of John LaFoy. Some of the holes are flat, but most include undulations. Bentgrass covers the fairways and greens.

General public play at this fine old course is limited to after noon. Guests at the inn can play anytime.

High Hampton offers a mature track with plenty of variety. Its most remarkable feature is the yardages. For example, the par 5 No. 3 measures a significant 572 yards; next up is the par 4 No. 4, just 229 yards. This pattern is repeated often. But don't be fooled into thinking the short holes are easy. You'll be shooting to small crowned greens that become extremely fast in the spring and fall. On the longer holes, including two monster

Profile: Dan Maples

Dan Maples, son of Ellis Maples, lives in Pinehurst. Dan was born in 1947 and was president of the American Society of Golf Course Architects in 1990. Before Dan had his driving license, he was handling earth-moving equipment, helping his father build golf courses.

Photo: The Architects of Golf

He attended Wingate Junior College and earned a bachelor's degree in landscape architecture from the University of Georgia in 1972. During the summer months, when he was not studying, Dan helped his father build golf courses. After two years as a professional at Palmetto Country Club, Dan joined the family firm and became a full partner after two years. In the early 1980s, he began his own firm based in Pinehurst. One of Dan's first designs, Oyster Bay Golf Links, was chosen by *Golf Digest* as the best new resort course in 1993. Dan's hobby is researching the history of course construction in Pinehurst.

Dan Maples

Maples is part of the ownership group at Longleaf, a course he designed. In Pinehurst, he also designed The Pit Golf Links. The two courses couldn't be more different, so it's difficult to characterize Dan's design philosophy — although both courses are challenging and fun. (Some would disagree that The Pit is a *fun* golf course.) Dan seems to enjoy, on just one hole, placing a tree right in the middle of a fairway or anywhere it's likely to cause the most trouble. He has designed a number of well-known courses in the Carolinas, including Cramer Mountain, Keith Hills, Marsh Harbour Golf Links, The Pearl Golf Links, Woodlake, Heritage Plantation and The Witch. He has also designed courses in Alabama, Georgia, Hawaii, Spain, Germany, Virginia and Tennessee.

Dan Maples is in mid-career now, but you can be sure that by the time he's finished designing courses, he'll be rated as one the best.

par 3s, you'll still find that the greens are not overly large. So, you'll need to be accurate to score well. The course presents a variety of fairway widths. You'll also find some imaginative tee sites. Interestingly, the course is devoid of bunkers, and water only comes into play on a few holes, most noticeably on the par 3

No. 8, where you might be tempted to take more club than you actually need.

Even if your golf isn't going too well, enjoy the setting; it has to be one of the finest of any public course in the mountains. Woods border a number of the holes, mountain streams crisscross the track, and there are wonderful views of the surrounding peaks from the elevated tees. You might think that 6012 yards isn't the longest course, but there are some significantly long holes where your drive through the chute has to be long and accurate. Don't be fooled by the distance; the course is tough enough for all levels of golfer. One throwback to the 1920s is the lack of yardage markers. Just like Ben Hogan and others of that era, you'll be on your own when it comes to choosing clubs — no cart-mounted laser-guided yardage aids here. Most holes offer a 150-yard marker, but that's it. It's rather interesting having to estimate yardage on your own.

Amenities include a practice green, range, chipping green, snack bar, bar, restaurant, locker room, rental clubs and a pro shop.

The course is walkable, you can walk anytime and you should walk. If you're not staying at the inn, you can only book a tee time one day in advance. Approximate cost, including cart, is $48; it's $37 if you're staying at the inn.

LAKE JUNALUSKA GOLF COURSE
19 Golf Course Rd.

Waynesville	*456-5777*
Championship Yardage: 4962	
Slope: No rating	*Par: 68*
Men's Yardage: 4579	
Slope: No rating	*Par: 68*
Ladies' Yardage: 3792	
Slope: No rating	*Par: 68*

There's evidence of the first nine holes of a golf course as far back as 1919; a new nine was added in 1993. The architect of the front nine is unknown, but Jim Moulin produced the back. The course is well-maintained, and efforts are ongoing to improve it. It's primarily wide open and set in rolling terrain. You'll find bluegrass in the fairways and bentgrass on the greens.

Lake Junaluska Golf Course is owned and operated by a conglomeration of Lake Junaluska Assembly, SEJ Administrative Council and the United Methodist Church. So if you want a beer with your mid-round hot dog, forget it. In fact, the brochure clearly states that the course has a "No alcohol — no profanity" policy. Two retired ministers serve as part-time rangers and golf-course maintenance experts. We played with one of the ministers who, at age 72, could still drive the ball more than 270 yards. And that's after having had surgery on three of his vertebrae!

This friendly course is an interesting old track with small greens. If the ground is hard, you'll have to take one less club than normal and let the ball run onto the greens. If you miss a green, you'll have to negotiate a tough chip or pitch up an embankment. A small pond and the occasional mountain stream come into play. You'll especially enjoy the 135-yard par 3, where the winds can sweep off the lake and influence a short shot to one of the smallest greens in Christendom. You might be tempted to think that the course is too short to be fun, but think otherwise.

There's plenty of entertainment here, and if you're not satiated after your round, you can pick up a copy of *Tee-Ology*, a book by John Freeman about golf's lessons for Christians and other seekers: a bargain at $10. If you like unmolested old courses without any gimmicks, take a look at this track.

Amenities include a practice green, snack bar, rental clubs and a pro shop.

The course is walkable anytime. You can book a tee time whenever you choose. Approximate cost, including cart, is $21.

LAKE TOXAWAY COUNTRY CLUB
353 W. Club Blvd.

Lake Toxaway	*966-4020*
Championship Yardage: 6234	
Slope: 122	*Par: 71*

Men's Yardage: 5594
Slope: 116   *Par: 71*
Ladies' Yardage: 4627
Slope: 109   *Par: 71*

If you want to play on this course, you have to stay at the inn.

The golf course at Lake Toxaway opened in 1960. According to *Architects of Golf*, R.D. Heinitsh designed the original layout. However, John LaFoy redesigned the course. LaFoy is a well-known architect who has designed fine tracks throughout the southeast. LaFoy apprenticed under George Cobb and made frequent visits to Augusta National to study the design. When Cobb was slowed by illness, LaFoy took over many well-known Cobb projects, including Linville Ridge. Most of the holes on the course are bordered by woods. The layout is undulating, with a number of significant elevation changes. You'll find bluegrass in the fairways and bentgrass and poa annua on the greens.

Lake Toxaway's course is well-designed and in a beautiful environment.

The course starts with a bang: a 445-yard par 4 uphill to a raised green fronted by a mean bunker. Is there a more difficult opening hole in western North Carolina? Things become a little more lenient on the rest of the front nine, but you'll find plenty of traps — some in the fairways, some around the greens. Most of the holes on the front boast just one bunker, but it's placed in a difficult spot and will force you to think about how heroic you plan to be on your approach shot: proof that you don't need a multitude of bunkers to make a hole interesting and challenging. Some bunkers have steep faces. The greens are midsize to large, crowned and sloped, with subtle undulations. The fairways are of a sensible width. Some of the greens are flanked by steep embankments, usually on the opposite side of the bunker. Note the Astroturf cart path next to

the green on No. 10: Is this still a free drop?

Things get more difficult on the back nine. First, there on more bunkers and some steeper embankments. On the 11th hole (where the Wards and their canine, Mulligan, live) you'll find a relatively gentle par 4. Then begins a long and treacherous series of holes, including a 429-yard par 4, a 659-yard par 5 and a 230-yard par 3. So don't be lulled into a state of semi-catatonic complacency when, upon first glance at the scorecard, you see a mere 6234 yards from the tips.

The course will be fun and entertaining for golfers of all levels. Go ahead and splurge on a night at the inn and enjoy yourself on this wonderful track. You'll love the golf as well as the opportunity to relax on the veranda overlooking the 10th tee, as you recount the gory details of your round, tell a few lies, collect on the bet and sip a cold beer.

Amenities include a practice green, range, chipping green, locker room, bar, snack bar, restaurant, rental clubs, a beverage cart and pro shop.

The course is walkable for the fit, and you can walk anytime. Book your tee with your room. Approximate cost, including cart, is $62.

MAGGIE VALLEY
RESORT AND COUNTRY CLUB

340 Country Club Rd.
Maggie Valley   926-1616
Championship Yardage: 6336
Slope: 121   *Par: 72*
Men's Yardage: 6031
Slope: 118   *Par: 72*
Other Yardage: 5344
Slope: 111   *Par: 72*
Ladies' Yardage: 4645
Slope: 105   *Par: 72*

The golf course at Maggie Valley opened in 1963. William Prevost Sr. designed the course, although *Architects of*

Golf also credits Emmett Mitchell as a designer. The course is relatively open, with trees defining the fairways on which you'll find bluegrass; on the greens, you'll find bentgrass. You'll also find it easiest to get a tee time at Maggie Valley if you're staying at the resort.

The advertisements exclaim: "You gotta meet Maggie!" And indeed you should. The 2-mile stretch of tourist traps that partly make up the town of Maggie Valley may lead you to think that the course is similar in its attitude towards aesthetics. Don't worry; the golf course at Maggie Valley is one of the better and prettier courses in the area. It has hosted four N.C. Open Championships, the women's state senior championship, the Western North Carolina PGA Assistant Pro Championship and a host of other competitions.

The back and front nines are quite different. The front winds along the valley floor, while the back is much hillier and presents some fine views from some of the tee boxes. Perhaps the front nine is a little tighter off the tee, although you might not notice a big difference. Problems come in the form of the streams that crisscross the course; take a good look at the layout on the scorecard and make a note of where the streams are. The bunkers are large and flat and will influence your approach shots. The greens are rolling, and a few are two- or even three-tiered; on some of the putting surfaces, just the slope and pitch will give you fits. The scorecard gives you green depths, which is useful considering the vastness of the greens. Despite all the hazards and undulations, Maggie is not overly penal, and you'll be able to score well here if you keep your game under control. In any case, you'll find excellent variety and interest here at Maggie Valley.

Amenities include a practice green, range, chipping green, locker room, bar, snack bar, restaurant, rental clubs, a beverage cart and pro shop.

The course is walkable for the fit, and you can walk after 2:30 PM. Book your tee time with your stay at the resort. Approximate cost, including cart, is $48 (the highest mid-season rate).

MEADOWBROOK GOLF CLUB

Meadowbrook Rd.
Rutherfordton   863-2690
Championship Yardage: 6378
Slope: 110   *Par: 72*
Men's Yardage: 5850
Slope: 105   *Par: 72*
Ladies' Yardage: 5208
Slope: 108   *Par: 75*

Meadowbrook, a Willie B. Lewis design, opened in 1964. The course is set on rolling terrain, with bermudagrass fairways and bentgrass greens. Some of the holes are open, others are bordered by woods.

This fun and relatively straightforward course has a mountain feel to it. If you hate bunkers, you'll love this course — there are none. Except for a few narrow fairways, you won't find a great deal of trouble off the tee. This is especially true on the front nine, which is more open than the back. Don't be fooled by the clubhouse: It looks like a hay storage facility. But the course is set in pretty surroundings and has a pleasant and peaceful ambiance not usually found on purely public courses. Credit the ever-underrated Willie B. Lewis. The greens are predominantly midsize to large, with subtle undulations. There's plenty of water to contend with from a mountain stream as well as a pond on two holes. This track is certainly worth a look if you're fond of courses with a traditional feel.

Amenities include a practice green, locker room, snack bar, restaurant, rental clubs and a pro shop.

You can and should walk anytime.

You can book a tee time whenever you choose. Approximate cost, including cart, is $20 weekdays and $25 on weekends.

MILL CREEK COUNTRY CLUB

100 Mill Creek Rd.
Franklin   524-6458
Championship Yardage: 6167
Slope: 115   *Par: 72*
Men's Yardage: 5775
Slope: 113   *Par: 72*
Ladies' Yardage: 4483
Slope: 113   *Par: 72*

Mill Creek Country Club opened in 1968. After numerous queries and additional research, we've discovered that no one knows who designed this course (Do you?). The layout is primarily wide open with some elevation changes. In the fairways and on the greens, you'll find bentgrass.

This mecca of golf in Franklin is a fun and straightforward course with plenty of challenge for golfers of all levels and abilities. The fairways provide various widths. The greens are small to midsize and protected by flat bunkers that could prove disastrous if your bunker technique isn't up to snuff. The greens are sloped. The most notable landscaping feature is the preponderance of mature willow trees, some of which come into play. You'll have some fine mountain views, particularly from the elevated tees. If you're in the area, stop by the course for a fun round.

Amenities include a practice green, chipping green, snack bar, rental clubs and a pro shop.

You can walk the course after 2 PM. Book a tee time two days in advance, if you wish. Approximate cost, including cart, is $38.

RED FOX COUNTRY CLUB

2 Club Rd.
Tryon   894-8251
Championship Yardage: 7104
Slope: 136   *Par: 72*
Men's Yardage: 6393
Slope: 124   *Par: 72*
Other Yardage: 5705
Slope: 111   *Par: 72*
Ladies' Yardage: 5286
Slope: 118   *Par: 73*

Red Fox Country Club opened in 1966. Ellis Maples designed the course — an open track, with woods and houses bordering some holes. In the fairways, you'll find bermudagrass; on the greens, bentgrass.

Red Fox is an excellent example of Ellis Maples' architectural talent. Maples took a pretty piece of land and turned it into a fine country golf course. The fairways are wide, and the greens are large and sloped; there are plenty of bunkers, mostly around the green complexes. (These are basic details that match many of Maples' courses.) The beauty of the course comes from the layout — the sweeping doglegs, the variety of shots you have to play and the subtle shaping of the large flat bunkers.

It's difficult to describe the essence of a fine old Maples course, so we recommend that you play this track and take in its attractions. Play it from the Red Fox tees (the tips) and you'll be in for a long day. If you're in for less of a challenge, choose the Other tees.

Amenities include a practice green, range, locker room, snack bar, rental clubs and a pro shop.

You must take a cart here, but you can book a tee time whenever you choose. Approximate cost, including cart, is $30 weekdays and $35 on weekends.

REEMS CREEK GOLF COURSE

Pink Fox Cove Rd.
Weaverville   645-4393
Championship Yardage: 6477
Slope: 130   *Par: 72*
Men's Yardage: 6106
Slope: 127   *Par: 72*

Photo: Clay Nolen

Hound Ears Club is one of the many magnificent courses in the North Carolina Mountains. George Cobb designed the course.

Other Yardage: 5357
Slope: 119   *Par: 72*
Ladies' Yardage: 4605
Slope: 114   *Par: 72*

Reems Creek Golf Course, a Martin Hawtree design, opened in 1989. This is a mountain track, and you'll find plenty of significant elevation changes. Most of the holes are open, and a few are bordered by woods. Bentgrass blankets the fairways and covers the greens.

Martin Hawtree is from England and is the third generation of the Hawtree family, famous for its fine and prolific designs, most of which are in the British Isles. Martin Hawtree has a doctorate in Land Planning from Liverpool University. His father, Fred, designed nearby Mount Mitchell Course. *Architects of Golf* lists European PGA Tour player Simon Gidman as an assistant in the design of Reems Creek.

Reems Creek is Martin Hawtree's only golf course in America. After playing it, you might be thankful that there isn't a second effort anywhere. It's a challenging track that's a sort of hybrid mountain/links course. The result is a difficult course that will test every aspect of your game and make you use every club in your bag.

The serious elevation changes mean that you'll often have to negotiate a serious uphill or downhill shot. The lack of length means that you'll be playing some target golf as well. If the bentgrass rough is grown up to any extent, then the fairways will play narrower than they look. Hit a straight drive and you're still not out of trouble. Your approach shot to the large green needs to be placed just right if you're going to score par. Some of the greens, particularly on the back nine, must slope up to six or seven feet from back to front. In fact, in our opinion some greens verge on being unfair. So make sure you check the pin placement and hit your approach shots to the sensible portion of the green. Oh, you'll also find plenty of mounding to help define the fairways and green complexes. Bunkers are everywhere as well, and Hawtree has taken a page out of Robert Trent Jones's book and made them cloverleaf-shaped. There are some grass bunkers around some of the greens as well.

Reems Creek seems to be a much admired and talked-about course among the local golfing population. If you're looking for a very challenging modern course in the Asheville area, you'll get all you can handle at this impressive track.

Amenities include a practice green, range, snack bar, grill, rental clubs and a pro shop.

You must use a cart at Reems Creek. You can book a tee time whenever you choose. Approximate cost, including cart, is $38 weekdays and $42 on weekends.

SAPPHIRE MOUNTAIN GOLF CLUB

30 Slicers Ave.
Sapphire   743-1174
Championship Yardage: 6147
Slope: 119   Par: 70
Men's Yardage: 5690
Slope: 118   Par: 70
Ladies' Yardage: 4515
Slope: 112   Par: 70

The course used to be called Holly Forest. The management attributes the current design to Ron Garl, although *Architects of Golf* attributes the design to Tom Jackson. Most of the holes are bordered by woods. The course is owned and operated by LinksCorp. You'll find bentgrass on the greens and in the fairways.

There are two other courses in the Cashiers area with the name Sapphire. Sapphire Mountain is the only course bearing the Sapphire nomenclature that's open to the public. The first thing you'll notice about the course is the somewhat bizarre routing, which must have been changed from the original. As your round progresses, you'll see that perhaps the re-routing was completed to produce the remarkable par 3s that define this course. Each one has its own character, and each is dramatic. For example, on the 203-yard 4th hole, you'll smack your tee shot to a green with a large rock on the left and a steep embankment to the right and front; and it's only the No. 14 handicap. Go figure. The 15th hole, just 138 yards, features an undulating island green. Although the par 3s are worth the price of admission, the 401-yard par 4 No. 14 is surely one of the most dramatic golf holes in the mountains. You have to drive from an elevated tee to a narrow landing area with a stream on the left-hand side. Your approach shot will travel to a significantly elevated two-tiered green. Miss the green to the right and your ball will be swallowed by a waterfall. A dramatic and difficult hole, par here is a good score. Overall, good variety, bizarre routing, tricky greens and some large bunkers will make your golfing life difficult and interesting. Oh, and if the greenskeeper lets the rough grow, then finesse shots become more difficult. In an area where most of the courses are private, Sapphire Mountain provides a modern public course in a pleasant setting.

Amenities include a snack bar, rental clubs, a locker room, bar, restaurant, beverage cart and pro shop.

Walking is not permitted here. You can book a tee time 30 days in advance. Approximate cost, including cart, is $25 weekdays and weekends.

SPRINGDALE COUNTRY CLUB

200 Golf Watch Rd.

Canton	*235-8451*
Championship Yardage: 6812	
Slope: 126	*Par: 72*
Men's Yardage: 6437	
Slope: 121	*Par: 72*
Other Yardage: 5734	
Slope: 113	*Par: 72*
Ladies' Yardage: 5421	
Slope: 121	*Par: 74*

All 18 holes at Springdale Country Club opened in 1970. Joseph Holmes laid out the original course, and according to the staff at Springdale, Fred Tingle revised the track. Most of the course is set in rolling terrain and includes some decent elevation changes. You'll find rye grass fairways and bentgrass greens.

The fairways vary in width. The greens vary in shape, but most are fairly large and undulating. A number of changes are under way, including the construction of a new practice putting green, the renovation of the practice range and the rede-

sign of all bunkers. Springdale also recently hired a full-time PGA professional as Director of Golf.

You don't have to stay at one of the guest cottages or at the inn to play here, but we recommend it. The resort is family-owned and operated and, according to the staff, enjoys strong repeat visits. The focus here is golf. As the brochure firmly states: "Here, the game of golf reigns supreme; no pools, spas or tennis courts." Hear, hear!

The golf course is a challenging mountain track with plenty of variety. Play it all the way from the back and you're in for a long day. Play it from the front and the course is kinder and gentler. Some fairways are narrow and bordered by woods, while others are wide and more forgiving. The back nine is more open than the front. You'll enjoy driving the ball from some of the elevated tees. We reviewed the course before the renovation of the bunkers, so we can't fairly comment on bunkering. The greens are midsize and sloped. Streams come into play on some of the holes. Overall , Springdale is a beautiful and fun course that will provide a challenge for any golfer.

And just in case you're worried about playing too slowly, each golf cart is equipped with an egg timer.

Amenities include a practice green, range, chipping green, locker room, snack bar, restaurant, rental clubs, a beverage cart and a pro shop.

You can walk anytime (if you can hack it . . . it's *not* advisable!). You can book a tee time whenever you choose. Approximate cost, including cart, is $35.

WAYNESVILLE COUNTRY CLUB INN

Country Club Dr.

Waynesville	*452-4617*

Carolina/Dogwood Course
Championship Yardage: 5798
Slope: 103   Par: 70
Men's Yardage: 5395
Slope: 100   Par: 70
Ladies' Yardage: 4927
Slope: 103   Par: 70

Dogwood/Blue Ridge Course
Championship Yardage: 5803
Slope: 105   Par: 70
Men's Yardage: 5258
Slope: 100   Par: 70
Ladies' Yardage: 4565
Slope: 100   Par: 70

Blue Ridge/Carolina Course
Championship Yardage: 5943
Slope: 104   Par: 70
Men's Yardage: 5493
Slope: 100   Par: 70
Ladies' Yardage: 5002
Slope: 104   Par: 70

Golfers started swinging at Waynesville Country Club Inn in 1926. According to *Architects of Golf*, the course has an interesting design history. Little known is the fact that Donald Ross designed the initial routing. John Drake finished the construction of the course. Ross Taylor revised the layout. Then Tom Jackson arrived to add the third nine and revised the course in 1989. If you ask in the pro shop who designed the course, they'll tell you it was Tom Jackson. In the fairways, you'll find bluegrass; on the greens, you'll find bentgrass.

The inn here is a magnificent structure. You can get on the course even if you're not staying here, but you'll probably find it easier to get a tee time if you are. You can also rent a condo or vacation cottage, or whatever it's called these days. All sorts of packages are available.

Due to the invasion of a tournament, we were unable to look around the course, but we were informed that the Carolina course is predominantly flat, the Dogwood nine is hillier, and the Blue Ridge course is even hillier still. All three nines

are relatively open, with trees delineating the fairways. The greens are on the small side of medium; they are sloped with all sorts of subtle undulations. You won't find a huge number of bunkers on the course, but you will have to negotiate a stream that meanders lazily through the tracks. We're also told that the elevated tees provide excellent views. Based on the design, the pedigree and the quality of the inn, you'll definitely want to take a look at the courses here at Waynesville Country Club Inn.

Amenities include a practice green, locker room, bar, snack bar, restaurant, rental clubs and a pro shop.

Walking is restricted. You can book a tee time with your reservation or one day in advance. Approximate cost for 18 holes, including cart, is $41.

Boone/Blowing Rock Area

BOONE GOLF CLUB

Fairway Dr.
Boone   264-8760
Championship Yardage: 6401
Slope: 120   Par: 71
Men's Yardage: 5859
Slope: 112   Par: 71
Ladies' Yardage: 5172
Slope: 103   Par: 75

Boone Golf Club, an Ellis Maples course, opened in 1959. The course is flat in places, rolling in others, with bentgrass fairways and greens.

At Boone Golf Club we found a formidable and mature Ellis Maples design that's close to Boone and well worth a visit. One of Maples' sons, Joe, was formerly the head pro here. Ellis Maples had been an architect for just six years when the Boone club was built, and you'll see many of the features that later came to be standards on his other fine courses.

You won't find a great deal of trouble

off the tee, but it will help to be long from the tips. Trees border many of the fairways. The greens are midsize and undulating — in fact, we noticed some buried elephants on a couple — so make sure your approach shots are well-placed. You'll also find some intelligent and sneaky bunker placement around the greens. A couple of small tributaries of the New River come into play on some holes.

If you're in Boone and looking for a fine Ellis Maples' design, drop by for 18 holes. You won't be disappointed. The club boasts about 500 members.

Amenities include a practice green, a restaurant, rental clubs and a pro shop.

Nonmembers can walk after 2 PM. You can book a tee time seven days in advance. Approximate cost, including cart, is $40 weekdays and $45 on weekends.

HAWKSNEST SKI AND GOLF

2058 Skyland Dr.	898-5135
Seven Devils	(800) 822-4295
Championship Yardage: 6244	
Slope: 117	Par: 72
Men's Yardage: 5953	
Slope: 110	Par: 72
Other Yardage: 5181	
Slope: 102	Par: 72
Ladies' Yardage: 4799	
Slope: 120	Par: 72

Hawksnest opened in 1965. A committee of local residents designed the course. Most of the holes are bordered by woods. In the fairways, you'll find bluegrass; on the greens, you'll find bentgrass. If you arrive at the course and it's dumping snow, leave your sticks in the car, strap on your skis and head for the slopes above the first tee.

Standing on the area just outside the pro shop, with the course spreading out below, you might think that this layout is wide open. It isn't. Place your driver in the trunk of your car unless you can keep the ball extremely straight: If you miss the fairway, you're in the thick woods and reaching into your bag for a fresh ball. Narrow fairways aside, Hawksnest proves that designing a golf course by committee can work successfully. With the mountainside above you and magnificent views from some of the tees, this course is surely one of the most striking in the mountains. You'll find a pleasant mix of flat holes and those with elevation changes, which include terraced fairways. The greens are medium-size and sloped just enough to make for some tricky putts. Miss the green and you may find your ball in a bunker, but it's more likely that you'll be playing from the well-prepared chipping areas. It's always nice to find a course that rewards skillful chipping. To score well here, choose less club than you think you'll need off the tee, keep your ball in play and shoot for the middle of the greens.

Amenities include a practice green, range, chipping green, locker room, snack bar, rental clubs and a pro shop.

You can walk after 6 PM if you've got the stamina. You can book a tee time seven days in advance. Approximate cost, including cart, is $32 weekdays and $36 on weekends.

HOUND EARS CLUB

N.C. Hwy. 105 S.
Blowing Rock   963-5831
Championship Yardage: 6165
Slope: 122   *Par: 72*
Men's Yardage: 6036
Slope: 120   *Par: 72*
Other Yardage: 5639
Slope: 115   *Par: 72*
Ladies' Yardage: 4959
Slope: 110   *Par: 73*

The golf course at Hound Ears Club, designed by George Cobb, opened in 1963. We found a pleasant mix of open and wooded holes. The fairways are covered with bluegrass; the greens, bentgrass.

You can't walk off the street and play at Hound Ears; you must stay at the well-appointed lodge. It may be worth your while if you're looking for a first-rate mountain resort, away from it all in a peaceful and pampered setting. Both the course and the lodge seem to be extremely popular with the well-to-do seasoned-citizen set. And with good reason: The golf course is a fine example of an excellent mountain track. Some of the holes are flat, while others offer dramatic elevation changes. The fairways are predominantly wide, and the greens are large and undulating. The three-tiered 12th green, a par 5 hole, must surely be one of the most difficult in western North Carolina; a three-putt is an accomplishment. Most of the greens are built-up and protected by bunkers that should only be a hazard if the pin is placed nearby and you play for the pin. Hit your approach shot to the middle of the green and you'll be fine. As for water, there's the Watauga River and a tributary stream; both come into play on a number of holes. There's also a pond on the back nine that could prove irritating. Make sure you look at the card.

We would be remiss if we failed to describe, or at least tried to describe, the general ambiance of the course. The mountains rise above you, streams burble as you pull your club back, you drive your cart under ancient and cool rhododendron bushes, and you feel relaxed and at ease with the world. Until, sadly, you pull your tee shot into the woods.

Amenities include a practice green, range, snack bar, rental clubs and a pro shop.

The course is walkable for the fit, and you can walk before 8 AM and after 6 PM. Book your tee time in conjunction with the lodge. Approximate cost, including cart, is $48 weekdays and weekends.

JEFFERSON LANDING

N.C. Hwy. 16-88
Jefferson   (910) 246-5555
Championship Yardage: 7111
Slope: 121   *Par: 72*
Men's Yardage: 6424
Slope: 115   *Par: 72*
Other Yardage: 5720
Slope: 109   *Par: 72*
Ladies' Yardage: 4960
Slope: 103   *Par: 72*

The golf course at Jefferson Landing opened in 1991. Dennis Lehmann and Larry Nelson designed the course; you may know Dennis Lehmann as the associate of Jack Nicklaus responsible for Elk River in Banner Elk — a private course rated as one of the finest in North Carolina. The course, for a mountain track, has a remarkably wide-open feel; also remarkable is its occasional flatness. In the fairways, you'll find an interesting combination of bluegrass and fescue; on the greens, you'll find Pencross bentgrass.

First, a note about the resort and the development. At Jefferson Landing, you can purchase a preexisting home or homesite, stay at the well-appointed lodge or rent a townhouse for a week . . . it's up

Photo: Asheville Convention and Visitors Bureau

Mountain golf courses are among the prettiest in the Carolinas, particularly in the fall. Not all mountain courses feature steep terrain.

to you. And you can enjoy an adult beverage or two. We mention that because Ashe County is as dry as the Sahara Desert when it comes to adult beverages.

And, of course, you can play golf. The layout, while relatively fresh, is straightforward and well-designed. There are no trick holes; there are no frivolously designed holes. There's plenty of water in the form of streams and ponds, but it doesn't always come into play. Quite a few tee boxes provide dramatic downhill tee shots. From the back tees, at a whopping 7111 yards, the course will give you all the challenge you want and then some: Water comes into play more often from the tips.

The strength of the course lies in its tremendous variety — again, not in tricks or gimmicks. What you see is what you get from the tee as well as with respect to your approach shots. The well-kept Pencross bentgrass greens provide an excellent example of why this type of green should be the grass of choice on putting surfaces in the next century: It's true, resilient, fair and easier to maintain than pure bentgrass. The greens are medium-size, as are the bunkers protecting them, and are flattish and tricky. The management is in the process of planting a large number of trees on the course to help define the fairways. Overall, Jefferson Landing is worth a visit if you're looking for a fine mountain golf course with good amenities and pleasant surroundings. Aim for the middle of the fairway and the middle of the green and you'll enjoy your round.

Amenities include a practice green, range, chipping green, snack bar, rental clubs, a beverage cart and pro shop.

The course is not walkable. You can book a tee time whenever you choose. Approximate cost, including cart, is $39 weekdays and $49 on weekends (including Fridays).

MOUNTAIN AIRE GOLF COURSE

1104 Golf Course Rd.
West Jefferson   (910) 877-4716
Championship Yardage: 6107
Slope: No rating   Par: 71
Men's Yardage: 5571

Slope: No rating	Par: 71
Other Yardage: 4935	
Slope: No rating	Par: 71
Ladies' Yardage: 4143	
Slope: No rating	Par: 71

Strangely, no one seems to know when Mountain Aire opened or who designed the course. It *is* known that the course is primarily open in design and features some dramatic topography. In the fairways, you'll find bluegrass; on the greens, you'll find bentgrass.

Deep in the heart of Jefferson County, you'll find Mountain Aire perched on the side of a significant and pretty mountain. The result is a course with stunning elevation changes, most noticeably on the 452-yard par 4, where you tee off from what seems like the top of a cliff. The left side of the fairway features an embankment dotted with grassy pot bunkers — a unique hole. Also interesting is the 2nd hole — a par 3 listed as 89 yards, although it may be even less.

We looked hard to find a hole here that's flat . . . we couldn't find one. Thus expect to hit either uphill or downhill on just about every shot. The greens are predominantly small and slightly sloped. Overall, Mountain Aire is a pleasant course, affording fine views and some challenging holes.

Amenities include a practice green, range, snack bar and rental clubs.

The course is walkable for the physically fit, and you can walk anytime. You can book a tee time whenever you choose. Approximate cost, including cart, is $28 weekdays and $32 weekends.

MOUNTAIN GLEN GOLF CLUB
N.C. Hwy. 194
Newland   733-5804
Championship Yardage: 6723
Slope: 129   Par: 72
Men's Yardage: 6195

Slope: 119	Par: 72
Ladies' Yardage: 5506	
Slope: 110	Par: 72

Mountain Glen Golf Course opened in 1964. This George Cobb design features rolling, relatively open terrain, with trees delineating the bluegrass fairways. The greens are bentgrass.

Mountain Glen is an example of a Cobb resort/vacation course with excellent routing. Cobb believed that this type of course should be more straightforward and less fraught with difficulty than a country club course that a member might play many times a year. After all, you're on vacation! If you still want a challenge, play it from the back tees. Actually, the course is quite long from the Ladies' tees.

The fairways are medium-width, and the greens are medium-size and sloped, with subtle breaks. Mountain streams comprise most of the water hazards. There's plenty of bunkering around the greens, so plan your approach to avoid them. Most of the bunkers are built to catch shots that are wide and short. If you don't like the look of a bunker, take an extra club or two. This is a fun and relatively challenging course that's worth the price of admission. An interesting local rule is that no beginning golfers are allowed on the course on weekends and holidays before 4 PM. A good move.

Amenities include a practice green, chipping green, locker room, snack bar, rental clubs and a pro shop.

The course is pleasantly walkable, and you can walk anytime (hooray!). You can book a tee time seven days in advance. Approximate cost, including cart, is $35 weekdays and weekends.

OLDE BEAU GOLF CLUB
U.S. Hwy. 21
Roaring Gap   (910) 363-3333
Championship Yardage: 6705

Slope: 131	Par: 72
Men's Yardage: 6264	
Slope: 129	Par: 72
Seniors Yardage: 5720	
Slope: 120	Par: 72
Ladies' Yardage: 4960	
Slope: 118	Par: 75

The golf course at Olde Beau opened in 1990. Billy Satterfield designed and owns the course and the surrounding development. Olde Beau features some significant elevation changes, and woods border most of the holes. In the fairways, you'll find an interesting combination of bluegrass and rye; on the greens, you'll find bentgrass.

Olde Beau is named after Beau the dog — the apple of Satterfield's eye. There's a memorial to Beau next to the 15th green. Satterfield must have enjoyed Beau's company because the course named in honor of his canine friend is one of the most magnificent testaments to golf and golf course architecture in the mountains. It's open for limited public play; once all the lots have been developed, it may become members only. It's actually easier to get to the course from Charlotte and the Triad than from the central mountains. Go ahead and make the trip from wherever you are.

Mr. Satterfield is not a well-known designer; in fact, this may be his only course. But Olde Beau is certainly evidence that you don't have to be a big-name architect to produce a stunning course. You'll be faced with a variety of shots off the tee and an even wider array of approach shots. The fairways vary in width; the green complexes, in size, shape and bunkering. Each shot requires thought and planning. Our advice is to steer clear of the trouble and take the bailout options — where they exist!

The front nine is challenging enough to make you happy after just nine holes. But the course really begins on the 10th tee, when you leave the snack bar with hot dog and adult beverage in hand. The 12th, 13th, 14th and 15th holes are breathtaking in their intensity, design, complexity and views. These holes are literally built on the side of a mountain. The panorama from the 15th green, where Olde Beau rests in peace (save the occasional "Fore!"), is unlike any other in the mountains. It's worth the price of admission to say that you scored a par on this tough target hole. The 17th hole, a severe dogleg left with a severe drop off, is a memorable par 5. After your round, relax with a drink in the fine clubhouse and reflect on the memory of Olde Beau and his amazing legacy.

Amenities include a practice green, range, chipping green, locker room, bar, snack bar, restaurant, rental clubs and a pro shop.

The course is not walkable and you must use a cart. You can book a tee time two weeks in advance. Approximate cost, including cart, is $40 weekdays and $50 on weekends (including Fridays).

THE VILLAGE OF SUGAR MOUNTAIN GOLF COURSE

Village of Sugar Mountain	
Banner Elk	898-6464
Championship Yardage: 4488	
Slope: 94	Par: 64
Men's Yardage: 4198	
Slope: 91	Par: 64
Ladies' Yardage: 3470	
Slope: 90	Par: 64

The golf course at Sugar Mountain opened in the early 1970s, according to local legend. The staff here did not know who designed the course, and we couldn't glean any information from our typically reliable text sources; but if we could warrant a guess, it might be Russell Breeden.

Some holes are set in open terrain, while others are wooded. The course is primarily flat, with some minor elevation changes. Fairways are bluegrass; greens, bentgrass.

Sugar Mountain is best known as one of the largest ski areas in the Southeast. It's still small by Western standards, but it's very popular and often very crowded. A large, multistory concrete-sided building, which looks like an East German apartment complex, is annoyingly perched on top of the mountain and must surely win the prize for the structure most deserving of the wrecking ball.

Architectural snafus aside, the Village of Sugar Mountain offers a fine and somewhat unique golf course. This par 64 course is defined by its nine varied, interesting and thoroughly hazardous par 3s. The other holes offer decent length and width off the tee, although a few are tighter. It looks like little earth was moved during construction. A couple of streams provide hazards, as do some large bunkers. The greens are built-up and medium-size; they are primarily sloped and slightly undulating. This friendly course is a good place for the beginner and interesting enough for the better and more experienced player who will be happy to keep the score close to par. Overall, Sugar Mountain is a course where residents and visitors alike will have a lot of fun.

Amenities include a practice green and rental clubs.

The course is walkable, and you should walk here; we were told that several octogenarians keep themselves going by walking the course on a regular basis. Hey, maybe it'll work for you. You can book a tee time five days in advance. Approximate cost, including cart, is $29 weekdays and $30 on weekends.

Hickory/Lenoir Area

GRANADA FARMS

10 River Dr.	
Granite Falls	396-2313
Championship Yardage: 6661	
Slope: 121	Par: 72
Men's Yardage: 5835	
Slope: 112	Par: 72
Ladies' Yardage: 4821	
Slope: 103	Par: 72

According to *Architects of Golf*, Granada Farms opened in 1978, although the pro shop staff cite a somewhat earlier date. Tom Jackson designed the course on rolling terrain. Some of the holes have an open feel, while others are bordered by woods and houses. Bermudagrass blankets the fairways; bentgrass covers the greens.

A well-struck 4-wood from the textile mills of Granite Falls sits Granada Farms Country Club, a housing development with one of Tom Jackson's first solo designs. Since this effort, Jackson's stock has risen: The houses around his golf courses are bigger, the mounds around the greens are more ominous, the greens are more demonic and the distance from the back tee has increased.

Granite Farms is a good example of why Jackson became such a hot designer in the Carolinas. You'll also see the links elements that have continued to define Jackson's work since the construction of Granada Farms. The fairways here are mostly wide, with bunkers and the occasional mound coming into play. The greens are midsize to large, and the green complexes include a multitude of bunkers, mounds and hollows. Water comes into play on a few holes and is ingeniously employed. The course is certainly worth a look if you're in the area, especially if you're a fan of Tom Jackson.

Amenities include a practice green,

range, locker room, snack bar and pro shop.

The course is walkable (amazing for a Tom Jackson course), and you can walk after noon on weekends and anytime during the week. You can book a tee time whenever you choose. Approximate cost, including cart, is $20 weekdays and $23 on weekends.

GRASSY CREEK
GOLF AND COUNTRY CLUB

101 Golf Course Rd.
Spruce Pine   765-7436
Championship Yardage: 6277
Slope: 120   Par: 72
Men's Yardage: 5744
Slope: 116   Par: 72
Ladies' Yardage: 4797
Slope: 109   Par: 72

Grassy Creek opened the first nine holes in 1956 and the next nine holes in 1966. The course is laid out on rolling terrain. Fairways combine bluegrass and bentgrass; greens are bentgrass.

At Grassy Creek we found a fine, mature course that's more challenging than it looks. Hit a long or wild hook off the first tee, and your ball will land smack in the middle of a McDonald's drive-through. After this, the course becomes a lot prettier. It's predominately tight off the tee, although you can escape by hitting onto the adjacent fairway. The greens are sloped, sometimes crowned, and small to midsize on the front nine and slightly larger on the back. Many of the greens are protected by bunkers of various sizes and shapes. Some of the greens are flanked by steep embankments. A mountain stream comes into play on some holes. Have a go here if you're looking for a relaxed outing.

Amenities include a practice green, range, chipping green, locker room, snack bar, restaurant, rental clubs and a pro shop.

You can walk this course anytime except Saturday before noon. You can book a tee time seven days in advance. Approximate cost, including cart, is $32 weekdays and $35 on weekends.

LENOIR GOLF COURSE

N.C. Hwy. 18
Lenoir   754-5093
Championship Yardage: 6385
Slope: 112   Par: 71
Men's Yardage: 5886
Slope: 106   Par: 71
Ladies' Yardage: 4943
Slope: 103   Par: 71

Lenoir Golf Course, a Donald Ross design, opened in 1927. Lenoir is not only open, it's one of the flattest courses you'll see anywhere outside the coastal plains. You'll find bermudagrass on the fairways and bentgrass on the greens.

This course has a strong membership, so much so that it restricts public play on weekends. Our advice is to take a sick day and spend some time at this fine old course. The staff in the pro shop said that a few changes have been made to the original design. Nevertheless, you'll find plenty of examples of what made Ross "The Man" when it came to golf course architecture and why so many of today's modern earth-moving designs seem superfluous. There's tremendous beauty in simplicity, and plenty of difficulty as well. Ross designs have stood the test of golfing time, and this course is an excellent example.

This course is so open, in fact, that wayward drives will find the next fairway and still leave you a shot at the green. The greens are small and sloped and often flanked by one or two simple, flat bunkers. We challenge you to get up and down from one of them! There aren't that many relatively unmolested Ross designs around and even fewer that are open to the public. If you're a Ross fan, you'll want to play this course. It's also a great value.

Amenities include a practice green, locker room, bar, snack bar, restaurant and pro shop.

You can walk anytime and you won't need a tee time during the week. Approximate cost, including cart, is $22.

MARION LAKE CLUB

N.C. Hwy. 126	
Nebo	652-6232
Championship Yardage: 6110	
Slope: No rating	Par: 70
Men's Yardage: 5710	
Slope: No rating	Par: 70
Ladies' Yardage: 4826	
Slope: No rating	Par: 74

The first nine at Lake Marion opened in 1923; the second nine opened in the early 1970s. The track is set in rolling terrain. In the fairways, you'll find 421 bermudagrass; on the greens, you'll find common bermudagrass. No one is certain about who designed this course, although a staff member said many knowledgeable golfers believe that the layout of the original nine smacks of Donald Ross, and the second nine is the work of Russell Breeden.

Here at Lake Marion, you'll find a country course in a pleasant setting. The older holes, on the back nine, feature small greens, and you can run the ball up to the hole if the ground gets hard. The greens are generally medium-size on the front and often flanked by steep embankments that you'll want to avoid. The back nine features some pretty views of the lake. The 14th hole features a tee shot near a very pretty house just 30 yards from the tee. This popular course is worth a visit.

Amenities include a practice green, range, locker room, snack bar and pro shop.

You can walk this course and book a tee time whenever you choose. Approximate cost, including cart, is $39 weekdays and $49 on weekends.

MOUNT MITCHELL GOLF CLUB

7590 N.C. Hwy. 80 S.	
Burnsville	675-5454
Championship Yardage: 6475	
Slope: 121	Par: 72
Men's Yardage: 6110	
Slope: 116	Par: 72
Ladies' Yardage: 5455	
Slope: 117	Par: 72

Mount Mitchell Golf Course opened in 1975. Fred Hawtree designed the course on a valley floor, thus it's predominantly flat. You'll find bentgrass in the fairways and on the greens.

Fred Hawtree is the son of Frederic George Hawtree, well-known in the United Kingdom as one of the great designers in the first half of the 20th century. Fred Hawtree continued his father's design excellence. After a distinguished record in World War II, including a stint as a POW in a Japanese camp, Hawtree designed and built numerous courses in England and France in addition to a few in Germany, Iran, the Netherlands, South Africa, Spain, Switzerland and Wales. Mount Mitchell is his only course in the United States. Fred Hawtree's son, Martin, continued the architectural firm and is, himself, a

Half your shots are played with your putter. Is half your practice time spent with putter in hand?

prolific designer. You can see an example of Martin's (demonic) work at Reems Creek Golf Course just north of Asheville in Weaverville (see the write-up in this chapter).

Comparing Reems Creek to Mount Mitchell is like comparing the musical artist formerly known as Prince to Mozart. Whereas Reems Creek is a masterpiece of modern earth-moving prowess, Mount Mitchell is a kinder, gentler course. Rumor has it that Ben Wright and Charlie "Choo-choo" Justice had houses on the course at one stage. Justice would sit on his porch and let golfers know how the putts were breaking.

The routing is magnificent. There are no bad holes, and each shot requires thought and a degree of precision. The holes have a gentle shape and appearance yet are quite challenging, due mostly to the tightness off the tee and the potential for big score disasters posed by mountain streams and several bunkers. It's probably one of the prettiest public courses in the mountains. As you drive up to the course through the winding mountain road and come upon the crosscut fairways, you can't help drooling a little at the sight.

The key to scoring well here is keeping the ball in play. If you're wild with your driver, lock it in the trunk and rely on your short game to keep you out of the big number dog house. The greens offer a great deal of variety. Some are sloped, others are tiered, others still are undulating.

Even though the course is a little remote, take time to get here, particularly in the fall, when the greens are lightening fast and the trees blaze with color.

Amenities include a practice green, locker room, snack bar, restaurant, rental clubs and a pro shop.

The course is walkable for the fit, and you can walk after 1 PM Monday through Thursday. You can book a tee time two weeks in advance. Approximate cost, including cart, is $40 weekdays and $45 on weekends.

ORCHARD HILLS GOLF CLUB

Colony Springs Rd.
Granite Falls   728-3560
Championship Yardage: 6134
Slope: 111   Par: 72
Men's Yardage: 5673
Slope: 106   Par: 72
Ladies' Yardage: 4803
Slope: 105   Par: 74

W. Pitts designed Orchard Hills, which opened in the 1950s. The course is set on undulating terrain, with bermudagrass fairways and bentgrass greens.

At Orchard Hills, we found a mature, sloped and predominately open course, with a number of uphill shots. You won't find a lot of trouble off the tee. There is a small stream that comes into play on a few holes and a pond could affect one hole. The greens are midsize and sloped, and you'll find some bunkers protecting them.

Amenities include a practice green, range, chipping green, locker room, snack bar and pro shop.

You can walk anytime during the week and after 2 PM on weekends. You can book a tee time as early as Tuesday for the following weekend. Approximate cost, including cart, is $22 weekdays and $26 on weekends.

QUAKER MEADOWS GOLF CLUB

N.C. Hwy. 181
Morganton   437-2677
Championship Yardage: 6704
Slope: 111   Par: 71
Men's Yardage: 6133
Slope: 108   Par: 71
Ladies' Yardage: 5625
Slope: No rating   Par: 71

The golf course at Quaker Meadows opened in 1969. This Russell Breeden design is open and primarily flat, including bermudagrass fairways and bentgrass greens.

We failed to find any Quakers, but we did find a fine, well-designed Breeden course. Typical of a Breeden track, we found little trouble off the tee, save the occasional stream or out-of-bounds area. The greens are classic Breeden: large, undulating, sloped and flanked by well-shaped and strategically-placed bunkers which vary in intensity depending on pin placement. The course is clearly popular with the local golfing population and with good reason — it's playable, fun and challenging, without being tricked up. At par 71, the course offers significant distance from the tips. Only one hole presents a significant water hazard.

Amenities include a practice green, range, locker room, snack bar, restaurant, rental clubs and a pro shop.

You can walk this course anytime except weekends before 2 PM. Book a tee time whenever you choose. Approximate cost, including cart, is $20 weekdays and $24 on weekends.

Around the Mountains...

Fun Things To Do

North Carolina's mountains present a playground unlike any other. It's perfectly possible to not play golf here and still find plenty to do.

Hang on. Did we really say that?

Let's try again. You'll find plenty to do here once you've finished playing golf.

That's better.

Once you've finished playing, try mountain biking, antique hunting, roller coasters and horseback riding. In fact, there's enough going on to fill a book, and we suggest *The Insider's Guide® to North Carolina's Mountains* as an excellent resource. Look for it at fine bookstores, call (800) 716-1388 to order a copy or use the handy order form at the back of this book.

Here are just a few major attractions that you shouldn't miss if you're in the mountains:

In Boone, check out **Horn in the West,** 264-2120, an outdoor drama depicting the trials and travails of those who settled the North Carolina mountains, including Daniel Boone. It's two hours of history and entertainment rolled into one. The season lasts from mid-June to mid-August.

Tweetsie Railroad, between Boone and Blowing Rock, is a great place to take the family. In addition to the 100-year-old locomotive there's much to see, do and sample, including a petting farm, Mouse Mine #9, caramel apples and a Ferris wheel and other rides. Call (800) 526-5740 for more information. The season runs from May to Labor Day.

If you're not particularly claustrophobic, **Linville Caverns** is an entertaining option. The caves were initially discovered by Native Americans in the 1820s. The limestone caverns also served as hideouts for Civil War deserters. It's a great place to see some serious caves and experience total darkness when the guides cut the lights. Call 756-4171 for more information.

For those of you who prefer life in the fast line to life underground, the **New Asheville Speedway** in Asheville (surprise!) will satisfy your need for speed. This short track used to be a regular NASCAR stop; despite the absence of the big boys, it's still competitive. Enjoy racing action every Friday night from April to September. The speedway's slogan, "Each year,

Photo: NC Travel and Tourism

Springtime in the mountains is a great time for golf.

80,000 fans buy seats, but they only use the edge," sums it up. Call 254-4627 for more information.

There are quite a few "touristy" spots in the North Carolina mountains, and Maggie Valley might be the most touristy of them all. One of the major attraction here is the well-known **Ghost Town in the Sky**, Soco Road, 926-1140 or (800) GHOST TOWN. You must take the incline railroad or a chair lift to get here. The Wild West theme is accentuated by gun fights, jail breaks, bank robberies, country music and Indian dances. You'll also find more than 20 rides, including the Red Devil roller coaster. There is also tons of food to eat, most of it deliciously loaded with calories. The Ghost Town in the Sky is open 9 AM to 6 PM from May to October.

No trip to Asheville is complete without a visit to what many must consider North Carolina's premier attraction, the **Biltmore House**. The aforementioned *Insiders' Guide® to North Carolina's Mountains* devotes an entire chapter to the Biltmore Estate — and justifiably so. George Vanderbilt completed this magnificent château in 1895, and the home is still in the possession of his descendants who graciously open it to the public. In addition to the house, check out the estate's winery; some currently produced wines are gaining significant praise from wine connoisseurs. The Biltmore House itself boasts more than 225 rooms, 50 of which are open to the public.

There are plenty of annual events but perhaps the best time to see the estate is during the Christmas holidays when the house is decorated in a fashion that will drop your jaw. You'll also find four places to eat: **Deer Park Restaurant**, the **Stable Cafe**, the **Winery Cafe** and **The Bistro**.

For more information about the Biltmore Estate, call (800) 543-2961.

WATERFALLS

No trip to the mountains is complete without a trip down a waterfall. Or if you're not the type to envelop yourself in a barrel and take the plunge, then at least you should go see one. It's probably safer. A number of golf courses in the mountains feature waterfalls of various shapes and sizes — often where you least expect them. Following is a selection of non-golf course waterfalls:

Avery County: Elk Falls' 65 feet of power cascade into one of the largest post-waterfall pools in the mountains. Travel north on U.S. Highway 19 E. to Elk Park. Turn right on Elk River Road and proceed 4 miles to a parking area next to the Elk River. Hike the short trail to the falls.

Burke County: One of the best-known of all mountain waterfalls, **Linville Falls** tumults down the deep Linville Gorge. The upper and lower falls are equally dramatic. Access Linville Falls at milepost 316.3 on the Blue Ridge Parkway, where there's a visitors center for your convenience.

Transylvania County: One of the most accessible of all mountain waterfalls, **Looking Glass Falls** is also one of the prettiest. It's on U.S. Highway 276, 5.5 miles into Pisgah Forest and the junction with U.S. Highway 64. Your total hike from car to view and back may be less than 30 feet.

Jackson County: You're an eight-hour drive to the beach, so take what you can get and lounge and sunbathe on the sand next to the pool at the foot of **Silver Run Falls**. Why not bring your 60-degree wedge and practice getting out of bunkers? Drive south from Cashiers on N.C. Highway 107 for 4 miles. Park at the gravel-covered pull-off on the left. Follow the short path to the falls.

BLUE RIDGE PARKWAY

One of the most remarkable attractions, if we could call it such, is the Blue Ridge Parkway. Construction began in 1935, part of a government project designed to employ then-unemployed people during the Great Depression. The roadway links Great Smoky Mountains National Park in North Carolina and Shenandoah National Park in Virginia. Thus a large portion of the Parkway winds through the North Carolina mountains. In some cases, it's a useful if somewhat circuitous route to some of the golf courses. Mount Mitchell Golf Course, for example, is just a few miles from the Parkway.

Cruising this picturesque roadway provides some of the greatest motoring pleasure anywhere. As you enter, a sign reads "No Commercial Vehicles;" thus, your journey will not be cluttered by the inevitable fast food joints and tourist traps that are sadly all too common on other mountain roads. It's the sort of road that makes you wish for an Italian sports convertible with a close-ratio stick shift, a rocket under the hood and a suspension so tight that you go around curves like you're on rails. This is real motoring.

Regularly during your trip, you'll be tempted to stop at one of the wonderful overlooks to take in the view. There are also numerous trails and picnic tables for your convenience. Like the mountains themselves, the Parkway changes dramatically by season. Enjoy the colorful fall. Get up early in the morning and rise above the clouds. Dip into morning fog so thick you can't see five feet in front of you. But drive safely; if you're in the driver's seat, keep your eyes on the road and your hands upon the wheel. Catch the views at the overlooks, not from behind the wheel.

The Parkway emergency number is (800) 727-5928. For general Parkway information, call 298-0398.

SKIING

It's actually quite a good idea to plan a trip with both golf and skiing in mind — if you're that ambitious. If it's cold, then it's quite likely that the course you came to play will be closed. If it's warm, then you won't be able to ski but will be able to play golf.

Skiing in the North Carolina mountains is not like skiing in the West. Most of the time, 99 percent of the snow is man-made and tends to get pretty icy. If there's real snow, it may be wet — which will turn icy in the late-afternoon shadows. About once every five years a winter of big storms will create optimal snow conditions, even if the runs tend to be a little short. We're sure you've heard that a bad day on the golf course is better than a good day in the office. Well if you take the same attitude about skiing in the North Carolina mountains, you'll be just fine.

The major ski areas include:

Hawksnest Golf and Ski Resort, 1800 Skyland Drive, Banner Elk, 963-6561, offers 11 slopes: two beginner, five intermediate and four advanced, with a 619-foot vertical drop. The golf course here is interesting too (see our review in this chapter).

Beech Mountain Ski Resort, Beech Mountain, 387-2011, is the highest ski resort in eastern North America, at approximately 5,500 feet. It's got quite a complex attached to it, including shops, ski rental, restaurants, an ice rink and a nursery. There are 14 slopes in all with a vertical drop of 830 feet. Ample accommodations are available as well at the resort.

Sugar Mountain, Banner Elk, 898-5421, is 5,300 feet above sea level and there are 18 slopes. Tackle the whopping (for North Carolina) 1,200-foot drop over and over again until the lactic acid buildup makes your quadriceps scream "No more!" Plenty of chair lifts assure you won't have to wait too long between runs. Ski rentals, lessons, lockers, a nursery and a cafeteria are available.

Appalachian Ski Mountain, Blowing Rock, 295-7828, is a family-owned resort that's been in business since 1962. There are eight slopes with a vertical drop of 365 feet. Check out the giant fireplace in the Bavarian-style lodge overlooking the slopes.

Where to Eat

There are hundreds of excellent restaurants in the mountains. While we're confident that the head pro at the golf course you're visiting can provide a sound dining recommendation, here are a few places you might want to go to celebrate that 76 you just posted (even if it was for nine holes). Be aware that America's bout with temperance lives on in full force in a number of counties in the North Carolina mountains. If you're in the mood for a bottle of claret to wash down your steak, you might be out of luck. *In vino non veritas.*

FAMOUS LOUISE'S
ROCK HOUSE RESTAURANT
U.S. Hwy. 221
Linville Falls   765-2702
$-$$ No credit cards

Louise's Rock House sits right on the border of three counties: Burke, McDowell and Avery. While this might lead to an intra-county identity crisis, it also leads to good food in a storied atmosphere. The building used to be a Prohi-

bition-era roadhouse before becoming a restaurant.

The food here is primarily down home. Menu items include pork loin, country-style steak, roast beef, turkey with all the fixins', fried chicken and a full complement of side dishes. There's also seafood delivered three times weekly from the coast.

TUMBLEWEED GRILL & MICROBREWERY
122 Blowing Rock Rd.
Boone   264-7111
$-$$

Tumbleweed serves up a great combination of fine Mexican food and excellent hand-crafted beer in an intimate atmosphere. Tumbleweed is popular and small, so you might want to make a reservation if you're on some sort of official schedule (but who *is* in the mountains?). Otherwise, enjoy an ale while you wait for your table.

At your table, why not enjoy another beer with your chipotle shrimp Caesar salad or Anasazi chicken sautéed with ancho chiles and goat cheese and rounded off with a Madeira wine sauce and tobacco onions. Yum! Have another beer, and the excess nature of your caloric intake will soon match the excess nature of the lies you'll be telling about how you got up and down for birdie from the stream on the back nine at Boone Golf Course. Yeah, right.

BOSTON PIZZA
501 Merrimon Ave.
Asheville   252-9474
$

Boston Pizza is about a John Daly drive away from the University of North Carolina at Asheville. There's a sort of college-campus beer-and-pizza ambiance to the place, which is also well-suited for families. When school's in session, and the weather is a little chilly, you'll probably run into a few students who look like they're right out of the Seattle "grunge" scene, donning oversize faded sweaters and Kurt Cobain look-alike three-day beard growth.

Alternative music scene aside, the pizza at Boston Pizza is wonderful. You can also devour subs and other Italian staples. This is a student hangout: Beer is never in short supply.

THE GROVE PARK INN
290 Macon Ave.
Asheville   252-2711
$$-$$$$

Even though your taste in accommodations might be on the lower end of the scale, we recommend that you splurge on the culinary delights at the Grove Park Inn, in part because there's a strong chance (particularly if you ask) that your table may overlook the golf course. You'll be dining next to a Donald Ross masterpiece. And you'll be dining in the hotel with the greatest golf history outside of Pinehurst. There are other places for blowouts in Asheville, but this one has golf attached to it. You can eat just a stone's throw away from where golfing giants once smacked the ball around.

You'll find three restaurants: Blue Ridge Dining Room, Sunset Terrace and Horizons. Book a tee time on Sunday afternoon and precede your best-ever round with the awe-inspiring brunch in the Blue Ridge. Or have lunch at the Sunset Terrace, with its wonderful views, after an early morning round. Perhaps you're entertaining guests for golf and dinner at Horizons. . . . It's hard to miss here.

LOUIE MICHAUD'S
MOUNTAIN BROOK CENTER
Mallard Sq.
Highlands   526-3573
$$-$$$

We'll risk the cliché, but there's something for everyone here at Louie

Michaud's: pasta, steak, ribs, lamb, chicken and big salads. Try the prime-rib buffet on Wednesday and the seafood buffet on Friday. There's also a belly-bulging brunch buffet on Sundays.

PEPPER'S RESTAURANT
2066 Blowing Rock Rd.
Boone   262-1250
$-$$

Pepper's has been well known in Boone for more than 20 years. Pepper's is particularly popular due mainly to the light, airy interior with its wooden floors and comfortable booths. The specialties here include seafood, pasta and sandwiches. Or try the mountain trout served à la Pepper.

RELIA'S GARDEN RESTAURANT
U.S. Hwy. 19-74
Bryson City   488-9186
$-$$

Relia's is just 20 minutes from Bryson City at the Nantahala Outdoor Center. You must cross a steel bridge over the Nantahala River to get to the restaurant. If the weather's right, you should sit on the open-air porch overlooking the herb and vegetable gardens which supply the restaurant. Talk about seeing what you're eating! Thus, you'll find a fresh touch here that few other restaurants can match. Go for the trout or one of the many vegetarian dishes.

Where to Stay

The variety of accommodations in western North Carolina is as massive as the mountains themselves. All the major chains have built a significant presence here. In addition, there are some wonderful old inns and hotels that date back

Photo: Ahseville Convention and Visitors Bureau

With severe elevation changes and superb views, golf in the mountains is both a challenge and a visual feast.

to the 19th century. Numerous small and intimate bed and breakfast inns dot the pastoral landscape. Many of the places to stay are affiliated with a golf course and can help you secure a tee-time.

THE SWITZERLAND INN
Blue Ridge Pkwy., MP 334
Little Switzerland   (800) 654-4026
$-$$$$

Just a well-struck 5-iron from the Blue Ridge Parkway, this fine old inn offers 55 rooms and outstanding view of the mountains. Enjoy fine dining here as well. It's a friendly place, and you'll end up meeting and mingling with other guests — perhaps even sharing a tee time at a local course. Fall is the peak season.

INN ON MAIN STREET
88 S. Main St.
Weaverville   645-3442
$

You can't miss the Inn on Main Street. It's the big, blue house on (you guessed it!) Main Street. The house dates back to 1900, when it was built as a combination office and home for Dr. Zebulon Richardson, a physician who may have left his practice every Wednesday afternoon for his customary and sacred 1:34 tee time. Who knows. The inn has been renovated recently, and the rooms are elegantly furnished with fine antiques.

THE PHELPS HOUSE
BED & BREAKFAST INN
W. Main St.
Highlands   526-2590
$

You'll find lots of charm in this modestly priced B & B that's close to all the fine golf courses in the area. The house dates back to 1885. Each room has a private bath. You'll get a massive and hearty

breakfast to push you along while you walk your 18 holes of choice.

DAYS INN - BLOWING ROCK
U.S. Hwy. 321 Bypass
Blowing Rock   295-4422
$$-$$$

This Days Inn offers a good value in an area replete with golf courses. Choose from a variety of configurations among the 118 guest rooms. Also enjoy the enclosed atrium with hot tub.

BEST WESTERN MOUNTAINBROOK INN
U.S. Hwy. 19   926-3962
Maggie Valley   (800) 752-6230
$$-$$$

In this busy tourist town, the Best Western offers a range of amenities including a pool, hot tub and your own personal rocking chair where you can sit, relax and watch the mountains. You're within walking distance of many of Maggie Valley's attractions.

THE BURGISS FARM
BED AND BREAKFAST
N.C. Hwy. 18
Laurel Springs   (910) 359-2995
$$

Innkeepers Tom and Nancy Burgiss have created a fun atmosphere and offer great hospitality. Additions to this 1897 farmhouse mingle Old World charm with modern conveniences like private baths, a massive great room, a wet bar and a large Jacuzzi room. All this means great privacy, which makes the inn quite popular with honeymooners.

Enjoy select items from Nancy's breakfast menu, which must be one of the most creative around. It features such delicacies as Hawaiian pancakes and baked fruit.

THE RAGGED GARDEN INN

Sunset Dr.
Blowing Rock   295-9703
$$-$$$

The first thing you'll notice at the Ragged Garden Inn is the stunning stone staircase in the grand hall. You'll also notice the English-style flower gardens and the chestnut bark siding found on older homes in this region. Innkeepers Joyce and Joe Villani tap into their extensive experience as restaurateurs in Connecticut and Florida to produce a sumptuous breakfast. Each of the inn's five guest rooms has a private bath. The inn is open from April to January; a good time to be here is in the spring when the garden is at its best.

ESEEOLA LODGE

U.S. Hwy. 221
Linville   733-4311
$$$$

The original Eseeola Lodge, destroyed by fire in 1936, opened somewhere near the turn of the century, and thus there's a great deal of history and tradition associated with this well-known establishment. The railroad made this remote section of the mountains somewhat accessible, and well-heeled vacationers made Eseeola a fine establishment frequented by the well-to-do of the Southeast. The rates, which in the middle of summer are upwards of $250 per night (including dinner and breakfast), are still geared toward the monied, so be prepared to shell out some serious plastic if you're going to stay here.

Still, it's well worth it if you enjoy excellent service, fine food and wonderfully appointed rooms. There are 29 rooms in all, most with private porches, surrounding a large main room with an inviting fireplace. Next to this main gathering room is the Lodge dining room. Gentlemen must wear a jacket and tie for dinner.

One of the biggest benefits of being a guest at the Lodge is access to one of the best golf courses in the Carolinas — Linville Golf Club. Golf packages are only available in May, June, September and October and are quite popular due to the quality of the course and accommodations. Donald Ross designed the course in 1924, and it's still relatively untouched. It's mostly flat with beautiful mountain views, small streams and somewhat narrow fairways. The greens can be some of the fastest anywhere in the spring and fall.

If golf is not your game, Eseeola offers tennis on clay courts, swimming and croquet. There are 2,000 acres for hiking and fishing and special recreation programs for children as well.

MAPLE LODGE

Sunset Dr.
Blowing Rock   295-3331
$$-$$$

If you're looking for a wonderful and homey place to stay in the mountains, look no further than the Maple Lodge. You'll find a place that's graceful, simple, elegant and convenient to Main Street in Blowing Rock and to the Blowing Rock Stage Company, which performs in the summer months.

There are 12 guest rooms at the Maple Lodge, and each room is named after a flower. Each room offers a private bath, and some even come complete with crocheted canopies — how about that for elegance! Your room fee includes a large breakfast that will set you up perfectly for the rest of the day. The spread includes muffins (homemade) and other breads, egg dishes and fresh fruit. The meal is served in the sun room, overlooking the flower garden. Innkeeper Marilyn Bateman will make sure your stay here is memorable and relaxing.

Photo: Bill Woodward

Wicked Stick's hole #5 is a beautiful par 3, but pay attention to the wind above the trees. Short and to the right is trouble. Bail out to the left. The mounds will act as a backstop for the long tee shot.

Inside
The Grand Strand
of South Carolina

The Grand Strand is a 60-mile stretch of coast which extends from Southport, North Carolina, to Georgetown, South Carolina. Anchored by the booming tourist resort of Myrtle Beach, the area includes more than 90 golf courses today, and enough are currently under construction to top the hundred mark well before the turn of the century. More than 3 million paid rounds are played here every year.

In addition to Myrtle Beach, the Grand Strand includes North Myrtle Beach and Little River in the northern part of South Carolina and Calabash and the Brunswick Island area in the southern part of North Carolina. Also, the Grand Strand stretches south from Myrtle Beach to Surfside, Murrells Inlet, Litchfield, Pawleys Island and Georgetown.

Golfing on the Grand Strand

The golf season on the Grand Strand is year-round, with the busiest and most expensive golf peaks being spring and fall. However, the busiest, thus most expensive, hotel season is summer, when families and students of all ages throng to the clean white sands of the public beaches along the Atlantic.

At least a hundred hotels offer golf packages that include accommodations, tee times and usually breakfast. Some will also package theater tickets or dinner if you are interested in a simple plan for the family. The golf package usually is the way to go,

unless you live here or own your own condo for annual golf vacation stays. In addition to the cost savings of a hotel's golf package, the convenience is built in. You can request that the golf director of the hotel book the room and the tee times. Hotels specializing in golf packages do staff a golf department where knowledgeable employees can book via computer on courses of your choosing or, on your first trip here, you may want to ask for the golf director's recommendations of the most convenient, most challenging, easiest or something in a particular price range.

We've listed most of the best courses; however, everyone's definition of the best course differs. Other courses are available, and still more will open over the next year; we'll list them in our next edition.

All courses on the Grand Strand have eight or more different rate periods during the year. Then within those periods, summer and winter specials, afternoon and twilight deals, coupon discounts, locals' rates or short-term memberships are sometimes offered. The greens fees listed here indicate the widest price range. The time of year and day will be reflected in each course's daily fees, and we recommend that you ask for details when you book your tee time directly. If you book through a hotel as part of a golf package, you will pay less than the daily fee. Several of the top-rated courses carry surcharges that are not itemized in packages; be sure to inquire when booking your golf

GOLF COURSES ON THE GRAND STRAND OF SOUTH CAROLINA

Course Name	Type	# Holes	Par	Slope	Yards	Walking	Booking	Cost w/ Cart
Angels Trace								
North Course	public	18	72	129	6216	call	anytime	$50
South Course	public	18	72	132	6442	call	anytime	$50
Arcadian Shores Golf Club	resort	18	72	131	6485	no	365 days	$20-78
Arrowhead Country Club								
Lakes/Cypress Course	public	18	72	122	6242	no	365 days	$23-79
Azalea Sands Golf Course	public	18	72	116	6287	yes	365 days	$20-54
Bay Tree Golf Plantation								
Gold Course	public	18	72	128	6390	yes	365 days	$34-55
Green Course	public	18	72	126	6492	yes	365 days	$35-55
Silver Course	public	18	72	122	6363	yes	365 days	$35-55
Beachwood Golf Club	public	18	72	117	6344	no	365 days	$2
Belle Terre	public	18	72	n/r	6666	no	395 days	$54-71
Blackmoor	public	18	72	118	6217	no	365 days	$32-81
Brunswick Plantation & Golf Links	semiprivate	18	72	124	6215	no	7 days	$30-55
Buck Creek Plantation								
Cypress/Tupelo Course	public	18	72	126	6306	no	365 days	$25-68
Meadow/Cypress Course	public	18	72	119	6211	no	365 days	$25-68
Tupelo/Meadow Course	public	18	72	119	6115	no	365 days	$25-68
Burning Ridge								
East Course	semiprivate	18	72	119	6216	no	365 days	$20-58
West Course	semiprivate	18	72	114	6237	no	365 days	$20-58
Caledonia Golf & Fish Club	public	18	70	115	6104	no	365 days	$51-96
Carolina Shores Golf & Country Club	public	18	72	122	6231	no	3 days	$25-55
Colonial Charters Golf and Country Club	semiprivate	18	72	119	6337	no	365 days	$24-49
Cypress Bay Golf Club	public	18	72	110	6101	yes	365 days	$20-58
Deer Track Golf resort								
North Course	semiprivate	18	72	121	6511	yes	365 days	$24-55
South Course	semiprivate	18	71	119	6143	yes	365 days	$24-55
Dunes Golf and Beach Club	private	18	72	130	6565	no	365 days	$100

Eastport Golf Club	public	18	70	III	5400	no	365 days	$24
Heather Glen Golf Links								
1 Red/2 White Course	public	18	72	110	6337	no	365 days	$25-81
2 White/3 Blue Course	public	18	72	109	6510	no	365 days	$25-81
3 Blue/1 Red Course	public	18	72	126	6427	no	365 days	$25-81
Heritage	public	18	71	122	6575	no	365 days	$52-72
Indigo Creek Golf Club	semiprivate	18	72	120	6185	yes	365 days	$20-38
Island Green Country Club								
Dogwood/Holly Course	semiprivate	18	72	III	5847	yes	365 days	$23-42
Holly/Tall Oaks Course	semiprivate	18	72	III	5864	yes	365 days	$23-42
Tall Oaks/Dogwood Course	semiprivate	18	72	III	5705	yes	365 days	$23-42
Legends								
Heathland Course	public	18	71	121	6190	no	365 days	$87
Moorland Course	public	18	72	130	6125	no	365 days	$87
Parkland Course	public	18	72	127	6425	no	365 days	$87
Litchfield Country Club	resort	18	72	130	6342	yes	365 days	$40-69
Long Bay Club	public	18	72	130	6565	no	365 days	$50-97
Marsh Harbour	public	18	71	121	6000	no	anytime	$52-72
Myrtle Beach National Golf Club								
North Course	public	18	72	109	6033	yes	365 days	$25-50
South Course	public	18	72	118	6089	yes	365 days	$25-50
West Course	public	18	72	113	6113	yes	365 days	$25-50
Myrtle West Golf Course	semiprivate	18	72	118	6191	no	365 days	$25-58
Myrtlewood Golf Course								
Palmetto Course	semiprivate	18	72	118	6495	no	365 days	$24-62
PineHills Course	semiprivate	18	72	119	6112	no	365 days	$24-62
Ocean Harbour Golf Links	resort	18	72	127	6592	no	7 days	$25-76
Ocean Isle Beach Golf Course	public	18	72	122	6146	yes	365 days	$20-43
Ocean Ridge Plantation								
Lion's Paw Golf Links	public	18	72	130	6457	no	anytime	$30-80
Panther's Run Golf Links	public	18	72	134	6706	yes	anytime	$30-80
Oyster Bay Golf Links	public	18	71	130	6560	no	365 days	$87Pawleys
Plantation Golf & Country Club	public	18	72	132	6522	no	365 days	$47-82

Course Name	Type	# Holes	Par	Slope	Yards	Walking	Booking	Cost w/ Cart
Pearl Golf Links								
East Course	public	18	72	132	6543	no	365 days	$69
West Course	public	18	72	131	6738	no	365 days	$69
Pine Lakes International Country Club	semiprivate	18	72	118	6522	no	365 days	$47-110
Possum Trot Golf Course	public	18	72	113	6388	yes	365 days	$32-57
Quail Creek Golf Course	semiprivate	18	72	116	6331	yes	365 days	$20-58
River Club	semiprivate	18	72	125	6240	yes	365 days	$40-74
River Hills Golf and Country Club	public	18	72	123	6400	no	365 days	$25-60
River Oaks Golf Plantation								
Bear/Fox Course	public	18	72	118	6314	no	365 days	$20-55
Fox/Otter Course	public	18	72	118	6345	no	365 days	$20-55
Otter/Bear Course	public	18	72	119	6425	no	365 days	$20-55
Robbers Roost Golf Club	public	18	72	129	6725	no	365 days	$29-40
Sea Trail Plantation & Golf resort								
Byrd Course	resort	18	72	126	6263	no	365 days	$34-58
Jones Course	resort	18	72	126	6334	no	365 days	$39-63
Maples Course	resort	18	72	117	6332	no	365 days	$34-58
Surf Golf and Beach Club	semiprivate	18	72	119	6360	no	365 days	$43-70
Tidewater Golf Club and Plantation	public	18	72	126	6000	no	365 days	$63-98
Tradition Club	public	18	72	n/a	6500	yes	365 days	$43-61
Waterway Hills								
Lakes Course	public	9	36	115	3001	yes	365 days	$29-54
Oaks Course	public	9	36	118	3080	yes	365 days	$29-54
Ravine Course	public	9	36	112	2579	yes	365 days	$29-54
Wicked Stick	public	18	72	n/r	6156	no	365 days	$30-65
Wild Wing Plantation								
Avocet Course	public	18	72	119	6614	no	365 days	$100
Falcon Course	public	18	72	117	6674	no	365 days	$100
Hummingbird Course	public	18	72	123	6310	no	365 days	$100
Woodstork Course	public	18	72	111	6598	no	365 days	$100
Willbrook Plantation Golf Club	semiprivate	18	72	127	6077	yes	365 days	$33-63
The Witch Golf Links	public	18	71	121	6011	no	365 days	$46-83

The Grand Strand of South Carolina

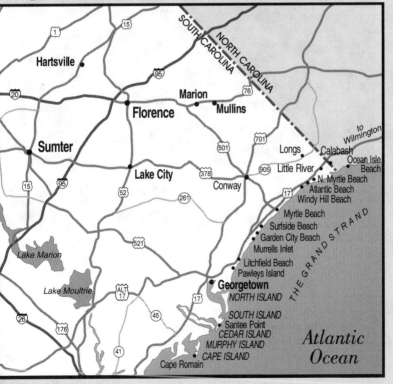

Photo: Wild Wing Plantation

Wild Wing's Wood Stork course was recognized by Golf Digest in the "Places to Play, 1994-95" as a Top 100 Great Value Course in America and a four-star award winner.

package. The package prices may not include that surcharge for certain courses, and you don't want any surprises taking a bite out of your budget. Most courses welcome walk-ons, yet they are sometimes so full that tee times are not available. Tee times are accepted up to a year in advance by most courses, and prebooking is recommended if you are picky about the course, day or time you play.

Ladies are welcome on all courses any day. Walking is permitted on certain courses, but not every day, so you should inquire specifically if that is your interest.

Refer to our list of accommodations for a few hotels that offer golf packages. For a complete listing, call **Myrtle Beach Golf Holiday** at (800) 845-GOLF. Do make reservations before your arrival. Maybe you remember the days of driving to the beach on a whim, arriving in the middle of the night and finding a room. Well, those days are long gone, folks. During certain weeks, which you might not even suspect, every single bed is full. In addition to the beach, the golf courses, the theaters and retail shops that attract tourists, conventions of all shapes and sizes bring the remainder of the area's 12 million annual visitors.

Getting around on the Grand Strand is fairly simple. Myrtle Beach itself is just a long, skinny island bordered on the east by the Atlantic Ocean and on the west by the Intracoastal Waterway. U.S. Highway 17, which we call Highway 17, stretches the length of the coast, and you can find a multitude of golf courses, restaurants and accommodations right on this route without any possibility of getting lost. Highway 17 is also called The Bypass where it branches and attempts to circumvent the main part of Myrtle Beach; and U.S. Highway 17 Business is called Kings Highway where it runs through the city. Both roadways run back together, so you still can't get lost no matter which north-south route you choose. Both route you by golf courses, as does almost any turn you take. Other main routes to the beach area from the west are S.C. Highway 9, referred to as Highway 9, and U.S. Highway 501. Many major golf courses also line these routes. And that's about all you need to know of our geography to get around just fine.

The greatest confusion tourists encounter is in learning that Myrtle Beach and North Myrtle Beach are two different cities, and both have their east-west streets labeled numerically and geographically. For instance, 17th Street could exist in four different places — north or south in either city. Remember to pay attention to the exact addresses in that respect.

One location you will need to find that isn't labeled is Restaurant Row. It's a 2-mile strip of some of the best restaurants around, just north of Myrtle Beach on Highway 17. Nowhere does a sign proclaim that you are there, but you'll know it; otherwise, any local can direct you. Refer to our list of some favorite places to eat all along the Strand and feel free to try others. Plenty of good food is a staple of our Southern hospitality.

If you should encounter heavy traffic, seemingly standing still on occasion, don't worry; it will only be a problem for a couple of miles, and probably only during happy hour and dinner hour, when locals just want to get home and visitors want to eat. You're probably on vacation anyway and don't need to rush to get anywhere. That same traffic is nowhere to be found when you're on the way to your early morning tee time. The minor traffic congestion, which is the major topic of locals' conversation, is nothing like that of a big city. However, the city leaders do recognize the need to bypass the bypass, and planning is under way to relieve traffic worries.

What to Bring

Bring your golf clubs, and that's all that matters, because that's the most important activity along the Grand Strand. Just wait — you'll see that golf really is our consuming passion. If you don't bring your clubs, or if a companion decides to take up the game while here, rental clubs are available at almost all courses.

Golf in the Carolinas is a vacation in more ways than one. The pace is slow, and our way of life is relaxed. You can pack casual attire and bathing suits for the summer. Or just buy it in the pro shop or at virtually any corner shop once you've arrived. Wear golf shirts and Bermuda shorts for golfing. Pack sweaters or jackets for winter trips. Don't worry about dressing up for dinner along the coast, because everyone is in the resort mode. Shorts are also acceptable dinner attire at many restaurants.

You might need your camera, because no one will ever believe the story about the alligator unless you can prove it.

You need to bring your family for sure. Even if you're planning a "strictly golf" trip, so much is available for non-golfer family members that everyone can have a good time. The beach is the most important attraction from sometime in March through November, with only a few cool days scattered throughout. Water parks and miniature golf are plentiful for the children's entertainment. World-class shopping abounds from basic malls to outlets and specialty shops. And country music performances and dinner shows delight the kid in all of us.

For complete information on the area, pick up a copy of *The Insiders' Guide® to Myrtle Beach and the Grand Strand*, available in bookstores nationwide or through the convenient order form in the back of this book.

Note that the area code for all South Carolina courses and businesses listed in this chapter is 803; for North Carolina courses and businesses it's 910.

Grand Strand Golf Courses

ANGELS TRACE GOLF LINKS
#2 Causeway Dr.
Ocean Isle Beach, N.C.   579-2277
North Course
Championship Yardage: 6640
Slope: 139   Par: 72

Men's Yardage: 6216
Slope: 129   Par: 72
Other Yardage: 4524
Slope: 115   Par: 72
Ladies' Yardage: 5316
Slope: 111   Par: 72

This public, 36-hole complex opened in November 1995. It's near The Pearl and a number of other popular courses on the southern edge of North Carolina where Calabash runs into Sunset Beach, which runs into Ocean Isle Beach. No houses are around the courses, and no noise or distractions will hinder your golf game here.

This Clyde Johnston course goes with the lay of the land with natural streams running through it. Gentle mounds and a few man-made ponds add to the character. No. 5 and No. 9 are bulkheaded. No. 5 is the signature. It's a par 4 dogleg left where the first shot is a placement shot and the second must carry over water. Traps are inside the fairway; two are in front and one on the side of the green, which is on a hill with oyster shells around it. At least nine holes have water coming into play. Some good long par 5s are here, and some require you to be careful where you hit. Tees, fairways and rough are bermudagrass, and greens are bentgrass. Fairway width varies from wide to narrow. It's a tough course, but popular for its playability. The average golfer will enjoy it.

Greens fees with cart cost an average of $50. Rates will vary during eight different seasons for the area's courses. Ladies are welcome anytime. Call for information about walking and amenities.

South Course
Championship Yardage: 6876
Slope: 139   Par: 72
Men's Yardage: 6442
Slope: 132   Par: 72
Other Yardage: 5590
Slope: 119   Par: 72
Ladies' Yardage: 4811
Slope: 122   Par: 72

Photo: Liz Mitchell

Jimmy D'Angelo is sometimes called Mr. Myrtle Beach Golf.

This course was also designed by Clyde Johnston and showed similarities to the North Course. Greens fees with cart average $50. No restrictions are placed on ladies' play. Call for more information; this course was just ready to open when this book went to press.

ARCADIAN SHORES GOLF CLUB

701 Hilton Rd.	449-5217
Myrtle Beach	(800) 248-9228
Championship Yardage: 6938	
Slope: 136	Par: 72
Men's Yardage: 6485	
Slope: 131	Par: 72
Other Yardage: 5994	
Slope: 116	Par: 72
Ladies' Yardage: 5276	
Slope: 117	Par: 72

This 18-hole course was designed by Rees Jones in 1974. It was rebuilt during 1994 and was in excellent condition and quite popular for the 1995 season. Arcadian Shores includes 64 creatively placed sand bunkers among natural lakes and elevated lush bentgrass greens. Water comes into play on eight holes. The fairways are wide and beautifully tree-lined. A challenging hole is No. 2, a 178-yard par 3. Your shot must travel over water and up a small hill to a fairly large green. The par 4 14th hole is one of the prettiest on the course. If your drive is lucky enough to make it to the top of a knoll, your ball will roll, leaving a relatively easy second shot over water to the green.

The course offers rental clubs, a driving range, practice green, pro shop, bar and restaurant. Ladies are welcome and encouraged by twilight clinics and discounted greens fee offered one afternoon each week during the summer. Also, locals are eligible for a special membership.

Greens fees average $78 and include cart. Walking is not allowed. Arcadian Shores accepts tee times 365 days in advance.

Arcadian Shores is affiliated with the oceanfront Hilton Hotel, and the golf course is across the street. The course is bisected by Hilton Road, which connects to U.S. 17 from the oceanfront.

ARROWHEAD COUNTRY CLUB

1201 Burcale Rd.	236-3243
Myrtle Beach	(800) 236-3243
Lakes/Cypress Course	
Championship Yardage: 6666	
Slope: 130	Par: 72
Men's Yardage: 6242	
Slope: 122	Par: 72
Other Yardage: 5713	
Slope: 115	Par: 72
Ladies' Yardage: 4812	
Slope: NA	Par: 72

Raymond Floyd and Tom Jackson unveiled this creation in November 1994. The first 18 of 27 holes opened with large bermudagrass greens and unique bermudagrass fairways due to numerous undulations, an unusual feature for a lowlands course, according to Floyd.

The nine-hole Lakes Course measures 3317 yards from the championship tees. The nine-hole Cypress Course measures 3349 yards among hardwoods standing in coastal wetlands.

The signature 13th hole is a beautiful 355-yard, par 4, crossing the water twice and overlooking the Intracoastal Waterway. The use of mounds, pristine woodlands and lakes coming into play on 17 holes makes the first 18 holes a challenging course. One of the tough holes is number two on the Cypress, a narrow par 5 with water on the left side of the tee shot, then a lay-up, then the green sits right on the edge of the water, and you cross it again.

The nine-hole Waterway Course opened in the fall of 1995. You guessed it; it also wraps along the snaking Intracoastal and calls upon all your skills to avoid water hazards.

The national trend toward 27-hole courses is growing, and the Arrowhead owners are delighted to have more to offer. They also promote their proximity to the airport for visiting golfers in a rush.

Arrowhead Country Club is the first Floyd signature course in South Carolina. Floyd won the GOLF MAGAZINE SENIOR TOUR Championship played in Myrtle Beach in November 1994, a very good year for him. He previously won three major U.S. championships, 22 events on the regular PGA tour and nine tournaments in less than two full years on the Senior Tour.

Jackson has been involved with 75 golf course projects, including design and construction of six Myrtle Beach area courses.

Rental clubs, a driving range, putting green, pro shop, locker room, bar and restaurant are available. No restrictions are placed on ladies' play.

Walking is not allowed at Arrowhead. Greens fees include cart and average $79. Tee times may be booked up to a year in advance.

AZALEA SANDS GOLF CLUB

U.S. Hwy. 17 S.	272-6191
North Myrtle Beach	(800) 253-2312
Championship Yardage: 6902	
Slope: 123	Par: 72
Men's Yardage: 6287	
Slope: 116	Par: 72
Ladies' Yardage: 5172	
Slope: 119	Par: 72

This 18-hole course, designed by Gene Hamm, was built in 1972. It's 6902 yards of golfing pleasure, according to Manager Dick Hester. Tifdwarf greens are set among lakes, bunkers and trees. One of the toughest holes is the 18th, a 540-yard par 5. Another challenging hole is a 195-yard par 3. The 5th hole requires a shot over a lake to a green well guarded by bunkers.

Amenities include practice greens, bar, snack bar, beverage cart, pro shop and rental clubs. No driving range is provided. No restrictions are placed on ladies' play.

The greens fee ranges from $20 to $54 and includes carts. The 12-month VIP membership for $25 is one great deal; with membership, a round costs $20. Azalea Sands accepts tee times 365 days in advance. Walking is allowed certain times of year, and a pull cart costs $3.

The course is centrally located just minutes from several of the largest golf equipment shops and a couple of miles from Barefoot Landing for lunch or dinner.

BAY TREE GOLF PLANTATION

S.C. Hwy. 9   249-1487
North Myrtle Beach   (800) 845-6191

You can't miss this golf course on Highway 9 because of its gigantic golf ball — which doubles as a water tower for the Little River area. Bay Tree has three 18-hole courses, all designed by George Fazio and Russell Breeden. In 1972, Bay Tree Golf Plantation was the first to build three courses simultaneously at the same site. It's a popular club for local memberships among the North Myrtle Beach crowd. All three courses have plentiful water hazards and bermudagrass fairways which are overseeded in rye during the winter.

The clubhouse offers a bar and restaurant at the 55th hole, a pro shop and men's and ladies' locker rooms. A driving range, practice green and rental clubs are available.

Greens fees range from $20 to $40, and carts are an additional $15. Check for afternoon specials. All accept tee times 365 days in advance, and walking is allowed.

Gold Course

Championship Yardage: 6942

Slope: 135	Par: 72
Men's Yardage: 6390	
Slope: 128	Par: 72
Ladies' Yardage: 5264	
Slope: 117	Par: 72

One of the most challenging holes on this course is the par 4 13th. Water runs down the entire left side of the fairway and behind the green. It also has a pond to the right of the fairway that may come into play. The 16th hole is interesting in that the tee and fairway flank Highway 9 in front of the towering golf ball. Several fairway bunkers may come into play with errant tee shots. The LPGA championship played on this course in 1977 was the first nationally televised tournament from the Grand Strand.

Green Course

Championship Yardage: 7044

Slope: 135	Par: 72
Men's Yardage: 6492	
Slope: 126	Par: 72
Ladies' Yardage: 5362	
Slope: 118	Par: 72

Insiders' Tips

Proper attire is required on most golf courses. Wear collared golf shirts and Bermuda shorts of standard length for summer dress. Socks are optional on most courses. Jeans, T-shirts, tank tops, short shorts and bathing suits are inappropriate attire.

*More than 4,000 golfers participate in the DuPont World Amateur
Handicap Championship played in Myrtle Beach*

The Green Course features narrow fairways. You're immediately initiated to the difficulty of this course on No. 1, a 563-yard par 5, where you must traverse water to reach a narrow green. Water comes into play on many holes, including the par 4 11th, where a hazard intersects the fairway. Your tee shot must lay up short of the water. The green is guarded by bunkers on the front and back.

Silver Course
Championship Yardage: 6871
Slope: 131   Par: 72
Men's Yardage: 6363
Slope: 122   Par: 72
Ladies' Yardage: 5417
Slope: 116   Par: 72

Bay Tree rebuilt and reshaped its Silver Course and reopened it in the fall of 1995. Greens, tees and traps were restructured and senior tees added. The fine Fazio design and undulations didn't change. The greens were made much larger and some trees removed. Target mounds behind some of the greens are helpful for approach shots. Many believe it to be the locals' favorite, and it's often preferred by women. Since Bay Tree opened its 54

holes, no major changes were made until the 1995 restructuring of the Silver Course; the Gold and Green courses are slated for overhaul during each of the next two years.

BEACHWOOD GOLF CLUB

1520 U.S. Hwy. 17 S.   272-6168
North Myrtle Beach   (800) 526-4889
Championship Yardage: 6825
Slope: 120   Par: 72
Men's Yardage: 6344
Slope: 117   Par: 72
Other Yardage: 5817
Slope: 115   Par: 72
Ladies' Yardage: 5052
Slope: 111   Par: 72

The 18-hole course, set between the Intracoastal Waterway and the Atlantic Ocean, as are many Grand Strand courses, was designed by Gene Hamm and built in 1968. Its lush fairways and bermudagrass greens meander through tall pines and lakes and host abundant native wildlife. The signature finishing hole, a par 3, plays 239 yards and calls for a long accurate shot to reach a green protected by three bunkers.

The practice facility is multifaceted, with two large greens, a driving range with multiple target areas, a chipping green and practice bunker. A complete pro shop, snack bar and lounge welcome you.

Greens fees range upward from $22. The course accepts tee times 365 days in advance. Walking is not allowed.

BELLE TERRE

U.S. Hwy. 501	449-4470
Myrtle Beach	(800) 340-0072

Championship Course

Championship Yardage: 7013	
Slope: Not rated	Par: 72
Men's Yardage: 6666	
Slope: Not rated	Par: 72
Other Yardage: 6274	
Slope: Not rated	Par: 72
Other Yardage: 5867	
Slope: Not rated	Par: 72
Ladies' Yardage: 5049	
Slope: Not rated	Par: 72

Belle Terre is planned as a 54-hole complex. Two championship courses and an 18-hole executive course all were designed by Rees Jones. The name Belle Terre (beautiful earth) came from Jones's description of the property. Each championship course measures a full 7000 yards. One championship course and the executive course opened in the fall of 1995. The executive course includes par 3s and 4s for an overall par 58. A new feature offered here is the motorized pull-cart for those who desire walking. The driving range is lighted and features rolling terrain and tees on each end.

"The soil and natural shape of the land allow for subtle elements of an old-style classic design, giving the holes clear definition so that a player can stand on the tee and have a clear perspective without using gimmicks. The subtleties make the course different every time you play it," Jones said.

Walking is not allowed on the Championship Course. Greens fees, with cart, are $54 to $71.

BLACKMOOR

S.C. Hwy. 707	
Murrells Inlet	650-5555
Championship Yardage: 6614	
Slope: 126	Par: 72
Men's Yardage: 6217	
Slope: 118	Par: 72
Other Yardage: 5774	
Slope: 111	Par: 72
Ladies' Yardage: 4807	
Slope: 115	Par: 72

This 18-hole course was built in 1990 and was the first in the Myrtle Beach area designed by Gary Player. Bermudagrass greens and fairways are always perfectly maintained. Several blind shots to the green will remind you to study the course layout. As with several on the southern end of the Grand Strand, Blackmoor was built on the site of a rice plantation along the Waccamaw River. The natural lakes, cypress trees and moss-draped oaks lend their tranquility to the course. From the back veranda of the clubhouse, you can oversee the finishing hole, listen to the birds and commune with nature.

The course includes a bar, snack bar, beverage cart, pro shop and rental clubs. Blackmoor offers a practice green and a chipping area as well as a driving range.

Greens fees range from a $32 summer rate to $81 during prime golfing season, with carts included. Walking is not allowed. Tee times are accepted 365 days in advance.

BRUNSWICK PLANTATION & GOLF LINKS

U.S. Hwy. 17	287-PUTT
Calabash, N.C.	(800) 848-0290
Championship Yardage: 6779	
Slope: 131	Par: 72
Men's Yardage: 6215	

Slope: 124	Par: 72
Other Yardage: 5791	
Slope: 118	Par: 72
Ladies' Yardage: 5210	
Slope: 115	Par: 72

The links-style course was designed by Willard Byrd and opened in 1992. Fairways are bermudagrass, and greens are bentgrass.

The signature hole is the 15th, a par 3 surrounded by oyster shells and water. It's a carry of 197 yards off the back tees over water. No. 4 is a long dogleg right, with water on one side and sand on the other.

Amenities include practice greens, driving range, pro shop, bar and snack bar, beverage cart and rental clubs.

Greens fees range from $30 to $55. Walking is not allowed.

BUCK CREEK GOLF PLANTATION

| S.C. Hwy. 9 | 249-5996 |
| North Myrtle Beach | (800) 344-0982 |

Cypress/Tupelo Course

Championship Yardage: 6865	
Slope: 132	Par: 72
Men's Yardage: 6306	
Slope: 126	Par: 72
Other Yardage: 5744	
Slope: 115	Par: 72
Ladies' Yardage: 4956	
Slope: 124	Par: 72

Meadow/Cypress Course

Championship Yardage: 6751	
Slope: 126	Par: 72
Men's Yardage: 6211	
Slope: 119	Par: 72
Other Yardage: 5688	
Slope: 111	Par: 72
Ladies' Yardage: 4972	
Slope: 117	Par: 72

Tupelo/Meadow Course

Championship Yardage: 6726	
Slope: 128	Par: 72
Men's Yardage: 6115	
Slope: 119	Par: 72
Other Yardage: 5574	
Slope: 115	Par: 72
Ladies' Yardage: 4684	
Slope: 117	Par: 72

This club's three nine-hole courses are played as three 18-hole pairs. All are naturally beautiful and are kept in top condition. This 137-acre natural wetland sanctuary is home to many varieties of wildlife. The preserve presents seasonal water hazards, and accuracy and shot placement are a must. All courses were designed by Tom Jackson, built by John McWhite and opened in 1990. All have bermudagrass greens and plentiful water hazards.

No. 9 at Tupelo and No. 2 at Cypress are tough holes. The 9th at Tupelo is a big dogleg left, and you can easily miss the green into traps or wetlands. The Cypress No. 2 is a par 5 where long hitters off the tee must be aware of the water on the right. Your second shot will be crucial because you must carry water. You must aim for the right side of the green because if you shoot left you may be in another water hazard. If you get to the front of the green without getting wet, you will be in position for a pitch to the green. The Meadows No. 4 par 3 is tricky. The large green is well-bunkered on the front and left. The prevailing wind is in your face. Choose the right club, and place your shot between the bunker and the water.

A putting green, driving range, pro shop, rental clubs, snack bar and bar are offered. No restrictions are placed on ladies' play.

Walking is not allowed. The course accepts tee times 365 days in advance, and greens fees range from $25 to $68, including cart.

BURNING RIDGE

| U.S. Hwy. 501 | 347-0538 |
| Myrtle Beach | (800) TEE-OFFS |

Both the East and the West courses of Burning Ridge are 18 holes. These adjacent courses were built in 1980 and 1987, respectively; both were designed by Gene

We're No. 1

*With such outstanding courses and the comfortable year-round climate,
is it any wonder South Carolina courses rank at the top?*

South Carolina is now the leading golf vacation destination in the country, according to *Golf Digest's* recent report based on its 1994 subscriber study.

For the first year, South Carolina ranked higher than Florida (and all other destinations) in the states visited on respondents' last three domestic golf vacations. South Carolina attracted a net 36 percent compared to Florida's 33 percent. North Carolina ranked third with a net 13 percent.

To the state's leaders as well as the golf community, this designation is a giant leap in achieving the destiny they've envied. The Grand Strand area, sprawling around Myrtle Beach, is home to almost half of the state's courses. It dubbed itself "America's favorite golf resort" years ago and waited with some degree of impatience and a steady pace of construction and marketing for a study to prove the assertion accurate. Now, you can almost hear the golf gurus saying, "I told you so," although they don't even need to say it. Everyone else saw it as inevitable.

A 1994 study by the South Carolina Department of Parks, Recreation and Tourism (PRT) reported that the state's economy gained more than $644 million from golf course operations alone in 1992-93. When transportation, hotels, restaurants and other expenditures are factored in, the figure rises to $1.5 billion.

"Golf is a key example of what this state has to gain by aggressively and intelligently marketing its best resources," said Grace G. McKown, PRT director, who is happy to recognize a good thing for her state when she sees it.

"Attracting more golfers means more jobs, more income and more tax revenue for the state," said Governor David M. Beasley in announcing that the state will continue to promote itself internationally by focusing attention on its outstanding golf at more than 200 courses.

All of this is supporting evidence that you're welcome here in South Carolina, whether to play a round of golf or to relocate and enjoy a new lifestyle. It didn't get to be the golfers' top choice by being anything less than the best.

Hamm. They incorporate numerous lakes and huge molded bunkers.

The complex has a practice green, a practice sand trap, driving range, pro shop, bar and restaurant, beverage cart and rental clubs. No restrictions are placed on ladies' play.

Greens fees range from $20 to $58, including cart. Free cart fees are available for juniors during the summer. Burning Ridge is part of the Links Group of courses, all of which accept tee times 365 days in advance from their central toll-free reservation number, noted above.

East Course

Championship Yardage: 6780

Slope: 132	Par: 72
Men's Yardage: 6216	
Slope: 124	Par: 72
Other Yardage: 5724	
Slope: 114	Par: 72
Ladies' Yardage: 4524	
Slope: 115	Par: 72

The par 3 No. 12 is 210 yards over water from the men's tees. You must choose the right club, and you must be long and left because your tee shot must carry over water in front and on the right.

West Course

Championship Yardage: 6714

Slope: 122	Par: 72
Men's Yardage: 6237	
Slope: 114	Par: 72
Ladies' Yardage: 4831	
Slope: 118	Par: 72

No. 14, a 577-yard par 5, is a slight dogleg left which usually plays into the wind. If you want to play 36 holes in one day this is an ideal place to be, because

the saying at Burning Ridge goes: The first 18 was so good, we decided to stay. Any hooks or shanks will definitely find water since water is in view on every hole on this course. You must pick the spots to be aggressive because of this liquid hazard.

CALEDONIA GOLF & FISH CLUB

King River Rd.	237-3675
Pawleys Island	(800) 483-6800

Championship Yardage: 6503

Slope: 130	Par: 70
Men's Yardage: 6104	
Slope: 115	Par: 70
Other Yardage: 5738	
Slope: 116	Par: 70
Ladies' Yardage: 4968	
Slope: 113	Par: 70

Caledonia opened in early 1994 and has drawn rave reviews from some of the country's most discriminating golfers. The 18-hole course was built on the site of a historic colonial rice plantation along the Waccamaw River. The centuries-old live oaks will capture your attention; you'll think you're driving onto a movie set. After your round, the rocking chairs beckon from the back porch of the antebellum style clubhouse overlooking the 18th green. You just might want to live here forever.

Mike Strantz, former assistant to Tom Fazio, was the architect who made a splash with Caledonia — his first course. Caledonia complements the surrounding natural landscape. Greens are tifdwarf. Tees are marked with replicas of the native waterfowl that inhabit the plantation's rice fields: wood duck, mallard, redhead and pintail. Gently sloping fairways with unique landing areas, vast waste bunkers and tough approach shots offer extreme challenges. The hunting and fishing retreat that predates the golf course maintains its old shed — where Thursday night socializing remains a time-honored tradition.

The course offers a putting green, a driving net in lieu of a range, a pro shop, a three-hole Par 3 course, men's and women's dressing rooms and a comfortable bar and restaurant with good food. No restrictions are placed on ladies' play.

Summer greens fees, including cart, are $51; spring fees are $96. Tee times are accepted a year in advance. Walking is not allowed.

CAROLINA SHORES
GOLF & COUNTRY CLUB

U.S. Hwy. 17 N.	579-2181
Calabash, N.C.	(803) 449-2657
Championship Yardage: 6783	
Slope: 128	Par: 72
Men's Yardage: 6231	
Slope: 122	Par: 72
Ladies' Yardage: 5385	
Slope: 122	Par: 72

The 18-hole course opened in 1974. It was designed by Tom Jackson. The greens and fairways are tifdwarf bermudagrass.

The toughest hole, ironically, is the 1st — a long par 5 with a lot of sand and protected by water in front. The course is known for its challenge: Note the 96 sand bunkers and 10 lakes. The layout of the front nine definitely brings water into play.

Practice greens, a driving range, pro shop, locker room, bar, snack bar, beverage cart and rental clubs are offered.

Greens fees range from $25 to $55, including cart. Walking is not allowed.

COLONIAL CHARTERS
GOLF & COUNTRY CLUB

S.C. Hwy. 9	
Longs	249-8809
Championship Yardage: 6769	
Slope: 124	Par: 72
Men's Yardage: 6337	
Slope: 119	Par: 72
Other Yardage: 6001	
Slope: 115	Par: 72
Ladies' Yardage: 5079	
Slope: 120	Par: 72

This course's most difficult hole is the 18th. It's been called so many names, ranging from one of the 10 toughest "Hell Holes" to the Number One hole in Myrtle Beach "Dream 18." Go ahead and play it and tell us what you think. It always generates comments.

The 18-hole course was built in 1988, designed by John Simpson.

Swing analysis, lessons, club fitting and club repair are available here. Colonial Charters also has rental clubs, a practice green, driving range, bar, restaurant and locker room, and ladies' play is unrestricted. A special program encourages juniors to play free during the summer.

Greens fees are seasonal and range from $24 to $49. Walking is not allowed. You may book tee times 365 days in advance.

CYPRESS BAY GOLF CLUB

U.S. Hwy. 17	249-1025
Little River	(800) TEE-OFFS
Championship Yardage: 6502	
Slope: 115	Par: 72
Men's Yardage: 6101	
Slope: 110	Par: 72
Ladies' Yardage: 5004	
Slope: 113	Par: 72

The Russell Breeden-designed 18-hole course was built in 1972. Locals like it a lot for its ample supply of water and sand. The picturesque 8th hole challenges you with 190 yards over water.

No driving range is provided, but rentals clubs are. After your round, unwind at the bar and restaurant.

Greens fees range from $20 to $58, including cart. Cypress Bay accepts tee times 365 days in advance. Walking is allowed.

DEER TRACK GOLF RESORT

U.S. Hwy. 17 S.   650-2146
Surfside Beach   (800) 548-9186

Both the North and the South courses (18 holes each) were designed by Bob Toski and Porter Gibson and built in 1974. Owner-operator Gary Schaal, past president of PGA of America, is better known in golf circles nationally and beyond than he is in Myrtle Beach, where he maintains a somewhat low profile and runs his golf courses just like any other businessman.

The complex offers practice greens, rental clubs, driving range, pro shop, bar, restaurant and beverage cart. Locker rooms are available for members only.

Greens fees range from $24 to $55, including cart. Walking is allowed. Tee times may be booked 365 days in advance.

North Course

Championship Yardage: 7203
Slope: 121   Par: 72
Men's Yardage: 6511
Slope: 121   Par: 72
Ladies' Yardage: 5,353
Slope: 119   Par: 72

Bermudagrass fairways and elevated bentgrass greens are featured here. No. 8 is a long and narrow hole that plays 458 yards from the back tees — beware of this one! The signature hole on the North Course is the 17th, a par 3 that requires a tee shot to an island green.

South Course

Championship Yardage: 6916
Slope: 119   Par: 71
Men's Yardage: 6143
Slope: 119   Par: 71
Ladies' Yardage: 5,226
Slope: 120   Par: 71

The South Course has bermudagrass greens, more water hazards and more narrow fairways than the North Course. The signature hole is No. 4, a 204-yard par 3 that requires a tee shot to a peninsula green.

THE DUNES GOLF AND BEACH CLUB

9000 N. Ocean Blvd.
Myrtle Beach   449-5914
Championship Yardage: 7165
Slope: 138   Par: 72
Men's   Yardage: 6565
Slope: 130   Par: 72
Other Yardage: 6175
Slope: 118   Par: 72
Ladies' Yardage: 5390
Slope: 127   Par: 72

Robert Trent Jones Sr. designed this 18-hole course in 1948. It's the only private course in Myrtle Beach that you can play — if you stay with a member accommodation. Several major hotels maintain memberships with this premier course. When you book your golf vacation, check with several hotel golf directors to locate a member property if you want to get on the Dunes. Also, reciprocal agreements allow for members from other clubs to play as well. The PGA seniors end their season here, and the Golf Writers Association of America has played its annual championship at the Dunes for 42 years. Everyone wants to play this course.

The Dunes features bentgrass greens and superior water hazards. Several holes overlook the Atlantic Ocean. The signature hole is the 13th, a par 5 that plays alongside a large lake. *Sports Illustrated* named it one of the best 18 holes in America. The championship tee on num-

ber 18 recently was enlarged and realigned toward the drive-landing area, and another men's tee was added to change the angle of play and stretch the hole to 405 yards.

The clubhouse includes bar, grill room and dining room, and the pro shop recently was expanded. The food is always good, especially the pastry chef's creations. The club houses one of the last vestiges of the good-ole'-boy days: a men-only lounge.

Members enjoy a pool, tennis courts, memberships for juniors, weekly bridge and frequent dances. Locker rooms are spacious. Driving range and practice green are provided, as well as rental clubs.

Greens fees are approximately $100, including cart. Tee times are accepted 365 days in advance. Walking is not allowed.

EAGLE NEST GOLF CLUB

U.S. Hwy. 17 N.	249-1449
Little River	(800) 543-3113

Championship Yardage: 6901
Slope: 120	Par: 72
Men's Yardage: 6417	
Slope: 116	Par: 72
Other Yardage: 5594	
Slope: NA	Par: 72
Ladies' Yardage: 5105	
Slope: 115	Par: 72

According to legend, it's actually an osprey nest tucked high in the tree on the way to the 8th hole. Don't worry about it too much; you'll keep busy enough looking for your own birdie. The course provides a wonderful guide to its birds as well as how to shoot for them. We haven't found ours yet, but we're willing to keep looking.

This 18-hole course, designed by Gene Hamm and built in 1972, is

...ong woods, water and marsh
...s three tough finishing holes.
...the signature hole, a par 3
...a small green. Bermudagrass
greens are perfectly kept and are a pleasure to play.

Rental clubs, a driving range and a restaurant are available.

Greens fees average $42, including cart. The course accepts tee times 365 days in advance and does allow walking.

EASTPORT CLUB

U.S. Hwy. 17 N.	249-3997
Little River	(800) 334-9035
Championship Yardage: 6047	
Slope: 116	Par: 70
Men's Yardage: 5400	
Slope: 111	Par: 70
Ladies' Yardage: 4560	
Slope: 114	Par: 70

Architect Dennis Griffiths designed this track as a finesse course. He did not produce the typical beach layout when he created this 18-hole design, built in 1988. It has narrow bermudagrass fairways and large bentgrass greens and is bordered on the east by the Intracoastal Waterway.

Holes No. 1 through 15 are short, and the course lulls you up to this point. Then, the last three holes are uncharacteristically difficult. The course is mostly flat, with occasional uneven lies. Some tree-lined fairways have doglegs. On the 3rd hole, your second shot will vary depending on the placement of your tee shot over the lake. The friendly ducks sometimes try to help find the ball.

Rental clubs are available, as are a bar and restaurant. Eastport has neither a driving range nor a practice green.

Greens fees average $24, including cart. The course accepts tee times 365 days in advance. Walking is not allowed.

HEATHER GLEN GOLF LINKS

U.S. Hwy. 17 N.	249-9000
Little River	(800) 868-4536

Inspired by Glen Eagles and St. Andrews, the Scottish tradition is unmistakable on this 200-acre historic site. The three nine-hole courses with bentgrass greens are a collective masterpiece — designed by Willard Byrd and Clyde Johnston, built in 1987 and named America's top new course of that year by *Golf Digest*. The 50-foot elevation changes, gigantic 100-year-old pine trees, pot bunkers and waste areas transport you from South Carolina to Scotland for a few hours. The 18th-century clubhouse, authentic Scottish pub and pro shop add to your day's pleasure here. Be sure to say hello to our friend Sam. He and his kilts are about as authentic as you can get.

Rental clubs, a driving range, putting area, locker room and beverage cart are available.

Heather Glen accepts tee times 365 days in advance. Greens fees range from $25 to $81, including cart. Walking is not allowed.

1 Red/2 White Course
Championship Yardage: 6786
Slope: 114   Par: 72

Men's Yardage: 6337
Slope: 110   Par: 72
Ladies' Yardage: 5949
Slope: 116   Par: 72

2 White/3 Blue Course
Championship Yardage: 6791
Slope: 111   Par: 72
Men's Yardage: 6510
Slope: 109   Par: 72
Ladies' Yardage: 6200
Slope: 114   Par: 72

3 Blue/1 Red Course
Championship Yardage: 6791
Slope: 130   Par: 72
Men's Yardage: 6427
Slope: 126   Par: 72
Ladies' Yardage: 5959
Slope: 117   Par: 72

The Red Course's par 5 No. 3 has a large fairway bunker on the right. The sloping green also has three smaller pot bunkers behind and left of the green. No. 8 on the White Course is a beautiful hole. You have a choice of playing it safe or going over the water. The right side of the fairway has mounds and bunkers, and the green has bunkers to the left and around the back. No. 1 on the Blue Course is a par 4, with a beautiful view of the hole from an elevated tee. The fairway is tilted from left to right, and the drive must be slightly left of center. What makes this hole especially tough is a large but hidden green. No. 5 is a short par 3 with huge mounds on the right and pot bunkers placed in the mounds at right, behind and guarding the left side of the green.

THE HERITAGE CLUB

Kings River Rd.
Pawleys Island   236-9318
Championship Yardage: 7100
Slope: 137   Par: 71
Men's Yardage: 6575
Slope: 122   Par: 71
Other Yardage: 6100
Slope: 115   Par: 71
Ladies Yardage: 5325
Slope: 125   Par: 71

The Heritage Club opened in 1986. It was designed and developed by Larry D. Young and was ranked in *Golf Digest's* 1990 Top-50 Public Courses. It is part of a golfing community built on 600 acres of giant magnolias, 300-year-old oaks, freshwater lakes and marshes. An avenue of oaks also leads to the Southern Colonial-style clubhouse that overlooks the Waccamaw River. The Heritage speaks of gracious Southern living and pays tribute to the rice culture of bygone days.

The 18 holes each have their own intriguing personalities. The par 3 13th requires a carry across water. The 4th hole features an avenue of centuries-old oaks alongside the fairway.

The driving range, putting green, pro shop, dining room and lounge are top-quality. Tee times are accepted up to a year in advance.

Greens fees, with cart, range from $52 to $72.

INDIGO CREEK

U.S. Hwy. 17 S.
Surfside Beach   650-0381
Championship Yardage: 6744
Slope: 128   Par: 72
Men's Yardage: 6185
Slope: 120   Par: 72
Ladies' Yardage: 4921
Slope: 120   Par: 70

The Willard Byrd 18-hole course was built in 1990. It sports bermudagrass greens, doglegs, bunkers and water. Note the 90 degree dogleg on No. 12 that crosses the same creek twice. Giant oaks draped with Spanish moss are standard in the Lowcountry, where time almost stands still.

The course offers rental clubs, a driving range and a bar and restaurant.

Greens fees average $40, including cart. Walking is not allowed.

ISLAND GREEN COUNTRY CLUB

455 Sunnehanna Dr.
Myrtle Beach   650-2186

Dogwood/Holly Course
Championship Yardage: 6272
Slope: 118   Par: 72
Men's Yardage: 5847
Slope: 111   Par: 72
Ladies' Yardage: 4510
Slope: 115   Par: 72

Dogwood/Tall Oaks Course
Championship Yardage: 6123
Slope: 118   Par: 72
Men's Yardage: 5705
Slope: 111   Par: 72
Ladies' Yardage: 4996
Slope: 116   Par: 72

Tall Oaks/Holly Course
Championship Yardage: 6243
Slope: 118   Par: 72
Men's Yardage: 5864
Slope: 111   Par: 72
Ladies' Yardage: 4704
Slope: 115   Par: 72

This 27-hole course was built in 1980 and has recently undergone major improvements under the management of the Links Group. Bermudagrass greens are nestled among azaleas and dogwoods, which always seem to be in bloom in Myrtle Beach. All three 18-hole combinations are similar, with narrow tree-lined fairways and small greens. The Holly Course features an island green on the 9th hole. Rental clubs are available as well as a bar and restaurant. There is no driving range however.

This is not an especially difficult course, except for that island green; therefore it can be enjoyed by all levels of golfers.

Island Green is not among the most expensive of places to golf either, ranging from $23 to $42, with carts included. Tee times are accepted 365 days in advance.

THE LEGENDS GOLF CLUB

1500 Legends Dr.
Myrtle Beach   236-9318

The three 18-hole courses are located just off U.S. Highway 501. The Legends Golf Club consists of the Heathland, Moorland and Parkland courses. These courses have been designed in three distinctively different architectural styles.

The Legends Group is owned and operated by Larry Young, one of the major names in the country's golf industry. In addition to The Legends Golf Club, the group's courses include Marsh Harbour, Oyster Bay and the Heritage Club.

The complex offers rental clubs, caddies, a driving range, bar, restaurant, pro shop and beverage cart.

Caddies are mandatory if you wish to walk. The courses accept tee times 365 days in advance, and many golfers book their next year's vacation before leaving for home. Greens fees range around $87, including cart.

Heathland at The Legends
Championship Yardage: 6785
Slope: 127   Par: 71
Men's Yardage: 6190
Slope: 121   Par: 71
Ladies' Yardage: 5115
Slope: 120   Par: 71

This 18-hole course is British-links style with bermudagrass greens — designed by Tom Doak and built in 1990. The first thing that may strike you upon approaching the three-course complex is the magnificent Scottish-style clubhouse, and you'll also notice the distinct absence of trees on the Heathland Course. In lieu of tree boundaries, Doak provided strategic bunkers and deep rough to make this course a challenge. Another difficulty comes from the presence of wind and its direction. Most of the bunkers that guard the greens are deep, in typical Scottish style, and shots from within them must be well-played in order to escape. No. 8 is the shortest hole on the course. Pin position is crucial here, since the front of the green has a severe contour. No. 14, a par 4, has one of the smallest greens on the course. The key here is to pick the right club.

Moorland at The Legends

Championship Yardage: 6799
Slope: 140   Par: 72
Men's Yardage: 6125
Slope: 130   Par: 72
Ladies' Yardage: 4905
Slope: 127   Par: 72

The 18-hole Moorland Course, with tifdwarf greens, was designed by Pete Dye and built in 1991. Dye created what is probably one of the most challenging golf courses on the East Coast. It has much natural growth, sand, water and waste areas combined with incredible undulations and many bulkheaded areas reminiscent of PGA West. This is a target golf course. The par 4 2nd hole has a sand trap running almost from tee box to green. No. 17, a par 3, has an island green with a twist: The green is an island in a sea of sand.

Parkland at The Legends

Championship Yardage: 7170
Slope: 138   Par: 72
Men's Yardage: 6425
Slope: 127   Par: 72
Ladies' Yardage: 5570
Slope: 127   Par: 72

These 18 holes were designed by The Legends Group and built in 1992.

The Parkland Course, with tifdwarf greens, is distinctly different from Heathland and Moorland because its fairways are tree-lined; it's not unlike the other two in that it has deep bunkers and undulating greens. Water and sand are dominant. The Parkland has a great finishing hole — a par 4 measuring 465 yards. The successful tee shot must be played on the right side of the fairway opposite two large traps. The most challenging hole is the par 5 15th, which has a big fairway. Wetlands cut this fairway

into halves. The fairway leading up to the green has seven traps that can cause trouble. No. 11 must be played to the left side. This 515-yard hole is a par 5. To reach the green, the ball must carry over water; if your shot is too long, four sand traps are waiting to catch your ball.

LITCHFIELD COUNTRY CLUB

U.S. Hwy. 17 S.	448-3331
Pawleys Island	(800) 344-5590
Championship Yardage: 6752	
Slope: 130	Par: 72
Men's Yardage: 6342	
Slope: 124	Par: 72
Ladies' Yardage: 5917	
Slope: 119	Par: 72
Other Yardage: 5264	
Slope: 119	Par: 72

One of the area's oldest and most prestigious clubs, Litchfield was designed by Willard Byrd. Its mature narrow fairways, lined with moss-draped oaks and large well-protected greens, wind through a former rice plantation to a traditional clubhouse. Although private, a limited number of guests are booked on this course.

Country club cottages are available for vacationers. The Lowcountry cuisine in the fine dining room is on par with the quality of the golf.

Greens fees range from $40 during the summer to $69, including cart. You may walk the course when you like, and you may also book a tee time 365 days in advance of your game.

THE LONG BAY CLUB

S.C. Hwy. 9	399-2222
Longs	(800) 344-5590
Championship Yardage 7021	
Slope: 137	Par: 72
Men's Yardage 6565	
Slope: 130	Par: 72
Other Yardage: 6139	
Slope: 126	Par: 72
Ladies' Yardage: 5598	
Slope: 127	Par: 72

Jack Nicklaus's signature mounds can't be missed as you approach North Myrtle Beach from Highway 9. The 18-hole course was built in 1989. It's rated by *Golf Digest* in the state's Top-10 Courses. It has tifdwarf greens.

The signature hole is No. 10 — a par 4. Your drive must be straight on this hole because a left or right shot will be in sand. You're surrounded by sand from your second shot. This sand trap is so big golfers have been known to drive their cart into it (don't). No. 13 is a par 3 of 123 yards with an island green. The abundance of lakes, mounds and bunkers is exciting on this course, which everyone wants to play.

The bar and restaurant are classy and comfortable. Rental clubs and a driving range are available.

Greens fees range from $50 to $97 and include cart. Walking is not allowed. Tee times may be booked 365 days in advance.

MARSH HARBOUR

Marsh Harbor Rd.	579-3161
Calabash, N.C.	(800) 552-2660
S.C. number	249-3449
Championship Yardage: 6690	
Slope: 134	Par: 71
Men's Yardage: 6000	
Slope: 121	Par: 71
Ladies' Yardage: 4795	
Slope: 115	Par: 71

Marsh Harbour sits on the North and South Carolina borders just south of Calabash (thus the numbers you can dial from both states). A good drive with a fade from the 10th tee in North Carolina will cross into South Carolina, then land on the fairway back in North Carolina.

Everyone seems to want to play Marsh Harbour — and its reputation is well-deserved. Salt marshes along the Intracoastal Waterway provide exciting scenery and exciting golf play. Larry Young built Dan Maples' design in 1980 and presented a

Pier of Distinction

Photo: Liz Mitchell

The Cherry Grove Pier features a unique double-deck spectator area.

It's a combination of a country club and a church, and you can arrive with or without a fishing pole. It's meeting the social, spiritual and recreational needs of many a soul. That's how Cherry Grove Pier is described by one of the regulars who frequents the North Myrtle Beach fishing spot.

Everyone knows everyone among a daily crowd, and they clearly get a lot more than fish from the experience. Cherry Grove is just across Hogg Inlet from the award-winning Tidewater Golf Club, and the vacationing anglers may fill the popular family-style motels quicker than the golfers if you aren't careful. It's another sport for the time left after golf.

Margaret Prince and her son, Ed, who own the pier, the restaurant and neighboring motels, welcome everyone who enjoys the sea. The pier is popular with locals and tourists for its July 4 fireworks and various gatherings. For the fishing, for the social network of good people, or just for some quiet time alone with nature, the Cherry Grove pier invites you for a breezy stroll on a hot day.

How many people are on the pier? Mrs. Prince says, "elbow to elbow and shoulder to shoulder," and most days that's what you see. A unique feature of the pier is the octagonal two-story gazebo perched on the end. It's the only two-story pier in South Carolina. The top level is for spectators. The bottom is reserved for serious fishing, and during tournament time it can't be disturbed.

A walk to the end of the 900-foot pier makes even a non-fisherman ready to join the club, whatever its affiliation. It's jammed with interesting people who share a camaraderie washed up by the sea. The hospitality is as wide as the ocean itself.

rare combination of elevated ground skirted by low-lying marsh.

The famous hole is the par 5 17th, featuring three distinct targets. Picture trees on the left and large bunkers on the right. You can handle the tee shot; then the second shot must carry across the marsh to a landing area with water on three sides . . . a toughie. Cross the marsh again to a green on the side of the marsh. Not too many of us make par on this one.

Greens fees, including cart, range from $52 to $72. While walking is not allowed, you may book your tee time whenever it's convenient for you.

MYRTLE BEACH NATIONAL GOLF CLUB

| U.S. Hwy. 501 | 448-2308 |
| Myrtle Beach | (800) 344-5590 |

This club has three 18-hole courses. All were built in the 1970s and designed by Arnold Palmer and Frances Duane. All feature bentgrass greens.

The Myrtle Beach National Golf Club owns another five courses on the Grand Strand, and their reservationist at Tee Time Central can quickly book your entire week for you with one easy phone call. They accept tee times 365 days in advance.

The course offers rental clubs, a driving range and bar and restaurant.

Greens fees change at least eight times a year based on the season, not including occasional afternoon and other specials; prices range from $25 to $50. Walking is allowed.

King's North

Championship Yardage: 6759
| Slope: 125 | Par: 72 |
Men's Yardage: 6033
| Slope: 109 | Par: 72 |
Ladies' Yardage: 5047
| Slope: 113 | Par: 72 |

Built in 1973, this course was one of the beach's initial courses and one of the first anywhere to feature an island green. Arnold Palmer and the Palmer Design Group oversaw substantial changes to the North Course in 1995.

What began as a minor update evolved into total design and visual enhancement. The bentgrass greens have been reshaped and enlarged and sodded with the new hybrid Crenshaw Bent. Trees were removed to open the course. Several fairways now feature increased undulation, and bunkers and lakes have been dramatically reshaped. The famous par 3 No. 3 has undergone a major enhancement with the addition of bulkheads and a new foot bridge. Increased greens fees have followed the course's redesign.

South Course

Championship Yardage: 6416
| Slope: 123 | Par: 72 |
Men's Yardage: 6089
| Slope: 118 | Par: 72 |
Ladies' Yardage: 4723
| Slope: 109 | Par: 72 |
Other Yardage: 5710
| Slope: 112 | Par: 72 |

This 18 hole course was built in 1975 and remodeled in 1990. It has flat fairways with some mounding. The smallest greens and greenside bunkers are on this course.

No. 5 is a par 4 dogleg, which is unintimidating unless you are short (your shot, not your person), and your second shot could be into a fairway pond that sits squarely in your line of fire. It's a 355-yard par 4. As you make the turn, No. 9 is a 390-yard par 4 where you must stay right because of the sand down three-fourths of the left side of the fairway. It's tough to make a birdie here because it's a small green. If you do hit the green, you'll probably be near the hole due to the size of the green. The 13th could be unlucky, as you must shoot over a sea of sand to an island green. It's a 166-yard par 3.

West Course

Championship Yardage: 6866
Slope: 119 — Par: 72
Men's Yardage: 6113
Slope: 113 — Par: 72
Ladies' Yardage: 5307
Slope: 109 — Par: 72

The 18-hole West Course, built in 1974, is the longest course at Myrtle Beach National. Although many tall pines line the fairways and can claim your ball, the course is considered wide open. No. 18 is the only hole on which you'll find a water hazard.

MYRTLE WEST GOLF COURSE

S.C. Hwy. 9 — 249-1478
Longs — (800) 842-8390
Championship Yardage: 6787
Slope: 132 — Par: 72
Men's Yardage: 6181
Slope: 118 — Par: 72
Other Yardage: 5555
Slope: 108 — Par: 72
Ladies' Yardage: 4859
Slope: 113 — Par: 72

Drive through the covered bridge to the Southern-mansion clubhouse. Take plenty of balls in case the numerous water hazards claim some, and enjoy the beautiful holes set among Carolina sand and tall pines. The 18-hole course was built in 1990, designed by Tom Jackson. The entire course is bermudagrass.

Pick the right tee for your level of ability, the professionals advise. Don't think you have to play macho golf. Where you tee it up defines the difficulty around the greens. No. 17 is one of the most difficult — 457 yards and usually playing into the wind.

Amenities include practice putting and chipping greens, a sand bunker, driving range, pro shop, rental clubs, a beverage cart during peak season and a bar and restaurant.

The course accepts tee times 365 days in advance. A rental cart is included in the greens fee, which ranges from $25 to $58. Walking is not allowed.

MYRTLEWOOD GOLF CLUB

48th Ave. N. — 449-5134
Myrtle Beach — (800) 283-3633

Myrtlewood offers back-to-back challenges, with two 18-hole courses along the Intracoastal Waterway. It's easily accessible on the U.S. 17 Bypass from any part of the Grand Strand.

Amenities include a driving range, practice green, rental clubs, a beverage cart, pro shop, bar and snack bar.

Greens fees range from $24 to $62, including cart. The complex accepts tee times 365 days in advance. Walking is not allowed.

Palmetto Course

Championship Yardage: 6957
Slope: 121 — Par: 72
Men's Yardage: 6495
Slope: 118 — Par: 72
Other Yardage: 6098
Slope: 115 — Par: 72
Ladies' Yardage: 5305
Slope: 117 — Par: 72

The Palmetto Course was designed by Edmund B. Ault and built in 1973. Its bentgrass greens are smooth, and its bermudagrass fairways are on open, rolling coastal terrain. No. 15 is a tough hole, because the long par 4 with water on the

Ask before packing your cooler onto the golf cart. Some courses do allow you to bring your own food or beverage, but several prohibit it because their beverage cart provides for your eating and drinking pleasure.

Insiders' Tips

right usually plays into the wind and demands a long second shot.

The signature hole is the 18th. You don't dare pull your tee shot because if you do your ball will land in the bottom of the Intracoastal Waterway. In fact, the entire length of the hole runs along the Waterway. The green is well guarded with bunkers in the front, left and right.

PineHills Course

Championship Yardage: 6640	
Slope: 125	Par: 72
Men's Yardage: 6112	
Slope: 119	Par: 72
Other Yardage: 5692	
Slope: 112	Par: 72
Ladies' Yardage: 4906	
Slope: 113	Par: 72

The PineHills course was the original Myrtlewood, built in 1966. It was rebuilt in 1993 — Arthur Hills' first design in Myrtle Beach. Bermuda fairways are full of plateaus, and bentgrass greens are situated in hollows or tucked into low hills. Bunkers are used sparingly, and water hazards are cleverly placed. No. 18 requires a good tee shot over water to a narrow green with bunker and water around it.

OCEAN HARBOUR GOLF LINKS

Sommersett Dr.	
Calabash, N.C.	579-3588
S.C. number	448-8398
Championship yardage: 7004	
Slope: 138	Par: 72
Men's Yardage: 6592	
Slope: 134	Par: 72
Other Yardage: 6148	
Slope: 127	Par: 72
Ladies' Yardage: 5358	
Slope: 126	Par: 72

An 18-hole course built in 1989, Ocean Harbour was Clyde Johnston's first design on the Grand Strand. It crosses the North Carolina-South Carolina border, so, like its neighbor, Marsh Harbor, is nice enough to give you a phone number for both states. On the 5th hole, you can drive from North Carolina into South Carolina then return on the 9th tee.

The 532-yard par 5 No. 7 is the signature hole. The teeing area is surrounded by a cedar grove. The marsh view and waterway view are spectacular. On each shot you will have to clear marshland. As if that's not hard enough, the green suggests an island appearance.

All 18 holes are tough; you'll encounter a lot of water. Fairways are bermudagrass, and greens are bentgrass. Saltwater marshes and natural elevation shape the course on 500 acres of grass bunkers and gentle rolling fairways. Sand bunkers and multiple ponds contribute to the endless challenges. The panoramic views include rare combinations of the Calabash River, the Atlantic Ocean and the Intracoastal Waterway. The clubhouse is a fine finishing spot with its view of the confluence of the waterway and the river.

Practice greens, a driving range, pro shop, bar, snack bar and rental clubs are available.

Greens fees range from $25 to $76, including cart, and tee times are accepted up to a year in advance. Walking is not allowed.

OCEAN ISLE BEACH GOLF COURSE

Pearl Blvd.	
Ocean Isle Beach, N.C.	579-2610
S.C. number	272-3900
Championship's Yardage: 6626	
Slope: 126	Par: 72
Men's Yardage: 6146	
Slope: 122	Par: 72
Ladies Yardage: 5075	
Slope: 116	Par: 72

This 18-hole course was designed by Russell Breeden and opened in 1976. The bermudagrass greens and fairways are carved through rolling terrain, towering pines and live oaks. A tough hole is the

Myrtle Beach Nightlife

It's the place for night life. Neon and noise are splashed across the middle of Myrtle Beach like you see in few other golf resorts. We never roll up the sidewalks; we begin the party late at night and continue until early morning. You have to sample it, even if you have to manage with only a few hours of sleep to make your early tee time. It's boisterous and sometimes bawdy, but, hey, it's all in fun.

The Southern-style jitterbug-type dance, which originated in North Myrtle Beach to the beach music of the 1960s, draws semiannual reunions of dancers and serious party-types from all over the world to North Myrtle Beach's Main Street at The Horseshoe. The dance is called The Shag, and you can take lessons if you missed learning it when you were younger, or you can watch the regular competitions and cheer for your favorites.

For games, dancing and a good time including good food, try Yesterday's NiteLife at 1901 N. Kings Highway. It includes a sports bar section with games for golfers, race car drivers and other sports enthusiasts.

A nearby favorite spot for dancing to the tunes spun by Jumpin' Jack Flash (a local DJ) is Studebakers at 2000 N. Kings Highway. Or you can check 2001, located at 920 Lake Arrowhead Road. It's three clubs with a piano bar, a disco and live performances, all in separate sections. This club almost always attracts a crowd of golfers and party people. Also for the extra late party crowd, Jamaica Joe's is a favorite hang out.

Player's Sports Lounge in the Galleria Shopping Center on Restaurant Row hosts live bands, pool tournaments, Ping Pong tables, 20 televisions and more sports games than you can play in one night.

Atlantis Nightlife on Highway 501 features a 4,000-gallon aquarium topped with a dance floor for the high-energy numbers, another club with live entertainers and a third club with acoustic guitarists performing.

The newest excitement is Celebrity Square's collection of 10 night clubs at Broadway at the Beach, opened in late 1995, and promising to rival any big city's nightlife. Live music ranges from blues to jazz to popular to country (of course) to you-name-it.

10th, where you have to hit over a ditch to a small green that will often bounce the ball off the back. It's frequently a bogey hole. No. 16 is a dogleg right that plays 451 yards from the championship tees.

Greens fees range from $20 to $43, including cart. Amenities include practice greens, a driving range, pro shop, rental clubs, a bar and a snack bar.

Ocean Isle is a quiet piece of golfer's paradise: No big city lights, but golf galore. While it's actually in North Carolina, the course aligns itself with the Myrtle Beach golfing scene. The Pearl (see our later entry) is the sister course to the Ocean Isle Beach Course, and you can spend many a vacation day trying to master the combination.

OCEAN RIDGE PLANTATION

351 Ocean Ridge S.W.   287-1717
Ocean Isle Beach, N.C.   (800) 233-1801
S.C. number   448-5566

Lion's Paw and Panther's Run were renamed in 1995 to become the 36-hole Ocean Ridge Plantation. The second nine of Panther's Run opened in October 1995.

Willard Byrd designed the first 18 holes, and Tim Nelson Cate designed the newer Panther Run. All have bermudagrass fairways and bentgrass greens.

Amenities include practice greens, a driving range, pro shop, bar, restaurant, beverage cart and rental clubs.

Greens fees range from $30 to nearly $80.

Lion's Paw Golf Links

Championship Yardage: 7003
Slope: 138   Par: 72
Men's Yardage: 6457
Slope: 130   Par: 72
Ladies' Yardage: 5364
Slope: 118   Par: 72

The toughest hole on Lion's Paw is No. 4, a 430-yard par 4. Water comes into play on 15 of the 18 holes on Lion's Paw. Fairways are somewhat narrow on the front nine but expansive on the second nine.

Panther's Run Golf Links

Championship Yardage: 7089
Slope: 140   Par: 72
Men's Yardage: 6706
Slope: 134   Par: 72
Other Yardage: 6267
Slope: 128   Par: 72
Other Yardage: 5546
Slope: 118   Par: 72
Ladies' Yardage: 5023
Slope: 116   Par: 72

On Panther's Run, the 5th hole is tough due to the great expanse of water to carry. The course along the nature preserve offers pretty scenery and marsh to clear on several holes. Five sets of tees allow every golfer to find a comfort zone. Wide fairways twist and turn around visually appealing lakes, brooks and waterfalls on the new nine. Deer, barn owls and waterfowl are frequently spotted along the course.

OYSTER BAY GOLF LINKS

Lakeshore Dr.   236-9318
Sunset Beach, N.C.   (800) 552-2660
Championship Yardage: 6785
Slope: 137   Par: 71
Men's Yardage: 6560
Slope: 130   Par: 71
Ladies' Yardage: 4825
Slope: 117   Par: 71

Oyster Bay is an 18-hole links-style course that is part of the popular Legends Group. It was designed by Dan Maples. Its trademark oyster-shell landscaping and walls have been incorporated into the design. Oyster Bay opened in 1983 and was recognized by *Golf Digest* as the best new resort course in the country that year and was ranked in the top 50 overall courses. It's one of the most beautiful courses to be found anywhere.

The 15th and 17th holes are par 3s with island greens. The 17th hole is played from oyster shell-walled tees. The island green is built on a mountain of shells. The 13th hole has a lake flanking the entire right side. The green is guarded by a large cavernous bunker.

Walking is not allowed at Oyster Bay. Amenities include rental clubs, a pro shop, bar, restaurant, beverage cart, driving range and practice green. Tee times are accepted up to 365 days in advance. Greens fees average $87 including cart.

PAWLEYS PLANTATION
GOLF & COUNTRY CLUB

U.S. Hwy. 17 S.   237-1736
Pawleys Island   (800) 367-9959
Championship Yardage: 7026
Slope: 132   Par: 72
Men's Yardage: 6522
Slope: 127   Par: 72

Jack Nicklaus' Long Bay showcases his signature mounds, surrounding this bunker at #10.

Other Yardage: 6127
Slope: 122   Par: 72
Ladies' Yardage: 5572
Slope: 130   Par: 72
Other Yardage: 4979
Slope: 126   Par: 72

A signature course by Jack Nicklaus, Pawley's Plantation offers exclusive play to members and guests of member hotels. Call the course or ask the golf director at one of the Sands Properties about how to get on this course. You may remember Pawleys Plantation best for the double green and dramatic split fairway. Lake and marsh views and bentgrass greens are spectacular, and similarly spectacular shots frequently are required to traverse the marsh.

The country club setting includes a clubhouse and lounge where breakfast, lunch and dinner are served. A pool and tennis court for guests are minutes from the beach.

Greens fees range from $47 to $82, including cart. Walking is not allowed. You may book your game at any time.

THE PEARL GOLF LINKS

1300 Pearl Blvd. S.W.
Sunset Beach, N.C.   579-8132
S.C. number   272-2850

The Pearl offers the East and West courses, both of which are 18-hole tracks, finely designed by Dan Maples and built on a 900-acre marsh preserve. Both courses were built in 1987 and feature bentgrass greens. The East Course is a traditional layout, and the West Course is links style. Both boast spectacular finishing holes. One finishes along the Calabash River, while the other finishes on a bluff overlooking the Intracoastal Waterway.

No two holes are alike, and you will definitely use all your clubs. The marsh views and natural wildlife in the undisturbed area are a visual feast. On the West Course, water and/or marsh is on every hole, and on the East Course water or marsh is on every hole except No. 8 and No. 15.

A pro shop, driving range, bar, restaurant and rental clubs are available.

Tee times may be booked a year in

advance, and greens fees average $69, including cart. Walking is not allowed.

East Course

Championship Yardage: 6749

Slope: 135	Par: 72
Men's Yardage: 6543	
Slope: 132	Par: 72
Other Yardage: 6250	
Slope: 127	Par: 72
Ladies' Yardage: 5125	
Slope: 129	Par: 72

No. 17 on the East Course is the signature hole. It's a slight dogleg left with three fairway bunkers, oyster beds and marsh down the left side. If you're long on approaching the green, a sand trap is in the back, not to mention the marsh again.

West Course

Championship Yardage: 7008

Slope: 132	Par: 72
Men's Yardage: 6738	
Slope: 131	Par: 72
Other Yardage: 6419	
Slope: 129	Par: 72
Ladies' Yardage: 5188	
Slope: 127	Par: 72

On the West Course, No. 16 is the signature. It's a 604-yard par 5 that bends twice before you get to the green. No only do you have to put up with marsh running down the complete right side of the fairway and green, but trouble is compounded by the addition of oyster beds, sand and marsh also down the right. An abundance of love grass on this course is especially on holes 1, 2, 9, 11 and 12. You don't have to know what it is. Just stay out of it.

PINE LAKES
INTERNATIONAL COUNTRY CLUB

5603 Woodside Dr.	449-6459
Myrtle Beach	(800) 446-6817

Championship Yardage 6609

Slope: 125	Par: 71
Men's Yardage: 6176	
Slope: 121	Par: 71
Ladies' Yardage: 5376	
Slope: 122	Par: 71

From the moment you walk into the clubhouse, you begin to soak up the tradition that Pine Lakes exudes. It's called the Granddaddy. "When I die, take me to the Granddaddy," a well-known writer instructed.

Pine Lakes International was the first golf course in Myrtle Beach, built in 1927. Robert White, the first president of the PGA and a native of St. Andrews, designed this 18-hole course. It was meant as a playground to complement the million-dollar Ocean Forest Hotel, an elaborate resort for the wealthy. Sunday afternoon croquet matches on its lawn continue another of its age-old traditions. Invitations to members of the neighboring Dunes Club announce the introduction of a "new game."

Among the many significant events Pine Lakes claims, one of the biggest is that *Sports Illustrated* was born here in 1954 when Henry Booth Luce and 66 other Time-Life executives came for a game and left with a brainstorm.

In 1995, it was the first Grand Strand course to lease a million-dollar fleet of carts with the Rolls-Royce design.

Today it retains the prestige its heritage demands. Scottish flavor and Southern gentility are reflected in every touch, beginning with the tartan-dressed starters, continuing with the mimosa Thomas serves as you approach the 3rd tee and culminating on cooler days with the signature clam chowder served at the turn. Its special Southern-style Manhattan recipe, heavy with red pepper, is said to add an extra 30 yards to your remaining drives. The cook will sign your score card if any of it is worth writing home about.

The fairways are wide and, while not overly tough, the course can be challenging, depending upon pin placements. Pine Lakes starts with a bang: a 563-yard par 3. The par 3 No. 7 is one of the country's most beautiful holes, according to the editors of *Golf Digest*. Greens are bermudagrass.

When your game is over, assistants will wash your clubs, shine your shoes and present your crying towel to remind you of this round.

Walking is not allowed. Booking tee times up to a year in advance is recommended. Rental clubs and a driving range are available. The bar, restaurant and pro shop are within the 60-room antebellum mansion, and a snack bar overlooks the pool.

Greens fees start at $47 during summer months and range to $110 in the high season. A cart is included.

POSSUM TROT GOLF CLUB

U.S. Hwy. 17	272-5341
North Myrtle Beach	(800) 626-8768
Championship Yardage: 6966	
Slope: 127	Par: 72
Men's Yardage: 6343	
Slope: 118	Par: 72
Other Yardage: 5505	
Slope: 108	Par: 72
Ladies' Yardage: 5153	
Slope: 111	Par: 72

One of the older courses on the Grand Strand, this 18-hole layout was built in 1968. It was designed by Russell Breeden. Greens and fairways are bermudagrass. High handicappers welcome the course's openness; yet the 50 bunkers and nine lakes and ponds combine with the length and finesse to challenge any golfer. Watch out for No. 11 — 430 yards uphill and into the wind from the men's tees. This course's signature hole is No. 13, a 163-yard par 3 full carry over water.

The extensive practice facility includes a driving range, sand bunkers and separate pitching, chipping and putting greens. Other amenities include a pro shop, bar, beverage cart, snack bar, locker rooms for men and women and rental clubs.

Greens fees range from $32 to $57, including cart. Walking is allowed after noon. The course accepts tee times 365 days in advance.

QUAIL CREEK GOLF CLUB

U.S. Hwy. 501	347-0549
Myrtle Beach	(800) TEE-OFFS
Championship Yardage: 6812	
Slope: 119	Par: 72
Men's Yardage: 6331	
Slope: 116	Par: 72
Other Yardage: 5955	
Slope: 114	Par: 72
Ladies' Yardage: 5287	
Slope: 112	Par: 72

Gene Hamm designed this 18-hole course in 1968. It has extra-wide fairways, large greens and easy playing conditions. No. 11 is a 526-yard par 5 that doglegs left. The somewhat large green is guarded front, left and right by bunkers. Somewhat unique to this course, water comes into play on only about six holes.

The clubhouse, including a bar and restaurant, was recently renovated. A driving range and rental clubs are available.

Part of The Links Group, this club accepts tee times 365 days in advance. Greens fees range from $20 to $58, including cart. Walking is allowed.

RIVER CLUB

U.S. Hwy. 17 S.	237-8755
Pawleys Island	(800) 344-5590
Championship Yardage: 6677	
Slope: 135	Par: 72
Men's Yardage: 6240	
Slope: 119	Par: 72
Ladies' Yardage: 5084	
Slope: 120	Par: 72

The River Club is an 18-hole Tom Jackson design. Its fairways are wide and open, and the large greens are undulating. More than 90 bunkers and plenty of water offer challenges to all skill levels. Its par 5 finishing hole wraps around a lake. Long hitters may be able to reach the green in two; however, if you miss, you can put at least a bogey on your scorecard.

Greens fees range from $40 to $74, including cart. Tee times are accepted up to a year in advance. Walking is allowed.

RIVER HILLS GOLF & COUNTRY CLUB

U.S. Hwy. 17 N.	399-2100
Little River	(800) 264-3810

Championship Yardage: 6829
Slope: 133	Par: 72

Men's Yardage: 6196
Slope: 123	Par: 72

Other Yardage: 5535
Slope: 113	Par: 72

Ladies' Yardage: 4861
Slope: 120	Par: 72

Tom Jackson designed this 18-hole course in 1988, with bermudagrass greens and fairways. Fairways are somewhat narrow, and water comes into play on 13 holes. The course is in a densely wooded setting and features 40-foot elevation changes. No. 5 is a challenge: a long par 4 uphill, with bunkers surrounding it.

A complete practice facility is available as are rental clubs, a pro shop, locker rooms for men and women, a beverage cart on busy days and a snack bar.

Walking is not allowed. The course accepts tee times 365 days in advance. Greens fees range from $25 to $60, including cart.

RIVER OAKS GOLF PLANTATION

3400 U.S. Hwy. 501	236-2222
Myrtle Beach	(800) 762-8813

Bear/Fox Course
Championship Yardage: 6778
Slope: 126	Par: 72

Men's Yardage: 6314
Slope: 118	Par: 72

Ladies' Yardage: 5133
Slope: 116	Par: 72

Fox /Otter Course
Championship Yardage: 6791
Slope: 125	Par: 72

Men's Yardage: 6345
Slope: 118	Par: 72

Ladies' Yardage: 5043
Slope: 118	Par: 72

Otter/Bear Course
Championship Yardage: 6877
Slope: 125	Par: 72

Men's Yardage: 6425
Slope: 119	Par: 72

Ladies' Yardage: 5188
Slope: 118	Par: 72

Three nine-hole courses make up the three 18-hole combinations that were completed in 1990. Tom Jackson designed the Bear Course, and Gene Hamm designed the Otter and Fox courses. Fairways and greens are bermudagrass. Wildlife, undulating greens, mounded fairways, finger-shaped sand bunkers and large lakes provide scenic beauty along the Intracoastal Waterway.

Water comes into play or at least is a major presence on the Bear Course, which many believe to be the most difficult of the trio. The 2nd hole on the Bear is . . . well, a bear . . . with water and sand prominently coming into play. Some doglegs on the Fox are difficult, although the course plays shorter than the others.

Practice greens, driving range, pro shop, snack bar, rental clubs and beverage cart are offered.

Greens fees range from $20 to $55 and include cart. Tee times may be booked a year in advance. Walking is not allowed.

ROBBERS ROOST GOLF CLUB

U.S. Hwy. 17 N.	249-1471
North Myrtle Beach	(800) 352-2384

Championship Yardage: 7148
Slope: 137	Par: 72

Men's Yardage: 6725
Slope: 129	Par: 72

Other Yardage: 6356

Who you are and what you think is important to us.

Fill out the coupon and we'll give you an Insiders' Guide® for half price ($7.48 off)

Which book(s) did you buy? _____

Where do you live? _____

In what city did you buy your book? _____

Where did you buy your book? ☐ catalog ☐ bookstore ☐ newspaper ad
☐ retail shop ☐ other _____

How often do you travel? ☐ yearly ☐ bi-annually ☐ quarterly
☐ more than quarterly

Did you buy your book because you were ☐ moving ☐ vacationing
☐ wanted to know more about your home town ☐ other _____

_____

Will the book be used by ☐ family ☐ couple ☐ individual ☐ group

What is you annual household income? ☐ under $25,000 ☐ $25,000 to $35,000
☐ $35,000 to $50,000 ☐ $50,000 to $75,000 ☐ over $75,000

How old are you? ☐ under 25 ☐ 25-35 ☐ 36-50 ☐ 51-65 ☐ over 65

Did you use the book before you left for your destination? ☐ yes ☐ no

Did you use the book while at your destination? ☐ yes ☐ no

On average per month, how many times do you refer to your book? ☐ 1-3 ☐ 4-7
☐ 8-11 ☐ 12-15 ☐ 16 and up

On average, how many other people use your book? ☐ no others ☐ 1 ☐ 2
☐ 3 ☐ 4 or more

Is there anything you would like to tell us about Insiders' Guides? _____

_____

_____

Name _____ Address _____

City _____ State _____ Zip _____

We'll send you a voucher for $7.48 off any Insiders' Guide© and a list of available titles as soon as we get this card from you. Thanks for being an Insider!

NO POSTAGE
NECESSARY
IF MAILED
IN THE
UNITED STATES

BUSINESS REPLY MAIL

FIRST-CLASS MAIL   PERMIT NO. 20   MANTEO, NC

POSTAGE WILL BE PAID BY ADDRESSEE

THE INSIDERS GUIDE
PO BOX 2057
MANTEO NC   27954-9906

Photo: Arrowhead Country Club

Raymond Floyd opened his first signature course in South Carolina — with 18 holes in 1994 and another nine in 1995 — at Arrowhead.

Slope: 120   *Par: 72*
Ladies' Yardage: 5387
Slope: 116   *Par: 72*

Designed by Russell Breeden, the 18-hole course opened in 1969, with tifdwarf bermudagrass on the tees, fairways and greens.

Breeden once said that No. 16 — a par 5 — was the greatest hole he had ever built. The par 5 is a slight dogleg left with a huge lake between the fairway and the green. If you hit a super tee shot, you have the option to go for it, but then you need a terrific second shot. Fairway bunkers are on the right, and greenside bunkers are left, right and behind. No. 14 is another interesting hole. It's a par 4, 390 yards, but the water butts up against the relatively small green, so the second shot is critical. No sand is on this hole, but your landing area for your drive is extremely narrow.

Water provides a challenge on several holes, and the course's length is a challenge in itself.

The Southern plantation-style porch around the clubhouse is a fine place to unwind after you've finished your round.

A driving range, rental clubs and a bar and restaurant are available.

Greens fees begin at $29 and go to $40, including cart. Walking is not allowed. You may book tee times a year in advance.

SEA TRAIL PLANTATION & GOLF LINKS
301 Clubhouse Rd.   *287-1100*
Sunset Beach, N.C.   *(800) 546-5748*

Sea Trail Plantation is a classy resort community set on 2,000 acres and featuring 54 signature holes of championship golf. The three 18-hole courses were designed by Dan Maples, Rees Jones and Willard Byrd, respectively, and named as such. Meeting and conference space plus golf packages make this resort a choice for many golf parties who want their townhouse or villa accommodations right on the course.

Sunset Beach is a great little North Carolina community (right over the border) with no resemblance to the neon hustle and bustle of Myrtle Beach. Views are of the golf courses or the river. The beach is about a mile away. Resort amenities include a bar, restaurant, pro shop, fitness room, pool, tennis club and biking and jogging trails.

Dan Maples Course
Championship Yardage: 6751
Slope: 121   *Par: 72*
Men's Yardage: 6332
Slope: 117   *Par: 72*
Other Yardage: 6035
Slope: 112   *Par: 72*
Ladies' Yardage: 5090
Slope: 108   *Par: 72*

This course was built in 1986 and promptly nominated by *Golf Digest* as one of the most outstanding resort courses in the country. Maples' Oyster Bay Golf Links is also located within Sea Trail Plantation, and his Marsh Harbour course is nearby. You can stay and play here for a long time if you're looking for some really fine golf.

The par 3 No. 3 is an intimidating hole because of a pond on the right of the green. This hole must be played to the middle or left of the pin regardless of where the pin is placed. The dogleg left par 4 7th hole needs to be played in the center of the fairway. The second shot must go over water to a kidney-shaped green. An island tee on the 13th is what makes this short par 4 interesting. Bunkers are on the left of the fairway. A good tee shot will leave a mid- to short-iron shot to a deceiving green.

Greens fees range from $34 to $58, including cart.

Rees Jones Course

Championship Yardage: 6761
Slope: 132   Par: 72
Men's Yardage: 6334
Slope: 126   Par: 72
Other Yardage: 5716
Slope: 118   Par: 72
Ladies' Yardage: 4912
Slope: 115   Par: 72

The Rees Jones course opened in the spring of 1990. Water comes into play on 11 holes. The par 3 No. 5 has many obstacles. Besides playing over water, it is surrounded by seven sand traps, to the rear, right and left; thus, club selection is crucial. Par 5 No. 8 needs a long tee shot if you hope to reach the green in two; however, you must be careful of the water in front of the green. It's better to lay up and hit the green in three.

Greens fees begin at $39 and go to $63, including cart.

Willard Byrd Course

Championship Yardage: 6751
Slope: 128   Par: 72
Men's   Yardage: 6263
Slope: 126   Par: 72
Other Yardage: 5590
Slope: 116   Par: 72
Ladies' Yardage: 4717
Slope: 121   Par: 72

The Byrd Course opened in the fall of 1990. It's built around lakes ranging from 14 to 20 acres. Shot-making finesse is called for here. The par 3 No. 2 is medium-length, but you must play over water. If possible, try to place your shot so you'll have an uphill putt. The par 4 No. 11 is a narrow dogleg right with four fairway traps. The green is long and narrow and slopes from back to front. Par 5 No.

18 requires a drive down the right-cer ter; otherwise, you're in water. You can reach the green in two with a long iron shot. If the hole is on the front of the green, try to stay below the hole.

Greens fees are $34 to $58, including cart.

SURF GOLF & BEACH CLUB

1701 Springland Dr.   249-1524
North Myrtle Beach   (800) 765-SURF
Championship Yardage: 6842
Slope: 126   Par: 72
Men's Yardage: 6360
Slope: 119   Par: 72
Ladies' Yardage: 5178
Slope: 111   Par: 72
Other Yardage: 5960
Slope: 114   Par: 72

This George Cobb classic was Myrtle Beach's third course when it opened in 1961. The 18-hole course recently was rebuilt and enhanced: Architect John LaFoy retained the traditional flavor while adding new challenges to the bermudagrass greens and fairways. The finishing hole is a dramatic par 3 over water. It's 219 yards, usually played against the ocean breeze.

The clubhouse opened in 1990 after a multimillion-dollar expansion and renovation. It's surrounded by an upper-class neighborhood just two blocks from the ocean. The bar, the food in the restaurant and the views are excellent.

Other amenities include a pro shop, driving range, practice green, locker rooms and rental clubs.

Tee times may be booked a year in advance. Greens fees range from $43 to

Limit conversation on the green. Concentration is critical to putting, and players should respect each other's time for mental preparation.

Insiders' Tips

g cart. Walking is not al-

GOLF CLUB & PLANTATION

...ver Neck Rd.   249-3829
Nortn myr... Beach   (800) 446-5363
Championship Yardage: 7150
Slope: 134   Par: 72
Back Yardage: 6530
Slope: 126   Par: 72
Men's Yardage: 6000
Slope: 118   Par: 72
Other Yardage: 5090
Slope: 132   Par: 72
Ladies' Yardage: 4665
Slope: 127   Par: 72

Ken Tomlinson's 18-hole creation was named the top new course of 1990 by both *Golf Digest* and *Golf Magazine*. It continues to draw rave reviews for its bentgrass greens and bermudagrass fairways set on a wooded peninsula between the Atlantic Ocean and the Intracoastal Waterway. The 3rd, 4th and 12th greens are on the marsh, and the 13th is on Cherry Grove Inlet and the Atlantic.

You might feel intimidated at the par 4 No. 5 because of the extremely large sand trap right off the tees. Also, the green is guarded on the left and right by traps. Par 3 No. 17 plays over water to a green that is bordered by four sand traps. The signature hole is No. 13.

Rental clubs, a driving range, putting greens, a pro shop, bar and grill and new clubhouse with restaurant are available.

Tee times may be booked 365 days in advance. Walking is not allowed. Greens fees range from $63 to $98, including cart.

THE TRADITION CLUB

1027 Willbrook Blvd.   626-1658
Pawleys Island   (800) TEE-OFFS
Championship Yardage: 6717
Slope: No rating   Par: 72
Men's Yardage: 6170
Slope: No rating   Par: 72

Other Yardage: 5554
Slope: No rating   Par: 72
Ladies' Yardage: 4924
Slope: No rating   Par: 72
Forward Yardage: 4148
Slope: No rating   Par: 72

This stunning 18-hole course was crafted by Ron Garl from acres of natural sand waste areas. Recently opened in the fall of 1995, it includes an island par 3 as well as a par 3 strategically set in the center of a vast waste area. Large rolling greens are set among the sand and towering Carolina pines. Garl created multiple teeing areas to determine the ideal ladies' yardage. This experiment has garnered national attention as has the Links Group's addition of this track to their nine-course collection along the Grand Strand.

The elaborate world-class practice area includes a 43,000-square-foot putting green, a multilevel chipping and pitching area, practice sand bunkers and target greens framed by sand and water to make practice itself an unforgettable experience.

Tee times may be booked a year in advance. Greens fees, including cart, range from $43 to $61. Walking is allowed after 3 PM.

WATERWAY HILLS GOLF COURSE

U.S. Hwy. 17 N.   449-6488
Myrtle Beach   (800) 344-5590

One of the most unusual to access, this club includes three nine-hole courses on the west side of the Intracoastal Waterway. You can only get to them by the lift over the waterway. If you're afraid of heights and the rocking ride of a ski lift, you won't know what you're missing. Wilderness surrounds these courses — and they're especially popular for that reason. One of the pros says there's an advantage to having nothing but wildlife around the courses.

These tracks were built in 1975, designed by Robert Trent Jones Sr., with bermudagrass greens. The terrain is rolling, and water comes into play a great deal.

Amenities include a bar, restaurant, driving range and rental clubs.

Walking is allowed, and pull carts are available. Tee times are accepted a year in advance and may be reserved through the same toll-free number for bookings at Myrtle Beach National Golf Club.

Greens fees range from $29 to $54, including cart.

Lakes Course
Championship Yardage: 3190
Slope: 121   Par: 36
Men's Yardage: 3001
Slope: 115   Par: 36
Ladies' Yardage: 2490
Slope: 115   Par: 36

Hole No. 9 is a dogleg left, a 390-yard par 4. It has a nice wide fairway, but a trap is left and right of your landing area. If you hit the landing area right, you have a nice iron shot to the undulating green, which is guarded on the right by two small traps.

Oaks Course
Championship Yardage: 3271
Slope: 119   Par: 36
Men's Yardage: 3080
Slope: 118   Par: 36
Ladies' Yardage: 2579
Slope: 118   Par: 36

Every single hole on the Oaks is straightaway. No. 3 is a par 4 of 422 yards, which shoots straight, as you suspect it should, but halfway down the fairway are lakes on each side. If you go long on your drive either left or right, your ball will be wet.

Ravine Course
Championship Yardage: 2927
Slope: 121   Par: 36
Men's Yardage: 2579
Slope: 112   Par: 36
Ladies' Yardage: 2335
Slope: 112   Par: 36

The 8th hole, a 470-yard par 5, is straightaway. If you try to go for the green in two, two bunkers could possibly be a hindrance, as could a greenside bunker on the front. There's yet another bunker behind the green.

WICKED STICK GOLF LINKS
U.S. Hwy. 17 S.   650-2146
Surfside Beach   (800) 548-9186
Championship Yardage: 7001
Slope: Not rated   Par: 72
Men's Yardage: 6507
Slope: Not rated   Par: 72
Other Yardage: 6080
Slope: Not rated   Par: 72
Ladies' Yardage: 4911
Slope: Not rated   Par: 72

John Daly's first-ever signature course, Wicked Stick opened in 1995. Daly served as consultant to architect Clyde Johnston. The course was developed by Southpark Golf Group Ltd. Partnership, a group led by past president of the PGA of America Gary Schaal.

This 18-hole links-style course features expansive dunes fields, large sand waste areas with gorse-like vegetation, pot bunkers and strategically placed water hazards. A select number of Daly signature tees offer additional length and difficulty, but generous landing areas help the average player.

Greens fees range from $30 to $65, including cart. Walking is allowed after 12 noon.

WILD WING PLANTATION
U.S. Hwy. 501   347-9464
Myrtle Beach   (800) 736-WING

Wild Wing Plantation is a 72-hole golf reserve, and it is truly a showcase for good golfers — many think they've gone to heaven. Japanese-owned and operated, it shows a distinct Oriental influence in the clubhouse and in its attention to detail and perfection. The plantation is set on

1,050 acres of natural beauty west of Myrtle Beach.

Almost every golfer loves the aesthetics and the variety of Wild Wing's courses; beginners might not excel on its tough courses, but they will enjoy nature while they improve. Some golfers could spend a four-day golf trip just at Wild Wing and be more than content with the diversity of the four courses.

The courses' bird names are not just incidental. All of these species have been sighted. On the Falcon Course, for example, a falcon sometimes just sits on a mound watching a hole, even when a foursome is wildly driving onto the green or all around it. The operations staff is studying flora that will attract the specific fowl to their namesake courses.

The pro shop, bar and restaurant are award winners. A beverage cart, driving range, practice greens and rental clubs are available.

Tee times are accepted up to a year in advance. Greens fees range from $42 to $85 at the Wood Stork and Hummingbird courses and from $60 to $103 on the Avocet and Falcon courses, including a cart in all cases. Each cart is equipped with a water cooler; you may not take a personal cooler. Walking is not allowed.

Falcon Course

Championship Yardage: 7082
Slope: 134	Par: 72

Men's Yardage: 6697
Slope: 128	Par: 72

Other Yardage: 6089
Slope: 117	Par: 72

Ladies' Yardage: 5190
Slope: 118	Par: 72

The Falcon Course, 18 holes built in 1994, was designed by Rees Jones in a "modern traditional" style. With an abundance of mounding, narrow fairways and small bentgrass greens, the Falcon offers diversity in design and play while creating a visually exciting experience. Jones, the renowned golf course architect, said, "The natural appearing features help to contain errant balls and provide a variety of approach shots." Right! We know of a number of errant balls that weren't exactly contained. Both nines feature large lakes. This course contains Wild Wing's most dominant feature, a 515-yard bunker, which separates the 12th and 13th holes.

Avocet Course

Championship Yardage: 7127
Slope: 128	Par: 72

Men's Yardage: 6614
Slope: 119	Par: 72

Other Yardage: 6028
Slope: 114	Par: 72

Ladies' Yardage: 5298
Slope: 118	Par: 72

The Avocet course opened in 1993 and was recognized by *Golf Digest* among the Top 10 Best New Resort Courses for 1994. It was designed as a signature course by Larry Nelson. Bentgrass greens are elevated, and one is a double green. Some fairways are double, and some tees are elevated.

Hummingbird Course

Championship Yardage: 6853
Slope: 131	Par: 72

Men's Yardage: 6310
Slope: 123	Par: 72

Other Yardage: 5796
Slope: 123	Par: 72

Ladies' Yardage: 5168
Slope: 123	Par: 72

The Hummingbird Course, 18 holes by Willard Byrd, opened in 1992. It's a links-style course with bentgrass greens, native grasses around its perimeter, strategically placed lakes and open fairways. It has an array of pot bunkers and waste areas.

Wood Stork Course

Championship Yardage: 7044
Slope: 126	Par: 72

Men's Yardage: 6106
Slope: 111	Par: 72

Ladies Yardage: 5409
Slope: 121   Par: 72

The Wood Stork Course, 18 holes also designed by Willard Byrd, opened in 1991. Its parklike setting features significant natural hazards: The first eight holes play through wetlands; the next 10, through a pine forest.

WILLBROOK PLANTATION GOLF CLUB

U.S. Hwy. 17 S.   237-4900
Pawleys Island   (800) 344-5590
Championship Yardage: 6704
Slope: 125   Par: 72
Men's Yardage: 6106
Slope: 118   Par: 72
Ladies' Yardage: 4963
Slope: 118   Par: 72

Dan Maples designed this 18-hole course on rice plantation wetlands between Litchfield Beach and Pawleys Island.

The par 4 No. 5 is a 383-yard hole. Your drive has to carry water onto the fairway that has a nice landing area, and the second shot also has to carry water onto a small green that gives the appearance of an island green, surrounded by water on three sides. You won't have to play the island green until you get to the 127-yard par 3 No. 6.

Public play is limited, with members given preference. A new clubhouse opened in the fall of 1995.

Greens fees are $33, including cart, with a summer coupon published regularly in the Myrtle Beach Sun News, and $46 in the high season, with a $17 additional cart fee. Booking is accepted a year in advance.

THE WITCH

1900 S.C. Hwy. 544   347-2706
Conway   (803) 448-1300
Championship Yardage: 6702
Slope: 133   Par: 71
Men's Yardage: 6011
Slope: 121   Par: 71
Ladies Yardage: 4812
Slope: 109   Par: 71

The Witch is an 18-hole course built in 1989 and designed by Dan Maples, with bermudagrass fairways and bentgrass greens. This course was built in the middle of a swamp. Wetlands come into play on almost every hole, and bridges wind through the course for about 4,000 feet. The 15th hole is a par 4 requiring a carry over wetlands of as much as 200 yards. The 9th hole features an island fairway surrounded by wetlands; it requires a carry over wetlands on the tee shot and the second shot.

Practice greens, a pro shop, beverage cart, rental clubs, a driving range, bar and restaurant are available.

The course accepts tee times 365 days in advance. Greens fees range from $46 to $83 and include a cart. Walking is not allowed.

Around the Grand Strand...

Fun Things To Do in Myrtle Beach

Entertainment comes in many forms along the Grand Strand. On those days when you're not playing golf, or if you and your family come here for golf combined with vacation, you have an almost endless choice of activities.

You only have to look at the **ocean** for the most obvious entertainment. If the sedentary life of sunbathing while reading a book isn't for you, you can rent a jet ski, take a sail boat ride out into the wild blue yonder or do a little parasailing. All of these can be done for a minimal cost. Or rent a bike, with the kids on funny low-slung three-wheeled banana bikes and wheel along the sand until you've seen it all. Of course that ocean can also provide you fun in the form of

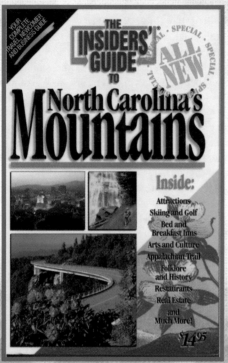

fishing, whether you are on one of the many piers, doing a little surf fishing or catching the big ones out in the Gulf Stream on a charter. Several charters you can choose are in Murrells Inlet, Little River or Calabash.

Speaking of water, just wait 'til you see the giant water slides on a 10-acre water park at **Myrtle Waves**, located off U.S. 17 Bypass at 1001 10th Street N. Since this is obviously fun that's dictated by the season (we don't care how far north you live, your kids will definitely be cold here if they're wet and outside in the winter), call 448-1026 for information on hours and rates.

When the sun goes down you don't have to sit around and clean your clubs to get ready for your tee time tomorrow. The fun, entertainment and enjoyment can continue when the moon comes out. The beach is alive with music at one of the many theaters. Calvin Gilmore has entertained visitors for years here with his theaters, which include **The Carolina Opry** in Myrtle Beach, and his unplugged concept, **Jubilee**, in North Myrtle Beach.

Fantasy Harbour also has live entertainment theaters with the Gatlin Brothers, Ronnie Milsap, Fantasy On Ice, Medieval Times and the Cercle Theater.

The group Alabama has their theater at **Barefoot Landing** where they appear several times each year. Guest performers have included Barbara Mandrel, Waylon Jennings and other familiar names to the country music lover.

The **Palace Theater** is a new attraction that will offer a varied list of entertainers, opening in 1995 with Bill Cosby, Kenny Rogers and The Righteous Brothers (not all together of course).

You may want to add a little culture to your trip, and this can be accomplished with a single trip to **Brookgreen Gardens**, the world's largest outdoor sculpture garden. This is a beautiful slice of Lowcountry landscape, displaying more than 500 pieces of sculpture. Wildlife and botanical gardens boast more that 2,000 different plants. Children and adults will enjoy this visit.

Shopping is always on the agenda when you are visiting Myrtle Beach, and with the 1995 opening of the **Myrtle Beach Factory Stores** the variety is even larger. Other familiar places are the **Outlet Park at Waccamaw** and **Barefoot Landing**. Also a 1995 addition to that list is **Broadway at the Beach**, a unique place to eat, shop and be entertained.

The Grand Strand has much to offer the vacationer who comes here to play golf. It's possibly the capital of miniature golf, not to mention the ever popular **Pavilion**, which has been spinning its Ferris wheels for years and luring every kid to rides and amusements that delight the entire family. You might go home tired, but never bored.

Where to Eat

Dining along the Grand Strand is neither for the timid nor the dieter. The Myrtle Beach Area Chamber of Commerce has counted 1,800 restaurants and claims that the area has more restaurants per capita than San Francisco — usually considered the benchmark for abundant and noteworthy restaurants. Personally, we haven't been able to keep count in Myrtle Beach, but we are diligently trying.

The food is outrageously delicious, no matter what your preference might be. Of course, fresh seafood is the local specialty, and you will encounter Calabash-style (lightly breaded and fried) cuisine throughout the area. Calabash is

Photo: Micheal Sleary

Litchfield Country Club.

actually a little fishing village on the southern edge of North Carolina. Many seafood buffets throughout the area offer all-you-can-eat choices, predominantly Calabash-style. Please don't even think about cholesterol. Anything so tasty just has to be good for you.

The other primary variety of local specialty is Lowcountry cooking. The Lowcountry stretches from the southern end of the Grand Strand throughout the Charleston and Hilton Head areas. Wealthy plantation owners settled in the Lowcountry, and their style of cooking depended heavily on locally produced fish, fowl and vegetables. The preparation took its flavorful hints from slaves who brought their ancestral memories of Creoles, sauces and stews from the French.

Plenty of ribs, steaks, burgers, and chicken are equally delicious if you don't want seafood. Also, vegetarian specialties, Italian and Oriental delicacies are equally superior.

Yes, as you might have guessed, we love food almost as much as we love golf.

If your area has a links-style course, play it one day in a howling gale or light rain to get a sense of what it's like to play in Scotland where the game began.

Insiders' Tips

CHESTNUT HILL

9922 U.S. Hwy. 17
Myrtle Beach   449-3984
$$$

Chestnut Hill offers fine dining in a casual atmosphere overlooking a beautiful marsh. Friendly service adds to the experience, and you'll want to come back often. Seafood, steaks, chicken and home-baked breads are the specialties.

JOE'S BAR & GRILL

U.S. Hwy. 17 S.
Myrtle Beach   272-4666
$$$

The selection of beef, veal, seafood and poultry is good. The atmosphere is golf shirt, but the meal is coat and tie.

ROSSI'S

9600 U.S. Hwy. 17 N.
Myrtle Beach   449-0481
$$$

Italian is the specialty here, including homemade pasta, but every choice is fine. We've never had a bad meal here. Golfers will find their own special corner, and everyone will have fun.

VILLA MARE

7819 N. Kings Hwy.
Myrtle Beach   449-8654
$$

Please don't tell all of your friends about this fabulous Italian restaurant. Don't tell anyone the food is the best, the most quantity and the least expensive. This is a secret place among locals, and we don't want it to get so crowded that we can't get our table. Lunch and dinner are real treats.

SEA CAPTAIN'S HOUSE

3002 N. Ocean Blvd.
Myrtle Beach   448-8082
$$$

This is one of the oldest and best of the local establishments. All the recipes are special Southern secrets. A long wait for a table is common, but you can enjoy watching the waves break and the sea gulls flocking to the lights. Think about splurging on a special dessert. You'll never find anything remotely comparable. During early breakfast, you can watch the dolphins play. Lunch and dinner also provide experiences to remember.

THE OLD PRO'S TABLE

U.S. Hwy. 17 S.
Myrtle Beach   272-6060
$$$

You'll find the area's only collection of golf antiques here as well as quality steaks or seafood for dinner. This famous haven of golf atmosphere is convenient and accessible from any golf course and across from Barefoot Landing. On a good day, you won't have to wait too long.

SAM SNEAD'S TAVERN

9708 N. Kings Hwy.
Myrtle Beach   497-0580
$$

Sam Snead's serves good food for dinner only. It's owned and operated by the same group as the popular Thoroughbred's next door, but the sporty atmosphere is even more pleasing for a casual meal. Even better than the food is the memorabilia collected by Snead, arguably the greatest golfer of all time. The fourth such restaurant in the country to open, this is a real museum. Snead occasionally greets visitors with his homespun philosophy explaining his self-taught golfing success.

CAROLINA ROADHOUSE

4617 S. Kings Hwy.
Myrtle Beach   497-9911
$$

The Roadhouse is patterned after the supremely popular California Dreaming restaurants in Charleston and Columbia.

Photo: Michael Slear

Pine Lakes International Country Club.

It smells like the fresh cedar of its rafters combined with fresh rolls and fries you can watch being prepared. This restaurant is open for dinner only.

DICK'S LAST RESORT

Barefoot Landing
North Myrtle Beach 272-7794
$$

Yes, Dick's even serves golfers, and the same rough and rude service is dished out to all who want to be loud and crazy in this popular nightspot where the food is actually served in a bucket and eaten with fingers. If you can manage to get here for Elvis's birthday, you will know he's alive and well in Myrtle Beach like no where else on earth.

THE ISLAND CAFE

U.S. Hwy. 17 S.
Pawleys Island 237-9527
$$

Locals frequent this cafe once a week for the lobster night. Everyone driving from one golf course to another on the South Strand stops here for a sandwich for lunch.

CONCH CAFE

1482 N. Waccamaw Dr.
Garden City 651-6556
$$$

Jimmy Buffet would be at home here, or maybe he was here when he wrote some of his tunes. Don't come here in a rush. Come after a round of morning golf on the South Strand and plan on a long cool salty drink with a sandwich.

FLO'S PLACE RESTAURANT & RAW BAR

U.S. Hwy. 17 Bus.
Murrells Inlet 651-7222
$$

Flo's is one of the only places we know of that offers alligator ribs. Flo's recipes, including the alligator and crawfish specialties, came from her childhood in Loui-

siana where her father regularly brought home such delicacies. Try the stewpot, which has some of everything mixed in. Plan to hold on to your hat unless you want to find it hanging from the rafters where Flo's collection sports hundreds of them. Flo's Place is fun and friendly, and it hangs over the marsh, creating a definite backwoods bayou feeling.

DRUNKEN JACK'S RESTAURANT & LOUNGE

U.S. Hwy. 17 Bus.
Murrells Inlet 651-2044
$$$

Plan to arrive long before you expect to be hungry, because the wait "in-season," as locals say, may be more than an hour or two. The downstairs lounge provides a view and a drink, and if you can wait, the seafood choices upstairs are worth it.

Where to Stay

Most of the major hotels on the Grand Strand offer golf packages. The following offers a variety of suggestions from basic golfer's accommodations to luxury resorts for a special family vacation.

SEA MIST OCEANFRONT RESORT

1200 S. Ocean Blvd. 448-1551
Myrtle Beach (800) SEA-MIST
$$

Sea Mist is one of the largest resorts that caters to golfers. Perfect for families, it offers supervised and structured summer programs for children. Many activities are within walking distance of the Sea Mist.

KINGSTON PLANTATION— A RADISSON RESORT

9800 Lake Dr.
Myrtle Beach 449-0006
$$$$$

This is one of the classiest resorts if

Photo: S.C. Department of Parks, Recreation and Tourism

Carolina pines flank the fairways of this Grand Strand gem.

you want to splurge on an oceanfront suite and spend some time; also villas for foursomes are practical if you're only here for golf. Be sure to enjoy the oceanfront pool and bar, plus the fine dining for a weekend dinner buffet. An indoor pool and health club also are on the property. The Arcadian Shores Golf Course is across the street, and many nightspots are an easy drive from the Radisson.

SANDS OCEAN CLUB RESORT
9550 Shore Dr.
Myrtle Beach   449-6461
$$

Suites or efficiencies are convenient to all major golf courses. The area is popular during summer when the neighboring Ocean Annie's Beach Bar offers live music, and lots of fun folks dance away the days and nights here. It's easy to walk to a few shops or, during November, to slip across the footbridge to the Dunes Club for the SENIOR TOUR Championship.

OCEAN CREEK
10600 N. Kings. Hwy.   448-8446
Myrtle Beach   (800) 443-7050
$$$$

Choose the towers on the oceanfront, or choose a short walk back to a villa on the 57-acre resort that welcomes golfers. The freshwater creek running through the property provides a unique change for the occasional golfer who doesn't like the ocean. The family who doesn't golf will love to scoot across Highway 17 to spend a day at Barefoot Landing where shopping and dining make up an award-winning center.

THE INN AT MYRTLE BEACH
7300 N. Ocean Blvd.
Myrtle Beach   449-3361
$$

This looks like a regular medium-size motel and is priced accordingly,

but it's far better quality than most, offering attractive furnishings and spacious rooms. If you bring a big family, consider the penthouse suite for a pleasant view, screened porch and plenty of rooms.

MYRTLE BEACH MARTINIQUE
7100 N. Ocean Blvd.
Myrtle Beach   449-4441
$$$

One of Myrtle Beach's nicest hotels, The Martinique offers just about any size room, efficiency or suite your group will need. The restaurant and bar are worth a stop, and this accommodation is convenient to northerly, southerly and centrally located golf courses.

OCEAN DUNES/SAND DUNES RESORT
201 74th Ave. N.
Myrtle Beach   449-7441
$$$

This resort caters to golfers — it's convenient to any golf course. Many rooms are oceanfront, and you can get on some private golf courses through this group's experienced and competent golf department. A full range of amenities are available on the premises for the non-golfers, and shopping areas also are nearby.

DUNES VILLAGE RESORT
5200 N. Ocean Blvd.
Myrtle Beach   449-5275
$$

The Dunes Village has the feel of a small family resort where everyone knows your name. Catering to golfers, the resort offers an attractive year-round pool and is a nice spot for the whole family to enjoy. The breakfast here is legendary, and you will likely return to this same home at the beach year after year.

Rees Jones opened Belle Terre in October 1995.

CORAL BEACH RESORT

1105 S. Ocean Blvd.
Myrtle Beach   448-8421
$$$

Have you ever taken a group to the beach only to encounter an unusually rainy week with nothing to do outdoors? If so, you'll want to consider staying at the Coral Beach. Of course, we know it never rains on the golf course, but sometimes it rains on the kids' pool parties. This quality hotel has a bowling alley on the sixth floor, arcade games and a regular entertainment center of its own. It also caters to golf groups, as you'll surmise from the memorabilia adorning its version of the 19th hole.

SHERATON MYRTLE BEACH RESORT

2701 S. Ocean Blvd.
Myrtle Beach   448-2518
$$$$$

The Sheraton is one of the truly nice spots to find a room, efficiency or suite. Golfers and their families will enjoy several pools, a health club and good food and drink in a welcoming setting. It's close enough to "downtown" Myrtle Beach to easily access any golf course, restaurant or entertainment on the north or south end of the Strand.

LITCHFIELD BEACH AND GOLF RESORT

U.S. Hwy. 17 S.   237-3000
Litchfield   (800) 845-1897
$$$$$

If you or someone in your party plays tennis, wants to find a spa and health club or simply wants to retreat from the busy resort area to the quiet marshes of the South Strand, this is the place for you. Everything you could need is here, and it's surrounded by several notable golf courses. The restaurant is great, entertainment is nearby and specialty shops are easily accessible. At Litchfield, you could completely miss Myrtle Beach and still have the vacation of a lifetime.

SWAMP FOX RESORT

2311 S. Ocean Blvd.
Myrtle Beach   448-8373
$$

The Swamp Fox boasts more oceanfront footage than most hotels. A quality and experienced golf department will help you book any package, including theater if desired. Choose from rooms or suites in its new tower or older motel. Little ones will enjoy the Lazy River, and everyone will be pleased with the adjoining Gabriel's Restaurant.

THE CARIBBEAN

3000 N. Ocean Blvd.   448-7181
Myrtle Beach   (800) 845-0883
$$$

New oceanfront suites in the tower sleep extras in the living room, and the breakfast included with your golf package will give you the real flavor of a local Myrtle Beach favorite — next door at the Sea Captain's House. Non-golfing family members hang out at the pool or roam a few blocks to the mall.

CLARION WINDS HOTEL

310 E. First St.   579-6275
Ocean Isle Beach   (800) 334-3581
$-$$

This lovely oceanfront hotel is part of the North Carolina Golf Coast Association that is seeking to develop its own identify separate from the Myrtle Beach or Wilmington areas between which it lies. The 73 rooms include oceanfront rooms and one-, two- or three-bedroom suites overlooking subtropical gardens and a 7-mile island beach. The four-bedroom spa houses (which sleep eight) are ideal for golf groups. All five luxurious houses include full kitchens, great rooms and large Jacuzzis.

Caledonia Golf & Fish Club.

Photo: Michael Slear

Golf packages with guaranteed tee times and discounted rates are offered on 20 high-quality Brunswick County courses within a five- to 15-minute drive and a total of some 86 championship courses in the Myrtle Beach area. Golfers are welcomed at a weekly reception during the prime golf seasons — spring and fall. Also, the continental breakfast buffet is more than the usual continental fare — it's pancakes, waffles or cereal.

If you aren't looking for the big city lights and other attractions, come here for great golf and great beach access in the family-type Ocean Isle area.

Golf Equipment

You'll find anything you need on the Grand Strand. You won't have any trouble finding a store, and what you'll find will amaze you by being bigger and better than anything you can find elsewhere. If you're in the market for new clubs, wait until you get here to shop. In addition to the following suggested equipment shops, professionals at many of the golf courses offer custom fitting. Ask a local golfer if you have any questions.

When golf shopping on the Grand Strand, check out any or all (if you have a week or more to spend just shopping!) of the following golf equipment retailers: **Nevada Bob's**, 3100 N. Kings Highway, Myrtle Beach, 448-1779, or 2006 U.S. Highway 17, North Myrtle Beach, 272-4705; **Golf Dimensions**, 2301 U.S. Highway 17 S., North Myrtle Beach, 272-4630; **Martin's Golf and Tennis**, 1615 U.S. Highway 17, North Myrtle Beach, 272-6030; 2204 U.S. Highway 17 N., 448-7525, or U.S. Highway 501, 236-7878, in Myrtle Beach; or

1010 U.S. Highway 17 S., Surfside, 238-1643; **Scottish Pride Golf**, 1500 U.S. Highway 501, Myrtle Beach, 946-9464; **Clubmaker's Golf**, 2016 N. Kings Highway, Myrtle Beach, 626-0099; **Wild Willie's**, U.S. Highway 501, Myrtle Beach, 249-9722 or (800) 249-9722; and **Sam's Discount Golf & Tennis Inc.**, 3300-C U.S. Highway 17 S., North Myrtle Beach, 272-6998.

Golf Instruction

Most of these golf schools offer any type of package you'll need to improve your golf game. Call for specific information or ask at any course you choose to play about private lessons by their professional staff. The area code for the following businesses is 803.

We recommend the following: **Myrtle Beach Golf Academy** at The Legends, (800) 882-5121; **The Links Group Golf School** at The Tradition Club, (800) TEE-OFFS; **Phil Ritson Golf School** at Pawleys Plantation Golf & Country Club, (800) 624-4653 or 237-4993; **Swing's The Thing Golf School** at Colonial Charters Golf & Country Club, 249-8809; **The Classic Swing Golf School** at Deer Track Golf Resort, (800) 548-9186 or 650-2545; **Riley School of Golf** at Wild Wing Plantation, (800) 84-RILEY; and **Myrtle Beach Golf School**, (800) 94-SWING.

Photo: The Charleston Area Convention & Visitors Bureau

Exploring Charleston's many beautifully restored homes is a pleasant pastime when you're not golfing.

Inside
Charleston/Hilton Head/ Beaufort, South Carolina

The Lowcountry stretches south along the South Carolina coast from Georgetown to Hilton Head. Lowcountry defines the marshy terrain and is often used to define the golf courses, the food, the culture, the architecture and the lifestyle of this area.

Charleston speaks of history with an irresistible charm and beauty. Walking the cobblestone streets of downtown or taking a guided tour by water or by horse and carriage, you may believe it's still the 17th century. Wandering among the military sites, homes, churches and formal gardens is a great way to enjoy Charleston when your golf game is finished. You'll seldom see so many architectural treasures as the huge mansions of pastel colors, and all are preserved in their original antebellum splendor. Charleston is an important Southern city displaying faint touches of modernity and a California lifestyle in its streetlife.

As the home of the annual Spoleto Festival USA — the world's largest arts festival in terms of the actual number of events offered — each May, Charleston offers cultural entertainment opportunities unlike most Southern cities. Art, music, drama and dance are reflective of international influences, not of a Southern city torn by its country's Civil War. Yet the carefully preserved traditions of the African culture are proudly shared by Gullah presentations so moving that you may feel the prickle of goose bumps.

Be sure to sample some she-crab soup, shrimp and grits and other local seafood, as well as some Lowcountry recipes, including black bean specialties and frogmore stew (just so you'll know, it doesn't even have any frogs in it). In fact, more grits are sold in these low coastal plains than anywhere else in the world, and the small town of St. George capitalized on this by instituting the World Grits Festival, celebrated each April. If you really want to learn about some Southern food, watch for the frequent food-related festivals throughout the coastal Carolinas from spring through fall, featuring shrimp, Cajun specialties and other tasty regional fare.

Golf follows the gracious Southern style with tradition and quality. Many clubhouses return you to a veranda with wooden rocking chairs, where you can look out over the rolling fairways, sip a cool mint julep and recount your winning shots. Charleston was the home of Harleston Green and The South Carolina Golf Club, the first golf course and golf club in America, respectively, both established in 1786. Today the area offers more than 20 outstanding courses and a relaxing pace, well-known since the 1991 Ryder Cup put Kiawah's Ocean Course in the international spotlight.

Included in the Charleston area are North Charleston, Summerville, Mt. Pleasant, McClellanville and St. George. Also, the islands are important vacation spots away from the bustling city life:

GOLF COURSES IN CHARLESTON/HILTON HEAD/BEAUFORT, SOUTH CAROLINA

Course Name	Type	#Holes	Par	Slope	Yards	Walking	Booking	Cost w/ Cart
Callawassie Island Club								
Dogwood Course	semiprivate	9	36	n/r	3239	no	call	$52-73
Magnolia Course	semiprivate	9	36	n/r	3275	no	call	$52-73
Palmetto Course	semiprivate	9	36	n/r	3187	no	call	$52-73
Charleston Municipal Golf Course	public	18	72	110	6161	yes	7 days	$20-23
Charleston National Country Club	semiprivate	18	72	129	6482	PM	60 days	$34-56
Coosaw Creek Country Club	semiprivate	18	71	124	6068	yes	call	$38-44
Country Club of Beaufort at Pleasant Point	semiprivate	18	72	115	6112	yes	call	$24
Country Club of Hilton Head	semiprivate	18	72	128	6543	no	call	$55-73
Crowfield Plantation	semiprivate	18	72	120	6471	yes	call	$20-49
Dunes West Golf Club	semiprivate	18	72	125	6392	no	365 days	$42-72
Golden Bear Golf Course/Indigo Run	semiprivate	18	72	125	6643	no	call	$55-73
Hilton Head National Golf Club	public	18	72	119	6260	no	call	$40-66
Island West Golf Club	public	18	72	124	6208	no	call	$49-62
Kiawah Island								
Marsh Point Course	resort	18	71	126	5841	no	call	$94
Ocean Course	resort	18	72	139	6824	no	call	$110
Osprey Point Course	resort	18	72	124	6015	no	call	$100
Turtle Point Course	resort	18	72	132	6396	no	call	$100
Oak Point Golf Club	public	18	72	128	6468	yes	call	$40
Ocean Point Golf Links	resort	18	72	124	6060	yes	call	$39-54
Old South Golf Links	public	18	72	119	6354	PM	call	$48-75
Oyster Reef Golf Course	semiprivate	18	72	123	6440	no	call	$63-79
Palmetto Dunes Golf Course								
Arthur Hills Course	resort	18	72	120	6122	yes	call	$36-75
George Fazio Course	resort	18	70	123	6239	yes	call	$36-75
Robert Trent Jones Course	resort	18	72	119	6148	yes	call	$36-75

Course Name	Type	#Holes	Par	Slope	Yards	Walking	Booking	Cost w/ Cart
Palmetto Hall Plantation								
Arthur Hills Course	semiprivate	18	72	123	6582	yes	call	$36-75
Robert Cupp Course	semiprivate	18	72	126	6522	yes	call	$36-75
Patriots Point Golf Links	public	18	72	113	6274	call	call	call
Port Royal Golf Club								
Barony Course	resort	18	72	122	6038	yes	call	$32-76
Planters Row Course	resort	18	72	126	6009	yes	call	$32-76
Robbers Row Course	resort	18	72	129	6188	yes	call	$32-7
Sea Pines								
Harbour Town Course	resort	18	71	126	6119	no	call	$105-175
Ocean Course	resort	18	72	119	6213	no	call	$105-175
Sea Marsh Course	resort	18	72	117	6129	no	call	$105-175
Seabrook Island								
Crooked Oaks Course	resort	18	72	121	6387	yes	call	$50-75
Ocean Winds Course	resort	18	72	125	6395	yes	call	$50-75
Shadowmoss Plantation	semiprivate	18	72	117	6399	weekdays	call	$24-32
Shipyard Golf Club								
Brigantine Course	resort	9	36	n/r	2959	after 5 PM	call	$38-80
Clipper Course	resort	9	36	n/r	3132	after 5 PM	call	$38-80
Galleon Course	resort	9	36	n/r	3035	after 5 PM	call	$38-80
The Golf Professionals Club								
Champions Course	semiprivate	18	72	119	6430	yes	call	$22-25
Players Course	semiprivate	18	72	101	5659	yes	call	$22-25
The Links at Stono Ferry	resort	18	72	112	6085	no	call	$38-41
Wild Dunes								
Harbor Course	resort	18	70	117	5900	no	call	$35-75
Links Course	resort	18	72	121	6131	yes	call	$55-110

Charleston/Hilton Head/Beaufort

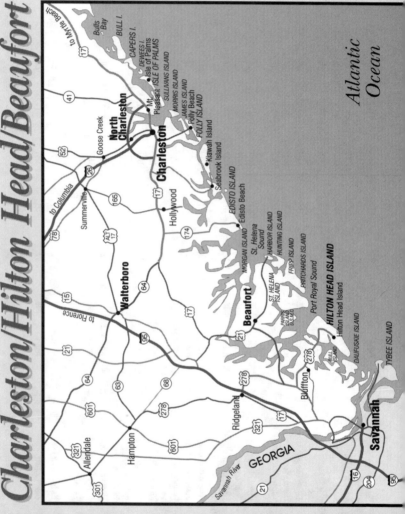

Atlantic Ocean

to Myrtle Beach

Bulls Bay

BULL I.

CAPERS I.

DEWEES I.

Isle of Palms

ISLE OF PALMS

SULLIVANS ISLAND

MORRIS ISLAND

JAMES ISLAND

Folly Beach

FOLLY ISLAND

Kiawah Island

Seabrook Island

EDISTO ISLAND

Edisto Beach

North Charleston

Goose Creek

Charleston

Hollywood

Summerville

to Columbia

Walterboro

to Florence

MORGAN ISLAND

St. Helena Sound

HARBOR ISLAND

HUNTING ISLAND

ST. HELENA ISLAND

FRIPP ISLAND

PRITCHARDS ISLAND

Beaufort

PARRIS ISLAND

Port Royal Sound

HILTON HEAD ISLAND

Hilton Head Island

DAUFUSKIE ISLAND

Bluffton

Ridgeland

Hampton

Allendale

GEORGIA

Savannah River

Savannah

TYBEE ISLAND

Edisto, Kiawah, Seabrook and Sullivans Island, Folly Beach and Isle of Palms. Each boasts its own character and attracts its own type of visitor or resident. Sample each until you find your own niche for seclusion or activity.

You'll also discover more than 20 courses in the Hilton Head and Beaufort areas. Beaufort (pronounced *beu-ford*) lies a few miles inland on the way south from Charleston to Hilton Head. Beaufort's entire town is a historic landmark and a treasured find for any history or antiques buffs. Interested browsers should schedule extra time for roaming around here after the golf game.

Golf, tennis and relaxing are the major activities on Hilton Head Island and outlying Fripp Island. Hilton Head is a 12-mile strand showcasing the white sands of the Atlantic beaches and the undisturbed natural beauty of flora and fauna. It is best known for the Heritage Golf Classic that was first played here on the Harbour Town Golf Links in 1969. Every spring, the party returns, and the plaid winner's jacket is passed to another of the world's best golfers. No amusement parks, unobtrusive shopping areas and a quiet way of life lead many to vacation or retire here. It's the most peaceful resort if you're looking for luxury, sophistication and good taste. Internationally known for its golf and tennis resorts and its fine quality, Hilton Head prides itself on catering to the crème de la crème rather than offering something for everyone. If that's your style, you will feel right at home here. Just don't expect anything too much more strenuous than a tennis match or a round of golf.

Additional information is available in *The Insiders' Guide® to Greater Charleston* or by calling the Charleston Trident Chamber of Commerce, 577-2510; the Charleston Area Convention and Visitors Bureau, 853-8000; the Edisto Chamber of Commerce, 869-3867; the Greater Beaufort Chamber of Commerce, 524-3163; the Hilton Head Island Chamber of Commerce, 785-3653; or the Greater Summerville Chamber of Commerce, 873-2931.

Note that the area code for all golf courses and businesses listed in this chapter is 803.

Lowcountry Golf Courses

CALLAWASSIE ISLAND CLUB
S.C. Hwy. 6, 176 Callawassie Rd.
Callawassie Island   521-1533
Dogwood/Palmetto Course
Championship Yardage: 6822
Slope: 130   Par: 72
Men's Yardage: 6426
Slope: 125   Par: 72
Ladies Yardage: 5166
Slope: 123   Par: 72
Other Yardage: 6053
Slope: 123   Par: 72
Magnolia/Dogwood Course
Championship Yardage: 6956
Slope: 138   Par: 72
Men's Yardage: 6514
Slope: 132   Par: 72
Ladies' Yardage: 5237
Slope: 126   Par: 72
Other Yardage: 6124
Slope: 129   Par: 72
Palmetto/Magnolia Course
Championship Yardage: 6956
Slope: 132   Par: 72
Men's Yardage: 6462
Slope 129   Par: 72

Ladies' Yardage: 5201
Slope: 120   Par: 72
Other Yardage: 6035
Slope: 124   Par: 72

The three nine-hole courses at Callawassie Island Club — to be played in tandem pairs to create an 18-hole round — were designed by Tom Fazio and built in 1986. Fazio says it's one of his best; of course, he likes all of his designs, as well he should.

Callawassie Island is an 880-acre sea island that sits among the marshlands between the Colleton and Chechessee rivers. A short drive from Charleston or Hilton Head and just past Beaufort, this island showcases a delightful piece of nature where birds and wildlife disregard your golfing, and your round is relaxed and easygoing but not necessarily easy golfing.

The order of difficulty is Magnolia, Dogwood then Palmetto. The Dogwood is the newest, and its four finishing holes along the river lend dramatics to your game. Greens are tifdwarf, and fairways are bermudagrass. The signature hole at Callawassie is the par 4 No. 9 on the Magnolia Course, where you must hit over a marsh onto an island green. The 4th hole on the Dogwood is tough — a 450-yard par 4 with a wetlands hazard on the right that narrows your driving area. On 15 of Callawassie's 27 holes, you will encounter marshland or ponds.

Practice greens, a driving range, a pro shop, rental clubs, a locker room, bar and restaurant are available.

Greens fees range from $52 to $73, including cart. Walking is allowed for members only. Advance bookings are accepted up to 40 days before play.

By the way, if you've never seen a black river, spend an extra few hours and paddle a kayak along some barely discovered wa-

Photo: The Charleston Area & Visitors Bureau

The sea, sun, sand... and golf — the perfect vacation.

ter where you will find nature like nowhere else. It could be within sight of I-95, and you still can hear not a sound — save an occasional chirp or splash. If you should find Tulifinny Joe's Outpost in Ridgeland (we'll give you the number — 726-5334 — to help in the search), where the best kayaks and guides hang out, be sure to ask Leon, Judy or Em to tell you all about this location where the Waterway was born.

CHARLESTON MUNICIPAL GOLF COURSE

2110 Maybank Hwy.
Charleston   795-6517
Championship Yardage: 6411
Slope: 112   *Par: 72*
Men's Yardage: 6161
Slope: 110   *Par: 72*
Ladies' Yardage: 5202
Slope: 114   *Par: 72*

This 18-hole course, managed by the city, is Charleston's oldest course — built in 1929. It's a well-run public course, with bermudagrass greens and fairways. Greens fees for visitors are $11 on weekdays and $14 on weekends, and carts are an additional $9; late-afternoon greens fees specials are offered for $5. The course hosts 54,000 rounds of play a year, in part because it has less water than many courses, the fees are affordable and booking a round is relatively easy. Calling a week in advance is recommended.

Practice greens, a driving range, rental clubs, a pro shop, snack bar and bar are available. On busy days, a beverage cart is also available.

Walking is allowed. The scenic 13th, 14th and 15th holes are on the marsh and the Stono River.

CHARLESTON NATIONAL COUNTRY CLUB

U.S. Hwy. 17 N.
Mt. Pleasant   884-7799
Championship Yardage: 6928
Slope: 137   *Par: 72*
Men's Yardage: 6482
Slope: 129   *Par: 72*
Other Yardage: 6061
Slope: 122   *Par: 72*
Other Yardage: 5509
Slope: 114   *Par: 72*
Ladies' Yardage: 5103
Slope: 126   *Par: 72*

The existing 18-hole course was designed by Rees Jones and opened in 1990. (The original Jones-designed course was destroyed by Hurricane Hugo in 1989.) It is home to the Citadel and the College of Charleston golf teams. Fairways and greens are bermudagrass. Marshland and bridges characterize this course.

One of the pro's favorite holes is the par 4 12th, a dogleg right with a big pond on the right and marsh on the left. It requires a fairly long but accurate tee shot. You have very little rough and are in a hazard if you shoot left or right. Your second shot (ostensibly) is to an elevated and undulating green surrounded by bunkers and backed by the Intracoastal Waterway, which usually wafts a gentle breeze over the green. Another challenging hole is No. 6, a par 4 — challenging not because of its length but because of its hazards. Your tee shot needs to hit a landing area to prevent hitting a second marsh that you can't see from the tee. Then your second shot will be over a marsh onto the narrow green.

A practice green, driving range, rental clubs, bar and restaurant are available. Members may access locker-room facilities, a pool and a tennis center. The pro-shop staff is very cordial and ready to answer questions and meet golfers' needs.

Greens fees range from $34 on off-season weekdays to $56 on in-season weekends, including cart. The course is open to the public year round, and tee times are accepted 60 days in advance. Walking is allowed on a limited basis dur-

ing afternoons only. Senior discounts are available to golfers age 65 and older. Dress code requires a collared shirt and no jeans, fairly standard for Carolina courses and enforced stringently here.

COOSAW CREEK COUNTRY CLUB
4210 Club Course Dr.
North Charleston   767-9000
Championship Yardage: 6593
Slope: 129   Par: 71
Men's Yardage: 6068
Slope: 124   Par: 71
Ladies' Yardage: 5064
Slope: 115   Par: 71

Arthur Hills designed this 18-hole course that opened in 1993. It is situated on 645 acres of woods and wetlands and features bentgrass fairways and bermudagrass greens. A few holes have marsh and a bit of rolling ground somewhat unique to the Lowcountry. This course places a premium on accuracy rather than length, making the approach shot and the short game the keys to scoring well. The best opportunities for scoring are on the front nine, as the course takes charge on the back nine, with more of the water and wetlands coming into play.

Hole No. 11, a 224-yard par 3, requires that your tee shot crosses water and wetlands three times. The tee shot on No. 12, a 596-yard par 5, must cross a lake then avoid a pot bunker in the middle of the fairway. The second shot must be played long and left to avoid pine trees on the right side of the fairway at the entrance to the green. The difficult No. 14 requires a perfect drive, then still leaves another 200 yards over a marsh. The signature hole is the 16th, a 516-yard par 5 from the back tees, requiring a 3-wood off the tee to drive over a big pond. Then a 40-foot elevation change down, then back up, from tee to green provides a unique situation.

Two practice greens, a driving range and club rental are available. A pro shop, shower facilities and a grill room are on site. A beverage cart makes the rounds on weekends and holidays.

Greens fees range from $38 on weekdays to $44 on weekends year round, including cart. Walking is allowed with some restrictions, depending on how busy the course is. Tee times are accepted one week in advance.

COUNTRY CLUB OF BEAUFORT
AT PLEASANT POINT
8 Barnwell Rd.
Beaufort   522-1605
Championship Yardage: 6506
Slope: 118   Par: 72
Men's Yardage: 6112
Slope: 115   Par: 72
Ladies' Yardage: 4880
Slope: 120   Par: 72

Russell Breeden designed this 18-hole course in 1970. Fairways and greens are bermudagrass.

The signature hole is the 18th — a slight dogleg left with a lagoon on the right and oaks on the left — which returns to the clubhouse. The 7th hole requires a carry over water on the right and offers a special challenge to a golfer who needs the roll.

A driving range and a putting, chipping and sand practice area are available. You'll also find club rentals, a pro shop, locker room, bar and snack bar.

Walking is allowed. You can generally book about a week in advance, but if you have a big group, they'll be happy to work with you to book an earlier reservation. Rates begin at $24 for summer afternoon play, including cart.

COUNTRY CLUB OF HILTON HEAD
70 Skull Creek Dr.
Hilton Head   681-4653
Championship Yardage: 6919

Paradise in Paradise

Discover the Joy and Wonder of Hilton Head Island at Club Sea Crest

Hilton Head Island is famous the world over for the outstanding quality of its golf courses, tennis facilities and beaches. Club Sea Crest is a well-established vacation center located right in the heart of Hilton Head Island. At Sea Crest, you can plan your vacation at your pace! We can arrange non-stop activity or just the occasional round of golf or round of tennis - leaving you plenty of time to soak up the sun, relax, or enjoy the magnificent coastline.

And at Sea Crest, we love families. Choose from any number of Sea Crest's outstanding programs designed specifically for children and teens and all staffed by qualified leaders and instructors.

So if you're looking for a vacation you won't forget right in the middle of Paradise, then come see us at Sea Crest on Hilton Head Island.

Club Sea Crest

A Holiday for the Whole Family that You'll Never Forget

For reservations, call (803) 842-4210, ext. 13. We can't wait to see you!

Slope: 132	Par: 72
Men's Yardage: 6543	
Slope: 128	Par: 72
Other Yardage: 6162	
Slope: 124	Par: 72
Ladies Yardage: 5373	
Slope: 123	Par: 72

Part of Hilton Head Plantation's complex, the 18-hole course was designed by Rees Jones and built in 1985. It features bermudagrass greens and fairways.

The 12th green is on the Intracoastal Waterway, and others run near it as well as along freshwater ponds and marshlands. Several holes are long par 5s, two of them measuring more than 575 yards each. For instance, No. 18 is 579 yards uphill from the back tees. All in all, you will encounter 13 doglegs as well as water hazards on 14 holes. Elevation changes are constant, including some tees, landing areas and greens. And what about that punch-bowl-shaped green on the 6th?

A practice green, driving range, pro shop, beverage cart and club rental are available.

The greens fees, including cart, range from $55 to $73. Walking is not allowed. They do their best to accommodate advance tee times of as much as 120 days.

CROWFIELD PLANTATION

300 Hamlet Cir.

Goose Creek	764-4618
Championship Yardage: 7003	
Slope: 134	Par: 72
Men's Yardage: 6471	
Slope: 120	Par: 72
Other Yardage: 6701	
Slope: 128	Par: 72
Ladies' Yardage: 5682	
Slope: 115	Par: 72

Tom Jackson and Bob Spence designed this 18-hole course in 1990 with bermudagrass greens and fairways.

They planned to take advantage of the wetlands and forests of an 18th-century plantation. Dense hardwoods surround every hole, and the layout has rolling terrain and plentiful bunkers. Accuracy is essential on this course. The signature 7th hole is a par 5, measuring 513 yards from the back tees, and mounds are abundant. All greens are elevated, and the course offers extraordinary character and subtleties for the Lowcountry. Every hole has three or more sand traps. Water hazards are small rather than large bodies of water.

Practice greens, a driving range, pro shop, a bar and restaurant and rental clubs are offered. Personalized instruction is available at the driving range.

The cost ranges from $20 to $49, including cart. Walking is allowed during the week or after 2 PM on weekends. Out-of-towners trying to make vacations plans can call at any time to book an advance tee time; otherwise, if you're in town, count on an advance booking of one week.

DUNES WEST GOLF CLUB

S.C. Hwy. 41

Mt. Pleasant	856-9378
Championship Yardage: 6871	
Slope: 131	Par: 72
Men's Yardage: 6392	
Slope: 125	Par: 72
Ladies' Yardage: 5278	
Slope: 118	Par: 72

This Arthur Hills design is an 18-hole course that opened in 1991 and has received national attention for its bermudagrass-covered dunes along the Cooper River, set among ancient oaks draped with Spanish moss. It's part of a residential community 10 miles northeast of Charleston. The clubhouse was built on the foundations of an old plantation house.

As with all Lowcountry courses, marshland is dominant — although it doesn't always come into play. The course is somewhat open. High rough and copi-

ous sand give trouble around the greens. The signature hole is 18th, a straightforward par 4 with two different greens. A short green that plays about 420 yards is in the marsh; the far green plays at 454 yards from the back tees and requires a shot over the marsh to the green for the second shot. Live oaks line the right side of the fairway, and woods are on the left.

Amenities include practice greens, a driving range, rental clubs, a pro shop, bar, restaurant and beverage cart.

Tee times are accepted a year in advance. Fees range from $42 to $72, including cart. Walking is not allowed.

GOLDEN BEAR
GOLF COURSE AT INDIGO RUN

72 Colonial Dr.
Hilton Head   689-2200
Championship Yardage: 7014
Slope: 129   Par: 72
Men's Yardage: 6643
Slope: 125   Par: 72
Other Yardage: 6184
Slope: 119   Par: 72
Ladies' Yardage: 4974
Slope: 120   Par: 72

The chief architect for this Nicklaus design (and 'nicknamesake' course) was Bruce Borland. Fairways and greens are bermudagrass. Lagoons and freshwater wetlands are sprinkled among oak, cypress and pine forests around the fairways and greens. Mounding and elevation are minimal.

One of the most challenging holes is 446-yard No. 11, a long dogleg left with water to the left of the green. The par 5 15th, a dogleg right of 512 yards, has a substantial landing area for your tee shot. As long as you pass the trees on the right side of the fairway, you should have a somewhat easy shot to the green.

Practice greens, a driving range, pro shop, rental clubs, a bar and grill and a

beverage cart all add up to an enjoyable golf excursion.

Greens fees range from $55 to $73, including cart. Individuals can book tee times 30 days in advance; if you book through a golf package, that time increases to 120 days. Walking is not allowed.

THE GOLF PROFESSIONALS CLUB

93 Francis Marion Cir.
Beaufort   524-3635
Champions Course
Championship Yardage: 6811
Slope: 124   Par: 72
Men's Yardage: 6430
Slope: 119   Par: 72
Ladies Yardage: 5241
Slope: 121   Par: 72

The Champions Course has the reputation of being demanding for its difficult doglegs and for requiring a number of placement shots. Fairways are somewhat narrow. The starting hole is the signature, a 90-degree dogleg left, 225 yards from the tee, then 200 yards to the green after a good tee shot.

Players Course
Championship Yardage: 5929
Slope: 104   Par: 72
Men's Yardage: 5659
Slope: 101   Par: 72
Ladies' Yardage: 5192
Slope: 107   Par: 72

The Players Course is a good recreational golf course for people of all abilities. The average golfer can make pars and an occasional birdie on this fun course. No. 18 is a great finishing hole with a well-bunkered elevated green.

Designed by Southern Turf Nurseries, the two 18-hole courses were built in 1969. Fairways are bermudagrass. Practice greens, driving range, pro shop, club rental, locker room and bar are available. New guest houses are at The Golf Professionals Club, and packages are offered.

Kiawah Island is a favorite choice for many family vacations.

Walking is allowed. One of the true bargain courses, greens fees include a cart and are $22 during afternoons and $25 during mornings year round. Tee times can be booked a couple of weeks in advance.

HILTON HEAD NATIONAL GOLF CLUB

1100 U.S. Hwy. 278
Bluffton   842-5900
Championship Yardage: 6779
Slope: 124   *Par: 72*
Men's Yardage: 6260
Slope: 119   *Par: 72*
Other Yardage: 5589
Slope: 115   *Par: 72*
Ladies' Yardage: 4649
Slope: 109   *Par: 72*

Gary Player designed this 18-hole course in 1989. Fairways and greens are bermudagrass, and the course is always in superb condition.

There is no residential development here, just marshland. The 9th is a tough hole due to its length, and you're almost always driving into the wind to an elevated green. Marshland lines the entire right side. The No. 17 signature hole is a par 3 with a fountain guarding the front. Other than the 17th, the narrow fairways and lack of marsh resemble a Northern course more than a typical Carolina layout.

A driving range, practice greens, pro shop, bar, restaurant and rental clubs are available.

Walking is not allowed. Greens fees are $40 to $66, including cart. Tee times can be made up to 90 days in advance.

ISLAND WEST GOLF CLUB

U.S. Hwy. 278
Hilton Head   757-6660
Championship Yardage: 6803
Slope: 129   *Par: 72*
Men's Yardage: 6208
Slope: 124   *Par: 72*
Ladies' Yardage: 4938
Slope: 116   *Par: 72*

Fuzzy Zoeller designed the 18-hole course in 1992, and the architect was Clyde Johnston. The 150-acre coastal forest includes live oaks and tall pines around lush wetlands and richly colored bermudagrass greens and fairways.

The course caters to the novice as well as the veteran and exudes Fuzzy's trademark sense of fun. The forward tees are well-placed for ladies or juniors; on 12 holes they are in front or to the side of carry-over water or wetlands. Shooting from the back tees . . . well, you'll have the carry on those 12 holes to have the opportunity to test your skills. Island West starts with a par 5 that is not overly difficult and ends with a unique large double green on No. 8 and a beautiful No. 9. The signature hole is the 17th, which plays to the double green.

Practice greens, a driving range and beverage cart are available. The Southern-style clubhouse houses a bar and grill and a pro shop.

Book your tee time up to one year in advance of your game. Greens fees and cart range from $49 to $62. Walking is not allowed.

KIAWAH ISLAND

S.C. Hwy. 700
Kiawah   768-2121, (800) 654-2924
The Ocean Course
Tournament Yardage: 7371
Slope: 149   *Par: 72*
Championship Yardage: 6824
Slope: 141   *Par: 72*
Men's Yardage: 6244
Slope: 134   *Par: 72*
Ladies' Yardage: 5327
Slope: 133   *Par: 72*

Pete Dye's 1991 course gained immediate fame when it hosted the 1991 Ryder Cup, and you'll most certainly feel like part of a great tradition when you play here. It's simply one of the best, one of the toughest and one of the most scenic courses in the area.

All 18 holes offer panoramic views of the Atlantic Ocean, and 10 play directly along the ocean. Dunes, marshes, water, sand bunkers and rolling greens all make you work at playing, but you'll never complain given such beautiful surroundings.

Make bookings through the resort for an all-inclusive package with every amenity. Greens fees are at least $110, including cart. Sorry, fitness buffs — walking is not an option.

Osprey Point

Championship Yardage: 6688	
Slope: 124	Par: 72
Men's Yardage: 6015	
Slope: 118	Par: 72
Ladies' Yardage: 5122	
Slope: 120	Par: 72

Tom Fazio used four lakes to challenge you on 15 holes, and moguls will determine the route of your golf ball past marshes and lagoons, sometimes into forests of pines, palmettos, magnolias and oaks. This 18-hole course, opened in 1988, is wider and more forgiving than the other Kiawah courses.

Strong holes include the 453-yard par 4 No. 9 and a pair of par 3s longer than 200 yards. Also, strategic short par 4s tempt the big hitters.

Greens fees are more than $100, including cart. Book tee times through the resort for the best prices. No walking is allowed.

Marsh Point

Championship Yardage: 6334	
Slope: 126	Par: 71
Men's Yardage: 6007	
Slope: 120	Par: 71
Ladies' Yardage: 4944	
Slope: 122	Par: 71

Gary Player places a premium on accurate shot placement, and that is reflected in this 18-hole course, opened in 1976. Undulating greens and narrow marsh-lined fairways are well guarded with water on 13 holes but offer a good game to players of all levels. It's a short course, but one not to be considered too easy.

Dramatic contouring within the putting surface makes precise iron play a prerequisite to good scoring. A halfway house is at No. 10.

Greens fees are $94, including cart, and should be booked through the resort. Walking is prohibited.

Turtle Point

Championship Yardage: 6914	
Slope: 132	Par: 72
Men's Yardage: 6025	
Slope: 122	Par: 72
Other Yardage: 6489	
Slope: 127	Par: 72
Ladies' Yardage: 5285	
Slope: 122	Par: 72

Jack Nicklaus designed this 1981 18-hole course with a finishing hole along the ocean. Two other holes along the Atlantic are also spectacular. Lagoons, oak-lined fairways, the ocean and the winds blowing off the Atlantic all contribute to the difficulty here. A keen eye and deft touch are required to master the gentle breaks of this course. Turtle Point is always on any list of top resort courses.

Greens fees are more than $100, including cart, and can be booked through the resort as part of a fine package including many amenities. Walking is not allowed.

THE LINKS AT STONO FERRY

5365 Forest Oaks Dr.	
Hollywood	763-1817
Championship Yardage: 6606	
Slope: 115	Par: 72
Men's Yardage: 6085	
Slope: 112	Par: 72
Other Yardage: 5710	
Slope: 111	Par: 72
Ladies' Yardage: 4928	
Slope: 119	Par: 72

Carolina Women Teaching Women

Women are different. They play golf differently. They need to be taught differently, says Marlene Floyd, Ladies Professional Golf Association member, tour player and women's instructor extraordinaire.

The North Carolina native and several other female professionals from the Carolinas teach 12 schools for women only each year at Palmetto Dunes in Hilton Head. The two-day sessions allow only 10 or 12 students and begin indoors with lectures and photographs of good golfers in action. Then, they progress outdoors with gimmicks and weighted clubs that teach the students exactly how to tilt, how to swing, how to grip, what to do and, more importantly, what to feel.

Floyd teaches golfers to understand the swing and, thus, to become more proficient at the game. She explains exactly how centrifugal force works and what the body should be experiencing during the actions required of golf. She demonstrates where the elbows should be, what the

Michelle Dobek at the LPGA Peninsula Club.

Photo: Lake Norman Magazine

wrist should do and what else it takes to reach the green.

"A woman has to be more proficient than a man because of lack of muscle, lack of wrist, hand and forearm strength," Floyd said. She emphasizes the difference between men and women, explaining the different center of gravity and the changes in forearm and hand action.

Floyd's father and mother and her famous brother Raymond Floyd, a star on the regular and now the senior PGA tours, all played, and finally Marlene began the game when she was in her 20s and dating a golf pro. She began her schools for women in 1993 and had previously taught for 14 years. The family was named "Golf Family of the Year" in 1988 by the New York Metropolitan Golf Writers Association.

For information on Marlene Floyd Golf Schools for Women, call (800) 637-2694. The cost of each two-day school is $435, which includes a narrated videotape of the personalized instruction.

Ron Garl designed this beautiful resort in 1989 as a Southern experience that can include a polo game after your round of great golf. It lies along the Intracoastal Waterway toward the mainland. It has bermudagrass greens and fairways.

The signature hole is the 14th, a par 3 measuring 157 yards. The tee box is built out into the Intracoastal Waterway, and the carry is about 120 yards to the green over marsh and wetlands. Water is prevalent on the back nine and comes into play on five holes.

Practice greens, a driving range, pro shop, rental clubs, a bar and restaurant and a beverage cart are available.

The cost of a round is $21 on weekdays and $24 on weekends, and you book a tee time one week in advance. The cart fee is $17. Walking is not allowed.

OAK POINT GOLF CLUB

4255 Bohicket Rd.

Johns Island	768-7431
Championship Yardage: 6759	
Slope: 136	Par: 72
Men's Yardage: 6468	
Slope: 132	Par: 72
Other Yardage: 5996	
Slope: 128	Par: 72
Ladies' Yardage: 4671	
Slope: 121	Par: 72

Clyde Johnston designed this 18-hole course with fairways and greens of bermudagrass. Wildlife is prevalent on this course.

Water comes into play on 16 of the 18 holes. The 3rd hole is a 90-degree dogleg with an island green, measuring 367 yards from the back tees. The 11th is a 193-yard par 3 from the back tees with a narrow driving area flanked by water on the right and left; there's water just left of the green as well.

Rental clubs, a pro shop, practice green and driving range are offered.

Cost is $40 year round, including cart. Walking is permitted after 2 PM, and you can book up to 60 days in advance.

OCEAN POINT GOLF LINKS

250 Ocean Point Dr.

Fripp Island	838-1521
Championship Yardage: 6590	
Slope: 129	Par: 72
Men's Yardage: 6060	
Slope: 124	Par: 72
Ladies' Yardage: 4950	
Slope: 113	Par: 72

The 18-hole George Cobb course was built in 1964. It's a private course open to resort guests, and attractive golf packages are available for every season. Greens and fairways are bermudagrass.

The 18th, a 486-yard par 5, is the signature hole. It's right on the ocean, bordered by the Fripp Inlet. Typical of an oceanside hole, it's usually windy here. Another classic hole is the 9th, a 365-yard par 4 that also borders the beach, and you can expect the ocean breeze to affect the flight of your golf ball. Tight fairways are sandwiched by generous water and woods. Many of the holes have ocean views so beautiful they are a potential distraction to the golfing, but your best judgment is required to succeed on this course.

A practice green, driving range, rental clubs, pro shop, bar, restaurant and beverage cart are available.

Walking is allowed here. Greens fees, including cart, range from $39 to $54. You can book well in advance of your requested tee time, usually at least 60 days.

On Fripp Island, tennis, boating, beach activities and fine dining are all within easy access, so you won't need to venture out into civilization.

OLD SOUTH GOLF LINKS

50 Buckingham Plantation Dr.

Bluffton	785-5353
Championship Yardage: 6772	

Photo: Hilton Head Island Chamber of Commerce

The MCI Heritage Classic is played each April on Harbour Town Golf Links.

Who can concentrate on putting with such a dramatic background?

Slope: 125
Par: 72
Men's Yardage: 6354
Slope: 119
Par: 72
Other Yardage: 5779
Slope: No rating
Par: 72
Ladies' Yardage: 4776
Slope: 123
Par: 71

This Clyde Johnston course is 18 holes of bermudagrass greens and fairways, and it's open to the public year round.

Johnston's Old South golf links is a tribute to a man working within nature's guidelines. You will experience natural amenities and fabulous views playing this course. Johnston said, "The variety of the setting from oak forest to open pasture to tidal marsh provides an opportunity to vary the design elements and strategy of play." This all adds up to marvelous diversity. It's a beautiful course featuring seven marsh-front holes and three spectacular island greens among live oaks scattered on rolling terrain. The clubhouse verandas overlook the large putting green and the lagoon, a reminder that you're in the Lowcountry, not in Scotland as the links might persuade you to believe.

The par 4 16th is the signature hole, with two carries over marsh. Lateral water hazards are characteristic. The 7th also requires a shot over water.

The course offers rental clubs, practice greens, a driving range, pro shop, bar, restaurant and beverage cart.

Walking is allowed after 2 PM. Bookings can be up to 60 days in advance. Cost ranges from $48 to $75, including cart.

OYSTER REEF GOLF COURSE

155 High Bluff Rd.
Hilton Head
681-7717
Championship Yardage: 7027
Slope: 131
Par: 72
Men's Yardage: 6440
Slope: 123
Par: 72
Other Yardage: 6071
Slope: 118
Par: 72
Ladies' Yardage: 5288
Slope: 118
Par: 72

Bermudagrass greens and fairways characterize the 18-hole Rees Jones course built in 1982 — part of the Hilton Head Plantation complex.

Nine ponds and 66 bunkers contribute to the fairness of the nicely laid out course where every hole is challenging. Doglegs are surrounded by mounds and fairway bunkers. Exact approach shots are required to the large greens with well-defined tiers. The 6th is the signature hole. It overlooks Port Royal Sound, and beautiful oak trees surround the green. It's a par 3 of 192 yards from the tips.

A chipping green, practice green and driving range and club rentals are available. You can also enjoy a pro shop, bar, restaurant and beverage cart. The locker room is for members only. Rates range from $63 to $79, including cart and greens fee. Walking is not allowed. You may call up to 90 days in advance to book a tee time.

PALMETTO DUNES GOLF COURSE

Palmetto Dunes Resort, 1 Trent Jones Ln.
Hilton Head   785-1138

The three 18-hole courses provide an outstanding golf experience on Hilton Head. The oldest of the trio, the Robert Trent Jones course, involves a winding lagoon on 11 holes, and stray shots can easily find their way into one of the many fairway bunkers or lagoons. The Arthur Hills layout, heavily wooded with trademark elevation changes and rolling fairways provided by sand dunes, was overhauled and reopened in the fall of 1995. All greens were rebuilt, some tee areas expanded and the irrigation system reworked.

Unrestricted walking is allowed on all courses any time and any day. According to management, an increasing number of good players are asking to walk, keeping with golf tradition and reaping the fitness benefits. Greens fees, including cart, begin at $36.75 and go to $74.50. Specials are available when booking through the resort. Advance bookings are accepted up to 30 days.

Arthur Hills Course

Championship Yardage: 6651	
Slope: 127	Par: 72
Men's Yardage: 6122	
Slope: 120	Par: 72
Ladies' Yardage: 4999	
Slope: 113	Par: 72

The par 4 12th hole has water running along an entire side from tee to green. The par 5 13th hole, 507 yards from the blue tees, is built for the long driver — your tee shot must carry over water. Your second shot entails a fairway wood, but you must be careful because both fairway and green are guarded by a lake bordering the right side.

George Fazio Course

Championship Yardage: 6534	
Slope: 126	Par: 70
Men's Yardage: 6239	
Slope: 123	Par: 70
Ladies' Yardage: 5273	
Slope: 117	Par: 70

This is a straightforward course with water only coming into play on six holes, which makes it forgiving though not easy. Sixteen of the tees and greens recently were rebuilt to bring a 1990s look to the older layout. The fairways are open on the front nine but are more severe on the back nine. The finishing hole has a large bunker right off the tee that must be carried with your tee shot, and your second shot must also carry a bunker to a short fairway leading up to the green. This course has only two par 5s and three par 3s.

Robert Trent Jones Course

Championship Yardage: 6710	
Slope: 123	Par: 72
Men's Yardage: 6148	
Slope: 119	Par: 72
Ladies' Yardage: 5425	
Slope: 117	Par: 72

A winding lagoon system comes into play on 11 of 18 holes here. You go out from the clubhouse to the left of the water, make the turn and return on the right side. The fairways are open and the greens are large. The majority of the holes on the back nine involve water; exceptions are the 10th, 11th, 16th and 18th. The signature is the 10th, a par 5 that plays into an ocean breeze and view.

The course was recently named to *Golf*

for Women magazine's top 100 most "women-friendly" golf courses nationwide.

PALMETTO HALL PLANTATION

108 Fort Howell Dr.
Hilton Head   689-4100

The Arthur Hills course opened in 1991, and the Robert Cupp course opened in 1993. Unrestricted walking is allowed on the Cupp course, a recent change that management believes will please many good golfers who respect the game's tradition.

Greens fees, including cart, range from $35 to $74.50. Bookings are accepted 60 days in advance.

Arthur Hills Course
Championship Yardage: 6918
Slope: 132   *Par: 72*
Men's Yardage: 6582
Slope: 123   *Par: 72*
Other Yardage: 6257
Slope: 117   *Par: 72*
Ladies' Yardage: 4956
Slope: 119   *Par: 72*

Oaks, pines and lakes wrap the rolling curves of this course. Some greens are edged with bunkers, and water is involved in 12 of the 18 holes, providing a formidable challenge. The par 5 490-yard 5th hole, for instance, has water up the entire right side of the fairway, so all shots must be placed to the left. Save some strength for the signature par 4 434-yard 18th hole, which has water running all the way up the left side of the fairway.

Robert Cupp Course
Championship Yardage: 7079
Slope: 141   *Par: 72*
Men's Yardage: 6522
Slope: 126   *Par: 72*
Other Yardage: 6042
Slope: 120   *Par: 72*
Ladies' Yardage: 5220
Slope: 126   *Par: 72*

As with many courses along the South Carolina coast, this course has a lot of water and marshland, although they may not always come into play. The course is somewhat original with straight lines and sharp angles evolving from Cupp's computerized design. The 6th hole is a par 5, 542 yards from the back tees. It doglegs left, and your tee shot must carry over water. A good second shot will be played to the right because the green is bordered by a pond on the left and rear. The 12th hole is a beautiful 208-yard par 3 with sand guarding the left front and side of the green.

PATRIOTS POINT GOLF LINKS

U.S. Hwy. 17 Bus.
Mt. Pleasant   881-0042
Championship Yardage: 6838
Slope: 118   *Par: 72*
Men's Yardage: 6274
Slope: 113   *Par: 72*
Ladies' Yardage: 5582
Slope: 115   *Par: 72*

This is an 18-hole public course just across the Cooper River bridges in Mt. Pleasant. It was designed by Bob Spence and opened in 1981. The views of the ocean are amazing, as are the panoramas of Shem Creek, James Island, Patriots Point and Sullivan's Island. The wind coming in from Charleston Harbor is a factor on most shots here, and it adds multiple dimensions to the course.

The signature hole is the par 3 17th, 139 yards from the back tees, with the green stretching into the harbor itself. This is a real test for a birdie.

Amenities include a pro shop, rental clubs, a driving range, grill and snack bar.

Patriots Point's rates range from $28.50 in weekdays to $32.50 on weekends, including cart. Walking is generally allowed except on weekends before noon. Call whenever you wish for an advance tee time and they'll do their best to accommodate you.

PORT ROYAL GOLF CLUB

10A Graslawn Ave.
Hilton Head   686-8801

The three 18-hole courses offer enough variety to keep you interested for three good rounds any time. All fairways and greens are bermudagrass.

A pro shop, locker rooms, a bar and restaurant, rental clubs, practice greens and a driving range round out the resort's golf amenities.

Walking is allowed occasionally on all of these courses during the winter, but you should ask before making plans to walk. Fees range from $32 to $76, including cart and greens fees. The staff at this course is very helpful and will work with you to book an advance tee time whenever you call.

Barony Course
Championship Yardage: 6530
Slope: 124   Par: 72
Men's Yardage: 6038
Slope: 122   Par: 72
Ladies' Yardage: 5253
Slope: 115   Par: 72

The Barony Course was built in 1963 and designed by George Cobb. The 12th on the Barony is a good par 4 measuring 428 yards. Water flanks the right and left of the fairway. Most of the greens are small with numerous bunkers, some deep and wide surrounding the greens. This course brings shot-making ability to the forefront and down plays long drives and iron shots.

Planters Row Course
Championship Yardage: 6520
Slope: 128   Par: 72
Men's Yardage: 6009
Slope: 126   Par: 72
Ladies' Yardage: 5126
Slope: 116   Par: 72

Planters Row was built in 1983 and designed by Willard Byrd. On Planters Row, the hole to fear is the 12th. It's narrow, measures 424 yards and requires a carry over water to the green. The course ends with a 480-yard par 5, with woods to the left and water to the right of the fairway. A good shot will set up your pitch to the elevated green.

Robbers Row Course

Championship Yardage: 6711
Slope: 134   Par: 72
Men's Yardage: 6188
Slope: 129   Par: 72
Ladies' Yardage: 5299
Slope: 114   Par: 72

The Robbers Row Course was designed by George Cobb and Pete Dye and built in 1967. It was recently redesigned by Pete Dye who added several water hazards. On Robbers Row take note of the 10th — a long, slight dogleg right that plays par 4 at 454 yards. Most greens are guarded by bunkers, thus requiring precise shot placement.

SEABROOK ISLAND

1002 Landfall Way   768-2529
Seabrook Island   (800) 824-2475

This resort includes a medical center, boat docking and an equestrian center that will rent you a ride to the trail or the beach. Other resort amenities are clay tennis courts and an excellent beachfront with sailing and fishing arrangements. Babysitters are registered at Seabrook, and you can ask the front desk personnel for assistance with scheduling one.

Golf packages arranged through the resort are recommended for great family vacations. These courses are only available to resort guests or island residents.

Amenities include a clubhouse with a large pro shop and private instruction.

Walking is allowed on both courses during afternoons. Appropriate golf attire is a must. Greens fees are $50, and high-season rates elevate to $75, including carts.

Crooked Oaks

Championship Yardage: 6862
Slope: 126   Par: 72
Men's Yardage: 6037
Slope: 117   Par: 72
Ladies' Yardage: 5250
Slope: 119   Par: 72
Other Yardage: 6387
Slope: 121   Par: 72

Crooked Oaks is an 18-hole Robert Trent Jones Sr. course that opened in 1981. The course is placed in the forest and the black water lagoons, and the greens are small. Crooked Oaks is true Scottish style in that the clubhouse is not at the turn; you play nine out and nine back, and restroom facilities are provided at the 9th hole. As you make the turn, you'll find No. 9, a 170-yard par 3 with a large bunker guarding the front left of the green. The 18th hole, a par 4 of 427 yards, requires that you carry a large body of water before reaching the fairway.

Ocean Winds

Championship Yardage: 6805
Slope: 130   Par: 72
Men's Yardage: 6037
Slope: 120   Par: 72
Other Yardage: 6395
Slope: 125   Par: 72
Ladies' Yardage: 5524
Slope: 127   Par: 72

Ocean Winds, opened in 1973, offers

Charleston Reception & Transportation Center was created from an old freight depot and showcases unique architecture of its own while serving as a visitor center.

18 holes designed by Willard Byrd. The greens are large, the layout is flat, and the breeze at this oceanside course is prevalent (hence its name). Only five holes on Ocean Winds do not have water. The 3rd is a 516-yard straightaway par 5, and you must avoid the sand on the entire right side of the green. The 6th hole is another par 5, with water bordering the entire left side of the fairway . . . so play to the right. Also be aware of the bunker on the left side of the green.

SEA PINES RESORT

11 Lighthouse Ln.
Hilton Head   **(800) 925-4653**

These three 18-hole courses are among the most popular on Hilton Head Island and offer preferred tee times and reduced rates to resort guests. Afternoon summer specials may offer you two courses for $125. That's a bargain. Afternoon summer specials at Harbour Town are $105. A more typical price is $164 or more, including cart. Enjoy a half-day school plus 18 holes of golf and cart on the Sea Marsh Course for $165. Eight

hours of beginner golf instruction are also available for $200.

Harbour Town Golf Links

Championship Yardage: 6919
Slope: 136   *Par: 71*
Men's Yardage: 6119
Slope: 126   *Par: 71*
Ladies' Yardage: 5019
Slope: 117   *Par: 71*

The MCI Heritage Classic is played each April on Harbour Town — designed by Pete Dye and Jack Nicklaus in 1969. It's always ranked among the world's top golf courses. The well-protected greens are some of the smallest of any tournament course. The par 4 18th hole is well-known in golf circles for its wind hazard off the sound.

Ocean Course

Championship Yardage: 6614
Slope: 125   *Par: 72*
Men's Yardage: 6213
Slope: 119   *Par: 72*
Ladies' Yardage: 5284
Slope: 111   *Par: 72*

The Ocean Course was designed by George Cobb in 1962 and remodeled by Mark McCumber in 1995. Multiple tees accommodate all skill levels, and the restructuring preserved traditional beauty while modernizing.

Sea Marsh Course

Championship Yardage: 6515
Slope: 120   Par: 72
Men's Yardage: 6129
Slope: 117   Par: 72
Ladies' Yardage: 5054
Slope: 123   Par: 72

The Sea Marsh Course was designed by George Cobb in 1964 and remodeled in 1990 by Clyde Johnston. The Sea Marsh's varied layout often crosses lagoons or marshes. Fairways are wide, and oaks, pines and palmettos surround them. Medium-size greens are bunkered and slope from back to front, requiring exact approach shots.

SHADOWMOSS PLANTATION

20 Dunvagen Dr.
Charleston   556-8251
Championship Yardage: 6701
Slope: 123   Par: 72
Men's Yardage: 6399
Slope: 117   Par: 72
Other Yardage: 6129
Slope: 112   Par: 72
Ladies' Yardage: 5169
Slope: 120   Par: 72

Russell Breeden designed this course with bermudagrass greens and fairways. It opened in 1970 and was extensively renovated in 1986 with the addition of several water hazards.

Beware of the par 5 8th hole, 533 yards from the back tees, with water lining both sides of the fairway and cutting across the path of your second shot. It's a dogleg right with bunkers surrounding the green. The two par 3s on the back are tough also. Wa-

ter hazards are primarily off to the side, and they don't come into play if your ball is anywhere near where it should be.

A pro shop, locker room, bar, snack bar, beverage cart, club rental, driving range and practice green are available.

Greens fees are $24 during the week, $30 on weekends; during the spring and fall seasons, fees increase to $28 and $32, including cart. Walking is allowed Monday through Friday only. If you're an out-of-towner, you can book your tee time up to three months in advance.

SHIPYARD GOLF CLUB

45 Shipyard Dr.
Hilton Head   689-5600

Three nine-hole layouts include the Brigantine, Clipper and Galleon courses. Fairways and greens are bermudagrass. Oaks, pines, magnolias, lagoons and ponds populate these courses and demand driving accuracy and putting delicacy. Water comes into play on 25 of the 27 holes.

Amenities include a practice putting and chipping green and a driving range. A pro shop, locker room, bar and restaurant, beverage cart and club rental are all on-site. The course also offers memberships.

Summer rates begin at $38 for late afternoon specials and increase to $80 during the spring season, including greens fees and cart. Walking is allowed after 5 PM during the summer.

Galleon Course

Championship Yardage: 3364
Slope: No rating   Par: 36
Men's Yardage: 3035

An Inviting Island

The Native Americans left a legacy for us to enjoy on the 10 miles of wide, sandy Kiawah Island. It's close enough to Charleston for easy access, yet it's worlds apart from everything. Its name came from the Indians who lived here during the 1600s and used the island resources for hunting and fishing. The Kiawahs disappeared, as did most tribes that inhabited the Carolinas during that period.

George Raynor, who was believed to be a pirate, was given title of the land by the Lords Proprietors. The island passed to daughters, granddaughters and husbands of that family during the next 50 years.

Then the Vanderhorst family acquired the island and kept the property for 200 years. During the Revolutionary War, sick and wounded junior officers were allowed passes to rest on Kiawah Island. Soldiers from the War of 1812 were located on the island to protect the city of Charleston. During World War II, U.S. Army teams patrolled the island's coast with horses and jeeps. After the Civil War, Arnoldous Vanderhorst IV returned home, and many of his former slaves returned to the island, enabling planting to resume. He was killed in a hunting accident, and his ghost has been reported on the island on many occasions, but the family rarely returned.

In 1951, a lumberman, C.C. Royal, purchased Kiawah Island, and in 1974 it was developed into a world-class resort and residential area. The undisturbed Atlantic beach has been preserved in a natural state as much as possible for the sake of the sealife. Dolphins play along the coast, and beachcombers can unearth a wide variety of shells. Sea turtles frequently come to the shore at night during nesting season, and each lays up to 150 eggs.

The resort includes four golf courses, two tennis complexes, three pool complexes, the 150-room Kiawah Island Inn, four restaurants and lounges. Also, 350 villas and 22 private homes are for rent. Regional influences are noticed in the cuisine, such as fresh seafood, locally grown vegetables, herbs and spices.

Kamp Kiawah is a supervised program for half-days or full-days for children ages 3 to 11, and it offers a fun-filled day while parents enjoy their time on the golf course. A teen program includes late night movies, photo scavenger hunts, basketball and volleyball tournaments, dance contests, billiard tournaments and pizza parties. Families find sand sculpture contests, movies, jeopardy, bingo, ice cream socials and aqua aerobics planned. Interpretative nature excursions are guided by staff biologists. They include off-island tours by boat or tractors, marsh creek canoe excursions, birding walks, night beach walks and bike tours. A full marathon is enjoyed each December by more than 3,500 runners. An annual triathlon takes advantage of the beach and trails of the island. The Charleston Symphony Orchestra plays twice a year. Need we say more? This island entices the vacationer with any level of relaxation or excitement that is wanted.

Call 768-2121 for complete information.

Slope: No rating   Par: 36
Ladies' Yardage: 2658
Slope: No rating   Par: 36

The Galleon is a George Cobb design. A nice par 3 is No. 5 — 179 yards and fronted by two bunkers that may come into play if your shot is short.

Fairways are defined by trees; they are of medium width allowing space to work the ball. The Galleon's second hole is its signature, a dogleg left, par 5, with a bunker to the left that can be carried by a long hitter. Then you have a chance to go for the elevated green, which has water in front and bunkers to left, front, right and rear. The uphill shot cannot be short or it falls back into the water.

Clipper Course

Championship Yardage: 3466
Slope: No rating   Par: 36
Men's Yardage: 3132
Slope: No rating   Par: 36
Ladies' Yardage: 2733
Slope: No rating   Par: 36

The only hole on this George Cobb design that doesn't involve water is the par 4 427-yard 6th.

This was the original back nine for the Galleon when the course began as an 18-hole layout. One of the Clipper's spectacular holes is the 9th, which doglegs left, has bunkers to the right of the fairway and one on the left corner that is difficult to carry. From there in, the hole is well-bunkered. The green is somewhat elevated and has bunkers 100 yards out and to the green. Shots that miss the green will be in these bunkers.

Brigantine Course

Championship Yardage: 3352
Slope: No rating   Par: 36
Men's Yardage: 2959
Slope: No rating   Par: 36
Ladies' Yardage: 2457
Slope: No rating   Par: 36

Tree lines also define the fairways here. The 5th hole, a par 3, is 180 yards from the back tee. A bunker circles the left back portion and around two-thirds of the green. It's a slight downhill shot with water from the tee to the green. A good carry is required.

Watch out for the 6th hole on this Willard Byrd design — a long par 4 with bunkers by the landing area and water on the left. Likewise, beware No. 9 — a par 5, 523 yards, with water running down the complete side of the fairway.

Private homes and rental condominiums surround this course but blend with the pines and don't distract from the golfing experience.

WILD DUNES

Isle of Palms   886-6000, (800) 845-8880

Just a 20-minute drive east of Charleston on the southern tip of the Isle of Palms lies this special resort that features two championship 18-hole courses designed by Tom Fazio. It's also a top-rated tennis resort, and the white, sandy beach runs for more than 2 miles. A fitness center, marina and 20 pools round out the resort amenities. The drive over the causeway to the isle — the new connector to which you will hear locals refer — is a prelude to the treats that await you on this tropical paradise. You can really feel the transition into modern-day resort mode as you drive onto the isle and leave behind any ideas of historical tours or city traffic. Villas and homes for vacation rental have views of the golf course, the ocean, woods or marsh.

Though the rates vary slightly for the two courses, the advance reservation policy is the same for both:

If you're staying at the resort, you may book a tee time through them up to a year in advance. If you're not a guest and are calling for weekend play, do so seven days in advance; for week days, call 30 days in advance.

Golfer's Delight

From the first tee, enjoy golf at its finest and Southern Hospitality that only the newly renovated Radisson can provide.

Your Package Includes:

- Luxurious suite accommodations
- Deluxe Continental Breakfast buffet
- One round of golf per day (including cart)
- Welcome golf amenity
- State and local taxes

Please note that some courses may require a surcharge and tee times must be cancelled within 72 hours of play.

Participating Golf Courses:

- **Palmetto Dunes Golf**-Home of the Robert Trent Jones, George Fazio and Author Hills courses. Palmetto Dunes offers a choice for golfers of all skill levels.
- **Hilton Head National**-Home of the Amoco-Centel Golf Championship. This course is one of the top 25 on the island.
- **Indigo Run**-One of the newest courses on the island. Indigo Run offers a special charm in a serene setting.
- **Old South**-Provides a challenging, enjoyable game while experiencing the uniqueness of the course and spectacular views.
- **Port Royal Golf Club**-Three challenging courses, Planters Row, Robbers Row, Baroney and the well-renowned, Shipyard Golf Club.
- Other participating courses-**Harbour Town Golf Links, Country Club of Hilton Head, Island West, Rosehill Country Club, Callawassie Country Club**

Radisson
SUITE RESORT

Hilton Head Island
Call our Golf Coordinator Today!
RADISSON SUITE RESORT
12 Park Lane, Hilton Head Island, SC 29928
803-686-5700

The Harbor Course

Championship Yardage: 6446
Slope: 124   *Par: 70*
Men's Yardage: 5900
Slope: 117   *Par: 70*
Ladies' Yardage: 4774
Slope: 117   *Par: 70*

A target golf course, Harbor involves water or marsh on 17 holes and is peppered with heavy bunkering. Fazio claims this 1986 course as one of his favorites. It's laid out similar to a Scottish design at St. Andrews, with eight holes out and ten back in. Instead of a clubhouse at the finish, a halfway house is located in the middle of everything between the 4th and 5th holes as well as between the 12th and 13th. Bermudagrass greens and fairways are popular. The signature 17th is a 460-yard par 4 that traverses the marsh at Morgan Creek. Marshland and water are mixed on this winding course.

Practice greens, club rental, a pro shop, bar, deli and pizzeria add to the pleasant atmosphere.

Rates range from $35 during off-season afternoons to $75 during spring and fall, including cart. Walking is not allowed on this course.

The Links Course

Championship Yardage: 6722
Slope: 131   *Par: 72*
Men's Yardage: 6131
Slope: 121   *Par: 72*
Ladies' Yardage: 4849
Slope: 121   *Par: 72*
Other Yardage: 5280
Slope: 125   *Par: 72*

This course opened in 1980. The signature holes are the 17th and 18th. Seventeen is a par 4 on the ocean, and it tees off going down the right along the Atlantic to a tucked-in green. It's 405 yards from the back tees. The 18th is a dogleg right

Photo: Mitch Willard

The Charleston Museum in the oldest museum in America.

and a beautiful driving hole, finishing with a well-bunkered and undulating green.

A driving range and practice green are available here. Also, it has a pro shop, locker room, club rental, full restaurant and bar.

Fees range from $55 to $110, including cart. Summer afternoons are the cheapest times to play. Walking is allowed.

Around Greater Charleston...

Fun Things To Do

It's important to stop at the **Charleston Visitor Reception & Transportation Center** at 375 Meeting Street when you first arrive in the area. You can park there and tour the downtown without the headache of searching for elusive parking spaces. Also, you'll enjoy the video display and the quantity of free maps and brochures describing the spots you'll want to tour. Guided walking tours for the hearty, bus tours for the less adventur-

ous, water tours by reservation or the famous carriage tours are our preference when we want someone to explain what it is we're seeing. The architecture and the culture of the past two centuries are preserved and displayed in a magnitude in Charleston that is found in few other areas. Among the churches, house museums and formal gardens are stories of earthquakes, fires, hurricanes and wars. The center is open daily from 8:30 AM to 5:30 PM.

Charles Towne Landing, located on S.C. 171 between I-26 and U.S. 17, is an unusual state park. It's an interpretation of the first English settlement in South Carolina, which occurred on the plantation site in 1670. The exhibits and the animals in natural habitat will interest the whole family. The park is open year-round. For more information, you may call 556-4450.

The **Charleston Museum** at 360 Meeting Street is the oldest museum in America. It showcases the memorabilia of early Charlestonians and defines the social and natural history of the coastal region. A special Discover Me room will occupy your children for hours, as they can touch things as well as learn about toys and clothes from past children's lives. Call for information about hours and prices, 722-2996.

The Battery is a seaside park where you can walk or drive among the cannon, statues and monuments telling of people and events of the American Revolution and the Civil War. Once a significant defense site for the city, it now plays host to laughing children, biking athletes, strolling retirees and blushing brides.

Other activities in the Charleston area that are worth including in planning a golf trip are the numerous festivals. Whether you love seafood, music, crafts or any combination, you will find a festival that shows it all. We recently enjoyed B. B. King and a number of lesser-known groups during the popular annual jazz festival, where young and old spend the day in the park sunning and schmoozing and soaking up the brass vibrations.

One of the great parts of the Charleston experience still remains the beach activity on the neighboring islands, such as Isle of Palms, Sullivan's Island and Johns Island. Think about biking, walking, fishing, swimming or just relaxing with a book while watching the kids shovel sand over your feet.

Where to Eat

We've found an abundance of great restaurants throughout the Charleston and Mt. Pleasant areas, on both sides of Shem Creek — the port for the area's fishing fleet. Our picks are in Charleston, primarily downtown, because it's such a neat town we want to make sure you enjoy it. We offer our recommendations based on the quality of food, of course, as well as on the service and all-around dining experience, but also for the downtown atmosphere itself. It's only a few miles from wherever you will golf or stay. You can put your vehicle into a parking garage since street parking spaces are hard to find. Then walk around and get a feel for the place — the cobblestone streets, the beautifully restored buildings, the market in the town's center. Late-night dinners are fashionable, and jazzy dessert cafes or watering holes are open into the wee hours for the crowd that mingles college students with fun-loving golfers and Charleston professionals.

BOCCI'S ITALIAN RESTAURANT
158 Church St.   720-2121
$-$$

Some of the best crusty bread you will ever sample is made at Bocci's. Try to save room for the pasta with special sauces, then pastries galore. You could be in Northern Italy if you didn't step out into the bustling historic downtown of Charleston after a lusty lunch or dinner experience here.

CHEF & CLEF RESTAURANT
102 N. Market   722-0732
$-$$$

This is a great place for a late Sunday morning champagne brunch while you listen to fine jazz. Dinner is good also, or stop by for dessert after a dinner elsewhere and a downtown walk. The different floors for different music styles are interesting and always popular with every age group.

82 QUEEN
82 Queen St.   723-7591
$$-$$$

Fine wines accompany elegant dinners of Lowcountry foods served in a historic building created from two townhouses wrapped around a garden courtyard. It's one of the locals' favorite spots for lunch, after work socializing or dinner.

LOUIS'S CHARLESTON GRILL

224 King St.   577-4522
$$$-$$$$

Nationally recognized as one of the country's best restaurants, Louis's provides a culinary experience beyond that of any ordinary dining room. You should definitely choose this for one of your most special meals. Louis Osteen uses regional foods splashed with ingenious touches of Lowcountry tradition and prepared with his traditional French training. Take some extra time, and maybe a few extra bucks, and you'll savor the evening you spend with Louis.

VICKERY'S

15 Beaufain St.   577-5300
$-$$$

Many of the appetizers are large enough for an average eater's entree. Try something made with black beans and dirty rice, and go ahead and pour pepper gravy over your fries so you'll know you've been to the South for a meal. The original Vickery's is in Atlanta, so if it's good enough for both of these Southern cities, it's worth a try for lunch or dinner. You'll see a college crowd mixed with professionals and golfers of all ages.

EAST BAY TRADING COMPANY

161 E. Bay St.   722-0722
$$-$$$

The atmosphere is casual and friendly set in a huge old warehouse where you can see several floors from your table or from the glass elevator. Food is very good here, and golfers will feel at home for happy hour and dinner. You can hang around the huge bar area and find a lot of people having fun.

CALIFORNIA DREAMING
RESTAURANT AND BAR

1 Ashley Pointe Dr.   766-1644
$-$$$

The view, the decor and the croissants drizzled with honey are enough to bring you back to this fine restaurant regularly. We know someone who will drive an hour to Charleston just to have lunch here. When you see the lines waiting for dinner, you'll also have another clue that it's the place to see and be seen. Try to book in advance for dinner, and bring a big appetite and people who like to have fun.

Where to Stay

Your best trip to Charleston will include someone special and a stay in one of the historic bed and breakfast homes downtown. Man or woman cannot live on golf alone, and a little history tinged with romance adds to any experience. When it's too dark to golf any longer, it's time to enjoy a winter fireplace in your bedroom or a summer sunset from the veranda while you turn the clock back several hundred years. We also recommend a few nice hotels and some basic places for a quick golf trip with no frills.

Insiders' Tips

Plan your shot and select your club while approaching your ball. Ready golf is the only good etiquette.

Please call for information, or to book reservations before arriving. You will find many venues filled during the height of summer tourist season and during some festival or convention weekends. Unless otherwise noted, accommodations are in Charleston proper.

HISTORIC CHARLESTON
BED AND BREAKFAST

60 Broad St.   722-6606
$$-$$$$

This organization represents more than 60 properties, all of which are private homes with owners who share their area's stories along with extraordinary beds and homemade Southern breakfasts. They include spacious and elegant suites in historic homes aged at least a century or two. The bed and breakfast inns are furnished with antiques and often have piazzas overlooking their own private garden or courtyard or maybe a lake, the Ashley River or the Charleston Harbor.

LAUREL HILL PLANTATION

8913 U.S. Hwy. 17 N.
McClellanville   887-3708
$$-$$$

This country bed and breakfast inn is halfway between Charleston and Myrtle Beach, and the location is ideal for reaching golf courses a few miles in either direction. Overlooking the marsh, islands, waterways and the Atlantic Ocean, the plantation house is a restored version of the 1850 historic home that was destroyed in the 1989 hurricane. Four charming guest rooms with private baths are lovingly furnished with simple traditional antiques. The hearty country breakfast will be a great start to a day of golf, and the serene fishing pond will be a place to return for

• **333**

recuperation from any stress your day may have inflicted upon you. If you had just putted a *little* higher on that 13th hole. . . .

THE OMNI HOTEL
AT CHARLESTON PLACE
130 Market St. 722-4900, (800) THE-OMNI
$$$$$

Located in the heart of the historic district, The Omni stands out for its elegance and newness in a city filled with otherwise restored antiquity. Splurge on the club floors where you receive personalized service fit for royalty. Louis's Charleston Grill, one of the best restaurants in America, is in this hotel, along with a complete health club, indoor-outdoor pool and world-class boutiques including Polo, Gucci and many names you will recognize. The location is easily accessible from any golf course, and you will find the downtown attractions a nice diversion.

HOLIDAY INN
U.S. Hwy. 17
Mt. Pleasant   *884-6000*
$$-$$$

Going above and beyond the clean and comfortable atmosphere at most Holiday Inns, this is an elegant property overlooking the harbor, just minutes away from Charleston or the golf courses in Mt. Pleasant. A pool, fitness center and sauna are available, and you will appreciate the concierge level service if you want to be treated accordingly.

HAMPTON INN-RIVERVIEW HOTEL
11 Ashley Pointe Dr. 556-5200, (800) HAMPTON
$$-$$$

This is a modern high-rise atypical of Charleston architecture but providing the standard quality and continental breakfast of a Hampton Inn, which we choose

in many cities, along with a view of the Ashley River. Also, it's convenient to California Dreaming Restaurant and not far from downtown for browsing or from the main routes to the golf courses.

WILD DUNES RESORT
Isle of Palms   886-9704, (800) 346-0606
$$$$

Boating, tennis, swimming, biking, dining and entertainment add to the golf amenities of this resort. The island is near Charleston but totally removed from the traffic or history. If you really want to play golf, and someone else in your party really doesn't, this resort is a perfect compromise with vacation villa rentals near all the choices for a leisurely stay.

SEABROOK ISLAND RESORT
1002 Landfall Way   768-1000
Seabrook Island   (800) 845-2475
$$$$-$$$$$

Ultimate golf, tennis, equestrian and senior citizen packages, along with villa rates are among the choices you will have here. If you're looking for a full family vacation with a multitude of activities along a sun-drenched Southern island, choose this resort, and you'll never want to leave.

Golf Equipment

Discount shopping for your golf equipment and accessories is popular in Charleston. Good choices that also have unusually wide selections for women are **Charleston Golf Center**, 1663 Savannah Highway, Charleston, 763-0800; **Pro Golf Discount**, 966 Houston Northcut, Mt. Pleasant, 881-2255; and **Edwin Watts**, 2037 Sam R. Henberg Boulevard, Charleston, 763-1995.

Photo: Hilton Head Island Chamber of Commerce

Harbour Town Golf Links at Sea Pines Resort in Hilton Head.

Golf Instruction

The best golf instruction will be found among the professionals at the top resorts. Call in advance to ask for an appointment. Other instruction is limited to **L.B.'s**, 6656 Dorchester Road, Charleston, 552-1717; and **The Practice Tee**, 3251 U.S. Highway 17 N., Mt. Pleasant, 884-1144.

Around Hilton Head...

Fun Things To Do

Golf is indisputably the most important of the things you can do on Hilton Head Island. Tennis is especially significant too. Fishing, parasailing, skiing, horseback riding, miniature golf and, of course, dolphin watching and beach walking are also worthy of some vacation time. Shopping includes some unique boutiques and an outlet mall — enough nice choices for the discriminating. Don't expect the neon resort atmosphere of Myrtle Beach with a zillion things to do or a college town with prolific nightlife like Charleston or Wilmington, North Carolina. Go for the sunsets and the sophisticated lifestyle of a privileged few. Just expect a memorable experience, and you've got it.

Where To Eat

Shrimp, oysters, crab and fish top the menu of local specialties. They're fresh today, and you can count on the hushpuppies and red rice to accompany the meal. Some 200 restaurants also provide enough variety of international cuisine and basics to please any appetite. Let us

know about your favorite places, and we'll consider the choices for our next edition. Here's a good start for sampling Lowcountry cooking at its best:

AUNT CHILADAS EASY STREET CAFE
69 Pope Ave.   785-7700
$-$$$

Choose Mexican, Italian, seafood, steaks or just about anything else you can think of, and it's probably here in quantities for the whole family for lunch or dinner. Don't go with us if you don't want to be embarrassed during the all-you-can-eat crab leg feast, which can be quite lengthy, but, oh, so delicious. The owner's Italian mother makes great Italian entrees, and steaks are outstanding, even though the restaurant claims a Mexican theme.

THE CRAZY CRAB
U.S. Hwy. 278   681-5021
Harbour Town   363-2722
$-$$$

Two locations are well-known by islanders and golfers, and everyone will send you there for lunch or dinner. Steamed seafood pots are usually a favorite. They have almost everything in them and require serious appetites. Dress is casual, and fun is a definite.

OLD OYSTER FACTORY
101 Marshland Rd.   681-6040
$$-$$$

Seafood and steaks are served at the site of the island's original oyster cannery, a landmark experience and location. The atmosphere is casual overlooking the water. Happy hour and dinner are enjoyed here.

HARBOURMASTER'S WATERFRONT
Shelter Cove Harbour   785-3030
$$$-$$$$

Fine dining in a dressy and elegant

restaurant is a treat here. Linen napkins and proper service are a treat for special occasions. The rack of lamb is tender and mouth-watering, and the beef and fish are also good. Call for reservations for dinner only.

Where to Stay

Resorts are the best choices for Hilton Head visits, as you'll find the top golf courses are easily booked through the resort. Also you will enjoy the luxury and the amenities, not to mention superbly prepared food. The beaches in Hilton Head are usually private, unlike those in much of the Myrtle Beach area; therefore, the premium beach access, as well as the best golf course access, usually comes through the top-quality resorts. For Hilton Head Central Reservations call 785-9050 or (800) 845-7018.

WESTIN RESORT & VILLAS

| Port Royal Plantation | 681-4000 |
| $$$$$ | (800) 228-3000 |

More than 400 rooms in a luxurious facility stretching along the beach, spacious meeting rooms, cafe, restaurant and bar, tennis, pools and, of course, championship croquet and golf are all around you. This top-quality resort offers easy Southern charm and some of the best-prepared food you will ever find in a hotel setting.

PALMETTO DUNES RESORT

| 4 Queens Folly Rd. | 785-1161 |
| $$$$$ | (800) 845-6130 |

Access to five fabulous golf courses is the best reason for choosing to stay at Palmetto Dunes. Villas are oceanside, on the harbor or on the fairway where you will enjoy the location, and your family will appreciate the pools, tennis and miles of beach.

HYATT REGENCY HILTON HEAD

1 Hyatt Cir.   785-1234, (800) 233-1234
$$$$$

The Hyatt has more than 500 rooms and provides a traditional quality accommodation. You can't go wrong here. The hotel features a health club, indoor and outdoor pools and children's wading pool. Bikes and scooters are available; tennis and racquetball courts are here. Golf courses are convenient.

PORT ROYAL VILLAGE

Port Royal Village 681-9325, (800) 673-9385
$$$

Near the 54 holes of Port Royal Golf Club, this collection of vacation villas and townhome rentals is near the beach as well; it also has a top-rate tennis complex. It has a pool and offers an hour a day at the racquet club. Tennis courts are of all three surfaces. The resort will package golf for you at several nearby courses in addition to the Port Royal Golf Club.

HAMPTON INN

1 Airport Rd.   681-7900, (800) 426-7866
$$$

Hampton Inns the world over are dependable if you are looking for a comfortable place that is not an expensive luxury resort. Continental breakfast is quick to grab on the way to an early tee time. An outdoor pool and exercise room are offered. Refrigerators are in suites. Babysitting services may be booked.

VACATIONS ON HILTON HEAD

The Plaza at Shelter Cove   686-3400
$$-$$$ (800) BEACH ME

A central reservation service claiming to be the largest service on the island, this company will arrange accommodations including a golf package in any price range requested. Discount greens fees and guaranteed tee times can be arranged on any public or semiprivate course, and a variety of accommodations is available with or without other amenities.

HILTON HEAD VACATION RENTALS

The Plaza at Shelter Cove   (800) 732-7671
$$-$$$

More than 125 villas, condos and rental homes are managed by this company. As part of your rental package, the staff will arrange your tee time on any of the public or semiprivate courses.

OCEANFRONT RENTALS

11 New Orleans Rd.   785-8161, (800) 845-6132
$$-$$$

This company manages about 175 properties that include your choice of luxurious or budget-type vacation rentals in all areas of Hilton Head. Golf packages can be arranged when you rent a villa or home of any size — from one to eight bedrooms. Some properties are on the ocean; others are on golf courses. Advance tee times are guaranteed on more than 30 area courses; free tennis, group rates and free accom-

Insiders' Tips

Take your practice swing while others are hitting.

panying non-golfer accommodations are offered.

Golf Equipment

Player's Golf is in the Shoppes on the Parkway and sells equipment, apparel and accessories; call 785-GOLF. **Nevada Bob's** is another large discount shop on the William Hilton Parkway, with better variety than the one in Myrtle Beach; call 686-GOLF. Also, **Las Vegas Discount Golf**, Buckingham Plantation Drive, 837-3399, is a new superstore that carries golf and tennis equipment.

Golf Instruction

One of the best places to study is where you can also play. The **Golf Academy of Hilton Head Island** helps you learn, then helps you receive a discount on greens fees at Port Royal and Shipyard. A full-day program includes four hours of instruction with video analysis, then lunch and 18 holes of golf. The half-day includes a three-hour lesson with video analysis. Special programs are designed for women and juniors, and a mini program will analyze and correct flaws in your swing. Call 785-4540 or (800) 925-0467.

Private instruction is available at many of the other fine resorts, including a variety of quality programs at **Sea Pines** where you can also study during the morning and play on the Sea Marsh Course during the afternoon. Call 842-1454 for information on a full-day, half-day, beginner or short clinic.

Santee National's course offers outstanding variety.

Inside
South Carolina's Midlands

South Carolina is constantly rated as one of the top golf destinations in the United States. Thus it should come as no great surprise that its capital city boasts a number of fine public courses as well as a few private ones you might be able to play as part of a package.

In general, you'll find an interesting mix of traditional layouts and modern layouts. Most of the facilities are first-class, and the courses are well-kept. Versions of bermudagrass predominate in the fairways, and bermudagrass rules on the greens. Only a handful of courses maintain bentgrass greens.

Note that although we provide week-day and weekend greens fees (sometimes including cart) for each course, these costs are subject to change at any time. We suggest you inquire about exact costs when you book a tee time.

Columbia is well-known for its volcanic summer heat. In fact, sometimes it's beyond volcanic. Greens tend to transition in June and October, so bear that in mind when planning a trip to the area. You should be able to play year round in Columbia, but spring and fall will be the most comfortable seasons.

It's not unlikely that many cities in America would gladly trade public courses with Columbia.

As in our North Carolina Mountains chapter, to help you better negotiate the large area that makes up the Midlands, we have divided this chapter into regional sections.

> Note that the area code for all golf courses and businesses listed in this chapter is 803.

Columbia Area Golf Courses

CHARWOOD —
THE COUNTRY CLUB OF PINERIDGE
4082 Bachman Rd.
West Columbia   755-2000

Charwood — The Country Club of Pineridge, offers three distinctly pleasing and pleasingly distinct nine-hole courses with plenty of variety and challenge. According to the staff, various improvements are currently under way, such as rerouting and rebuilding some holes. Particularly interesting are the nuggets of sagacity and advice included on the scorecard for each hole.

Amenities include a practice green, practice range, pro shop, bar, snack bar and rental clubs.

You can walk these courses and book a round anytime. Approximate cost for 18 holes, including cart, is $22 weekdays, $26 weekends.

Charwood Course

Back Yardage: 2898	Par: 36
Middle Yardage: 2777	Par: 36
Ladies' Yardage: 2306	Par: 36

The Charwood Course, also known as the White Course, boasts tight fairways, so accuracy is key off the tee. This nine-hole track is relatively short and poses no major problems until you get to the

GOLF COURSES IN SOUTH CAROLINA'S MIDLANDS

Name	Type	# Holes	Par	Slope	Yards	Walking	Booking	Cost w/ Cart
Beech Creek Golf Club	semiprivate	18	72	116	6397	restricted	anytime	$18-25
Bishopville Country Club	semiprivate	18	72	n/r	6448	anytime	anytime	$11.75-17
Bogeyville Golf Course	semiprivate	18	72	100	5514	anytime	anytime	$14-18
Calhoun Country Club	semiprivate	18	72	n/r	5954	restricted	anytime	$18-23
Cedar Creek Golf Club	semiprivate	18	72	119	6689	no	anytime	$25-35
Charwood								
Charwood Course	semiprivate	9	36	n/r	2898	anytime	anytime	$22-26
Ridgewood Course	semiprivate	9	36	n/r	3157	anytime	anytime	$22-26
Pinewood Course	semiprivate	9	36	n/r	3416	anytime	anytime	$22-26
Cheraw State Park	public	18	72	120	6129	anytime	anytime	$24-26
Chester Golf Club	public	18	72	n/r	6273	restricted	5 days	$24-31
Coldstream Golf Club	semiprivate	18	71	118	5733	restricted	10 days	$22-28
Cooper's Creek	semiprivate	18	72	115	6039	anytime	7 days	$22-28
Fox Creek	semiprivate	18	72	118	6493	restricted	anytime	25-30
Golden Hills Golf and Country Club	semiprivate	18	71	119	6011	anytime	2 days	$24-30
Green River Country Club	semiprivate	18	72	n/r	6257	restricted	anytime	$17-27
Highland Park Country Club	semiprivate	18	71	n/r	6100	anytime	anytime	$12
Hillcrest	public	18	72	114	6104	anytime	anytime	$20-22
Indian River	public	18	71	n/r	6052	restricted	anytime	$29-3
Lake Marion Golf Course	public/resort	18	72	113	6223	no	anytime	$25-37
Lakewood Links	semiprivate	18	72	116	6027	no	24 hours	$25-37
Lancaster Golf Club	public	18	72	n/r	6140	restricted	3 days	$29-32
LinRick	public	18	73	120	6293	anytime	2 days	$22-27
Mid-Carolina Club	semiprivate	18	72	116	6368	anytime	1 day	$25
Midland Valley Country Club	semiprivate	18	72	118	6182	anytime	anytime	$27-33

Name	Type	# Holes	Par	Slope	Yards	Walking	Booking	Cost w/ Cart
Northwoods	semiprivate	18	72	118	6485	restricted	7 days	$25-40
Oak Hills Golf and Country Club	public	18	72	117	6449	restricted	anytime	$32-37
Paw Paw Country Club	semiprivate	18	72	117	6649	anytime	anytime	$15-20
Persimmon Hill	public	18	72	117	6449	weekdays	anytime	$16-27
Pineview	semiprivate	18	72	116	6346	restricted	anytime	$16
Pocalla Springs	semiprivate	18	71	n/r	5882	anytime	anytime	$18-25
Sandy Pointe	public	18	72	116	6045	anytime	anytime	$27-36
Santee National	semiprivate	18	72	114	6125	restricted	anytime	$15-20
Sedgewood Country Club	public	18	72	n/r	6031	anytime	anytime	$21-28
Sweetwater Country Club	semiprivate	18	71	n/r	5830	anytime	7 days	$28-34
Timberlake Plantation	semiprivate	18	72	124	6226	anytime	7 days	$24-31
The Traces Golf Club	semiprivate	18	72	117	6449	restricted	anytime	$24-31
White Pines	public	18	72	111	5848	restricted	10 days	$25-30
White Plains Country Club	semiprivate	18	72	n/r	5874	restricted	3 days	

South Carolina's Midland

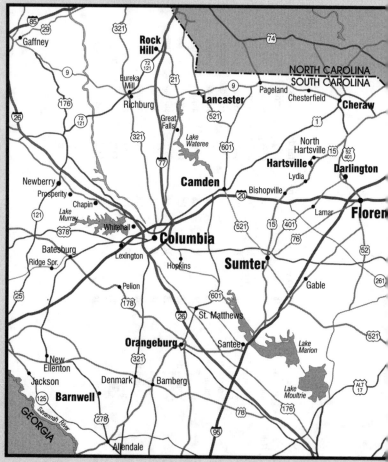

greens, which are sloped and probably tricky to hold when firm.

Ridgewood Course

Championship Yardage: 3157	*Par: 36*
Men's Yardage: 2945	*Par: 36*
Ladies' Yardage: 2478	*Par: 36*

The Ridgewood Course, or Blue Course, is slightly more open than the Charwood Course. The fairways are flatter and wider. The ball must carry bunkers to reach the built-up greens, which are predominantly flat. If the rough has been allowed to grow up around the greens, then getting up and down will not be easy.

Pinewood Course

Back Yardage: 3416	*Par: 36*
Middle Yardage: 3074	*Par: 36*
Ladies' Yardage: 2580	*Par: 37*

The Pinewood Course (a.k.a. Rose Course) is the most interesting and modern of the trio at Charwood. Needless to say, because the course is a typical modern design, there are mounds. This nine offers the most variety and challenge, big elevation changes and some fun driving holes. The fairways are tight in places, and the holes are relatively longer than on the counterpart courses.

COLDSTREAM GOLF CLUB

Lake Murray Blvd.
Irmo   *781-0114*

Championship Yardage: 6155	
Slope: 122	*Par: 71*
Men's Yardage: 5733	
Slope: 118	*Par: 71*
Ladies' Yardage: 5047	*Par: 71*

Coldstream, a Michael Mungo design, opened in 1975. Bermudagrass covers the fairways and greens. Some holes are flat, but most feature elevation changes. The course is part of a residential development near the shores of Lake Murray.

At Coldstream, we found narrow fairways, plenty of variety, a couple of spectacular holes and mostly small greens. Miss the green here and you may be in trouble: Your ball will roll into deep rough or bounce almost anywhere. Still, the relatively straightforward layout makes for a fun round if you're playing at a relaxed pace. If your approach shots are accurate, you'll score well. You'll enjoy the final hole on the front nine: a 196-yard par 3, which requires a downhill shot through a chute to a green backed by a series of hedges.

Amenities include a practice green, pro shop, bar, snack bar, occasional beverage cart and rental clubs.

Walking is allowed primarily on weekdays. You can book up to 10 days in advance. Approximate cost, including cart, is $22 weekdays, $28 weekends.

COOPER'S CREEK GOLF CLUB

Country Rd.
Pelion   *894-3666*

Championship Yardage: 6582	
Slope: 120	*Par: 72*
Men's Yardage: 6039	
Slope: 115	*Par: 72*
Ladies' Yardage: 4565	
Slope: 99	*Par: 73*

Cooper's Creek opened in 1973. Red Chase designed the course. Bermudagrass covers the greens and fairways, and most of the track is set in wooded terrain with some significant elevation changes.

Cooper's Creek offers tremendous variety in a pleasant country atmosphere. Each hole has a character all its own. Some fairways are wide, others are narrow. Some holes are flat, others may remind you of a roller-coaster ride. The greens differ in size, shape and undulation. We found that the course is fair and not overly penal, although your really awful shots will likely yield really awful results. Make sure you bring your brain to this course, as you'll have to use all your clubs and know when to use them. Concentrate, take what the course gives you, and you'll have lots of fun.

Amenities include a putting green, practice range, chipping green, locker room, snack bar and rental clubs.

If you're fit, the course is walkable, and you can walk anytime. You can book up to seven days in advance. Approximate cost, including cart, is $22 weekdays, $28 weekends.

GOLDEN HILLS GOLF AND COUNTRY CLUB

100 Scotland Dr.
Lexington   957-3355
Championship Yardage: 6461
Slope: 126   Par: 71
Men's Yardage: 6011
Slope: 119   Par: 71
Other Yardage: 5575
Slope: 115   Par: 71
Ladies' Yardage: 4957
Slope: 113   Par: 71

Golden Hills, a Ron Garl design, opened in 1987. Bermudagrass covers the fairways and greens, and most of the holes are set in woodland bordered by a residential development. The course combines undulating and flat terrain, and water hazards come into play on several holes.

Golden Hills used to be a pure linksland course, with tall, ball-eating rough bordering many of the fairways. The members apparently changed all that: What used to be rough is now fairway or light rough. But you'll still find plenty of tight holes, particularly on the back nine. Resist the temptation to swing the driver too much: In many instances, Golden Hills forces you to play target golf — the big stick will simply get you into big trouble.

As you drive up to the clubhouse, you come face to face with the terrifying 10th hole — a 361-yard par 4 requiring a tee-shot to a narrow downhill landing area fronted by a large pond. Once you've lobbed an accurate long iron down the fairway, you have to smack the ball about 140 yards over water to a thin green. Score par here and you should feel very pleased with yourself.

The course boasts tremendous variety; no two holes are the same. If you're up for a challenge that will test your brain as much as your swing, make sure you play Golden Hills. And as one member told us, "The course will give you all you want from the tips." (Note: "The tips" are the back tees, for those of you who might be unfamiliar with the jargon.)

Amenities include a practice green, pro shop, locker room, restaurant, pro shop, bar and rental clubs. The practice range is open to members only.

You can walk anytime, but it's a tough round on foot. Nonmembers can book two days in advance. Approximate cost, including cart, is $24 weekdays, $30 weekends.

INDIAN RIVER

200 Congaree Hunt Dr.
West Columbia   955-0080
Championship Yardage: 6507
Slope: No rating   Par: 71
Men's Yardage: 6052
Slope: No rating   Par: 71
Other Yardage: 5586
Slope: No rating   Par: 71
Ladies' Yardage: 4643
Slope: No rating   Par: 71

Indian River, a Lyndell Young-designed course, opened in 1992. Bermudagrass covers the well-maintained greens and fairways. The course is undulating on the front nine and somewhat flatter on the back. The holes are bordered by pine forest, wetlands or both, and water comes into play on several holes.

Indian River boasts a Scottish links-style design in a serene and peaceful wooded environment. The mix works well: Indian River is one of the more popular public tracks in the Columbia area. A modern course, you'll find mounds off the tee, wide and rolling fairways, decent variety and some fine views. And for a modern course (typically replete with tricks and trappings), Indian River is fair. We found little trouble off the tee but plenty of challenge around the sizable greens — some of the most undulating in the entire Midlands area. Pat yourself on the back for reaching the green in regulation, but realize that getting down in two will likely produce massive beads of perspiration on your sun-drenched forehead. It's important to look at pin placement and play your ball as close to the pin as possible if you plan to two putt these greens.

Indian River is definitely a course to visit if you're in the area, particularly if you enjoy putting challenges.

Amenities include a practice green, practice range, pro shop and snack bar.

You can walk the course anytime on the weekdays and after 2 PM on weekends, although it's not a particularly easy trek. You can book anytime. Approximate cost, including cart, is $29 weekdays, $35 weekends.

INDIAN TRAIL GOLF CLUB

1304 Willis St.

Batesburg	*532-9010*
Championship Yardage: 3027	*Par: 36*
Men's Yardage: 2867	*Par: 36*
Ladies' Yardage: 2182	*Par: 36*

Indian Trail opened in 1993. Tifton bermudagrass covers the fairways and greens, and the course winds through some wonderful wooded terrain in a peaceful country setting.

Indian Trail is the creation of Rudy Raborn, a Certified Public Accountant by day who has been moonlighting as a golf course owner and architect. Perhaps it's time for Mr. Raborn to leave his day job in the world of number-crunching and take up golf course layout full time.

To Raborn's credit, this pleasant and rolling nine-hole course boasts a truly competent design. The course will definitely make you think about your game and may even make you think of Robert Trent Jones: sensible use of water, bunkers and those "landing strip" tee boxes. The greens are primarily sloped but fair, as are the fairways, and the overall design is solid. To assure that you don't go home without a serious challenge, two of the greens slope away from the fairway.

The back nine is on the drawing board and should be ready sometime in 1997. If you're in the area, definitely drop by this course for a pleasantly challenging surprise. And if you have a bad round, who knows... perhaps Mr. Raborn will help you take it out on the IRS (there must be *some* allowance for a tax deduction based on pain and suffering incurred on the golf course!).

Amenities include a practice range, putting green, tax form preparation, snack bar and rental clubs.

Walking is allowed anytime, and you can book anytime as well. Approximate cost, including cart, is $16 weekdays, $18 weekends.

LINRICK GOLF COURSE

356 Campground Rd.

Columbia	*754-6331*
Championship Yardage: 6959	
Slope: 125	*Par: 73*
Men's Yardage: 6293	
Slope: 120	*Par: 73*
Other Yardage: 5255	
Slope: No rating	*Par: 73*
Ladies' Yardage: 5086	
Slope: No rating	*Par: 73*

LinRick Golf Course opened in 1971. This Russell Breeden design is operated by the Richland County Recreation Commission. Thus you might think of LinRick as Columbia's municipal course.

Bermudagrass covers the greens and fairways. Eight lakes bring water into play on several holes.

You might be asking, "Why a funny name like LinRick?" Well, the course is named after Thomas S. Lynton and J. W. Derrick, two gentlemen who played significant roles with the recreation commission. Instead of calling the course the Lynton-Derrick Columbia and Richland County Municipal Golf Course Open to All, they slimmed it down to LinRick. Wise decision.

Nomenclature aside, LinRick is an outstanding public course. The Russell Breeden design features lots of water, wooded terrain, doglegs, plenty of challenge, picturesque holes and midsize greens. We have a sneaking suspicion that Russell Breeden must be fairly happy with this layout, particularly the final five holes — among the most challenging and picturesque on the course. We found wide fairways on the front nine and narrower fairways on the back. The residents of Columbia should be proud that the city is represented by a course such as LinRick.

Amenities include a practice range, putting green, pro shop, snack bar and rental clubs.

You can walk the course anytime. Book after 9 AM on Thursdays for the weekend and after 9 AM on Monday for a weekday. Approximate cost, including cart, is $22 weekdays, $27 weekends. You may purchase an annual greens fee pass for $330 per person.

MID-CAROLINA CLUB

3593 Kibler Bridge Rd.	364-3193
Championship Yardage: 6595	
Slope: 122	Par: 72
Men's Yardage: 6368	
Slope: 116	Par: 72
Other Yardage: 5791	
Slope: 111	Par: 72
Ladies' Yardage: 5351	
Slope: 123	Par: 73

Mid-Carolina boasts a fine and mature Russell Breeden design. The course is open to the public on weekdays only; on weekends, you must play with a member. Or better still, be a member. Greens and fairways are bermudagrass. The course is development-free and set in wooded terrain.

Mid-Carolina is a good example of a well-maintained Russell Breeden course. Four sets of tees provide challenge for golfers of all levels. Some of the bunkers are larger than those on other Breeden designs. There's water on nearly half the holes, and it's most noticeable on three of the par 3s.

The course offers some dramatic elevation changes on the back nine. We overheard one regular player telling an assembled group that he had gone without his driver for the past 13 years in favor of a fourth wedge. What he's trying to say is that you won't need to smack the ball a long way to score successfully at Mid-Carolina. Play it from the tips and the course is less than 6600 yards. The premium here is on accuracy off the tee, not distance. This is particularly true on some of the dogleg holes and some of the tighter holes on the back nine.

Insiders' Tips

To speed up play, particularly when the course is busy, be generous with your "gimmee" putts. Players behind you will be irritated if you take two minutes lining up a three-footer.

Amenities include a practice range, putting green, chipping green, pro shop, snack bar and rental clubs.

You can walk the course anytime. The public can book up to a day in advance. Approximate cost, including cart, is $25.

NORTHWOODS GOLF CLUB

201 Powell Rd.
Columbia   786-9242
Championship Yardage: 6800
Slope: 122   Par: 72
Men's Yardage: 6485
Slope: 118   Par: 71
Other Yardage: 5936
Slope: 113   Par: 72
Ladies' Yardage: 4954
Slope: 116   Par: 72

Northwoods opened in 1990. Bermudagrass covers the fairways and greens. Some holes are set in wooded terrain while others are wide open. The course is hillier on the front nine than on the back, where there is more water.

Northwoods is a modern course designed by P. B. Dye, one of the leading proponents of the modern layout. If you've never played a Dye course and you're within striking distance of Columbia, then you *must* play here. Standing on some tees can be a mind-bending experience. Standing in the middle of the fairway can be a mind-bending experience. Standing in the middle of a bunker where the lip is above your head can be a mind-bending experience. You get the picture — there are plenty of major elevation changes. In addition, there are some massive greens with equally massive undulations, uneven stances in the fairway and some incredible blind shots. Hit a perfect drive down the middle of the fairway on the 14th, and you're faced with a wedge into the green. The only problem is that you can't see the green, such is the size of the mounds in between you, your ball and the green.

Did we mention the bunkers? At Northwoods they come in every shape and size, including a couple that could only have been created through the detonation of a large incendiary device. Have fun at Northwoods, but don't be surprised if the course beats you up — physically and mentally. We warned you!

The course is walkable for the very fit, and pedestrian play is allowed on weekdays and weekends after 1 PM. If driving your round, carts must stay on the path. You can book up to seven days in advance. Approximate cost, including cart, is $25 weekdays, $40 weekends.

OAK HILLS GOLF AND COUNTRY CLUB

7629 Fairfield Rd.   735-9830
Columbia   (800) 263-5218
Championship Yardage: 6894
Slope: 122   Par: 72
Men's Yardage: 6449
Slope: 117   Par: 72
Other Yardage: 5666
Slope: 111   Par: 72
Ladies' Yardage: 4829
Slope: 110   Par: 72

Oak Hills Golf and Country Club opened in 1991. Steve Melnick, who plays on the PGA Tour, and D.J. DeVictor teamed up to design this fine modern track. The course is laid out on terrain that provides a good mix of open and wooded holes. Water frequently comes into play. Recently, the course added 1,452 tons of bunker sand, 648 tons of top soil and more than 140,700 square feet of sod. Bermudagrass covers the fairways and greens.

We found plenty of entertainment and variety at Oak Hills. Greens, fairways, bunkers and water hazards vary in dimension. However, the course provides excellent sight lines, so there are few blind shots. Keep the ball in play off the tee and prepare for an approach shot that you may have to play from an uphill or downhill stance.

Undulating bands of green beckon golfers in South Carolina's Midlands.

Get the ball to the green, and the slope will challenge your abilities with the blade.

Many of the holes are majestically framed by trees. With four sets of tees, there are challenges for golfers of all abilities. Overall, the course is friendly, playable, challenging, pretty and popular.

Amenities include a practice green, practice range, pro shop, locker room, bar, restaurant, beverage cart and rental clubs. An interesting touch is the yardage book inside the golf cart.

Walking is restricted, but you may book anytime. Approximate cost, including cart, is $32 weekdays, $37 weekends.

PERSIMMON HILL GOLF CLUB

4322 W. Southborough Rd.
Florence   275-2561
Championship Yardage: 7063
Slope: 123   Par: 72
Men's Yardage: 6449
Slope: 117   Par: 72
Other Yardage: 5666
Slope: 112   Par: 72
Ladies' Yardage: 4829
Slope: 100   Par: 72

Persimmon Hill opened in 1962. The temperature on opening day — Labor Day — was 102° F. Russell Breeden designed this popular course. Bermudagrass covers the fairways and greens, and the design wanders through some wonderful and scenic pine forests.

The brochure for Persimmon Hill (an excellent name for a golf course, don't you think?) calls it "The Thrill on the Hill." We found it difficult to describe as a "thrill," but the course boasts an excellent layout. Russell Breeden might even tell you that it's one of his better tracks. The land provides great variety, and the layout makes commendable use of the natural features. You won't find tremendous trouble off the tee, but you will need to think around the spring-fed water hazards. The greens are large and rolling, and the bunkers are larger than we've seen on other Russell Breeden courses. Perhaps the course favors the long hitter. That's certainly the case on the monster 18th — a 630-yard par 5 that is the longest hole in South Carolina. Once you've played Persimmon Hill, you'll understand why it's one of the most understated yet popular courses in the area.

Amenities include a practice range, putting green, pro shop, snack bar and rental clubs.

Walking is allowed primarily on weekdays. You can book anytime. Approximate cost, including cart, is $25.

SEDGEWOOD COUNTRY CLUB

9560 Garner's Ferry Rd.
Hopkins   776-2177
Championship Yardage: 6810
Slope: No rating   Par: 72
Men's Yardage: 6031
Slope: No rating   Par: 72
Ladies' Yardage: 4841
Slope: No rating   Par: 72

Russell Breeden designed Sedgewood, which opened around 1965. Bermudagrass and native grasses cover the fairways and greens. The course is primarily flat on the front nine and somewhat more hilly on the back.

If you're a relaxed golfer who enjoys taking your shirt off while playing, not paying a fortune, but are into a challenge on a well-designed course, then Sedgewood is for you. And then there's the world's longest tee on the 18th hole: The tee box must stretch for more than 100 yards. If it's a hot day and you're on the putting surface, the sprinkler system — with sprinkler head positioned squarely in the middle of the green — may well cool you down. There are many fine holes on the course, but the track could benefit from a revamp.

Amenities include a practice green, practice range, pro shop, snack bar and locker room, although the latter amenity doubles as an auxiliary maintenance storage facility.

The course is walkable anytime. You can book anytime too. Greens fees, including open-air cart, are $15 weekdays, $20 weekends.

TIMBERLAKE GOLF CLUB

1700-A Amicks Ferry Rd.
Chapin   345-9909
Championship Yardage: 6703
Slope: 132   Par: 72
Men's Yardage: 6226
Slope: 124   Par: 72
Other Yardage: 5701
Slope: 117   Par: 72
Ladies' Yardage: 4829
Slope: 121   Par: 72

Timberlake Plantation, a Willard Byrd design, opened in 1987. Bermudagrass covers the fairways and greens. This well-maintained course winds around the wooded shoreline of Lake Murray, and water hazards come into play on several holes.

Timberlake Plantation is a magnificent modern course without too many of the huge mounds, bunkers and other absurdities often found on contemporary layouts. Byrd created an awesome and varied track that is fairly tight off the tee box yet lots of fun around the sloped greens. If the rough is grown up any, you'll need to be particularly careful off the tee. Many of the holes are straightforward, but the last four seem more difficult and breathtaking. The crème de la crème here is the 18th hole, where Lake Murray guards the right side of the large green. Make par or birdie here and you'll have plenty to be happy about as you down a cold one at the 19th.

Timberlake provides an excellent example of how a modern course can be fun, challenging and visually appealing without being tricked-up. This course is a must-play if you're in the Columbia area.

There's a small marina adjacent to the new clubhouse, where you may be able to cruise up to the course in your speed boat! Call Timberlake to inquire about specific details.

Amenities include a practice green, practice range, pro shop, locker room, snack bar, beverage cart and rental clubs. An inn and restaurant are slated for completion in December 1995.

Walking is allowed anytime and is manageable if you're fit. You can book up to seven days in advance. Approximate cost, including cart, is $28 weekdays, $34 weekends.

Timberlake Plantation is a little tricky to find. Take I-26 toward Spartanburg. Take Exit 91 to Chapin and take a left into town. About a mile outside Chapin the road forks; veer right, and proceed for about 6 miles. The course is on the right.

Courses Available Through Packages

The Columbia Metropolitan Convention and Visitors Bureau offers a number of package deals that feature some of the better public courses in Columbia as well as some outstanding private courses. Those in the Columbia Golf Promotion include Crickentree, Cooper's Creek, Fort Jackson (on the U.S. Army base), Northwoods, Oak Hills, Timberlake Plantation, Windemere and The Woodlands. Call (800) 264-4884 or 254-0479 for more information.

Aiken Area Golf Courses

In Aiken, you're so close to the home of the Masters that you can almost smell the azaleas at Amen Corner. Sadly, your percent chance of playing at Augusta National is optimistically described as zero or less. Thankfully, there are plenty of golfing options in the Aiken area to keep you happy. And the area is sprouting some formidable new courses.

Aiken is in the heart of what's called Thoroughbred Country. This means that

when golfers aren't playing golf, they're breeding horses. Aiken itself has an old and pretty downtown area with some fine restaurants. The area has always been a retirement center, so if the average age of the foursome in front of you is 92 and they're all taking the slow boat to the 19th hole, don't be surprised. Decent people all, they'll probably let you play through. You'll find a wide variety of courses in the area, from the new and fantastic Cedar Creek to the venerable Midland Valley Country Club and the enigmatic Allendale County Golf Club, designed by a one-eyed millionaire with an incurable slice.

The soil is sandy, and pine forests dot the mostly country scenery. You'll find bermudagrass on the greens and fairways.

ALLENDALE COUNTY GOLF COURSE

Rte. 1, Barton Rd.
Allendale   584-7117
Men's Yardage: 3789
Slope: No rating   Par: 36
Ladies' Yardage: 2736
Slope: No rating   Par: 36

Allendale County Golf Course, formerly Allendale County Country Club (a real hit with alliteration fans ...), opened in 1952. The course was designed by Walker Smith, a millionaire with a glass eye who made his cash in the hat business. Smith, a left-hander with a chronic and incurable slice, designed the course to suit the needs of a left-hander with a chronic and incurable slice. That is to say, a lot of holes go left. So if you're a left-hander and your stock shot is a big, booming out-of-control fade, you'll love Allendale Golf Course.

The course was purchased in 1993 by Joe and Audrey Vuknic who spent many years running a course in the Hilton Head area. Allendale is being renovated, and the bermudagrass greens and fairways show signs of improvement. Set in rolling, fairly

Walking vs. Riding

Go ahead and walk — it's great exercise.

If you join the United States Golf Association (and you should), you may receive the pamphlet *A Call to Feet* urging more golfers to walk. In the pithily written document, the powers-that-be even refer to golf in a cart as "cart-ball." Pretty stern stuff from the men and women in Far Hills, New Jersey — home of the USGA — for whom golf "is a walking game."

An unscientific survey shows that most public courses in the Carolinas prefer that you use a cart when you play. The courses where walking is restricted far outnumber the courses where walking is unrestricted. Even on courses where walking is allowed, riders almost always outnumber the pedestrians. Many designers and architects, particularly in the last 10 years, have built courses where the only realistic option is to ride — especially true on courses built around a housing or condo development. Most modern courses feature significant distances between green and tee, making walking tedious if not impossible. The modern course that's walkable is a vanishing species. It's all quite sad.

Courses built earlier in the century are walkable and were built to be so. With the arrival of the cart, many of these courses built ugly ribbons of asphalt or concrete to accommodate the buggy. Many of these same courses started telling their customers when they could and could not walk. In addition to the unsightly cart path, the cart's boxy shape invades the beauty of the course. And if the cart is gas powered, it's also smelly and noisy.

From our observations and experience, there are numerous myths and problems that surround the cart issue. Many will tell you that cart fees generate income, but that's rarely true when you consider the costs of buying or leasing the cart, insurance, electricity, upkeep, gas, storage and cleaning. Seeing as more people like to ride in carts than walk, the cart generates greens fee income, due primarily to laziness. It's an unfortunate fact that some people simply wouldn't play the game if they couldn't ride. Thus a portion of the greens fee covers part of the cost of keeping carts ready and available; even if you walk, you're probably still paying for a cart.

Many amateurs (and course rangers) will tell you that play is faster in a cart. That may be so when the course is deserted; but that's not always the case when the course is busy. During or after rain, most courses make you keep the cart on the path. Thus a twosome will be forced to drive to a point parallel with the ball, walk to where the ball lies, hit the shot, walk back, and begin the process again. Under these circumstances, on a walkable course, two golfers walking will play faster than two golfers in a cart. Even a foursome of decent golfers will rarely delay a foursome that's riding.

And then there's the issue of aesthetics. The great golf course designers build courses so that the course is best viewed from the fairway, not the cart path. From the cart path, you're going to see woods, scrub and the backside of mounds. Walkers see the green complex and the fairway. Walkers see the golf course, not the cart path.

When you play golf, you should walk. In Scotland, where the game began, everyone walks. Courses are walkable, and the Scots know how to play in well under four hours. Most people we know play golf because it's a release from their indoor workplace. The game provides a well-deserved break from the office or factory, from traffic, and from the concrete jungles where we work and shop. So why the great need and desire to ride in a cart on a cart path?

The Scots realized, and still realize, the tremendous health benefits of playing golf. Many a recovering heart-disease victim is told to take lessons from a golf pro and take to the links for four hours of gentle walking. If a person with a heart problem can walk a golf course, then anyone can walk. On walkable courses, We've run into people who think that their poor knees mean that they have to ride in a cart. Garbage. The gentle yet beneficial exercise provided by walking the course can only help build up the leg and back muscles — which can only help ailing joints.

In the Carolinas, one of the only public-access golf courses with an established and well-run caddie program is Pinehurst Country Club. If you play there (you should at some stage in your life), take a caddie, for a caddie will make the course even more walkable, tell you where you should aim and tell you which way a putt will break. A caddie will rake the bunker after you've make a mess, will suggest what club might work and tell you exactly how far you are from the pin. This is pure golf, and caddies are part of what make Pinehurst so special. Wouldn't it be great if more public courses could follow their example?

Perhaps one day a course will sell its carts, blow up its cart paths, provide you with a walking bag or pull cart for free and restore a piece of tradition so sadly lacking in today's game. In this book we've included information about walking so those of you who are dedicated to the traditional game can indulge in the benefits — spiritual and physical — provided by walking your round of golf.

open terrain bordered by farmland and pine forests, the wide fairways provide a comfortable landing area off the tee. The small to midsize sloping greens, however, will test your ability to read putts. Some greens are protected by bunkers.

The Vuknics operate a small pro shop, bar and snack bar. There's also a practice putting green. Gone are the days when, according to local lore, Mr. Smith would instruct the greenskeeper to pull the flags out of the holes when a group he disliked was on the course. The atmosphere these days is friendly and relaxed. The calendar features five tournaments a year and a weekly captain's choice scramble, where, as we discovered, the aristocracy of Allendale County is more than happy to lighten your wallet.

Walking is allowed anytime, and you won't need a tee time. Approximate cost for 18 holes, including cart, is $15. Rental clubs are available.

BOGEYVILLE GOLF COURSE

500 Bogeyville Rd.
Bogeyville   649-3366
Blue Yardage: 5514
Slope: 100   *Par: 72*
Ladies' Yardage: 4622
Slope: No rating   *Par: 72*

Bogeyville Golf Course opened at least 30 years ago. The H. D. Wyman-designed course features bermudagrass on both the fairways and greens. Some holes are set in wooded terrain; others are wide open. Water hazards come into play on some holes. The course offers challenging golf in a peaceful country setting. Terrain is undulating, particularly on the back nine.

We found Bogeyville (what a name for a golf course!) somewhat remote, though the many and varied golfers who were playing in the middle of the week in the heat of the day apparently found it accessible. You'll certainly find plenty of vari-

ety on this course. There are some remarkable holes, including a par 5 on the front nine that literally makes a U-turn. The front nine opens with a drivable par 4. Water and bunkers come into play on this mature course bordered by pine trees and thickets, although there's decidedly more water and thicket on the back nine. The greens are predominantly flat; make sure, however, that you keep them in front of you — disaster lurks behind some of the greens.

Walking is allowed anytime, and you may book anytime as well. Approximate cost, including cart, is $14 weekdays, $18 weekends.

Bogeyville is definitely off the beaten path. The following directions should help: From Aiken, take U.S. Highway 1 N. past I-20 and look for a signpost for the course on your left. Take an unimproved road for about 3 (bumpy) miles, and the course will appear on your right.

CEDAR CREEK GOLF CLUB

2475 Club Dr.
Aiken   648-4206
Championship Yardage: 7206
Slope: 119   *Par: 72*
Men's Yardage: 6689
Slope: 119   *Par: 72*
Other Yardage: 6277
Slope: 115   *Par: 72*
Ladies' Yardage: 5231
Slope: 115   *Par: 72*

Cedar Creek, an Arthur Hills design, opened in 1992 and is part of a new upscale residential development. The fairways and greens are bermudagrass. Most holes are bordered by trees, and water, wasteland and creeks frequently come into play.

With Cedar Creek, Arthur Hills has given the golfing world a fine modern course. Challenges come from significant elevation changes, large hilly greens with surrounding bunkers, the occasional mound and some holes where you must hit the carpet. You may find yourself flirting with out of bounds on a few holes if you're wayward off the tee. For a modern course, the design is not overly tricked-up or difficult. If your last name is Daly and your first name is John, you'll want to play from the tips — a whopping 7206 yards. Thankfully, Arthur Hills also remembered the short people in the world: There's a 1000-yard difference between the championship and men's tees. Comparatively speaking, you'll have more fun from the men's tees if you're a mid- to high handicapper. If you're in the Aiken area, make sure you play this course. You may like it enough to plop down some cash for a house on the 18th!

Amenities at this top-notch facility include a practice green, practice range, pro shop, locker room, bar, beverage cart and rental clubs.

We do not recommend walking this course. You can book anytime, and the approximate cost, including cart, is $25 weekdays, $35 weekends.

HIGHLAND PARK COUNTRY CLUB
Highland Park Ave.
Aiken   *649-6029*
Men's Yardage: 6100
Slope: No rating   *Par: 71*
Ladies' Yardage: 4911
Slope: No rating   *Par: 71*

Highland Park opened its golf course in 1903. Bermudagrass covers the fairways and greens. The layout winds through some pretty pine forest and is mostly flat save a few elevation changes.

Highland Park is a venerable old club just a three-putt from booming downtown Aiken. While wandering around this ancient course, we almost felt the presence of the ghosts of great golfers striding up the fairways, a fleet of doting caddies in their wakes.

Sadly, this excellent layout could use some sprucing up. If someone with a love for old traditional courses would revamp it, perhaps Highland Park could become one of the better tracks around. Still, if you're in the area and want to see a wonderful traditional layout and have some fun, you'll enjoy Highland Park.

Amenities include a practice green, pro shop, locker room and rental clubs.

You can walk anytime, and you won't need a tee time. Approximate cost, including cart, is $12.

MIDLAND VALLEY COUNTRY CLUB
U.S. Hwy. 1
Aiken   *663-7332*
Championship Yardage: 6870
Slope: 126   *Par: 72*
Men's Yardage: 6182
Slope: 118   *Par: 72*
Other Yardage: 5748
Slope: 111   *Par: 72*
Ladies' Yardage: 5545
Slope: 123   *Par: 74*

Midland Valley Country Club opened in 1965. The course was designed by Ellis Maples. Jim Ferree, who plays on the PGA SENIOR TOUR, is the director of golf. Greens and fairways are bermudagrass.

Midland Valley is one of the better courses in the Aiken area. We found an excellent traditional design and a well-run, mature track. If you haven't played an Ellis Maples course, you should definitely visit this one. Attention is paid to details here: The course is meticulous, and yardage markers indicate the distance to the back, middle and front of the green. Towering pine trees and shrubs add to the ambiance, and water comes into play on a few holes.

Maples made excellent use of the sandy undulating terrain to produce a course with great variety and challenge. Maples courses are often defined by mid-size sloped greens protected by a bunker

One of the challenges at Paw Paw Country Club's course is to keep the ball straight down some relatively narrow fairways.

or two. One of the bunkers will front roughly half of the green. Thus, pin placement can play a significant role in what type of approach shot you'll play. If the pin is behind the bunker, risk it and go for it, or play it safe and aim for the unprotected part of the green. You'll also find some fun and exciting driving holes where placement is often more important than pure brute strength. Fans of mature, traditional courses will love Midland Valley.

Amenities include a practice green, practice range, pro shop, locker room, bar, snack bar and rental clubs.

Walking is allowed anytime, although the elevation changes will test your stamina. You can book anytime as well. Approximate cost, including cart, is $27 weekdays, $33 weekends.

PAW PAW COUNTRY CLUB

600 George St.
Bamberg   245-4171
Championship Yardage: 7063
Slope: 123   Par: 72
Men's Yardage: 6449

Slope: 117	Par: 72
Other Yardage: 5666	
Slope: 112	Par: 72
Ladies' Yardage: 4829	
Slope: No rating	Par: 72

Paw Paw sits peacefully in the heart of Bamberg County and is a quality course with a fine Russell Breeden layout. Bermudagrass covers the fairways and greens. We found a predominantly flat track with some shallow greens and fairway bunkers providing most of the difficulties. The fairways are lined with old Midland pines. You'll see the occasional mound here, but the challenge off the tee is keeping the ball straight down relatively narrow fairways. You'll also need to be accurate on your approach shot; if you miss the green here at Paw Paw, only a good chipping game will keep your score from ballooning. There's more water on the back nine than on the front.

Enjoy the difficult finishing hole — a 446-yard par 4 with just enough water to make you nervous. When you're looking for a straightforward yet challenging course, stop by Paw Paw.

Amenities include a practice range, putting green, pro shop and snack bar.

You can walk this course anytime if you wish, but it's truly a hike. You can book up to seven days in advance. Approximate cost, including cart, is $15 weekdays, $20 weekends.

SWEETWATER COUNTRY CLUB

U.S. Hwy. 64
Barnwell   259-5004
Championship Yardage: 6248
Slope: No rating   Par: 71
Men's Yardage: 5830
Slope: No rating   Par: 71
Ladies' Yardage: 4680
Slope: No rating   Par: 71

Sweetwater, a Russell Breeden design, opened in 1981. The course sits amidst rolling terrain, although many of the fairways are flat. Bermudagrass covers the fairways and greens. Water comes into play on a few holes.

Sweetwater boasts a fine design that's undergoing some improvements. The course is fair and not tricked-up. We found decent variety in a relaxed and pretty setting. The fairways vary in width and the greens vary in size and shape; a couple of greens are noticeably shallow, others are protected by large bunkers. Chipping areas are mown around the greens. Overall, Sweetwater is a thoroughly playable course.

Amenities include a practice green, practice range, pro shop, handicap computer and snack bar.

Walking is allowed anytime. You can book seven days in advance. Approximate cost, including cart, is $21 weekdays, $28 weekends.

Santee-Cooper Area Golf Courses

The Santee-Cooper area, including Orangeburg, Santee, Sumter, Manning and Moncks Corner, is defined by the mammoth bodies of water — Lake Marion and Lake Moultrie — and is home to some fine golf courses. There's a recreational atmosphere to the area and that extends to golf. A number of individuals from northern climes come here as an alternative to Myrtle Beach and Florida. This may explain why this area is surprisingly rich in quality golf courses. We didn't see a bad course in the area. The immediate area around Sumter is particularly strong. Why? Perhaps it's the presence of Shawn Weatherly, the 1980 Miss Universe. Perhaps it's the presence of Shaw Air Force Base. Or perhaps it's the water. Who knows.

Overall, you'll find courses from the modern to the traditional and back again. Spend a long weekend in the area playing golf and you won't be disappointed.

Packages are available through the Santee-Cooper Counties Promotion Commission, P.O. Drawer 40, Santee 29142, 854-2131.

BEECH CREEK GOLF CLUB

1800 Sam Gillespie Blvd.
Sumter   499-4653
Championship Yardage: 6805
Slope: 120   Par: 72
Men's Yardage: 6397
Slope: 116   Par: 72
Other Yardage: 5956
Slope: 111   Par: 72
Ladies' Yardage: 5247
Slope: 115   Par: 72

Beech Creek opened in 1990. James Goodson designed the course, which today is part of a residential development. The course is well-maintained and somewhat flat. Bermudagrass 419 covers the fairways, and putting surfaces are tifdwarf.

You'll find plenty of variety on this well-designed modern course. Fairways vary from tight to expansive, and greens vary in size and shape. You'll also find mounds, out of bounds, water, pot bunkers and other trappings of the contemporary layout.

Beech Creek is popular with members of the United States Armed Forces stationed at Shaw Air Force Base. The track is one of a host of fine courses in the surprisingly golf-rich Sumter area. For $30 or less per round, including cart, the course is also a fine value.

Amenities at Beech Creek include a practice green, practice range, pro shop, snack bar, yardage book and rental clubs.

Walking is restricted on weekends. You can book anytime. Approximate cost, including cart, is $18 weekdays, $25 weekends.

CALHOUN COUNTRY CLUB
U.S. Hwy. 176
St. Matthews   823-2465
Championship Yardage: 6339
Slope: No rating   *Par: 72*
Men's Yardage: 5954
Slope: No rating   *Par: 72*
Ladies' Yardage: 4812
Slope: No rating   *Par: 72*

The front nine at Calhoun Country Club opened in 1959, and the back nine opened a year later. Ashby Gressette designed the course. Bermudagrass covers the fairways and greens. The layout winds through some fine woodlands, providing a peaceful country setting. The front nine is open and includes some wide fairways. The back nine is narrower.

At Calhoun Country Club we found a fun and relatively straightforward course with plenty of elevation changes. The greens are mostly flat and slightly sloped; some are elevated and bunkered. Water comes into play on some holes, but overall, the course is not overly penal. Play Calhoun from the tips for the best challenge. On some of the tee shots, you'll be guiding the ball through a chute. The atmosphere at Calhoun is friendly and relaxed. However, if you're looking for an intense round, Calhoun's design is strong and varied enough to provide a test.

Amenities at Calhoun include a practice green, practice range, pro shop, men's locker room and snack bar.

The course is walkable anytime except weekends, when some restrictions apply. You can book anytime. Approximate cost, including cart, is $18 on weekdays and $23 on weekdays — an excellent value.

CRYSTAL LAKES GOLF COURSE
Dillon Park
Sumter   775-1902
Men's Yardage: 5870
Slope: 110   *Par: 72*
Ladies' Yardage: 5560
Slope: No rating   *Par: 72*

Crystal Lakes is Sumter's muni. The Eddie Riccoboni-designed track opened in 1990. Bermudagrass covers the fairways and greens.

Just a smooth 3-iron from Shaw Air Force Base, you'll find Crystal Lakes, a small, well-designed nine-hole course that is popular with local golfers. (yes, we know nine-hole course is an anomoly in this book,

To speed up play, park your cart or place you bag on the far side of the green so you can move along quickly when finished.

Insiders' Tips

but this one is a great golfing deal for 18 holes, especially for beginning players.) If your backswing is interrupted by the sonic boom of an F-15 practicing low-altitude bombing runs, it's okay to take a mulligan.

Aeronautics aside, there's an aquatic environment on the first four holes. The 1st hole is a par 3 over water "infested" by one alligator. Otherwise, Crystal Lakes is a fun, low-pressure, flat, walkable, user-friendly golf course that is challenging enough to entertain the mid- to low handicapper.

After your round, if you're not too frazzled by the reptile, bunkers and low-flying, first-strike aircraft, you can relax with a jovial round of darts in the game room adjacent to the pro shop.

Amenities include a practice range, putting green, pro shop, snack bar and rental clubs.

You can and should walk this course anytime. You won't need a tee time. Approximate cost for 18 holes, including cart, is $14. You can walk 18 holes for $6 on weekdays.

HILLCREST GOLF AND TENNIS CLUB

Old St. Matthew Rd.
Orangeburg   533-6030
Championship Yardage: 6722
Slope: 119   Par: 72
Men's Yardage: 6104
Slope: 114   Par: 72
Ladies' Yardage: 5208
Slope: 107   Par: 72

The golf course at Hillcrest Golf and Tennis Club opened in 1972. Russell Breeden designed the primarily flat track. Trees define the fairways, and water comes into play on a few holes but rarely poses a serious threat.

Hillcrest is owned by the City of Orangeburg. Wouldn't it be nice if every town in North and South Carolina could boast a solid, well-designed muni like

Hillcrest? We found a well-kept, well-marked, relatively straightforward course with plenty of variety and fun. Off the tee, the course is basically wide-open, with the occasional raised bunker lurking in the fairway. As you might expect with a Russell Breeden design, the greens are predominantly midsize with a couple of bunkers protecting the putting surface. The greens are undulating but fair. The key to scoring well here is solidly hit, accurate approach shots.

Amenities include a practice green, practice range, pro shop, locker room, snack bar and rental clubs.

The course is walkable anytime. You can book anytime too. Approximate cost, including cart, is $20 weekdays, $22 weekends.

LAKE MARION GOLF COURSE

S.C. Hwy. 6
Santee   854-2554, (800) 344-6534
Championship Yardage: 6615
Slope: 117   Par: 72
Men's Yardage: 6223
Slope: 113   Par: 72
Ladies' Yardage: 5254
Slope: 112   Par: 72

Lake Marion Golf Course opened in 1979 and is part of the Santee-Cooper Resort. Eddie Riccoboni designed the course. Bermudagrass covers the greens and fairways. Pine trees border most holes, and water comes into play on several.

At Lake Marion, we found a wonderful and friendly golf course with an understated charm usually found only at country club and private courses. This is definitely one of the must-play courses in this area and will be well worth the trip; the yardage book gives the distance from Chicago: 919 miles. Majestic pine trees frame majestic golf holes that you'll find both challenging and visually appealing. Design-wise, the brilliance and challenge of this traditional layout lies in the strategic placement of bunkers. Just one or two bunkers per hole are enough to guard the midsize to large greens. You'll have to think here and play sound strategic golf. You'll also have a lot of fun driving the ball from some of Lake Marion's elevated tees. Play your cards right on the greens and you'll make some birdies. This is the type of golf course you'll enjoy playing more than once. Be sure to purchase the witty, entertaining and thoroughly useful yardage book.

Amenities at Lake Marion include a practice green, practice range, extensive pro shop, locker room, snack bar, occasional beverage cart and rental clubs.

You need to use a cart to play. You can book anytime. Approximate cost, including cart, is $25 weekdays, $37 weekends.

LAKEWOOD LINKS GOLF CLUB

3600 Green View Pkwy.
Sumter   *481-5700*
Championship Yardage: 6857
Slope: 123   *Par: 72*
Men's Yardage: 6027
Slope: 116   *Par: 72*
Ladies' Yardage: 5072
Slope: 116   *Par: 72*

Lakewood Links opened in 1989 and is part of a residential development. Common bermudagrass covers the fairways, and 328 bermudagrass is used on the greens. Porter Gibson designed the course. Houses and pine trees border the holes, and water comes into play on 11 of them.

Lakewood Links is a links-style course with all the trappings of a modern layout built in tandem with a residential development. We found mounds, large, multilevel undulating greens, bunkers around the greens and in the fairways, out-of-bounds terrifyingly near the middle of the fairway, more mounds, plus significant

distances from green to the tee. The course is especially narrow on the back nine, so if you choose to break out your 300cc titanium-headed driver, make sure you bang it down the middle, otherwise you might be in for a long day. The par 4 10th hole is 461 yards from the back tees and 420 from the men's, yet the fairway at the 175-yard marker is just 25 yards wide. Therein lies the challenge of this course. You'll be entertained by the par 3s here. The course also features a significant number of doglegs.

Visually, the course is quite appealing. There are numerous ponds so packed with lilies, Monet would have felt like he was at home in Giverny.

Amenities at Lake Marion include a practice green, practice range, extensive pro shop, locker room, snack bar, occasional beverage cart and rental clubs.

Use a cart to play here. You can book 24 hours in advance. Approximate cost, including cart, is $25 weekdays, $37 weekends.

PINEVIEW

7305 Myrtle Beach Hwy.
Gable   *495-3550*
Championship Yardage: 7084
Slope: 122   *Par: 72*
Men's Yardage: 6346
Slope: 116   *Par: 72*
Other Yardage: 5951
Slope: 112   *Par: 72*
Ladies' Yardage: 5307
Slope: 119   *Par: 72*

Pineview opened in 1968 and was formerly known as Pineland Plantation. Bermudagrass covers the greens and fairways. The Russell Breeden design is primarily flat and is set in a pine forest.

Pineview is under renovation, and many improvements are being made at the facility, including a new clubhouse. Pineview has all the classic Russell Breeden touches: runway tee boxes, the occasional mound, slightly raised greens, one or two bunkers per green and putting surfaces that are more sloped than undulating. There isn't a lot of trouble off the tee, so if you're playing the course from the tips, go ahead and take out the big stick. Just make sure you put yourself in a good spot for your second shot. Water comes into play on a few holes at this relaxed, straightforward course that should improve over the next few years.

Amenities at Pineview include a practice green, practice range, pro shop, snack bar and bar.

You can walk anytime on weekdays and on weekends after 2 PM. You can book anytime. Approximate cost, including cart, is $16 weekdays, $27 weekends.

POCALLA SPRINGS COUNTRY CLUB

1700 U.S. Hwy. 15 S.

Sumter	481-8322
Championship Yardage: 6327	
Slope: No rating	Par: 71
Men's Yardage: 5582	
Slope: No rating	Par: 71
Ladies' Yardage: 4682	
Slope: No rating	Par: 71

Pocalla Springs Country Club, an Eddie Riccoboni design, opened in 1955. Bermudagrass covers the fairways and greens. This layout winds through primarily flat ground with lots of live oaks.

Pocalla Springs is a mature course that's popular with the local golfing population. You might take a look at the yardage from the back tees, giggle and think this is a silly track designed for "Oh honey, I'm *hot* today!" old-timers. Think again. According to the locals, Pocalla Springs's tight fairways, large greenside bunkers and minute greens will flat out "eat your lunch."

There are five par 3s on the course, and you'll come face to face with one of them as you drive up to the clubhouse: The 14th is

just 127 yards from the back tees, and the bunkers that surround and front the green each seem larger than the green itself, which is not much larger than a hot tub. Get the ball safely on the green and your birdie putt from the edge might be one of the shortest of your golfing life. Miss the green and you'd better know how to chip or use your sand wedge. You might want to pack away your driver in favor of a fourth wedge! Make sure you play this course if you get the chance.

Amenities include a practice green, practice range, pro shop, bar, restaurant, beverage cart and rental clubs.

You can walk and book a round anytime. Approximate cost, including cart, is $16.

SANTEE NATIONAL GOLF CLUB

S.C. Hwy. 6

Santee	854-3531
Championship Yardage: 6858	
Slope: 120	Par: 72
Men's Yardage: 6125	
Slope: 114	Par: 72
Other Yardage: 5415	
Slope: 116	Par: 72
Ladies' Yardage: 4748	
Slope: 116	Par: 72

Santee National opened in 1989 and is part of an upscale new residential development called Chapel Creek Plantation. Porter Gibson designed the course. Bermudagrass covers the greens and fairways, although bentgrass is used to cover the greens. Most holes are bordered by trees. Water, wasteland and creeks frequently come into play.

At Santee National, we found a modern yet fair course with outstanding variety. The front nine is relatively open; the back nine is more wooded and undulating than the front nine, which is fairly flat. There's such great variety at Santee National that it's difficult to characterize the

Russell Breeden:
Golf Course Architect

In the Midlands of South Carolina, one architect's name pops up over and over again: Russell Breeden. We spoke with the enthusiastic and active designer who will turn 80 years old in 1997. He lives near Greenville, in Mauldin.

Off the tee, a Breeden course is fair. You'll find the occasional bunker or raised bunker, but you'll be able to take out the driver most of the time. Greens are sometimes sloped, sometimes undulating, but are almost always protected by a bunker to the front left or front right and another off to one side. Greens are usually raised, and water often comes into play.

Perhaps what makes many of Breeden's courses so playable and popular are his excellent layout skills and use of the natural topography. If the landscape is picturesque, the golf holes will be as well. You won't find a lot of mounds or evidence that bulldozers moved a lot of earth.

Ironically, an architect that Breeden admires is Jack Nicklaus, one of the leading proponents of modern design. Go figure. He also admires one of the hottest architects around: Tom Fazio, who lives in North Carolina.

Breeden began his golfing career as a golf course superintendent in Virginia. He "studied" golf under the Scotsman Fred Findlay — who also tutored notable architect George Cobb.

Breeden estimates that there are 75 of his designs spread across North and South Carolina, Virginia and Kentucky. Among his favorites are Persimmon Hill in the Columbia area, Possum Trot in Myrtle Beach, Lanier Country Club in Spartanburg and Sleepy Hole in Portsmouth, Virginia — a course that hosted an LPGA event for five years.

Using his experience as a former superintendent, Breeden takes pride in overseeing a course's development from initial design and layout through its opening. He's currently working on one of Charlotte's new public courses, Charlotte National, and says he's too busy to plays these days.

If you've played a lot of golf in North and South Carolina, chances are you've played a Russell Breeden course. It's also a good bet that you enjoyed the course for its playability, fairness and quality of layout.

fairways and greens as large, medium or small. You'll see it all here! Big hitters off the tee will enjoy Santee National due to the lack of serious trouble spots in the fairways. The key to scoring well here is keeping your ball in play off the tee and hitting accurate approach shots as well as having a good day with the short game. Good chippers will have fun here. And, of course, because Santee National is modern, you'll find mounds of mounds!

Amenities at Santee National include a practice green, practice range, pro shop, bar, restaurant, beverage cart and rental clubs.

Only members can walk. You can book anytime. Approximate cost, including cart, is $27 weekdays, $36 weekends.

Pee Dee Country Golf Courses

Pee Dee Country, including Darlington, Florence, Dillon and Marion, boasts some fine golf courses in pleasant environments. You'll find a variety of courses, with a cluster of particularly good ones around Florence and Darlington.

Golf packages can be arranged through Swamp Fox Golf at (800) 845-3538 or Pee Dee Golf at 332-2611. These firms may be able to get you on some of the private courses in the area, including Ellis Maples' Country Club of South Carolina.

BISHOPVILLE COUNTRY CLUB

S.C. Hwy. 3
Bishopville   428-3675
Championship Yardage: 6877
Slope: No rating   Par: 72
Men's Yardage: 6448
Slope: No rating   Par: 72
Other Yardage: 5675
Slope: No rating   Par: 72
Ladies' Yardage: 5620
Slope: No rating   Par: 73

Bishopville Country Club opened in 1959. Bermudagrass covers the fairways and greens. Some holes are set in wooded terrain, while others are wide open. The course is primarily flat. Water hazards come into play on a few holes. Improvements and renovations were scheduled for completion in the fall of 1995. The course offers decent variety, sound design and the potential for a fun round.

Fairways at Bishopville are primarily wide and lack serious trouble spots, so feel free to take out the driver and take a big rip. Be careful, however, on the home-lined holes where the fairways narrow and the greens decrease in size. The 16th hole features what must surely be one of the smallest greens in the Carolinas. Streams, overgrown trenches and water hazards come into play on a few holes but only

pose a threat to the really wayward shot. The sloping greens are raised and flanked and protected by a variety of bunkers. A couple of the greens are domed. Large tufts of pampas grass are placed at potentially awkward positions around a few of the greens and provide a unique and potentially irritating hazard. Another interesting feature is a double green on the front nine.

Amenities at Bishopville include a practice range, putting green, chipping green, pro shop, snack bar and rental clubs.

Walking is allowed anytime. You can book anytime. Approximate cost, including cart, is $11.75 weekdays, $17 weekends.

FOX CREEK GOLF CLUB

S.C. Hwy. 151
Lydia   332-0613
Championship Yardage: 6903
Slope: 123   Par: 72
Men's Yardage: 6493
Slope: 118   Par: 72
Other Yardage: 5915
Slope: 112   Par: 72
Ladies' Yardage: 5271
Slope: 106   Par: 72

Fox Creek opened in 1987. According to the owners, a committee of architects designed the course. Bermuda 419 covers the fairways and tifdwarf covers the greens. Most holes are set in rolling, wooded terrain, and water hazards frequently come into play.

Fox Creek has amazing variety. Perhaps the design committee was comprised of 18 individuals, each responsible for designing one of the holes. The result is an interesting track featuring just about every design element in the book — you won't be bored at Fox Creek. In fact, you'll be challenged by the greens here. Tifdwarf is grainy, so make sure you take a look at the direction the grass is growing: It will affect your putt.

The course is completely house-free. You'll find yourself playing all sorts of shots at Fox Creek as you navigate this wonderful track. Resist the temptation to hit the driver too much: Keeping the ball in the right place at the right time is more important than pure distance.

You won't forget the 18th hole, a magnificent par 5 that doglegs left over water to a large two-tiered green. Overall, it's a playable, fun course with distinct differences from hole to hole. We think you'll find that the course is well worth the trip.

Amenities include a practice range, putting and chipping greens, a pro shop, snack bar, rental clubs and the occasional beverage cart.

If you're fit, the course is walkable. However, walking is restricted to weekdays. You can book anytime. Approximate cost, including cart, is $25 weekdays, $30 weekends.

GOVERNOR'S RUN

665 Club Dr.
Lamar   *326-5513*
Men's Yardage: 3296
Slope: Not available   *Par: 36*
Ladies' Yardage: 2720
Slope: Not available   *Par: 37*

Governor's Run originally opened as Lamar Country Club. A new back nine is scheduled to open by January 1996. Eddie Riccoboni designed the front nine, which is relatively flat with some mild elevation changes. The back was under construction the day we reviewed the course. We were told that the back nine will feature more undulation, contour and water. Common bermudagrass covers the fairways, and bermudagrass 328 covers the greens. The course is set in a peaceful country environment.

The front nine is relatively wide open and features a sensible design with a lack of serious trouble. The greens are predomi-

nantly medium-size and sloped. Chipping areas surround many of the greens. Bunkers come into play on several holes. Overall, the course is relaxed, fun, straightforward and fair. You'll enjoy driving the ball in this primarily wide-open design.

Amenities include a practice range, putting green, pro shop and snack bar. A new clubhouse is slated to open in 1996 and will boast a bar and grill.

You can walk this course and book a round anytime. Approximate cost, including cart, is $14 weekdays, $18 weekends.

SANDY POINT GOLF CLUB

S.C. Hwy. 4
Hartsville   *335-8950*
Championship Yardage: 6840
Slope: 122   *Par: 72*
Men's Yardage: 6045
Slope: 116   *Par: 72*
Ladies' Yardage: 5203
Slope: No rating   *Par: 73*

Sandy Point opened its J. B. Ammons design in 1982. Bermudagrass covers the fairways and bentgrass covers the greens. The course is set in wooded terrain. The back nine features more of a links design than the front — a parkland design.

At Sandy Point you'll find excellent variety, elevation changes and six holes where water comes into play. Most of the fairways are tight, so you'll need to be straight off the tee. If you play from the tips, you'll also need to be long with the big stick. Bunkers make you think about your approach shot. Once you reach the green, your short game will be challenged by small, undulating greens. Sandy Point is popular with the local golfing population.

Amenities include a practice green, pro shop, locker room and snack bar.

You can walk anytime. You can book anytime too. Approximate cost, including cart, is $18 weekdays, $25 weekends.

Photo: Josh Gibson/Santee Cooper Country

South Carolina's temperate climate makes for enjoyable golfing throughout the year.

THE TRACES GOLF CLUB

4322 W. Southborough Rd.
Florence   662-7775
Championship Yardage: 7063
Slope: 123   Par: 72
Men's Yardage: 6449
Slope: 117   Par: 72
Other Yardage: 5666
Slope: 112   Par: 72
Ladies' Yardage: 4829
Slope: No rating   Par: 72

James Goodson designed The Traces Golf Club, which opened in 1991. Bermudagrass covers the fairways and greens. Some holes are set in wooded terrain; others are wide open. The course is primarily flat. Water hazards come into play on several holes. The Traces has hosted Nike Tour qualifying play as well as the Powerbilt Tour.

Traces provides an excellent example of what a modern, popular golf course should be. Four sets of tees challenge all levels of golfer. The greens are massive and relatively easy to hit. There's potential trouble off the tee on some holes, but you'll be rewarded on most if you keep your ball in play. There are mounds, but they don't get in the way. The scenery is pretty, especially on the back nine. The key to scoring well here is a solid short game, particularly with your putter. You may hit a green and still have a 75-foot downhill slider. We watched one foursome on a par 3 hit decent but not perfect shots, and they all landed on the green. Getting the ball down in two was not as easy. The 12th and 13th are unforgettable holes. On No. 12, if you're playing from the back, you'll need all you have off the tee: The hole measures 471 yards. But the fairway is wide enough to be fair and allow you to hit the driver. The facility is well-run. If you're in the area, make sure you play this course; it's worth the drive from Columbia.

Amenities include a practice range, practice green, chipping green, pro shop, snack bar, beverage cart and rental clubs.

The course is walkable, although the back nine is a trek; walking is restricted on the weekends. You can book anytime. Approximate cost, including cart, is $24 weekdays, $31 weekends.

Olde English District Golf Courses

Olde English District — including Cheraw, Camden, Chester and Lancaster — is so named because the area was a significant base for the British Army in the Revolutionary War. This area is dotted with a number of fine golf courses. Cheraw State Park's modern course is probably the one you'll want to visit the most. Two of the three Springs Industries-owned courses, in Lancaster and Chester, are fine traditional courses worth a visit.

Note: Courses in the Fort Mill area are reviewed in The Charlotte Region chapter of this book.

CHERAW STATE PARK

S.C. Hwy. 52
Cheraw   537-0160, (800) 868-9630
Championship Yardage: 6928
Slope: 130   Par: 72
Men's Yardage: 6129
Slope: 120   Par: 72
Ladies' Yardage: 5408
Slope: No rating   Par: 72

Cheraw State Park is a modern course designed by Tom Jackson. Since the course is part of the park, you can camp nearby should you be a golfer who prefers a night spent in a tent vs. one in a dry, comfortable and air-conditioned motel room with a big TV and wide choice of stations. Fairways are bermudagrass and the greens are bentgrass. Laid out in a magnificent pine forest (with no houses in sight), the course is undulating and poses several water hazards, including a significant lake.

In this age of wholesale government downsizing, Cheraw State Park is a rare example of successful government intervention. Based on this effort, we can only hope that the State of South Carolina's budget includes significant earmarks for golf!

Truly, you'd be hard-pressed to find a better course in this area. It's a modern design, including the obligatory mounds, big bunkers and water plus large, undulating greens that will test your sanity and patience. The course features a number of doglegs. The variety here comes around the greens, where you'll find different contours and extensive bunkering.

The backbreaker hole is the 13th, a 492-yard par 4 (that's not a misprint). The hole doglegs left down a hill. Assuming you hit your drive 325 yards, you'll be faced with a long downhill approach shot to a shallow green fronted by water and backed by a cavernous bunker. Hit it hot and you're flying over the green. Hit it fat and you're in the drink. Good luck!

Make a daytrip from Charlotte, Columbia or wherever; it will be worth the effort. It might be of interest to some golfers that Cheraw is the home of jazz great Dizzie Gillespie.

Amenities include a practice green, chipping green, pro shop, snack bar, practice range, locker room and rental clubs. The clubhouse is particularly impressive.

The course is a hike, but you can walk anytime. You can book up to a year in advance. Approximate cost, including cart, is $24 weekdays, $26 weekends.

CHESTER GOLF CLUB

S.C. Hwy. 9
Chester   581-5733
Championship: 6811
Slope: No rating   Par: 72
Men's Yardage: 6273
Slope: No rating   Par: 72
Other Yardage: 5816
Slope: 112   Par: 72
Ladies' Yardage: 5347
Slope: No rating   Par: 72

Chester Golf Club, designed by Russell Breeden, opened in the early 1970s. The fairways are bermudagrass and the greens are bentgrass. Holes are mixed between wooded terrain and flat, open stretches. Water hazards come into play on eight holes. The greens are slightly raised, sloped and undulating. As you might expect with a Breeden course, each green is strategically protected by a couple of bunkers.

Chester Golf Club is part of the Springs Industries triumvirate of golf courses. The track is one of Breeden's better designs in that it makes tremendous use of the land. Hole after hole is magnificently framed by a backdrop of mature pines and hardwoods.

Dare we recommend that you make the trip from Charlotte or Columbia? Yes, of course we do! We ran into a number of regulars in the pro shop who were justifiably enthusiastic about their course. There's plenty of variety here, without modern trickery. And there are no houses to avoid.

The course closes with a bang, as you must smack the ball a long way over water with your second shot. The fairways vary in width, but the course allows and almost encourages you to bring out the big weapon on a few excellent driving holes. Chester is a thoroughly sensible, completely fair course in a wonderful setting.

Walking is allowed (and you should walk) on weekdays and after 1 PM on weekends. You can book on Monday for the weekend. Approximate cost, including cart, is $24 weekdays, $31 weekends.

GREEN RIVER COUNTRY CLUB

Country Club Rd.
Chesterfield   623-2233
Championship Yardage: 6706
Slope: No rating   Par: 72
Men's Yardage: 6257
Slope: No rating   Par: 72
Ladies' Yardage: 5328
Slope: No rating   Par: 73

The full 18-hole layout opened at Green River Country Club in 1982. The members designed the back nine. R.C. Goodson designed the front, which opened in roughly 1965. The course is set on rolling wooded terrain. Bermudagrass covers the fairways and greens.

The front nine at Green River is spectacularly understated and straightforward — you'll look at the course and think, "I'll devour this track." The fairways are wide open. A couple of holes bring water into play. Hit the driver on most of these holes, but be accurate — your second shot will have to avoid bunkers and reach the right part of the green for a birdie attempt. You'll use almost every club in the bag, yet the course comes without all the trappings of the modern layout. Chipping areas flank the greens — a nice touch.

With your scorecard reading two under and a hot dog firmly planted in your stomach, it's time to tackle the back nine — somewhat different from the front, though still fair. For starters, there are many more doglegs. The fairways are more rolling though still fairly wide. The greens vary in shape and size. The most difficult hole on the course is a terrifying par 5 that features a pond at the bottom of a large downslope (if possible, enlist the guidance of a member who knows how to score par). Overall, the back nine is more challenging, due primarily to the elevation changes and all the water. Still the course is a lot of fun; try to visit if you're in the area.

Amenities include a practice green, practice range, pro shop and snack bar.

Walking is allowed primarily on weekdays. You can book anytime. Approximate cost, including cart, is $17 weekdays, $27 weekends.

LANCASTER GOLF CLUB

Airport Rd.
Lancaster   285-5239
Championship Yardage: 6553
Slope: No rating   *Par: 72*
Men's Yardage: 6140
Slope: No rating   *Par: 72*
Ladies' Yardage: 5017
Slope: No rating   *Par: 73*

The front nine at Lancaster Golf Club opened in the 1930s. The course added a back nine more recently. The course is one of the three Springs Industries courses. Bermudagrass covers the fairways, and bentgrass covers the greens.

This popular course is well-kept and boasts a fair design that wanders through some beautiful woodlands. It's mainly flat, save a few minor elevation changes. The fairways are predominantly wide, and water only comes into play on three holes, including the 7th — an island green. Bunkers abound around the greens, so it's important to consider them if you play aggressively. Lancaster also boasts a golf ball-stealing fox.

There's a meeting and banquet facility on site. Other amenities include a practice range, practice green and snack bar.

Walking is restricted on the weekends. You can book up to three days in advance. Approximate cost, including cart, is $29 weekdays, $32 weekends.

WHITE PINES

614 Mary Ln.
Camden   432-7442
Championship Yardage: 6373
Slope: 115   *Par: 72*
Men's Yardage: 5848
Slope: 111   *Par: 72*
Ladies' Yardage: 4806
Slope: 12   *Par: 72*

White Pines opened in 1969. We could not determine the designer, so drop us a line us if you know. Bermudagrass covers the greens and fairways. The layout is mostly open and hilly.

To score well at White Pines, you must keep your ball in play. To do so, keep the ball out of the numerous ditches and water hazards; they have a yen for dimpled eggs. The greens vary in size, and most are undulating. Some are raised, and all are protected in some fashion by bunkers. Overall, we found a relaxed setting for a fun round of golf, where it helps to be accurate from tee to green.

Amenities include a practice range, putting green, pro shop, snack bar, locker room and rental clubs.

Walking is allowed primarily on weekdays. You can book up to 10 days in advance. Approximate cost, including cart, is $24 weekdays, $31 weekends.

WHITE PLAINS COUNTRY CLUB

White Plains Church Rd.
Pageland   672-7200
Championship Yardage: 6353
Slope: 117   *Par: 72*
Men's Yardage: 5874
Slope: No rating   *Par: 72*
Ladies' Yardage: 4602
Slope: No rating   *Par: 72*

White Plains, an Eddie Riccoboni design, opened in 1968. Bermudagrass covers the fairways and bentgrass is used on the greens. The layout is open and undulating, with trees bordering the course and defining the fairways.

At this friendly course, we found a playable and mostly straightforward track. In the heat of summer, White Plains, due to its openness, becomes white hot. The layout is challenging yet sensible, short yet demanding. The fairways are generally wide enough to let you pull out the driver. Greens are fairly large and primarily flat yet gently sloped. You'll end up using most of the clubs in your bag. If you get in trouble, you can only blame yourself (or your clubs). Overall, this is a fun course that can be as easygoing or as intense as you want it to be.

Amenities include a practice range, putting green, chipping green, pro shop, snack bar and rental clubs.

Walking is allowed primarily on weekdays. You can book up to three days in advance. Approximate cost, including cart, is $25 weekdays, $30 weekends.

Around the Midlands...

Fun Things To Do

There's plenty to see and do in the Midlands if you've left your clubs or desire to play golf behind. Don't believe it? Read on.

In **Columbia**, the **Greater Columbia Convention and Visitors Bureau** at 301 Gervais Street should be your first stop. There's plenty of information and advice as well as historical and audiovisual exhibits. This is also the site of the **South Carolina State Museum**. By appointment only, you can tour the **Governor's Mansion** on Tuesdays, Wednesdays and Thursdays. Call 737-1710.

On weekdays, you can tour the **State House**, where the legislature of South Carolina convenes. The **Columbia Mu-**seum of Art is at the junction of Senate and Bull streets. There's also the Movietonews Film Library in the **McKissick Museum** at The University of South Carolina. The **Fort Jackson Museum** in **Fort Jackson** is open from Tuesday through Sunday. And if you've got the kids with you, don't miss one of the finest zoos in the country: **Columbia Riverbanks Zoo** is about a mile west of Columbia off I-126/U.S. Highway 76 (take the Greystone Riverbanks Exit). No one is admitted after 4 PM.

Two steeplechase races take place in **Camden** each year — one in the fall and one in the spring. Camden is a beautiful small town, with quaint shops and restaurants.

Cheraw is another picturesque town, with a number of historical buildings. **Old St. David's Episcopal Church**, for example, dates back to 1770. There's a fish hatchery and aquarium in addition to **Cheraw State Park**, which offers camping, fishing, picnicking, lake swimming, rental boats, a bridle trail (that's horses, not newlyweds) and rental cottages.

If you're in **Aiken**, and you like horses, visit the **Thoroughbred Hall of Fame** in Hopeland Gardens (the city park) at the junction of Whiskey Road and Dupree Place. Visit the **Aiken County Museum** and the **Aiken State Park** as well.

For more information about the Aiken area, contact **Thoroughbred Country**, P.O. Box 850, Aiken 29802, 649-2248.

If you're in the **Pee Dee** area on Labor Day, spend a day at the **Southern 500 NASCAR Race** that's held at **Darlington Raceway** — the track they call "the lady in black." You might want to visit the **NMPA Stock Car Hall of Fame/Joe Weatherly Museum** in Darlington on S.C. Highway 34 next to the raceway. In **Florence**, there's the **Florence Air and Missile Mu-**

Photo: Josh Gibson/Santee Cooper Country

Pine trees border most holes at Lake Marion Golf Course in Santee.

seum, the **War Between the States Museum** and the **Francis Marion College Planetarium**. And, of course, there's South of the Border. . . .

For more information about the Pee Dee area, contact the **Pee Dee Tourism Commission** at 669-0950.

In the **Santee-Cooper** area, **Lake Marion** and **Lake Moultrie** offer some of the best fishing and watersports opportunities in South Carolina. There are fish camps dotted throughout the region.

In **Orangeburg**, visit **Edisto Memorial Gardens** on U.S. Highway 301. Also check out the **Orangeburg Arts Center** on Riverside Drive and the **Orangeburg National Fish Hatchery** on U.S. Highway 21 bypass south of Orangeburg.

Sumter, in addition to being the home of the 1980 Miss Universe, Shawn Weatherly, offers minor league baseball, **Swan Lake Iris Gardens**, the **Sumter County Museum** and the **Sumter Gallery of Art**.

For further information about the Santee-Cooper area, contact the **Santee-Cooper Counties Promotion Commis-**

sion at 854-2131. Call toll-free from outside South Carolina, (800) 227-8510.

Where to Eat

We're going to direct you to some restaurants that provide a welcome flair and diversion from the chain-run culinary scenery that tends to dominate the area.

THE CAPITOL CAFE

1210 Main St.
Columbia   *765-0176*
$

Just a smooth wedge from the shadow of the State Capitol building sits the Capitol Cafe, where you'll feel like you've stepped back in time a few years. You get the sense that the comfortable booths have hosted many a heated political conversation or that quite a few "I'll scratch your back if you scratch mine — and pass the mustard" deals have been made here. The menu offers home favorites ranging from toast to K.C. Sirloin steak. Conversation here centers of the fortunes of the University of South Carolina football team, debauchery, politics and the latest news from The Citadel.

THE SHERLOCK HOLMES
1440 Main St.
Columbia   779-3659
$

Head down a short flight of stairs and you might think you're walking onto the set of "Cheers" — only this place is slightly smaller and without the highly paid actors. Relax with a cold beer or engage in somewhat raucous conversation. Or hunker down and munch a tasty lunch from the pub-fare menu. Sherlock's specialty is a juicy pot roast, thinly sliced, served on a French roll with melted Swiss cheese and accompanied by dipping sauce. Or you might try the veggie lasagna washed down with a couple of Killian's Red ales. Good food, I presume, Watson?

HENNESSY'S RESTAURANT AND LOUNGE
Main & Blanding Sts.
Columbia   799-8280
$$$

At Hennessy's you'll be instantly impressed with the fine ambiance created by white tablecloths and linens. This is a downtown restaurant where you can have a good old-fashioned culinary blowout. And you won't be disappointed. Begin with Oysters Rockefeller or Maryland crab cake. Move on to she crab soup, then to Steak au Poivre or Shrimp Hennessy. Follow it all with something from the dessert tray. You won't be disappointed. There's also a variety of beer, wine and liquor. Go for it. But before you do, make a reservation.

BLUE MARLIN
1200 Lincoln St.
Columbia   799-3838
$$$

Bill Duke's latest effort is a retro-ambiance restaurant with dark wood paneling and some of the best Lowcountry cooking you'll find outside the Lowcountry. You'll also find steaks and pasta on the menu. How about shrimp and grits for your out-of-town guests? Or you might try the deviled crab or the plump oysters. Finish the meal with a homemade cobbler. You won't need a reservation and you should dress down, not up. Relax.

LONGHORN STEAKS, RESTAURANT AND SALOON
902-A Gervais St.
Columbia   254-5100
$$

This Texas-style eatery is perfect for a casual evening in a fun and laughter-filled environment. Devour a steak or try some uniquely prepared salmon — Longhorn style.

THE CHESTNUT GRILL
1455 Chestnut St. N.E.
Orangeburg   531-1747
$$

The Chestnut Grill used to be called Mr. Steak and, as that name implied, red meat is one of the more popular options on the menu. You'll find USDA choice steaks and prime rib plus tasty seafood and a remarkably extensive wine list, a full range of beer and spirits. There's also a children's menu as well.

Insiders' Tips

When you're on a green, fix your ball mark and one other. Pat down spike marks.

HOUSE OF PIZZA

910 Calhoun Rd.
Orangeburg   531-4000
$$

Greek-owned and operated the "Kali Orexi" is a great place for pizza as well as subs, sandwiches, salads, gyros, souvlaki, shish kabob and baklava. Round out your meal with a draft beer or a glass of Italian wine. You'll find another House of Pizza at 1338 Grove Park Road.

THE COUNTRY BARN RESTAURANT

S.C. Hwy. 151
Darlington   395-2257
$

The Country Barn restaurant presents an array of country cooking in their Country Cooking BUFFET (their caps). It's open Thursday to Saturday evenings from 11 AM to 9 PM and from 11 AM to 3 PM on Sundays. Also sample the salad bar and dessert bar. Things get really exciting on Friday when you'll find a sumptuous seafood buffet. The Country Barn also claims to be a "BBQ Specialist." Bring all the appetite you can muster.

LUI'S INN CHINESE RESTAURANT

807 Market St.
Cheraw   537-4889
$

You might not think of Cheraw as a place to find an outstanding, albeit small, Chinese restaurant; but Lui's Inn fits the bill. Just a few minutes from the challenging golf course at Cheraw State Park, you'll find all your favorite Chinese dishes, like hot and sour soup and General Chicken (he must have been the one who ran away). We suggest you try the surprisingly good shrimp curry.

THE PADDOCK RESTAURANT AND PUB

514 Rutledge St.
Camden   432-3222
$$

Camden is well known for its steeplechase, so it makes perfect sense that one of its better restaurants is called The Paddock. In addition to a range of drinking options, The Paddock offers a diverse menu that includes soups, salads, pizza, steaks, seafood (try the linguine in clam sauce) and chicken dishes — even lamb chops. If you can't find anything on the menu that excites you, you'd better check your pulse.

Where to Stay

There is no shortage of places to stay in the Midlands. Every motel chain you've ever heard of has a large presence.

ADAM'S MARK HOTEL

1200 Hampton St.
Columbia   771-7000
$$$$

This large, full-service hotel is right in the heart of downtown Columbia. You'll find a spacious room complete with one king-size or two double beds, color cable TV and a concierge lounge where continental breakfast is served daily. You'll also find a pool and a Jacuzzi. On site are meeting facilities, a gift shop, secretarial services and a health club. Inquire about golf packages.

BEST WESTERN AIKEN

3560 Richland Ave.
Aiken   649-3968
$$

Located within easy striking distance of beautiful downtown Aiken, the Best Western Aiken offers microwaves, TVs, refrigerators, coffee makers as well as VCRs and movie rentals. Some rooms even have in-room Jacuzzis. Amenities include a lounge, continental breakfast and meeting facilities. Note that the price increases somewhat the week the Masters takes place.

CLAUSSEN'S INN
2003 Green St.
Columbia   765-0440
$$$$

Claussen's is a Columbia landmark. This bed and breakfast inn is located in the heart of Five Points near the USC campus and the State Capitol. Rates include continental breakfast and turn-down service, with chocolates and complimentary wine, sherry and brandy in the lobby.

COURTYARD BY MARRIOTT
347 Zimalcrest Dr.
Columbia   731-2300
$$

This no-frills, down-to-earth lodging is convenient to Columbia's main thoroughfares. Amenities include a whirlpool, an outdoor pool, in-room coffee makers and ironing boards, cable TVs with pay-per-view movies plus a restaurant that's open for lunch and dinner. If you want to do some laundry, your detergent is free.

EMBASSY SUITES
I-126 at Greystone Blvd.
Columbia   252-8700
$$$$

The seven-story atrium makes this one of the most arresting hotels in the Columbia area. There's a complimentary cocktail reception in the evening, and breakfast is included in your room rate. In your room, you'll find a coffee maker and color cable TV.

COMFORT SUITES AIKEN
3608 Richland Ave. W.
Aiken   641-1100
$$

Tired after a long day in business meetings? Have a bad day on the course? Consider the small extra investment that will get you a Jacuzzi suite at the Comfort Suites. You'll also have a TV with cable in the room, and the price of admission includes access to the swimming pool and weight room. You can also book a meeting in the conference room.

HOLLEY INN
235 Richland Ave.
Aiken   648-4265
$$

When in Aiken, check out the charming Holley Inn — a place so old that the elevator is hand-operated and the floorboards in the hallways are uneven. Relax in the courtyard or sip a drink in the bar. The service in the Holley Inn Restaurant will remind you of a bygone era — when hotel guests were treated like royalty.

BEST WESTERN ORANGEBURG
475 John C. Calhoun Dr.
Orangeburg   534-7630
$$

The Best Western Orangeburg is a modern and convenient motel. The moderate room rate includes continental breakfast, cable TV with Showtime and access to the swimming pool. A conference room is also available should you want to organize a meeting.

DAYS INN CHERAW
820 Market St.
Cheraw   537-5554
$

The Days Inn Cheraw offers a comfortable and convenient place to stay in the town that's perhaps best known in the jazz world as the birthplace of Dizzie Gillespie. You won't find much about Dizzie here at the Days Inn, but you will be provided with a clean room and all the cable TV (with HBO) you care to watch. Other amenities include an outdoor pool and a daily continental breakfast.

HOLIDAY INN OF CAMDEN

U.S. Hwys. 1 & 601
Lugoff   *438-9441*
$$

The Holiday Inn Camden is actually just down the road in Lugoff, but it's near enough to Camden to warrant its name. The price of your room includes cable TV, access to an exercise room and a full breakfast buffet. If you're hungry, thirsty and in the mood for a dance, head for Plum's Restaurant and Lounge.

The Hickory Knob course at McCormick State Park is fun and challenging.

Inside
Upstate South Carolina

As you might expect in a state that's renowned for the quality of its golf courses, the Upstate of South Carolina is endowed with a fine portfolio of tracks that are open to the public. And more are on the way. First, for the sake of clarity, let's define the Upstate; we've included the Greenville-Spartanburg area all the way down to the Greenwood-Abbeville area that borders Georgia.

The Upstate area possesses some fine scenery. The southern reaches of the Appalachian Mountains dip into the Upstate, giving some of the courses a distinctive mountain feel. The area around Greenville is lush and rolling, providing excellent ground for the golf course architect and developer.

While Upstate is not exactly famous for golf courses, it is known for economic development and success. BMW recently built a massive factory in Greer. You can see it as you drive down I-85 from Spartanburg to Greenville: It's quite a sight. A number of enterprises have moved to the area or have sprung up as a direct result of the new facility. Aside from the manufacture of "Bimmers," the Upstate maintains a strong industrial base. Everywhere you go it seems there's a factory or a distribution facility just around the corner. And there are more coming. As we visited the Upstate, Fuji had just opened a plant outside Greenwood. Clearly, the people of the Upstate are hard-working and prosperous.

They also like to play golf. And they like to play on good courses. We played a number of fine tracks designed by such notable architects as Tom Jackson, Russell Breeden, Gary Player, P.B. Dye, George Cobb and Willie B. Lewis. In fact Breeden, Jackson and Lewis make their homes in the area, and George Cobb once lived here.

The area course that's on everyone's must-play list is The Cliffs at Glassy, a Tom Jackson design north of Greenville. The Cliffs is private, but it's worth your while to try to make friends with a member. If you can't get on The Cliffs, don't worry — there's plenty of other high-quality golf in the area.

A note about greens fees: As with all courses in the Carolinas, where golf is a year-round activity, expect seasonal variations and occasional discounts.

> Note that the area code for all golf courses and businesses listed in this chapter is 803.

Courses in Upstate South Carolina

BONNIE BRAE GOLF COURSE
1316 Fork Shoals Rd.

Greenville	277-9838
Championship Yardage: 6579	
Slope: 115	Par: 72
Men's Yardage: 6255	
Slope: 113	Par: 72
Ladies' Yardage: 5468	
Slope: 116	Par: 74

GOLF COURSES IN SOUTH CAROLINA'S UPSTATE REGION

Name	Type	# Holes	Par	Slope	Yards	Walking	Booking	Cost w/ Cart
Bonnie Brae Golf Course	semiprivate	18	72	113	6255	anytime	7 days	$24-27
Boscobel Golf Club	semiprivate	18	72	n/r	6184	anytime	2 days	$22-26
Carolina Springs Golf and CC								
Pines/Cedars Course	semiprivate	18	72	122	6248	anytime	5 days	$25-30
Pines/Willows Course	semiprivate	18	72	120	6416	anytime	5 days	$25-30
Cedars/Willows Course	semiprivate	18	72	117	6204	anytime	5 days	$25-30
Cobb's Glen Country Club	semiprivate	18	72	120	6470	restricted	2 days	$30-35
Cotton Creek Golf Club	semiprivate	18	72	113	6170	anytime	anytime	$20-25
Falcon's Lair	semiprivate	18	72	119	6444	anytime	7 days	$22-25
The Gauntlet Golf Club	semiprivate	18	72	130	6233	anytime	5 days	$25-30
Greer Golf and Country Club	public	18	72	116	5730	anytime	anytime	$25-28
Hickory Knob	public	18	72	n/r	5951	anytime	anytime	$22-26
Hunter's Creek								
Maple/Willow Course	semiprivate	18	72	n/r	6407	restricted	7 days	$26-35
Willow/Oak Course	semiprivate	18	72	n/r	6301	restricted	7 days	$26-35
Oak/Maple Course	semiprivate	18	72	n/r	6376	restricted	7 days	$26-35
Lakeview Golf Club	semiprivate	18	72	110	6016	anytime	3 days	$20-23
Links O'Tryon	semiprivate	18	72	122	6230	restricted	2 days	$35-45
Oak Ridge Country Club	semiprivate	18	72	111	5487	anytime	2 days	$20-25
Parkland Golf Club	semiprivate	18	72	120	6140	anytime	anytime	$13-22
Peach Valley Golf Club	public	18	70	92	5925	anytime	anytime	$17-21
Pickens Country Club	semiprivate	18	72	117	5966	anytime	2 days	$25-30
River Chase	semiprivate	18	71	114	6086	anytime	anytime	$39-49
River Falls Plantation	semiprivate	18	72	121	6238	no	anytime	$32-41
Rolling Green Golf Club (27 holes)								
First & Second Nines	semiprivate	18	71	118	5635	anytime	7 days	$21-23
Southern Oaks Golf Club	semiprivate	18	72	115	6449	anytime	2-7 days	$27-32
Stoney Pointe	semiprivate	18	72	117	6129	anytime	7 days	$25-30
Summersett	semiprivate	18	72	108	5420	restricted	anytime	$21-26
Table Rock	resort/semiprivate	18	72	114	6038	anytime	anytime	$19-23
Village Green Country Club	public	18	72	117	5873	anytime	2 days	$20-25
Verdae Greens Golf Club	semiprivate/resort	18	72	118	6249	restricted	7 days	$35-45

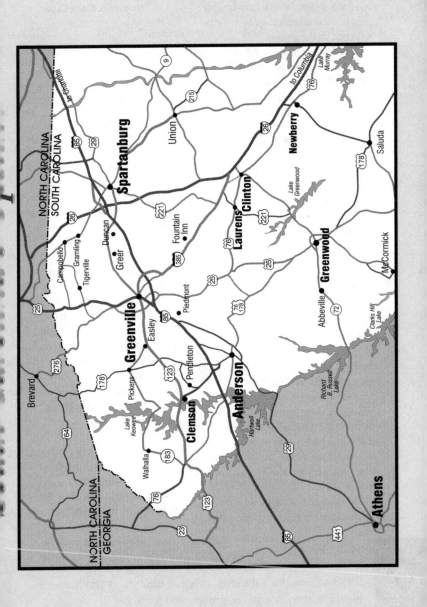

Bonnie Brae golf course opened in 1961. According to staff, Charles Willimon designed the course, which is set on wooded and mostly undulating terrain. You'll find bermudagrass in the fairways and on the greens.

Charles Willimon may not be the best-known architect in the great golfing state of South Carolina. That doesn't matter. Bonnie Brae is one of those golf courses that proves you don't necessarily need a big name architect for a fun and sensible track with excellent variety. And variety is the key here. There are large, small and mid-size greens; Mr. Willimon has provided some unique and interesting shapes as well. No two bunkers look the same. The fairways are wide in some places, narrow in others. It's just difficult to characterize this course, which is what makes it so interesting and popular with local golfers.

Willimon's design starts off with a bang: a 457-yard par 4. Bunkers are strategically placed on quite a few holes and influence approach shots to the sloped greens. On some holes, the superintendent left chipping areas. Water comes into play on a few holes but won't ruin your day unless you're hitting the ball just terribly. There's nothing earth-shattering or jaw-dropping about this course, but it's certainly worth a look if you're in the mood for a relaxed round on a well-designed, mature track.

Amenities include a practice green, range, snack bar, rental clubs, the occasional beverage cart and a pro shop.

The course is walkable anytime. You can book a tee time seven days in advance.

Approximate cost, including cart, is $24 weekdays and $27 on weekends.

BOSCOBEL GOLF CLUB

U.S. Hwy. 76
Pendleton   646-3991
Championship Yardage: 6449
Slope: No rating   Par: 72
Men's Yardage: 6184
Slope: No rating   Par: 72
Other Yardage: 5776
Slope: No rating   Par: 72
Ladies' Yardage: 5023
Slope: No rating   Par: 72

Boscobel opened in the 1930s. *Architects of Golf* lists Fred Bolton as the original designer, although Russell Breeden also has worked on the course. You'll find bermudagrass fairways and bentgrass greens set on rolling terrain.

Boscobel is a fun and challenging course, with pretty surroundings; it's also mature, with plenty of established trees. According to the locals, the course is "sneaky long" and plays every bit of its 6500 yards from the tips. You'll have to use all your clubs and marshal your short-game skills, considering the greens are predominantly small to midsize. You'll have plenty of tricky and downright difficult putts on these greens. The fairways vary in width. The front nine is hilly; the back is slightly flatter. And water is a factor on three holes. It's a challenging track.

Amenities include a practice green, locker room, bar, snack bar and pro shop. Boscobel is a good value.

Walk anytime you wish. You won't need a tee time during the week, and you can book for the weekend on Thursday. Approximate cost, including cart, is $22 weekdays and $26 on weekends.

CAROLINA SPRINGS
GOLF AND COUNTRY CLUB

1680 Scuffletown Rd.
Fountain Inn   862-3551

Pines/Cedars Course
Championship Yardage: 6676
Slope: 125   Par: 72
Men's Yardage: 6248
Slope: 122   Par: 72
Other Yardage: 5833
Slope: 116   Par: 72
Ladies' Yardage: 5084
Slope: 116   Par: 72

Pines/Willows Course
Championship Yardage: 6815
Slope: 123   Par: 72
Men's Yardage: 6416
Slope: 120   Par: 72
Other Yardage: 5988
Slope: 113   Par: 72
Ladies' Yardage: 5084
Slope: 119   Par: 72

Cedars/Willows Course
Championship Yardage: 6643
Slope: 121   Par: 72
Men's Yardage: 6204
Slope: 117   Par: 72
Other Yardage: 5773
Slope: 113   Par: 72
Ladies' Yardage: 4996
Slope: 113   Par: 72

Carolina Springs opened in 1968. Russell Breeden designed this course, with bermudagrass fairways and bentgrass greens set on hilly terrain. Most of the holes are wooded, while others are open. Improvements are currently under way.

This course is somewhat typical of a Russell Breeden track in that it presents plenty of difficulties while appearing straightforward. There's trouble off the tee in the form of the occasional raised bunker, but the fun begins when you consider your approach shot. Most of the green complexes include one, two or three bunkers; the green will slope to reward the bold. The greens are midsize to large, and on quite a few holes you can run the ball up to the pin. The beauty of the course is that each hole presents its own set of challenges and decisions. Water comes into play on a few holes but should only affect the truly awful shot. Play the course from the tips and you'll have your hands full.

On first inspection, there isn't a massive difference between the three courses; play them in any combination for a wonderful round. Take a look at this course, especially once all the improvements have been made.

Amenities include a practice green, range, snack bar, rental clubs, a beverage cart and pro shop.

The course is walkable anytime. You can book a tee time five days in advance. Approximate cost, including cart, is $25 weekdays and $30 on weekends.

COBB'S GLEN COUNTRY CLUB

2201 Cobbs Way
Anderson   226-7688
Championship Yardage: 7002
Slope: 129   Par: 72
Men's Yardage: 6470
Slope: 120   Par: 72
Other Yardage: 5952
Slope: 115   Par: 72
Ladies' Yardage: 5312
Slope: 121   Par: 72

Cobb's Glen opened in 1975. As you might expect, George Cobb designed the course, with help from John LaFoy, on pleasant rolling terrain. Houses and woods border many of the holes. In the fairways, you'll find bermudagrass; on the greens, you'll find bentgrass. The course may become completely private in 1996; stay tuned for updates.

At Cobb's Glen we found a fun, well-designed and somewhat challenging course that's well worth a visit if you're in the

Clemson/Anderson area. It's a hefty course from the back tees, so you might want to play it from the middle or front if your last name isn't Daly and your first name isn't John. If the bermudagrass rough is at all long, the fairways will be narrower than they look. Adding to the trouble off the tee are numerous fairway bunkers that are ready and willing to catch your ball. The greens are mostly large and undulating. These, too, are heavily bunkered. Water comes into play on a few holes, but the woods that border most of the holes pose more of a hazard. Cobb's Glen is mature and has a traditional feel.

Amenities include a practice green, range, locker room, bar, snack bar, restaurant, rental clubs, an occasional beverage cart and a pro shop.

The course is walkable for the physically fit, and you can walk late in the day. You can book a tee time 48 hours in advance. Approximate cost, including cart, is $30 weekdays and $35 on weekends.

COTTON CREEK GOLF CLUB

640 Keltner Blvd.
Spartanburg   583-7084
Championship Yardage: 6653
Slope: 116   Par: 72
Men's Yardage: 6170
Slope: 113   Par: 72
Ladies' Yardage: 5070
Slope: 118   Par: 72

Cotton Creek Golf Club opened in 1968. Russell Breeden designed this course, which is set on slightly rolling terrain. In the fairways and on the greens, you'll find bermudagrass.

Cotton Creek is a somewhat typical Breeden design. The routing and overall layout are sound. You'll find the occasional raised bunker in the fairway. The green complexes feature two or three bunkers, a pampas grass bush here and there, a slightly undulating putting sur-

face and some small mounds. One interesting touch is the addition of grass bunkers — a rarity on a Breeden course. Overall, this track is open, straightforward and fun, providing a venue for an enjoyable round of golf in a country setting. Keep the ball in play, smack it to the middle of the medium-size greens, two-putt, and you'll leave with a smile on your face. The back nine is a little tighter and a bit more wooded.

Amenities include a practice green, range, chipping green, locker room, bar, snack bar, restaurant, rental clubs, a beverage cart and a pro shop.

The course is walkable anytime, and you can book a tee time whenever you choose. Approximate cost, including cart, is $20 weekdays and $25 on weekends.

FALCON'S LAIR

1308 Falcon's Dr.
Walhalla   638-0000
Championship Yardage: 6955
Slope: 124   Par: 72
Men's Yardage: 6444
Slope: 119   Par: 72
Other Yardage: 5913
Slope: 113   Par: 72
Ladies' Yardage: 5238
Slope: 123   Par: 74

Falcon's Lair, a Harry Bowers design, opened in 1991 and features bermudagrass fairways and bentgrass greens set on undulating terrain.

After graduating from Michigan State with degrees in park planning and turfgrass science, Bowers joined Robert Trent Jones as an associate designer. He supervised several new designs and remodeled others. In 1991, Bowers and Curtis Strange built Odyssey Golf Course in Illinois.

Falcon's Lair is a challenging course that demands accuracy off the tee. Several greens are tricky and trouble spots exist on

Photo: Table Rock Resort

Many of the holes at Table Rock Resort are beautifully framed by trees.

almost every hole. There are some extremely pretty holes on the course as well.

Amenities include a practice green, range, chipping green, locker room, snack bar and rental clubs.

You can walk anytime; book a tee time up to seven days in advance. Approximate cost, including cart, is $22 weekdays and $25 on weekends.

THE GAUNTLET GOLF CLUB

253 Chinquapin Rd.
Tigerville   895-6758
Championship Yardage: 6713
Slope: 135   Par: 72
Men's Yardage: 6233
Slope: 130   Par: 72
Other Yardage: 5543
Slope: 124   Par: 72
Ladies' Yardage: 4545
Slope: 119   Par: 72

The Gauntlet Golf Club, a P.B. Dye design, opened in 1992. Most of the holes are bordered by woods and the course is very hilly. Fairways are bermudagrass; greens are bentgrass.

The Gauntlet is one-third of a triumvirate of perilous Carolinas golf courses including The Gauntlet at St. James Plantation in Southport, North Carolina, and Myrtle West Golf Club outside North Myrtle Beach.

Just a theory, but here goes: "P.B." in P.B. Dye stands for Pin Ball, which is what your ball will behave like if you miss the green just slightly or, on occasion, if you actually hit a green. Purely conjecture, mind you.

The Greenville version of The Gauntlet is set in the foothills of the Smoky Mountains and provides one of the greatest challenges in the Upstate — a challenge that borders on the absurd in places. Earth was moved. Sands were shifted. The sky was shaken. The golfing world has never been the same. No two holes are the same, but they're all extensively difficult. Score par on most holes and you should be extremely pleased with yourself. Each hole has a name with an Arthur and the Round Table motif. If the course beats you up in a particularly nasty fashion, our advice is to restore your sense of humor by renting *Monty Python and the Holy Grail.*

As you might expect with a modern course, there's plenty of mounds, bunkers, steep drop-offs, water, blind shots and uneven stances. Some holes defy description. The par 5 No. 16, a 521-yard monster, looks innocent enough off the tee, but that's because the shot is uphill to a flat landing area. From here, you can lay up to a series of terraced landing areas or go for it and fire away at a massive green divided by an elephant buried in the shallowest of graves. We tried to putt from one end to the other while keeping the ball on the green and failed miserably. You've been warned.

The Greenville-Spartanburg area is full of fine courses, but you'll want to visit here for the experience of having played a Dye course. Whether or not you'll return depends on your ability to suck up mental anguish. There's nothing that comes close to describing the semi-hallucinogenic thought processes that went into designing the aptly named Gauntlet.

Amenities include a practice green, range, chipping green, snack bar, rental clubs, an occasional beverage cart and a pro shop.

You'll only add injury to insult if you try to walk this course, but you can if you want to. . . . You can book a tee time five days in advance. Approximate cost, including cart, is $25 weekdays and $30 on weekends.

more holes in 1965. There's no record of any one designer. Bermudagrass covers the fairways; bentgrass, the greens.

As mentioned in this chapter's introduction, Greer is known around the world as the site of a new and massive BMW automotive factory. However, this friendly South Carolina town is also home to a decent golf course — proving you don't need a big name, hot-shot golf course architect. The track is popular with the locals, many of whom find time in their schedules to work out their beer drinking muscles in the clubhouse, which is well-equipped with a few card tables and a state-of-the-art (in 1954) television.

The course is relatively straightforward until you reach the undulating greens. The fairways are tree-lined. The course has a pleasant country ambiance, well-removed from the hustle and bustle of life in the rapidly expanding and booming Greenville-Spartanburg metropolis. Have fun.

Amenities include a practice green, range, locker room, bar, snack bar, restaurant, rental clubs, a beverage cart, TV and pro shop.

The course is walkable for the limber, and you can walk anytime. You'll need a tee time on the weekend. Approximate cost, including cart, is $25 weekdays and $28 on weekends.

GREER GOLF & COUNTRY CLUB

2990 Gap Creek Rd.
Greer   877-9279
Championship Yardage: 6321

Slope: 121	Par: 72
Men's Yardage: 5730	
Slope: 116	Par: 72
Ladies' Yardage: 5083	
Slope: 110	Par: 72

Greer Golf & Country Club opened nine holes in 1954. The club added nine

HICKORY KNOB STATE RESORT PARK GOLF COURSE

Rte. 1, Box 199-B
McCormick   391-2450
Championship Yardage: 6560

Slope: No rating	Par: 72
Men's Yardage: 5951	
Slope: No rating	Par: 72
Other Yardage: 4905	
Slope: No rating	Par: 72
Ladies' Yardage: 4905	
Slope: No rating	Par: 72

Hickory Knob State Resort Park Golf Course opened in 1982. Tom Jackson designed the course amid rolling wooded terrain. Fairways and greens are bermudagrass.

Hickory Knob is part of McCormick State Park. We found it to be an excellent course with plenty of challenge. Here's a good example of sound government! You won't find the abundance of mounds that typically defines Tom Jackson courses; the greatness lies in the variety. You'll find greens of all sizes and shapes. Some are sloped; others pitch and roll. Bunkering is extensive, and there's plenty of water, some of which comes from the picturesque lake bordering the course.

You won't have to bang the ball a mile here to score well, but you will need to keep it in play and take what the course gives you. You'll also have to carry the ball over water on a few occasions. Just the setting alone is worth the modest price of admission. Seek this place out.

Amenities include a practice green, range, chipping green, locker room, bar, snack bar and pro shop.

You can walk and book a tee time at Hickory Knob whenever you choose. Approximate cost, including cart, is $22 weekdays and $26 on weekends.

HUNTER'S CREEK

702 Hunter's Creek Blvd.
Greenwood   223-9286
Maple/Willow Course
Championship Yardage: 7089
Slope: No rating   Par: 72
Men's Yardage: 6407
Slope: No rating   Par: 72
Other Yardage: 5723
Slope: No rating   Par: 72
Ladies' Yardage: 4977
Slope: No rating   Par: 72
Willow/Oak Course
Championship Yardage: 6927
Slope: No rating   Par: 72

Men's Yardage: 6301
Slope: No rating   Par: 72
Other Yardage: 5704
Slope: No rating   Par: 72
Ladies' Yardage: 4931
Slope: No rating   Par: 72
Oak/Maple Course
Championship Yardage: 6920
Slope: No rating   Par: 72
Men's Yardage: 6376
Slope: No rating   Par: 72
Other Yardage: 5765
Slope: No rating   Par: 72
Ladies' Yardage: 5000
Slope: No rating   Par: 72

The Oak Nine at Hunter's Creek Plantation opened in 1995. Tom Jackson designed the course. Many of the holes are open, others are bordered by woods. You'll find bermudagrass on the greens and fairways. Please note that the course plans to become members-only sometime in 1996.

Hunter's Creek was under construction when we visited, but if the Maple and Willow nines will be anything like the Oak Nine, you're in for a modern treat. The courses feature plenty of mounds, tough greens, big tee shots and a variety of nasty bunkers. They will be extremely challenging from the back tees. If you're a fan of modern and difficult courses, you'll want to challenge this track before it's unavailable to the public.

Amenities include a practice green, range, chipping green, bar, snack bar, restaurant, rental clubs, a beverage cart and a pro shop.

The Oak Nine is walkable. You can book a tee time seven days in advance. Approximate cost, including cart, is $26 weekdays and $35 on weekends.

LAKEVIEW GOLF CLUB

315 Piedmont Golf Course Rd.
Piedmont   277-2680
Championship Yardage: 6455
Slope: 116   Par: 72

Men's Yardage: 6016	
Slope: 110	Par: 72
Ladies' Yardage: 5036	
Slope: No rating	Par: 73

Lakeview Golf Course opened in 1954. In the fairways, you'll find 419 bermudagrass; the greens are 328 bermudagrass. Although we searched high and low, we could not determine who designed this course.

Lakeview offers a fun and relaxing round in a pleasant country setting. Like its neighbor, Bonnie Brae, the course is set on gently rolling terrain. Some of the holes are wide open, while others are set in woodland. One of the first things you'll notice, depending on the time of year, is that the first fairway is crosscut — a landscaping touch evident from the elevated tee. The greens are small to medium-size and not overly undulating. The layout is predominantly straightforward: What you see is what you get. There's a distinct lack of water and heavy bunkering. Perhaps the back nine is a little tighter than the front. The course offers enough challenge and variety to keep the novice as well as the low-handicapper happy, which may explain its clear popularity.

Amenities include a practice green, range, chipping green, snack bar, rental clubs and a pro shop.

You can walk the course anytime. You won't need a tee time during the week, but you will need to call on Wednesday to book for the weekend. Approximate cost, including cart, is $20 weekdays and $23 on weekends.

LINKS O'TRYON

11250 New Cut Rd.	
Campobello	468-4995
Championship Yardage: 6728	
Slope: 130	Par: 72
Men's Yardage: 6230	
Slope: 122	Par: 72

Other Yardage: 5539	
Slope: 113	Par: 72
Ladies' Yardage: 5051	
Slope: 114	Par: 72

Links O'Tryon, a Tom Jackson design, opened in 1987. The course is set on gently rolling terrain bordered by woods and houses. Fairways are blanketed with bermudagrass, and greens are bentgrass.

Links O'Tryon is well-known in the Upstate as one of the area's finest courses. During our visit, the greens had been beaten up by a heat wave, the superintendent had recently received a pink slip and some maintenance improvements were under way. By the time this book is published and you're playing here, the course should be in good shape. It may also be completely private. So call before you play to make sure the general public can venture forth onto this fine course. For three years running, the course was voted No. 1 in Upstate South Carolina by *GolfWeek* magazine.

The course offers many Tom Jackson links-type touches. The course is somewhat forgiving and rewarding. Many of the holes are quite memorable. Perhaps this course is less penal than other Tom Jackson designs. The open aspect that defines most of the course and its proximity to the foothills of the Smoky Mountains mean that wind may be a factor in your round here, accentuating the "n'ae wind, n'ae golf" links effect.

But the key to this course's greatness is its variety. You'll have to place all of your shots to score well here. No two holes are the same. It's a great example of why Tom Jackson is such a well-respected architect. Bunkers come in all shapes and sizes; some are massive. Jackson took a page out of Robert Trent Jones's book with a couple of cloverleaf bunkers that are fun to look at but

Designer Profile: George Cobb

George Cobb (1914-1986) lived in Greenville, South Carolina, most of his life. Cobb graduated from the University of Georgia in 1937 with a degree in landscape architecture. The National Park Service employed him until he entered the Marine Corps as an engineering officer in 1941.

A scratch golfer, Cobb was asked to build a course at Camp LeJeune. Cobb was so unsure of his abilities as an architect, he hired Fred Findlay to design the course; Cobb supervised the construction. After World War II, Cobb entered private practice as a golf course architect and land planner.

George Cobb

Photo: The Architects of Golf

In the 1950s and '60s Cobb was a design consultant at Augusta National where he designed and built the par 3 course at Augusta. Cobb was a close friend of Bobby Jones, and you'll find examples of Cobb's drawing skills in Jones' autobiography.

Many Cobb-designed courses are private, and you'll find most of his public-access courses in resort areas. He tended to build difficult and long courses for private clubs but included more playability in his resort tracks. During the last 15 years of his career, he was assisted by John LaFoy. Many of Cobb's courses have hosted professional and amateur tournaments.

You'll find Cobb's work in Alabama, Florida, Maryland, Georgia, North and South Carolina, Tennessee, West Virginia, the Bahamas, Virginia and Minnesota.

In total, George Cobb worked on nearly 100 golf courses.

---

no fun to be in. Water comes into play on a few holes, but it shouldn't pose too much of a problem unless you're very wayward.

Amenities at this fine golfing facility include a practice green, range, chipping green, locker room, bar, snack bar, restaurant, rental clubs, a beverage cart and a pro shop.

The front nine is more walkable, and you can walk after 2 PM. Book a tee time whenever you choose during the week, but you'll need to call after 1 PM on Thursday to schedule for the weekend. Approximate cost, including cart, is $35 weekdays and $45 on weekends.

OAK RIDGE COUNTRY CLUB

5451 S. Pine St.
Spartanburg   582-7579
Championship Yardage: 6156
Slope: 121   Par: 72

Men's Yardage: 5487
Slope: 111   Par: 72
Ladies' Yardage: 4491
Slope: 112   Par: 72

Oak Ridge Country Club opened in 1980. George Cobb designed the course on picturesque rolling terrain. Fairways are 419 bermudagrass, and greens are bentgrass.

The course was remodeled in 1992. Much of the difficulty on this well-designed course comes from its hilly nature. At times, you might feel like you're on a mountain track. The greens vary in shape but are primarily midsize and sloped, with some subtle undulations. A combination scorecard/yardage book is a useful aid. You'll find bunkering in the fairways and around most of the greens. Keeping the ball in play on this somewhat short course is crucial, so you might want to leave your big stick in the trunk. The course narrows a touch on the back nine, and water comes into play on a few holes. You can't go wrong with a George Cobb design, so visit this course if you can. It's also an excellent value.

Amenities include a practice green, range, chipping green, snack bar, rental clubs, a beverage cart and pro shop.

The course is walkable for the physically fit, and you can walk anytime. You can book a tee time two days in advance. Approximate cost, including cart, is $20 weekdays and $25 on weekends.

PARKLAND GOLF CLUB

295 E. Deadfall Rd.
Greenwood   229-5086
Championship Yardage: 6520
Slope: 124   Par: 72
Men's Yardage: 6140
Slope: 120   Par: 72
Other Yardage: 5710
Slope: 114   Par: 72
Ladies' Yardage: 5130
Slope: 115   Par: 72

Parkland Golf Club opened in 1986. John Park designed the course on rolling wooded terrain, with bermudagrass greens and fairways.

Parkland is a fine country course — another example that proves you don't need a big name architect to create a formidable track. Overall, the layout is relatively flat and features a number of tricky holes surrounded by towering pine trees. Some of the holes are tight off the tee. Streams and ponds come into play, particularly on the back nine. You'll find a great deal of bunkering around the greens and an occasional bunker in the fairway. The greens undulate and vary in size. There's nothing tricked-up about the course; it exudes an old-style country club feel. Definitely play here if you can.

Amenities include a chipping green, snack bar and pro shop.

The course is walkable for the fit, and you can walk anytime. You won't need a tee time. Approximate cost, including cart, is $13 weekdays and $22 on weekends.

PEACH VALLEY GOLF CLUB

2363 Chesnee Hwy.
Spartanburg   583-2244
Championship Yardage: 6225
Slope: 109   Par: 70
Men's Yardage: 5925
Slope: 92   Par: 70
Ladies' Yardage: No rating
Slope: 97   Par: 76

Peach Valley opened in 1960. The course is set on open and primarily flat terrain. In the fairways, you'll find bermudagrass; on the greens, you'll find bentgrass and bermudagrass. Who designed this course? We don't know, and neither did anyone or any text source we consulted.

Peach Valley offers low-cost, worry-free, relaxed golf in a pleasant setting. Greens are raised and small to medium-size, with subtle slopes. The fairways are wide and open, so feel free to take out the boron-shafted big daddy you just purchased from the clubmaker in the pro shop and let it rip.

Amenities include a practice green, range, chipping green, snack bar, restaurant, rental clubs and a pro shop.

The course is walkable, you should walk here and can do so anytime (three cheers!). You can book a tee time whenever you choose as well. Approximate cost, including cart, is $17 weekdays and $21 on weekends.

PICKENS COUNTRY CLUB

1018 Country Club Rd.

Pickens	878-6083
Championship Yardage: 6250	
Slope: 120	Par: 72
Men's Yardage: 5966	
Slope: 117	Par: 72
Ladies' Yardage: 4912	
Slope: 115	Par: 72

Pickens Country Club opened in 1954 with nine holes; the club added a back nine in 1958. Willie B. Lewis designed the course. Woods border some of the holes, and most of the fairways are defined and delineated with evergreens and hardwoods. The course is set in rolling terrain; water only comes into play on a couple of holes. You'll find bermudagrass in the fairways and bentgrass on the greens.

At Pickens Country Club, we found a fine, mature, traditional layout. You won't find anything tricked-up or gimmicky here; it's fairly straightforward, the trees are mature and magnificent, there's barely a house in sight anywhere, and many of the holes sweep majestically right and left, giving you the feeling that you're on a country club track. You might ask yourself why today's modern courses aren't like this one.

Like a lot of older traditional designs,

you'll find that the degree of trouble off the tee depends on the length of the rough: If it's long and shaggy, you'll need to keep your ball in the short grass. The greens are small, undulating and, according the staff, fast outside the summer months. They're probably harder than they look. You won't find an overabundance of bunkers, although there are some strategically placed sand and grass bunkers to make you think about your approach shot.

The course offers a yardage book that includes swing thoughts and golf tips on each page, including one tip that encourages you not to over-think . . . a good example of yardage-book irony.

Amenities include a practice green, range, chipping green, locker room, bar, snack bar and pro shop.

You can walk anytime. Nonmembers can book a tee time two days in advance. Approximate cost, including cart, is $25 weekdays and $30 on weekends.

RIVER CHASE

459 Fairwood Blvd.

Union	427-3055
Championship Yardage: 6607	
Slope: 121	Par: 71
Men's Yardage: 6086	
Slope: 114	Par: 71
Ladies' Yardage: 5138	
Slope: 103	Par: 71

River Chase, a fine Russell Breeden design that opened in 1976, is set in rolling wooded terrain, with bermudagrass greens and fairways.

You'll find there isn't much room off the tee, which makes the course play longer — as if it weren't long enough already. The green complexes are challenging and feature numerous bunkers and extreme undulations.

The course was under renovation at press time, and many improvements are being made that should certainly make it worth a visit once complete.

Amenities include a practice green, range, locker room, snack bar and pro shop.

River Chase is walkable for the fit, and you can walk anytime. You can book a tee time whenever you choose. Approximate cost, including cart, is $39 weekdays and $49 on weekends.

RIVER FALLS PLANTATION

100 Player Blvd.
Duncan   433-9192
Championship Yardage: 6697
Slope: 127   Par: 72
Men's Yardage: 6238
Slope: 121   Par: 72
Other Yardage: 5702
Slope: 116   Par: 72
Ladies' Yardage: 4928
Slope: 125   Par: 72

Gary Player designed the golf course at River Falls Plantation, which opened in 1990. Most holes are bordered by woods, and some holes have a mountain feel. In the fairways, you'll find bermudagrass; on the greens, bentgrass.

Player did an excellent job here. He routed the course exceedingly well, and the result is a track with a number of memorable holes. We found outstanding variety: It's the sort of course where, as the old saying goes, you'll have to use every club in your bag. You'll find yourself being forced to plan a strategy on just about every hole. Some holes offer great elevation changes. Fairway widths vary a great deal, and on certain holes you'll want to throttle back with a long iron. On other holes, take out the big stick and fire away. Water frequently comes into play. The green complexes vary in size, shape and protection to the point where it's impossible to generalize. On certain holes, you might think of this course as a sort of kinder, gentler Dye-ish effort.

Amenities include a range, chipping green, locker room, snack bar, restaurant, rental clubs, a beverage cart and pro shop.

Walking is not allowed, but you can book a tee time whenever you choose. Approximate cost, including cart, is $32 weekdays and $41 on weekends.

ROLLING GREEN GOLF CLUB

386 Hester Shore Rd.
Easley   859-7716
First & Second Nines
Championship Yardage: 6116
Slope: 118   Par: 71
Men's Yardage: 5635
Slope: 118   Par: 71
Ladies' Yardage: 4546
Slope: 115   Par: 71

The course offers 27 holes.

The first nine holes at Rolling Green opened in 1968; the second nine opened two years later; and the third nine opened in 1991. William B. Lewis designed the first nine holes; the owners, the Dacus family, designed the second and third nine. The course is set in rolling terrain and is bordered by woods. Water comes into play on a number of holes. You'll find bermudagrass in the fairways and bentgrass on the greens.

As you might expect from a course built in three stages, each section has its own character and feel. The front nine is relatively narrow and pretty yet straightforward. You won't find any significant water on the front nine. The greens are medium-size, sloped and protected by bunkers. Keep the ball in play and you'll have some fun. On the second nine, the bunkers seem a little deeper and a bit more menacing; the greens are a little larger. The layout retains the traditional feel of the first nine. Water also comes into play. The third nine offers a bit more variety; the fairways are defined and delineated by evergreen trees. There are some significant elevation changes on the final nine plus a

Photo: Table Rock Resort

*Courses in Upstate South Carolina provide magnificent
scenery and interesting elevation changes.*

bit more water. Considering that the final nine is just a few years old, it feels remarkably mature. Overall, Rolling Green offers three fun, varied and interesting nine-hole layouts.

Amenities include a practice green, range, chipping green, locker room, bar, snack bar and pro shop.

You can walk anytime. Nonmembers can book a tee time seven days in advance. Approximate cost, including cart, is $21 weekdays and $23 on weekends.

SOUTHERN OAKS GOLF CLUB

105 Southern Oaks Dr.

Easley	*859-6698*
Championship Yardage: 6701	
Slope: 119	*Par: 72*
Men's Yardage: 6449	
Slope: 115	*Par: 72*
Other Yardage: 6044	
Slope: No rating	*Par: 72*
Ladies' Yardage: 5000	
Slope: 110	*Par: 72*

Willie B. Lewis designed Southern Oaks Golf Club, which opened in 1989. The course is set on gently rolling terrain and is predominantly open. Fairways are bermudagrass; greens, bentgrass.

An important fact about Southern Oaks: Head PGA professional Wayne Myers holds what might be the world-record golf score for 18 holes: 57. Obviously, there were numerous eagles and birdies during this impressive round, but don't think that Southern Oaks is a pushover. This is one of the finest courses in the Greenville-Spartanburg metroplex, and it surely rates as one of Willie B. Lewis' best efforts.

The course is modern inasmuch as it was built fewer than 10 years ago, but the design borrows more from the traditional than from today's trickery and treachery. In many ways Southern Oaks reminded us of Tanglewood in Clemmons, North Carolina, without all the bunkers. Most of the holes are open, thus you get a links effect here. Each hole has a distinct character. There's usually plenty of room off the tee. The greens are midsize to large, with plenty of slope and/or undulation. Bunkers come into play on quite a few holes, and water poses a hazard on several holes as well.

You'll enjoy the tee shot on the par 4 No. 3, where you must clear nearly 200 yards of water to reach a peninsula landing area; it's 465-yards from the back tees. There's also a 625-yard par 5 on the front nine. So make sure you bring your big stick and be ready to smack it on a few holes, although some holes favor placement over distance off the tee. Overall, Southern Oaks is a course you must play if you're a fan of traditional yet challenging golf courses. Southern Oaks is an excellent value, especially if you walk.

Amenities include a practice green, range, chipping green, locker room, snack bar/grill, rental clubs and a pro shop.

The course is walkable, you should walk and you can walk anytime (amazing for a modern course!). You can book a tee time for the weekend on the preceding Thursday, seven days in advance for the weekdays. Approximate cost, including cart, is $27 weekdays and $32 on weekends.

STONEY POINTE

709 Swing About Rd.
Greenwood   942-0900
Championship Yardage: 6681
Slope: 125   Par: 72
Men's Yardage: 6129
Slope: 117   Par: 72
Other Yardage: 5449
Slope: 111   Par: 72
Ladies' Yardage: 4962
Slope: 120   Par: 72

Stoney Pointe opened in 1991. Tom Jackson designed the course to be open in some places and bordered by woods and houses in others. In the fairways, you'll find 419 bermudagrass; on the greens, you'll find bentgrass.

Stoney Pointe is a wonderful design and, for our money, it's one of Tom Jackson's best efforts. In places, the course has a links feel, with mounds bordering the

fairways and undulations within them. Many are tight, with OB and water lurking off the tee. The greens vary in size, and many are sloped and rolling. If the rough is tall, you must avoid it to score well. The yardage book/scorecard is a useful aid. As with many Jackson courses, bunkers come in all shapes, sizes and depths. If the rough is grown up around the greens, it will hamper your finesse pitches and chips. You'll also find some grass bunkers — just to make the course all the more difficult. Stoney Pointe is a really fun and challenging course that you should play on more than one occasion. It's also a good value.

Amenities include a practice green, range, chipping green, locker room, bar, snack bar, rental clubs and a pro shop.

You can walk anytime and book a tee time seven days in advance. Approximate cost, including cart, is $25 weekdays and $30 on weekends.

SUMMERSETT

111 Pilot Rd.
Greenville   834-4781
Championship Yardage: 6025
Slope: 114   Par: 72
Men's Yardage: 5420
Slope: 108   Par: 72
Ladies' Yardage: 4910
Slope: 119   Par: 74

Summersett opened in the late 1930s. *Architects of Golf* lists Tom Jackson as the individual who revamped the track. This occurred back in 1979. The course is set on undulating terrain, and you'll find bermudagrass fairways and bentgrass greens.

Summersett is short from the back tees (6025 yards), but it's also tight off the tee. Tom Jackson resisted the temptation to lengthen the course to absurd proportions. Instead, it appears that the renovation made good use of the original routing, and the course was made more difficult by adding variable pitch and roll to the greens. There's plenty of variety here, and you'll discover it's most sensible to keep the driver in the bag, especially on the back nine.

With the foothills of the Smoky Mountains bearing down from above, the course has a mountainous feel; the rolling terrain makes for some interesting tee shots. It's definitely worth a visit if you're looking for a good game on a short but sensible course.

Amenities include a practice green, chipping green, snack bar, rental clubs, a beverage cart and a pro shop.

You may walk the course anytime except weekends before 2 PM. You can book a tee time whenever you choose. Approximate cost, including cart, is $21 weekdays and $26 on weekends.

TABLE ROCK RESORT

171 Sliding Rock Rd.
Pickens   878-2030
Championship Yardage: 6514
Slope: 118   Par: 72
Men's Yardage: 6038
Slope: 114   Par: 72
Ladies' Yardage: 5085
Slope: 112   Par: 72

The golf course at Table Rock Resort was designed by Willie B. Lewis and opened in 1983. Table Rock is a mountain course; most of the holes are bordered by woods, while others are wide open, with a couple of shared fairways. You'll find common bermudagrass in the fairways and 328 bermudagrass on the greens, although these are in the process of being changed to bentgrass; the complete change-over is expected sometime

in 1996. Water comes into play on a number of holes.

Improvements and changes were under way at Table Rock when we visited. The basic layout and design is sound, with some fine holes beautifully framed by trees. If everything goes according to plan, the modifications to the course should make it a fun and playable course.

Many of the fairways are narrow, particularly on the back nine where the course is less open and more wooded. There are a couple of fun driving holes where you need to bang it through a chute. Locals advise keeping the driver in the bag unless you can keep it straight. The greens are primarily small, flat and interestingly shaped; the change-over to bentgrass may alter that. Most of the holes are flat, although there are some significant elevation changes on a few. Water comes into play mainly in the form of pretty mountain streams that need be avoided: Take a picture, but don't let your ball anywhere near them. A couple of bunkers lurk here and there. But overall, Table Rock boasts a course with a lot of potential.

If you're fed up with golf, the resort offers horseback riding, walks, tennis or fishing in a stocked lake. Table Rock State Park is just a few minutes away.

Amenities include a practice green, range, chipping green, locker room, bar, snack bar, restaurant, rental clubs and an occasional beverage cart.

You can walk anytime, and the course is walkable for the fit. You can also book

Unless otherwise instructed, play "real" golf — play the ball where it lies.

anytime. Approximate cost, including cart, is $19 weekdays and $23 on weekends.

VERDAE GREENS GOLF CLUB

650 Verdae Blvd.
Greenville   676-1500
Championship Yardage: 6773
Slope: 126   Par: 72
Men's Yardage: 6249
Slope: 118   Par: 72
Other Yardage: 5470
Slope: No rating   Par: 72
Ladies' Yardage: 5012
Slope: 116   Par: 72

Verdae Greens opened in 1990. Willard Byrd designed this track amid rolling terrain. Many holes are bordered by woods. In the fairways, you'll find bermudagrass; on the greens, you'll find Pencross bentgrass.

Verdae Greens (an interesting name) is owned by Embassy Suites Hotels (note the large multistory Embassy Suites adjacent to the course. Call 676-9090 for reservations.). Thus the course is a magnet for golfers on corporate outings, retreats and getaways. This means that the foursome in front of you may comprise four golfers with sparkling bags enveloping more than $2,000 worth of titanium-shafted golf equipment, the latest in golf fashions, several sleeves of 100 compression Balata balls and plenty of adult beverages. Their goal is to play in less than nine hours. They play from the tips, plant balls in the woods all day, and report that they scored somewhere in the 80s before retiring to the bar before retiring to the seafood buffet before retiring to the bar again. Welcome to golf — corporate-retreat style.

S&P 500 aside, Verdae Greens is home to one of the finest and prettiest golf courses in the Greenville-Spartanburg area: an excellent example of Willard Byrd's magic. The course hosts a Nike Tour event. We found excellent variety and some serious challenges. Water comes into play often. The course is not overly long, but it's narrow and exacting in places. You'll need to play some target golf to play well. It's important to be in the right place at the right time. Bunkers lurk off the tee and around the greens, which are relatively large but mercilessly undulating at times.

If you're a mid-handicapper, play from the "Other" tees and you'll have a good time. If you're a corporate golfer, hit from the back tees, expense each sleeve of balls to the company account and be sure to write it off (oh, lighten up IRS; we're just kidding). This is a must-play course in the Greenville-Spartanburg area. A useful purchase is the witty yardage book: Heed its advice.

Amenities include a practice green, range, chipping green, bar, snack bar, restaurant, rental clubs, a beverage cart and pro shop.

The course is walkable for the fit and dedicated, and you can walk anytime on weekdays. You can book a tee time seven days in advance. Approximate cost, including cart, is $35 weekdays and $45 on weekends.

VILLAGE GREEN COUNTRY CLUB

S.C. Hwy. 176
Gramling   472-2411
Championship Yardage: 6372
Slope: 122   Par: 72
Men's Yardage: 5873
Slope: 117   Par: 72
Ladies' Yardage: 5280
Slope: 123   Par: 74

Village Green Golf Course opened in approximately 1965. *Architects of Golf* lists Russell Breeden as the course designer; give an assist to Dan Breeden. In the fairways, you'll find bermudagrass; on the greens, you'll find bentgrass.

Village Green is a fine course — a

Designer Profile: Tom Jackson

Born in Pennsylvania in 1941, Tom Jackson is one of the busiest architects in the Carolinas and with good reason: He has built some of the finest new public courses in our area.

Jackson graduated from the State University of New York at Farmingdale with a degree in ornamental horticulture. He also earned a degree in landscape architecture from the University of Georgia.

Photo: The Architects of Golf

Tom Jackson

In 1965, Robert Trent Jones hired Jackson to build several courses in the Southeast. Three years later, he joined George Cobb and eventually started his own firm in 1971. From his base in Greenville, Jackson has designed or remodeled more than 50 courses — and more are on the way. His best-known effort is a private course north of Greenville called the Cliffs at Glassy. This has been rated as the fourth most beautiful course in America by *Golf Digest*. You'll find Jackson's work in Florida, Alabama, South Carolina and Georgia.

Jackson aims to build roughly six or seven courses a year. And when he's not supervising the construction of a course, he's playing golf to a six handicap. Jackson has two sons who are now active in the business as associates.

Jackson builds courses to meet the needs and desires of his clients but likes to emphasize playability, particularly on public courses. Play a Jackson course from the tips and you'll likely find it difficult; play it from forward tees and the course will be manageable. Jackson employs some of the characteristics of a modern course, including big mounds, undulating greens and bunkers, but you won't find tricked up or completely impossible designs. You will find that his courses are among the more aesthetically pleasing — particularly those without houses.

If you believe that the greatest indication of an architect's prowess is the popularity of his/her courses with the people who plop down hard-earned cash to play them, you'll find Jackson's prowess quite remarkable. We think you'll always enjoy a round on a Tom Jackson course, regardless of your score, and you'll be tempted to play it over and over again.

playable and attractive track that provides good value for your hard-earned golfing dollar. The course features all the typical Breeden elements and includes a number of truly fine golf holes. There's a definite lack of hardship off the tee, and you'll have to plan your approach shot to avoid the bunkers and leave yourself a viable birdie putt. The back nine is slightly hillier. As the shadows lengthen at the end of the day, the subtle undulations in the green will become more evident. To score well, keep the ball in the fairway and avoid the deep rough around the greens. True to Breeden form, the course becomes a little tougher as you come home. Village Green is worth a visit.

Oh, and call ahead on the 9th and 18th tees for your Kenburger and adult beverage from Ken's Grill.

Amenities include a practice green, range, chipping green, bar, snack bar/grill (Ken's), rental clubs, a beverage cart and pro shop.

You can walk anytime (yeah!). No advance tee times are necessary during the week, but book on Thursday for the weekend. Approximate cost, including cart, is $20 weekdays and $25 on weekends.

WILLOW CREEK GOLF COURSE

205 Sandy Run	
Greer	476-6492
Championship Yardage: 6698	
Slope: No rating	Par: 72
Men's Yardage: 6222	
Slope: No rating	Par: 72
Other Yardage: 5640	
Slope: No rating	Par: 72
Ladies' Yardage: 4846	
Slope: No rating	Par: 72

Willow Creek Golf Course, a Tom Jackson design, opened in summer 1995. The course combines open holes as well as some bordered by woods. Water frequently comes into play. You'll find bermudagrass in the fairways and Crenshaw bentgrass on the greens.

We examined this new addition to the fine portfolio of courses in the Greenville-Spartanburg area just after it opened; the greens and fairways had not yet grown in, but the overall outlook is good, given the resources of the course's ownership, Danner-Eller enterprises. This combination also owns the Hermitage Golf Course in Old Hickory outside of Nashville, Tennessee — host to the Sara Lee Classic on the LPGA Tour. Needless to say, it doesn't hurt to have the area's hottest architect, Tom Jackson, as the big-name designer.

Willow Creek demonstrates that Tom Jackson is not a cookie-cutter designer. The course is flatter and apparently less penal than some of Jackson's other tracks: The mounds bordering the fairways aren't quite as large. Still, the course has a links feel, and if the wind is blowing, you're in for a challenge. The tee boxes are massive and, clearly, built to withstand the expected heavy play. The greens are also large, and the influence of the bunkering and slope of the green will vary depending on pin placement.

Based on the looks of the clubhouse and the track record of the ownership, there's an initial commitment to make this course one of the better facilities in the area; this should be achieved once the course has had some time to grow and mature.

Amenities include a practice green, range, chipping green, locker room, snack bar, restaurant, rental clubs and a pro shop. There's no beverage cart, because *your* cart is the beverage cart: The course supplies you with your own personal cooler.

The course is not especially walkable, but you're allowed to walk on weekdays. You can book a tee time five days in advance. Approximate cost, including cart, is $29 weekdays and $34 on weekends.

Around Upstate South Carolina...

Fun Things To Do

While you're driving through the Greenville-Spartanburg area in the reckless pursuit of golfing nirvana, you might begin to feel somewhat awed by the sheer volume of industry. On I-85, construction crews busily prepare new interchanges and add lanes in an effort to support all the traffic produced by the area's pulsing industrial base. People work hard here. And when their work is done, they like to play. And many of them play golf on the fine selection of aforementioned courses.

The visitor to the area might be tempted to wonder what there is to do besides view factories from arterial roads or play golf. Well, you'd be surprised. Downtown **Greenville** has undergone a fine renovation, and you'll find all sorts of eclectic opportunities for dining and drinking. The NFL's **Carolina Panthers** spend summer camp at Wofford College in Spartanburg. There's dirt track stock-car racing at the speedway in Gaffney. But most importantly, there's a serious threat that minor league glove-dropping ice hockey might soon come to the Greenville-Spartanburg area.

Here are just a few activities you might find interesting.

For starters, **Tours Around Greenville South** (TAGS), 123 W. Broad Street, Greenville, 467-8088, is a volunteer organization that assists visitors in seeing Greenville's special attractions. Give 'em a call; they'll point you in the right direction.

The **Greenville Braves**, AA affiliate of Major League Baseball's Atlanta Braves franchise, play at Greenville Municipal Stadium on Mauldin Road, Greenville, 299-3456. Take Exit 46 from I-85.

If you strike out at the ball park, a real hit, especially with the kids, is the **Greenville Zoo**, 150 Cleveland Park Drive, Greenville, 467-4310. You'll find 14 acres of exotic animal kingdom, featuring lions and other big cats, miniature deer, kangaroos, tortoises and myriad wild beasts roaming about in a natural setting. Go ahead and make your day (and your kids' day too) with a visit to Dirty Harry, the boa constrictor.

Another educational attraction is **Roper Mountain Science Center**, 504 Roper Mountain Road, Greenville, 281-1188. All types of fun and scientifically oriented activities await the entire family. There are observatory/planetarium shows, hands-on exhibits and nature trails. Go to the intersection of I-385 and Roper Mountain Road.

For more information about activities and events in the Greenville area, contact or stop by **The Greater Greenville Convention & Visitors Center**, 206 N. Main Street, Greenville, 233-0461. Or you may also call or write **Discover Upcountry Carolina Association**, P.O. Box 3116, Greenville 29602, (800) 849-4766.

In **Spartanburg**, there's plenty to do when you're not playing golf. Anyone interested in historic homes should see the **Thomas Price House**. It was built in 1795 and was the centerpiece of the Thomas Price Plantation; the house is brick with a steep gambrel roof and inside end chimneys. Call 476-2483 for more information.

Cowpens National Battlefield was the site of one of the more important battles in American history. On a grim January day in 1781, Gen. Daniel Morgan and his militia beat up a group of British soldiers in less than an hour. Part of the National Park System operates a visitor's center, auto trail, walking trail and picnic area. If you're a member of a YMCA, you can get more fit than you already are at the **Spartanburg YMCA**, 585-0306. This branch is the largest single-unit YMCA in the Southeast and features two indoor pools, basketball and handball courts, Nautilus equipment and a cardiac-rehab center.

For more information about Spartanburg, call the **Spartanburg Convention and Visitors Bureau** at 594-5050.

Where to Eat

There's no shortage of places to eat in the Greenville-Spartanburg area. Upstaters are a hard-working lot; they also like to eat, as evidenced by the plentiful locally-owned proprietorships where local folk have been feasting for years. You'll find all your favorite chain restaurants plus an excellent variety of ethnic- and regional-fare establishments from Chinese to Italian to down-home country-style favorites.

THE BLUE RIDGE BREWING COMPANY
217 N. Main St.
Greenville   232-4677
$$

Walk in the door, head straight for the bar and ask yon fair bartender for a pint of Colonel Paris Pale Ale, an outstanding hand-crafted beer the likes of which you won't find anywhere else in the Upstate. Then look around to discover that this relatively new establishment has an Old World

feel and a trendy, well-to-do younger clientele — although beer lovers of all sizes, shapes and ages seem to enjoy themselves here.

Sample other fine pints, including Dove Field Wheat, Strumhouse Scottish Red Ale and the Rainbow Trout Amber Ale. There's an abundance of food as well — basic appetizers, soups, salads and sandwiches plus some interesting pub-type entrees, including pan-seared trout and a half-rack of brewhouse ribs. There's pizza too. For brew-pub lovers, this is heaven.

ANNIE'S NATURAL CAFE
121 S. Main St.
Greenville   271-4872
$$

Annie's has a sort of European-style flair and atmosphere. Coupled with the great selection of foods health-conscious folks and vegetarians will savor, such as veggie lasagna and herbal teas, this place is a wonderfully unique addition to the downtown Greenville eating scene.

COUNTRY EARL'S CHOMPIN' & STOMPIN'
I-385 at Exit 31
Simpsonville   967-8569
$$

You'll get good, hearty country cookin' here at Country Earl's, in addition to a full evening of country entertainment. Indulge in fried chicken, beef tips, chicken and gravy and all your favorite fixins. And enjoy various bands, clogging exhibitions and all types of dancing to work off your meal. Tour-bus groups are welcome to come chomp and stomp.

PETER DAVID'S FINE DINING
921 Grove Rd.
Greenville 242-0404
$$

Peter David's offers an elegant atmosphere with affordable prices. Menu items include fresh seafood, beef, veal and a value-priced wine selection. The establishment is a member of the Blue Plate Society.

LONGHORN STEAKS
1793 E. Main St.
Spartanburg 585-9400
$$

On U.S. Highway 29 near Hillcrest Mall, this version of the popular chain offers all that you've come to expect from a Longhorn. Begin your meal with a beer and some sizzling appetizers, then delve into a thick and juicy steak cooked to your specifications. If steak is not your cup of tea, devour a chicken dish or try Longhorn's famous salmon. Round out the meal with a beer or a Texas-size bowl of ice cream.

STEFANO'S AUTHENTIC ITALIAN CUISINE
1560 Union St.
Spartanburg 591-1941
$$

Stefano's proclaims that it's Spartanburg's premier Italian restaurant. It's certainly worth a visit if you're a lover of Northern Italian cuisine. This large restaurant specializes in banquets and catering. You'll find your favorite pasta dishes as well as some unique recipes featuring chicken, veal and fresh fish. Wash down your Veal Valdostana with a bottle of Valpolicella and top it off with tarimisu.

YODER'S DUTCH KITCHEN
S.C. Hwy. 72 E.
Abbeville 459-5556
$$

It may come as some surprise to you that one of the top 10 Pennsylvania Dutch restaurants in the country is right here in the thriving submetropolis known as Abbeville. Yoder's declares itself a "nice place to bring your family or friends" except on Sunday, Monday and Tuesday when the restaurant is closed. There's a smorgasbord-style buffet, so if you're particularly hungry, you can indulge all you want here. Also try the lunch buffet Wednesday through Saturday. In addition to the tasty Pennsylvania Dutch treats, you can purchase whole pies, apple butter and cinnamon-nut rolls.

Where to Stay

With all the business activity in the Greenville-Spartanburg area, it's very important to book a room before you arrive, particularly for the weekday. Try to call up to two weeks in advance of your arrival if you can.

HYATT REGENCY GREENVILLE
220 N. Main St.
Greenville 235-1234
$$$$

Enter the spacious atrium lobby and you'll immediately be at ease in this outstanding hotel right downtown. There are 327 guest rooms, many with fine views. There's also a pool, health club and a full-service business center.

HOLIDAY INN EXPRESS
AT MCALISTER SQUARE MALL
27 S. Pleasantburg Dr.
Greenville 232-3339
$$

This Holiday Inn is off I-385 and U.S.

Highway 291, two blocks from the Palmetto International Exposition Center and close to McAlister Square Mall. Breakfast is included in your room rate. Amenities include fax and other business services and cable TV.

THE PHOENIX
246 N. Pleasantburg Dr.
Greenville   233-4651
$$

The Phoenix is a full-service inn with outdoor dining in the Courtyard Grille plus romantic dining in the Palms Restaurant. There's dancing and entertainment in The Bar. The Phoenix exudes a much more intimate setting than the typical motel.

PETTIGRU PLACE
302 Pettigru St.
Greenville   242-4529
$$$

Located in the heart of downtown, Pettigru Place offers five individually decorated guest rooms with private baths. Gourmet breakfast is included.

RESIDENCE INN BY MARRIOTT
9011 Fairforest Rd.
Spartanburg   576-3333
$$$

The Residence Inn chain tends to cater to the person who is staying in an area for an extended period: weekly and monthly rates are available. Residence Inn Spartanburg offers one- or two-bedroom suites, a fully equipped kitchen, a living room with a fireplace, cable TV with free HBO, complimentary breakfast and a swimming pool.

BEST WESTERN SPARTAN INN & CONFERENCE CENTER
I-85 Bus. & S.C. Hwy. 9
Spartanburg   578-5400
$$

This comfortable and accessible Best Western underwent a complete renovation just three years ago and is popular among the business traveler set. This hotel offers 122 rooms with free cable TV. There's a business center, banquet and meeting rooms, a tennis court plus an outdoor pool. Corporate rates are available. After your busy day of golf and business, retire to Bigoli's Restaurant and Lounge.

HOLIDAY INN GREENWOOD
1014 Montague Ave.
Greenwood   223-4231
$$

The Holiday Inn Greenwood offers 100 recently remodeled rooms as well as a courtyard with a pool and decks. It's a good value as well, particularly if you make use of the corporate, group and special weekend rates; kids and teens stay free. A free full breakfast and local calls are included in your room rate, and fax and copy services are available. Relax after golf in the Greenwood area in Simon's Bar and Grill or take in the bountiful Sunday brunch before you venture forth onto the links for your Sunday afternoon round.

Index of Advertisers

Index

ORDER FORM
Fast and Simple!

Mail to:
Insiders Guides®, Inc.
P.O. Drawer 2057
Manteo, NC 27954

Or:
for VISA or
MasterCard orders call
(800) 765-BOOK

Name _____

Address _____

City/State/Zip _____

Qty.	Title/Price	Shipping	Amount
	Insiders' Guide to Richmond/$14.95	$3.00	
	Insiders' Guide to Williamsburg/$14.95	$3.00	
	Insiders' Guide to Virginia's Blue Ridge/$14.95	$3.00	
	Insiders' Guide to Virginia's Chesapeake Bay/$14.95	$3.00	
	Insiders' Guide to Washington, DC/$14.95	$3.00	
	Insiders' Guide to North Carolina's Outer Banks/$14.95	$3.00	
	Insiders' Guide to Wilmington, NC/$14.95	$3.00	
	Insiders' Guide to North Carolina's Crystal Coast/$12.95	$3.00	
	Insiders' Guide to North Carolina's Mountains/$14.95	$3.00	
	Insiders' Guide to Myrtle Beach/$14.95	$3.00	
	Insiders' Guide to Atlanta/$14.95	$3.00	
	Insiders' Guide to Boca Raton & the Palm Beaches/$14.95	$3.00	
	Insiders' Guide to Sarasota/Bradenton/$14.95	$3.00	
	Insiders' Guide to Northwest Florida/$14.95	$3.00	
	Insiders' Guide to Tampa Bay/$14.95	$3.00	
	Insiders' Guide to Mississippi/$14.95	$3.00	
	Insiders' Guide to Lexington, KY/$14.95	$3.00	
	Insiders' Guide to Louisville/$14.95	$3.00	
	Insiders' Guide to Cincinnati/$14.95	$3.00	
	Insiders' Guide to the Twin Cities/$14.95	$3.00	
	Insiders' Guide to Boulder/$14.95	$3.00	
	Insiders' Guide to Denver/$14.95	$3.00	
	Insiders' Guide to Branson/$14.95	$3.00	
	Insiders' Guide to Civil War in the Eastern Theater/$14.95	$3.00	

Payment in full (check or money order) must
accompany this order form.
Please allow 2 weeks for delivery.

N.C. residents add 6% sales tax _____

Total _____

GOLF BALL GIVE-AWAY
THE GAME IMPROVEMENT
GOLF BALLS™

ACRA

- Reduces Hooks & Slices
- Mid-Size Low Spin
- Extra Distance

TOUR

- Two Piece Balata
- Distance & Accuracy
- Soft Feel, Pro Spin

TDX150

- New! Double Dimples
- Target Accuracy
- Extra Carry

LITE

- Slower Swing Speeds
- Lighter Weight
- Longer Distance

Fill out the following information and have a chance to win 3 dozen golf balls. Twenty winners will be chosen. Entries must be received by March 31, 1996. Find out how a Laser, Game Improvement Golf Ball can help your game.

Name: _____

Address: _____

City: _____ ST: _____ ZIP: _____

Avg Score: _____ Current ball played: _____

Avg Driver Distance: _____

Club used from 150 yards: _____

Golf Ball Characteristics

1- Not Important   5- Very Important

Distance_____ Spin_____ Durability_____ Control _____ Price _____

Have you ever purchased clubs to improve your game? _____

Have you ever purchased balls to improve your game? _____

HANSBERGER PRECISION GOLF
"GOLF BALL GIVE-AWAY"
P.O. BOX 300
PONTOTOC, MS 38863